For Cuba—for Freedom!

# For Cuba—for Freedom!

## An M-26-7 Leader Aiding the Castro Revolution from America, 1955–1961

RAUL ANDRES VILLAMIA
*with* RHONDA J. VILLAMIA
*and* PAUL J. GUZZO

*Foreword by* Emiliano "E.J." Salcines

McFarland & Company, Inc., Publishers
*Jefferson, North Carolina*

LIBRARY OF CONGRESS CATALOGUING-IN-PUBLICATION DATA

Names: Villamia, Raul Andres, 1925–2020, author. | Villamia, Rhonda J., 1954– author. | Guzzo, Paul author. Paul J. 1975– | Salcines, E. J. (Emiliano José), 1938– writer of foreword.
Title: For Cuba—for freedom! : an M-26-7 leader aiding the Castro revolution from America, 1955–1961 / Raul Andres Villamia ; with Rhonda J. Villamia and Paul J. Guzzo ; foreword by Emiliano "E. J." Salcines.
Description: Jefferson, North Carolina : McFarland & Company, Inc., Publishers, 2024 | Includes bibliographical references and index.
Identifiers: LCCN 2023020118 | ISBN 9781476690995 (paperback : acid free paper) ∞
ISBN 9781476649184 (ebook)
Subjects: LCSH: Villamia, Raul Andres, 1925-2020. | Revolutionaries—Cuba—Biography. | Cuban Americans—Florida—Tampa—Biography. | Political activists—Florida—Tampa—Biography. | Cuba—History—Revolution, 1959—Personal narratives. | Movimiento Revolucionario 26 de Julio.
Classification: LCC F1788.22.V34 A3 2023 | DDC 972.9106/4092 [B]—dc23/eng/20230512
LC record available at https://lccn.loc.gov/2023020118

BRITISH LIBRARY CATALOGUING DATA ARE AVAILABLE

**ISBN (print) 978-1-4766-9099-5**
**ISBN (ebook) 978-1-4766-4918-4**

© 2024 Rhonda J. Villamia and Paul J. Guzzo. All rights reserved

*No part of this book may be reproduced or transmitted in any form or by any means, electronic or mechanical, including photocopying or recording, or by any information storage and retrieval system, without permission in writing from the publisher.*

Front cover image: *inset*: Home of Dalia Mas Delgado where Fidel Castro stayed while in Tampa during his November 1955 visit. Standing: Dalia Mas Delgado, Hedda (woman), Leonardo Muniz. Sitting: Migdalia Valdes Mas (married to Dalia's brother Rolando), Castro, Raul Villamia. Tampa, (Ybor City) Florida, November 26, 1955. *Top*: Raul Villamia with sugar cane truck in support of Fidel Castro's rebels burning Cuba's sugar cane crops in protest of dictator Fulgencio Batista y Zaldivar (photograph by *La Gaceta*, appearing in their November 15, 1957, issue). Bottom: M-26-7 tie (all images from the collection of Raul Villamia).

Printed in the United States of America

*McFarland & Company, Inc., Publishers*
  *Box 611, Jefferson, North Carolina 28640*
  *www.mcfarlandpub.com*

To my dad, Raul Villamia,
who endeavored to live his life
by the words of José Martí
in his poem

Cultivo Una Rosa Blanca

*Cultivo Una Rosa Blanca*  *I Have A White Rose To Tend*
*En Julio Como En Enero*  *In July As In January*
*Para El Amigo Sincero*  *I Give It To The True Friend*
*Que Me Da Su Mano Franca*  *Who Offers Me His Frank Hand*

*Y Para El Cruel*  *And To The Cruel One*
*Que Me Arranca El Corazon*  *Whose Blows Break The Heart*
*Con Que Vivo,*  *By Which I Live*
*Cardo Ni Ortiga Cultivo...*  *Thistle Nor Nettle Do I Give....*
*Cultivo Una Rosa Blanca*  *For Him Too.... I Have A White Rose*

# Table of Contents

*Acknowledgments* ix
*Foreword by Emiliano E.J. Salcines* 1
*Preface* 3
*Introduction* 9

1. I Once Supported Fidel Castro Ruz — 11
2. Baseball and Bloodshed in Cuba — 14
3. Ybor City — 22
4. My Revolutionary Brother Mario — 27
5. Revolutions in Tampa — 48
6. Castro Comes to Tampa — 57
7. Dark Forces — 81
8. Meet Tampa's M-26-7 — 86
9. The Media's Role in the Revolution — 104
10. The Radicals — 115
11. New Leadership — 127
12. Mario's Missions — 130
13. A Revolutionary Hero Leads Us — 142
14. Gun Smuggling from Tampa — 153
15. Victory — 160
16. Fallout — 172
17. My Return to a Free Cuba — 180

| | | |
|---|---|---|
| 18. | Signs of Trouble | 188 |
| 19. | Visiting Santo Trafficante Jr. | 204 |
| 20. | New and Old Enemies | 211 |
| 21. | A Dead Revolutionary in Tampa | 215 |
| 22. | Who Freed the Gangster? | 217 |
| 23. | Creating José Martí Park | 219 |
| 24. | Battling the Consul | 227 |
| 25. | The End of Tampa's M-26-7 | 244 |
| 26. | The End to My Revolutionary Days | 255 |
| 27. | Saying Goodbye to Cuban Cigars | 257 |
| 28. | The Cuban Missile Crisis | 259 |
| 29. | The Assassination of JFK | 261 |
| 30. | My Brother Comes Home | 264 |
| 31. | Viva Cuba Libre | 269 |

*Chapter Notes*     271
*Bibliography*     283
*Index*     289

# Acknowledgments

Writing a book is like birthing a child. In the womb, all the parts patiently knit together as the whole is slowly formed. Many factors affect the incubation period, and wise investments made throughout the term net a good outcome: a healthy child. Likewise, those who invest their time, talent, experience, encouragement, and constructive advice during the writing process impact the outcome of the work.

Before I acknowledge the earthly "angels" who helped, I first of all want to give glory to the God of Abraham, Isaac, and Jacob, and His Son Jesus Christ, whom I endeavor to serve with my entire being. It was God's plan to have me be born at this precise moment in time, to precisely the two people—Raul Villamia and Nora Rodriguez—who would be my parents. And it is because of His divine orchestration that I am able to be here—now—sharing the story in this book. I thank God for inspiring me to preserve my dad's role and those of the others who played their respective parts in this unique period of history.

I am indebted to my father for his meticulously recalled memories and saved memorabilia from his years in the 26th of July Movement (M-26-7). It is because of his diligence in attention to detail and preservation of historical documents that this book exists.

I would like to thank my collaborator, *Tampa Bay Times* journalist and author Paul Guzzo, who helped "wrap" the eyewitness accounts with historical documentation via other archived sources, enabling the reader to better understand the individuals' experiences in the context of what was simultaneously taking place in the United States and Cuba.

I am grateful for my uncle Mario for so often sharing his story with me. His "drafting" my dad into the Cuban revolutionary movement is what sparked my dad's involvement. Mario also was a keeper of memories and documents. I very much appreciate the assistance his children Natacha Villamia Sochat, Arlene Villamia Drimal, Deborah Villamia, Michael Villamia, and Elizabeth Villamia Slattery provided me when I needed to catalog their father's various photos to be used as illustrations in the book.

# Acknowledgments

It was an honor having the late Angel Pérez-Vidal share his story and his book *Historia Íntima de la Revolución Cubana* with me and having his widow, Alma Rivera, continue to refresh my memory when I needed a bit of clarification.

Howard K. Davis's story was intertwined with Uncle Mario's and my dad's stories, and it was gratifying to have Howard share his experiences with me. Both Howard and Angel were dear friends of Mario's, becoming friends of my dad's throughout the revolutionary process.

I am grateful to Rafael García Bárcena y Valladares for sharing recollections of his beloved father, Rafael García Bárcena y Gomez, who founded the Movimiento Nacional Revoluciónario and organized the first conspiracy against Batista, in which Tampa M-26-7 members Juan M. Pérez, Carmelo Bueno, and Marcelino Golan were involved. I am glad to have met Juan and heard these details as only an eyewitness can share.

There are many others who shared their stories, and I appreciate their contributions. Each added his or her own puzzle piece, giving more clarity to the whole picture.

Patrick Manteiga, third generation publisher of *La Gaceta*, our nation's only trilingual newspaper (Spanish, English, and Italian), founded in 1922, continues the legacy started by his grandfather Victoriano Manteiga, who was personally named by Fidel Castro Ruz as president of the Tampa M-26-7 when established in 1955. *La Gaceta* chronicled many of the accounts contained in this book.

In certain respects, *La Gaceta* more thoroughly and consistently reflected these accounts than the English language newspapers. Since it was predominantly a Spanish-speaking community that supported the Cuban Revolution, *La Gaceta* would often feature news items that would never make it to the American papers.

I thank Patrick and his wife, Angie, for giving me unfettered access to the *La Gaceta* archives and for providing many of the photos included in the book.

The Honorable Emiliano "E.J." Salcines was the first to read the manuscript when it was still a work in progress. He marked his notes on the margins, and his input was immensely appreciated. I (and I would venture to say most) consider E.J. a living legend in Tampa, not only because of his many accomplishments in the field of law, but for his wealth of knowledge as a historian. I am honored that he has graciously written the foreword.

A debt of gratitude is owed to Heberto Norman Acosta, researcher at Cuba's Office of Historic Affairs (OAH) in Habana, Cuba and author of *La Palabra Empeñada, Tomo 1–2*. His two-volume exhaustive account of the Cuban Revolution from 1953 to 1956 was invaluable in providing many of the specific details surrounding Fidel Castro Ruz's 1955 visit to the United

## Acknowledgments

States to establish branches of his M-26-7. Thanks also go to fellow OAH researcher Elsa Montero Maldonado, OAH director Jorge Luis Aneiros, and the late former OAH director Eugenio Suarez Pérez for their provision of materials.

Habana City Historian, the late Eusebio Leal Spengler provided much appreciated enlightenment.

Julia E. Sweig, former deputy director of the Latin American Program at the Council on Foreign Relations and author of many books on Cuba, provided me copies of letters written by Uncle Mario or that mentioned him, which she references in her book *Inside the Cuban Revolution*. My thanks for these, as well as for her introducing me to Elsa at the OAH. Mario, his daughter Arlene, and I had the honor of meeting Julia at a talk she gave in Weston, Connecticut, in October 2009.

Questions arose as I fact-checked, and I directed these to Andrew T. Huse, author and curator of Florida Studies, Special Collections, at the University of South Florida Library; Gary R. Mormino, author and historian on the faculty of the University of South Florida; Louis A. Pérez, author and historian on the faculty of the University of North Carolina at Chapel Hill; Jennifer Dietz, archivist at the City of Tampa Office of the City Clerk; and researcher Jeannette Tamborello.

I appreciate the Facebook groups devoted to Tampa and Ybor City, members of which were also very helpful in providing details.

When I needed help identifying some of Dad's fellow baseball players on the 1948 Miami Tourists minor league team, Sam Zygner and Barbra Cabrera, authors of *Baseball Under the Palms: History of Miami Minor League Baseball*, "pitched" in. Barbra's father, the late Emilio Cabrera, and my dad played together in Cuba. Steve Smith, member of the Society of American Baseball Research, "slugged away" in this effort as well. I appreciate their collective "sleuthing" in matching name to face.

Chip Weiner came to the rescue when we were in need of scanning images that required a professional hand. Thank you, Chip, for your expertise and making yourself immediately available for this task.

My thanks to those who offered their emotional and spiritual support. From the moment the book was a mere thought, Rhonda Falk was my sounding board. She was my confidant as I considered how to move forward with it. I appreciate her encouragement buoying me as I navigated these unchartered waters.

I am grateful to my church prayer chains for covering me with their intercessions as I faced challenging moments along the way.

I would also like to thank those who have endorsed this book: Gary R. Mormino, Louis A. Perez, Jr., Maura Barrios, Andrew Huse, Carlos J.

Cano, Patrick Manteiga, and Manny Leto, some of whose words appear on the back cover as space permits. Your support is much appreciated.

My hope is that the hundreds of men and women who, from America's "sea to shining sea," dedicated their blood, sweat, and tears for the cause of Cuban freedom see themselves in these pages. Their toil is not forgotten. Though many may feel a sense of betrayal at the outcome, what was carried out by the M-26-7 in exile from October 1955 to January 1961 was done with a pure heart and righteous motives. That cannot be taken away.

Finally, to my family—son Wynter Galindez and his wife, Melissa Rose; son Javan Galindez; grandchildren Luna and Rio Galindez; and sister Denise Villamia—I am grateful for your love. We were blessed to have had Raul in our lives for as long as we did. May his story, preserved in this book, forever keep his memory alive.

And may it inspire others to give life to their loved ones' stories.

—Rhonda J. Villamia

# Foreword

### Emiliano E.J. Salcines

This is an interesting and revealing read. It is an untold history of the clandestine and undercover anti–Fulgencio Batista activities in Tampa, Miami, New York, and elsewhere in our country. They recruited supporters and volunteers, raising money to buy weapons, military equipment and supplies, and whatever was needed by the guerrilla rebels in different parts of Cuba—like the Sierra Maestra and Escambray Mountains—and smuggled those goods into Cuba, much like the 27 expeditionary "filibuster" boats from Tampa and other parts of Florida during the "Martí War" of Cuban independence (1895–1898).

The disclosures of real events made in these memoirs bridge the missing gaps that had existed for more than six decades. It was not anti–Batista groups in Miami alone and pro–Fidel Castro supporters in South Florida recruiting, raising funds, buying rifles, guns, incendiary devices, etc., shipping them to Cuba by whatever means they could find or afford, all in an effort to free their homeland from the grips of a totalitarian dictatorship. Villamia gives us real facts that supply missing links that let us understand better the big picture, especially Tampa's role.

To understand the underlying history this book talks about, it is important that the reader grasp the complex 20 years from 1932 to 1952, during which Cuba had 20 interim leaders. Since attaining their republic on May 20, 1902, Cubans everywhere, in and out of Cuba, have had an optimistic dream that united them: having a democratic nation where a constitution and rule of law governed, based on freedom and free enterprise—similar to their neighbor to the north. Those dreams were coming true with the adoption of their new and quite advanced 1940 Constitution and legitimate elections at all levels—national, regional, provincial, and municipal. But as presidential elections were about to take place, a sad military takeover on March 10, 1952, led by Batista interrupted the hopes and dreams of a real democracy and the ideals of rebuilding the Cuban political structure. Batista suspended constitutional guarantees from 1952 to 1959 as a strong-arm military dictator.

Batista fled the island on January 1, 1959. Ybor City and West Tampa rejoiced, believing that democracy and constitutional guarantees would soon hold sway in Cuba as in the United States. But the contrary soon became evident.

Castro "monopolized" the government, but a "democratic system" was not restored as he had promised. At the peak of his popularity as a "freedom fighter," he dismantled constitutional guarantees and installed a totalitarian Communist system as his Revolutionary Government.

This is a story of persons in Tampa and other parts of the United States who participated and played a role in overthrowing Cuban dictator Fulgencio Batista, after his disregarding the 1940 Cuban Constitution and the established electoral process. Yes, there were anti–Batista armed forces in the Sierra Maestra as well as the Escambray Mountains in Cuba, but there were other locations and venues *inside* the United States with the same objective: to restore the Constitution and due process of law in the island nation.

Villamia died in Tampa just after celebrating his 95th birthday. He had outlasted 10 U.S. presidents, a failed 1961 Bay of Pigs Invasión, the Cuban Missile Crisis "eyeball-to-eyeball" nuclear threat, the lack of compensation for the national expropriation of private property, a tsunami of boatloads of Cuban refugees seeking asylum. As the Castros kept governing Cuba uninterrupted, he even saw the first U.S. president to visit Cuba in 88 years.

The Castro that the Villamias had hoped was "the Messiah" had instead become "a menace."

Their revealing details and recollections were finally put down on paper with the help Raul's oldest daughter, Rhonda Villamia, and writer Paul Guzzo. I trust, with Villamia's memoirs, we now know "the rest of the story."

Retired Appellate Judge Emiliano "E.J." Salcines (1998–2012), a Tampa native, was the first American of Hispanic heritage to be elected state attorney (1969–1985). He is a former vice president of the Tampa Historical Society and trustee of the Tampa Bay History Center. A recipient of the Outstanding Spanish Letters Award from University of South Florida, he received the 2020 Cuban Cultural Heritage Herencia Award (Miami), the 2022 Cuban Medal of Honor San Carlos Institute (Key West), and the 2021 Medal of Honor, Florida Bar Foundation. He was knighted into the Royal Order of Queen Isabella by the King of Spain and awarded two additional Medals for Community Service from the government of Spain.

# Preface

My desire for preserving family history was sparked by the 1977 TV miniseries *Roots: The Saga of an American Family*, based on Alex Haley's novel. That is the earliest recollection of my starting to ask my family questions about our ancestry.

I grew up in a three-generation home environment in a close-knit Cuban, Spanish, Sicilian, and Irish family. Being the fourth generation in Tampa, Florida, and having been blessed with both my maternal great-grandparents, Hipólito Concepción and Maria Coniglio, until age 20, I was somewhat aware of my ancestral lineage. But in the ensuing years post–1977, I learned more.

My maternal great-grand-uncle Alfonso Coniglio was part of Tampa's cigar makers' immigrant labor union La Resistencia, having played a role in unionizing the cigar makers. He had an extensive library, and, whenever visiting him, I would find him in his study behind the garage, avidly reading. Ybor City was the older part of Tampa, which became the hub of the cigar industry in the early 1900s.

Alfonso's sister, my great-grandmother Maria, would often take me to visit her nephew Anthony "Chino" Coniglio Jr. at the Tampa Fire Rescue station in Ybor. Tony, the son of her brother Anthony, was a lifelong firefighter, retiring as chief in 1985, after having introduced significant fire department innovations.

Maria's sister Frances "Panchita" Coniglio Leto was mother of Ateo Phillip Leto, beloved principal of Chamberlain High School, who literally died at his desk, and for whom A. P. Leto High School was named. Sister Rose Coniglio Fernandez was owner of the King Bee grocery and butcher store in Ybor City. Her son-in-law was Tampa City Clerk William Ledgert Stark, in office from 1955 to 1973.

Background for my maternal grandparents Richard C. Rodriguez and Noemi "Norma" Concepción Rodriguez is referenced in the book, so I will not repeat it here.

On my paternal side, there were no family members in Tampa until the late '50s, when my aunt Barbara Villamia took up residence in Ybor. My grandfather Miguel Villamia Saa had passed away before I was born, and my grandmother Balbina Lagos lived in Cuba, so I only spent time with her during her few visits to Tampa. She died in Cuba days before my fifth birthday. I would occasionally see my cousins, Uncle Mario Villamia's children, when they came for visits or briefly lived in Tampa for a few months.

Though I did not have as much of Dad's family in close proximity as I did my mom's, which made up most of my childhood memories, there was one very memorable experience I shared with my dad: his involvement in the 26th of July Movement (M-26-7).

I have memories of, as a young child, accompanying Dad to M-26-7 activities—meetings, events—riding in the car with him and fellow members as they handed out flyers or did fundraising. I recall being fascinated by one particular member's name: Carmelo Bueno. My fascination was that his name reminded me of the word for "candy" in Spanish: *caramelo*. Funny the things that stay in one's head. I suppose for a five-year-old with a sweet tooth that would make an impact.

I had memorized the M-26-7 anthem and would often belt it out as I rode my tricycle in and out of my grandma Norma's garage. She would come out and try to silence me. Perhaps that might have been at the time relations between our countries were beginning to sour.

I also remember at one point my parents always trying to keep me from going into their bedroom closet. There was a long and thin object wrapped in cloth on the closet floor about which I suppose I was curious due to its shape. The content of the mystery package is revealed in the book.

As I started first grade, this new milestone of life kept me busy, and by then, the United States-Cuba tensions increased until relations broke the latter half of that school year. Even before school commenced, Dad and I had not been sharing as many M-26-7 activities as before. In the process of my writing this book with Dad, I subsequently came to understand the reason why: violence had begun to erupt as diplomacy deteriorated.

Once relations broke and the embargo was put in place, everything M-26-7-related ceased. I was occupied, going through my wonder years: elementary school, high school, and college. Time flew by. Then *Roots* was broadcast. I was already living in New York City. Mom and Dad had recently divorced, and Dad began coming up for visits.

I started asking Dad about his M-26-7 years. He would not share much because he did not think it worthy of sharing, always saying that his role was minimal and that it was his brother Mario who played the larger part. And, since the subject had been an "unmentionable" for so many years due to the polarizing political implications, he saw no value in revisiting it.

## Preface

Year after year, whenever I came down to Tampa with my sons, Wynter and Javan Galindez, during their summer vacation, or when Dad would come up to New York City for the Thanksgiving and Christmas holiday season, I would gently ask him about starting to record his experiences. He gave me the same excuses.

Then the event that marked and divided modern history happened: September 11, 2001.

Dad was actually with me that day. Wynter and Javan had graduated from college and high school, respectively, and Dad had come up for their commencement ceremonies in May and was staying through until the end of the holidays. We were at my Queens apartment watching the morning news when the broadcast was interrupted with the breaking news.

It did not seem real. We immediately went up to the roof and incredulously witnessed the unfolding events.

In the following days, I began volunteering at the WTC site. Within a few weeks, my sister, Denise Villamia, also began volunteering. I was there for the nine-month recovery-relief effort, an average of three days per week. At times, Denise and I would be on the same shift. Dad periodically came with me to the site, and on those occasions where Denise was there, it was a special moment of bonding for the three of us. Wynter and Javan also did some shifts with me.

While at Ground Zero, I met many family members and responders who had lost their loved one or fellow brother/sister in uniform. A few of my fellow volunteers were mothers or siblings of someone lost on 9/11. Words cannot adequately describe the sentiment of hearing a mother say she was volunteering because she wanted to be near the place where her child's final breath was taken and to support the workers who were searching for her child's remains.

During my time at the WTC site, the volunteers, families, and workers became an extended family. It was a phenomenon such as what happens with soldiers in the trenches during war. We were uniquely knit together by a tragedy that brought people from all walks of life to converge on this 16-acre spot that became a hallowed graveyard.

After the work at the WTC site ended, there were many activities that continued: 9/11 groups were formed, and events that brought our community together were had. Dad participated in these whenever he was in town.

My 9/11 experience set my life on a new trajectory. I became very cognizant that tomorrow is not guaranteed and developed a penchant for not putting things off for "someday." Thus, my desire to have Dad start writing his memoirs intensified. Each of the subsequent holiday seasons that he came up, I would broach the subject, but still no pen was put to paper.

As I entered each new year post–9/11, I sensed time more swiftly passing. My Dad was getting older. He was one of the very few original Tampa M-26-7 members remaining, and the only founding leader still alive. I suddenly was struck by that reality. Thoughts of all those who perished on 9/11 filled my mind; I wondered how many had stories we would never know. This saddened me. If Dad did not share his experience, he would take it to his grave.

Finally, during Dad's 2004 visit, I emotionally pleaded, trying to express how important it was that he do this, if only as his legacy to our family. He had played a role in United States-Cuba history, and it was crucial he preserve it while he still had a clear mind. Dad was always a humble person and often downplayed his achievements. I believe it was this trait that restrained him all those years. But by 2004, having shared 9/11 and many subsequent experiences with me and our WTC community, he understood, I believe, how fleeting life could be and how significant it was to me for him to share his story. So, on that visit, he sat at my dining room table and, in Spanish, started to write his memories on loose-leaf paper.

In the course of writing this, we had many three-way calls with my uncle Mario. The two brothers conversing about their respective and shared M-26-7 experiences sparked many formerly tucked away memories. As I began to appreciate the roles Mario's friends Angel Pérez-Vidal and Howard K. Davis played in the story, I started having conversations with each of them. This rippled out to others whose stories were also interwoven with Dad's and Mario's.

Thus, the book's core is based on the eyewitness accounts of these various individuals, with supplemental documentation per articles, letters, and memorabilia.

Though the original thought was for Dad to preserve his experiences as a legacy for our family, in the writing process I realized that there was only one account of which I was aware, written by someone who supported the Cuban Revolution while living in the United States: Angel Pérez-Vidal's book *Historia Íntima de la Revolución Cubana*. Angel lived in New York City from 1946 to 1959, when he returned to Cuba to serve in a high-level position at the presidential palace.

This all the more reinforced my belief that a book recounting the experiences of a number of stateside individuals who, from 1952 to 1959, dedicated their lives to the ousting of Cuban dictator Fulgencio Batista y Zaldívar was needed.

In 2010, journalist Paul Guzzo approached me about collaborating and joined me in this effort.

My hope is that, despite whatever posture the reader may have on United States-Cuba relations, this book would simply provide a very personal glimpse into a period of history where Cubans 90 miles away were united with those on the island in a desire to free their homeland from tyranny.

It was my fervent prayer that Dad would see this book published. God, however, had other plans. The Lord took Dad to his eternal home on December 2, 2020, after granting him his two desires: to reach age 95 and die at home surrounded by his family.

Interestingly, the two bookends of Dad's life were related to significant dates in Cuba's history.

He came into the world on November 30, the day that, 31 years later in 1956, would be the uprising in Santiago de Cuba led by Frank País, planned in concert with the landing of the *Granma* yacht bringing Fidel Castro Ruz and the other 81 revolutionaries to Cuba. The yacht was delayed and did not arrive until two days later.

Dad died exactly 64 years after the *Granma* landed on December 2, 1956.

His very life—from beginning to end—was Cuba....

Rest in peace, Dad, until we see each other again and spend eternity together!!

—Rhonda J. Villamia

# Introduction

For more than six decades, the name Fidel Castro Ruz has fomented debate and division. The Cuban community has passionately and at times violently expressed its support or disdain for the man who promised a new Cuba. And each person who has vociferously defended his respective sentiment has done so based on perhaps some very personal experience. No one can diminish what someone has lived and witnessed.

Regardless of the reader's feelings towards Castro, this book is not intended to challenge them. The book's mission is twofold: to provide the audience with a brief, general history of Cuba, and, most importantly, to share and preserve the story of individuals who, while living in the United States, played a role in removing from power the ruthless dictator, Fulgencio Batista y Zaldívar. Their time, money, and freedom were sacrificed in the process. And whether the liberation of Cuba by Castro was accomplished admirably or abominably, the reader may decide.

In myriad books about the Cuban Revolution, most of the credit for its success has been given to what happened in the Sierra Maestra mountains primarily, and in the other parts of Cuba secondarily. Little has been documented on the work done by the exile community in the United States that helped the revolution triumph by providing the public relations blitz needed to propel the 26th of July Movement to global recognition, raising the funds to train the rebels, and buying the weapons they carried.

This book endeavors to do just that. It provides an exhaustive account of the 26th of July Revolutionary Movement branch in Tampa, and those in New York City, Miami, and Key West to some extent, from the moment they were established in 1955 until diplomatic relations between Cuba and the United States were severed in 1961.

# 1

# I Once Supported Fidel Castro Ruz

My name is Raul Villamia, and I actively supported Fidel Castro Ruz during his successful Cuban Revolution.

Why?

I wanted Cuba to be free.

I was part of the Tampa branch of Castro's revolutionary organization known as the 26th of July Movement, or M-26-7 for short.

In 1955, Castro traveled throughout the United States and established chapters of his movement in cities with high populations of Cubans whom he knew would support his vision for Cuba as a nation free from the tyranny of then-President Fulgencio Batista y Zaldívar. I was personally selected by Castro to be the founding secretary of Tampa's branch, and I was later its president.

Our job was to collect money and supplies to support Castro's troops and to wage a public relations battle for the Revolution in the United States.

I have long wanted to tell my story but was hesitant to do so.

Following the revolution, we were hailed as heroes by our fellow Cubans in Tampa, who danced in the streets in celebration of Castro's victory.

But we were treated like enemies as relations between the United States and Cuba soured.

Our homes and businesses were vandalized. Some were violently attacked.

The FBI regularly followed us, questioned us, and treated us like traitors. We were called Communists and turncoats to both our native home of Cuba and our adopted home of the United States.

Some of my fellow members left Tampa or the United States altogether. Others, like myself, decided to fade into the background and never discuss our involvement.

It was something I kept to myself, but it was also something Tampa sought to hide. No one was willing to admit that the city played a role in Castro's victorious revolution. Some of the same Tampa Cubans who publicly celebrated the rise of Castro later condemned me for my work with Castro's movement.

For 65 years it seemed easier to hide my past than to explain what I did and why I had no shame in supporting Castro. It seemed easier to allow people to pretend that Batista was not a vicious tyrant and that Castro was not once seen by many as Cuba's savior.

Then, my older daughter, Rhonda, and I visited Cuba in April 1980. I again saw my homeland, the house in which I was raised, the streets on which I played, and old friends.

And in Cuba, it was also the first time in decades that I could openly talk of my time as a member of the M-26-7.

Coincidentally during that visit, dissidents seeking asylum occupied the Peruvian embassy in Habana. The entire island mobilized in a patriotic protest, each region of Cuba marching by the embassy with signs and posters demonstrating their disapproval of this action. Rhonda and I, along with my family, took part in the march. It was amazing to witness this unity of mind and purpose.

While there, I met with Gabriel Gil Alfonso, who had been the leader of Tampa's M-26-7 when Castro claimed victory. We spoke at great length about the time we spent together in Tampa. My daughter listened intently, mesmerized by what we had seen and done. She had lived some of the history with me. Though just four years old at the time of Castro's victory, she had memories of sitting on the floor in the back of M-26-7's headquarters during our meetings, but this was the first time she heard me speak so passionately about those days. Up until then, she only remembered names, faces, and places. Gil and I provided the stories of which each was a part.

Following the visit to Cuba, Rhonda encouraged me every so often to write my memoirs, to finally share my experiences as my legacy to our family and, maybe one day, to the world. I was surprised that she felt them worthy of conserving; I had not done much compared to others, so I did not see any value in recording them for posterity. I doubted people would want to read them. It had been a forbidden topic for years. Why bother to resurrect and preserve those memories? For what? To be negatively judged again? I was simply not interested, so the years passed, and my recollections remained in the recesses of my mind.

Then, the planes crashed into the World Trade Center on September 11, 2001. Many lives were lost, and many more were changed forever. My daughter, a New York City resident, was luckily among the latter.

She became involved in the nine-month relief effort at Ground Zero and was impacted by the tragedy's resultant uncertainty of life. And she

## 1. I Once Supported Fidel Castro Ruz

wondered how many stories were lost with those lives. How many lessons did those people keep locked inside that could have changed how others thought and lived? Once I was gone, she told me, my history would be gone forever, too. She said we could all leave this world at any time so I should begin writing down my memories, and that she would help me with the process.

She emphasized that I had played a part in the history of Tampa and Cuba and by virtue of that alone it was imperative that I tell my story.

I began to contemplate what she said and realized that I was the last surviving founding member of Tampa's M-26-7. If I did not tell our story, perhaps no one ever would.

My name is Raul Villamia, and I had a role in helping Fidel Castro Ruz win the Cuban Revolution.

# 2

# Baseball and Bloodshed in Cuba

One of my earliest memories is of bloodshed.

I was seven years old and living in Habana, Cuba. It was August 1933, not long after Cuba's president, Gerardo Machado y Morales, was forced to resign.

Machado was a tyrant who kept power by suppressing our freedom of speech through violence.

That was the case surrounding the death of a university student. The student was a political activist arrested for preaching that Cuba would never be free until we could practice a right as basic as freedom of speech. Ironically, and sadly, the lack of that freedom led to his death. He never made it to prison. He was never granted a trial. Instead, in an undeveloped area of the Cerro section called El Ensanche de la Habana, a place where witnesses would be few, if any, he was murdered by a law enforcement officer.

Years later, I became curious as to the identity of this student, so my daughter Rhonda reached out to the Habana City historian Eusebio Leal Spengler, whom we had the great honor of meeting during our 2010 visit to Cuba. The renowned historian furnished her with the following information, obtained from the Museo Municipal del Cerro (the Cerro Municipal Museum).

An engineering student by the name of Mariano Gonzalez Gutierrez was assassinated in the Cerro on January 15, 1933. His body was found near a building on Leonor Street between Vento and Carvajal Streets, where the students used to meet to conspire against Machado. He and others from the group had been taken to the 11th Police Precinct, where they were tortured and then brought back to the Leonor locale and shot to death.[1]

Though I will never be certain that Gonzalez was that student, historical records place him in that vicinity in that time.

On August 12, 1933, Machado's tyrannical government finally

Rhonda Villamia, Habana City Historian Eusebio Leal Spengler, and Raul Villamia, at Convento Santa Brigida in Old Habana, Cuba, August 2010 (from the collection of Rhonda Villamia).

collapsed. In the ensuing days and weeks, those persecuted by his thugs sought revenge.

I was outside my home playing stickball in the street when a horde of my neighbors rushed past me, screaming that the officer who had killed the student had been corralled and was going to be punished. I was not sure what was going on, but I did what any seven-year-old would do after seeing so many people he knew running in one direction in excitement—I followed.

The mob led me several blocks from my home to the same area where the student had been murdered. That undeveloped area looked like a thriving community that day due to a sea of people making their way there. My neighbors joined the crowd in surrounding the target of their excitement—Police Sergeant Peñate. I may not recall his first name, but even though it has been over 88 years since that day, I can still remember his last name. And I can still picture the look on his face when he realized he was going to die.

Being so small, I was able to weave my way through the crowd to the front of the viewing audience. Peñate was on his knees, weeping like a baby, begging for his life. He swore he was not the officer who killed the student. He swore he was innocent. The crowd was unmoved by his pleas. They were happy that the officer was going to receive the same treatment as the student—no trial, no judge, no jury, only punishment.

To the right of the weeping officer was the unofficial executioner. He had a pistol in his hand and pressed it hard against the officer's temple, denting his skin as though he wanted to kill him by shoving the gun through his head rather than with a bullet.

The officer wept harder, his tears forming puddles at his knees. The mob became so loud that they drowned out the officer's pleas, but I could read his lips. "Please no," he cried.

My heart began beating faster and faster as I tried to wrap my seven-year-old brain around what was occurring.

Three shots were fired into his head. The first shot killed him. The second and the third were just for effect and were fired so quickly that they pierced his skull before his body could collapse to the ground. As the blood poured from the officer's head and mixed with the salty puddle of tears, the executioner announced to the crowd that justice had been served.

In researching to substantiate the facts of this memory, I learned that there was an officer named José Peñate who was a Machado henchman. Newspaper articles state that on September 2, 1933, Peñate was killed. I believe this Peñate may be the one I remember, though I cannot be certain.[2]

That was the world in which I was raised.

Throughout most of my childhood, Cuba was in a constant state of unrest. Leaders ruled through fear and violence. Gangs sought revenge against the government through equally violent means. I grew up never knowing what true liberty was. It had been centuries since anyone in Cuba tasted an extended period of freedom.

Cuba lost its freedom in the late fifteenth century shortly after Christopher Columbus arrived. The island was inhabited by the Siboney, Arawak, and Taíno tribes at the time. Columbus claimed the island as a Spanish possession, and the indigenous people were enslaved. Spain then shipped African slaves to Cuba to help man the fields. Spain's economy flourished with the added income that Cuba's sugar, coffee, and tobacco crops brought. But the Cuban natives saw little of that profit.

As the years passed, the definition of a Cuban native changed. It was no longer just the aborigines of the island, but those of Spanish and African descent who were born in Cuba after their ancestors moved or were brought to the island. And they wanted Cuba to be free from Spain for the same reasons the United States colonies wanted to be free of England's rule—sovereignty.

Finally, in 1868, Cuba fought its First War of Independence, the Ten Years' War. Spain prevailed, but Cuba did not give up hope. In 1895, Cuba again fought for its liberty. For three years, the Cuban people battled Spanish combatants. The Spaniards were better equipped and trained, but Cuba's military was fueled by the desire to be sovereign. Waging an unconventional guerrilla war, Cuba could force the Spaniards from their island and win their liberation. Or so they thought.

As the hour of Spain's defeat approached, the United States swooped in with its military to "help" with the final push. Cuba did not ask for the assistance, nor did we need it. However, the United States needed Cuba to be its cash cow. Once the United States found a way to get its military onto the island, the "free" Cuban government was forced to listen to the U. S. government's demands.

The U.S. military remained in Cuba until 1902, when the Platt Amendment was signed. This amendment provided the United States with favorable tariffs on Cuban sugar plus the rights to land on which to build a naval base in Guantánamo. The amendment also stated that the United States could intervene in Cuban politics whenever it perceived a threat to American interests there, "interests" meaning "money." This meant that the United States could force a Cuban president from power if he passed a law that could financially hurt U.S. corporations doing business in Cuba. So, it was in the best interests of the Cuban president to kowtow to the U.S. government and their "interests."

The average Cuban was poor. Having never lived in a free capitalistic society, few had the type of money necessary to purchase interests in something like the sugar industry or to buy land. The best way to rebuild the nation would have been to give land to the people so they could begin to shape a Cuba run by Cuban people. Unfortunately, what happened was that in the three years after the United States troops left, the United States held a controlling interest in most of the island's major industries. Cuba was supposedly a sovereign country, but for all intents and purposes it was just a U.S. colony. The United States controlled the economy, and it controlled the government.

President after president was nothing more than a political puppet of the United States. For instance, Cuba's first president after winning its "freedom" was Tomás Estrada Palma. The United States did not agree with his politics and thus replaced him with appointed provisional governors: William Taft and Charles Magoon, both U.S. citizens. It is believed that the United States wanted Estrada replaced because he agreed to allow them to build "only" one naval base on the island. The United States wanted five.

Following Magoon's term, an election was held and won by José Miguel Gómez, a former general in the war against Spain and a popular figure with the United States because he was among those who signed the Platt Amendment.

And thus was the state of Cuban affairs for the next half century. Presidents remained in power until the U.S. government thought it was in their best interests to have a new president. The United States did not care how the Cuban president ran the country, only how he treated U.S. businessmen.

Machado is a perfect example. He was elected in a legitimate election in 1924 but, corrupted by the money and power of his position, organized a phony election in 1928 with himself as the only candidate. The United States never blinked as he terrorized Cuba for eight years. Then, in 1933, Machado began implying that it was time for Cuba to force the United States out of its government. For years, there were numerous groups of Cuban citizens, such as the students and laborers, who wanted Machado gone. But it was not until the United States supported his overthrow that it occurred. On August 12, 1933, he was forced from office in a bloodless coup steered by the United States.

Through the joint effort of traditional political parties, the military, and U.S. influence, Carlos Manuel de Céspedes, son of the leader of the 1868 First War of Independence (a.k.a. Ten Years' War), was named president. His term lasted only a few weeks.

That was when Fulgencio Batista y Zaldívar rose to power as a behind-the-scenes influencer.

On September 4, Batista promoted himself to colonel, took control of the Cuban military, and refused to support Céspedes. The Cuban president was forced to resign because a leader is powerless without a military.

A provisional government was formed that was composed of five representatives from anti–Machado factions. They named physician and University of Habana professor Ramón Grau San Martín the new president of Cuba.

One of Grau's first actions was to revoke the Platt Amendment. For this bold decision, Batista wrestled power away from Grau, in the same manner he did Céspedes, just months into his presidential term.

## 2. Baseball and Bloodshed in Cuba

Having rid the political system of his rivals, Batista selected presidents for the next few years; they stayed in office for as long as he wished. Batista was officially the chief of staff of the military, but his true position was that of presidential puppeteer. The official presidents were simply tokens. Batista wielded the real power. He controlled the military, the might of the nation.

In 1940, Batista decided he wanted to be the official face of Cuba. He called for a "democratic" election, declared his candidacy, and won a fraudulent contest.

Batista was as ruthless a leader as Cuba had ever seen. Murder and torture of dissidents was common. Compounding matters was that the military that carried out his orders was trained by the United States at their Cuban naval base. The greatest democracy in the world was enabling a dictator. Why did the United States support Batista? Because, for a kickback, he allowed the U.S. businessmen to build whatever they wished, and they were taking over the island's economy.

Batista ruled until 1944. He then retired to Miami, Florida, as a millionaire with money he earned through backroom deals with American businessmen. An election was held, and Ramón Grau San Martín once again was selected president. Cuba was free of Batista's iron grip. However, it was still financially owned by the United States.

Despite these conditions and even though I would one day work with Cuba's most famous revolutionary, as a child I had no interest in politics or revolution. The only thing I cared about was baseball.

My father, Miguel Villamia Saa, was born in Pontevedra, Galicia, Spain and immigrated to Cuba at the age of 13 with his older brother, José Villamia Saa. My mother, Balbina Lagos, was born in Lugo, Galicia, Spain and immigrated to Cuba with her sister Marcelina Lagos and her cousin Manuela Lagos. My mother's uncle, Constantino Lagos, was a close friend of my father's, and he introduced the two. They married in 1912 and started a family in Habana, having seven children: Miguel, Barbara, Fernando, Irene, Mario, me, and Marta. My father owned a stagecoach business, the equivalent to a modern-day livery service.

I was born in November 1925, the sixth of seven children. Four years later, before my memories began to develop, my father lost his life savings due to the Great Depression and the newly invented automobile. The horse and buggy were on the road to extinction. So, he pulled together what little money was left and bought a car with which he began a taxi service.

Still, my father never let on that we were struggling, nor did he talk politics around me. There were enough reminders of our government corruption. He did not want to add another. He wanted me to enjoy my childhood.

Miami Tourists minor league baseball team, Orange Bowl Stadium. Standing: Dave Coble (manager), Raul Villamia, Frank Tincup, Charles Haynes, William Stanton, Melvin Nee, Henry Dlugokecki, Arturo Seijas, George "Tiny" Parker (owner). Kneeling: Beverly "Frank" Tschudin, Antonio "El Pollo" Rodriguez, unidentified male, Bill Perrin, Robert Morem, unidentified male, Bill Cates (coach). Sitting: Barney Bridgers, Donald Hormann, bat boy, Gene Petty, Howard "Red" Ermisch. Unidentified players may be Bill Copcheck and Walt Widmayer. Miami, Florida, August 1948 (photograph by Ronald Thibedeau, from the collection of Raul Villamia).

As little kids, my friends and I spent every free moment playing baseball in the streets. Then, in my mid-teen years, I began playing amateur baseball as part of La Liga Nacional de Béisbol Amateur de Cuba (National Amateur Baseball League of Cuba). I was a star on the rise, a strong-armed pitcher who could hit the catcher's target with ease and throw a good fastball or a curveball to a batter whenever needed.

In 1947, after playing a game with my team, La Sociedad del Pilar, at the University of Habana baseball field, I was approached by a Washington Senators scout named Joe Cambria. He offered me a minor league contract. Just a few days later, I was in the United States, Big Springs, Texas, to be exact, playing in the Longhorn League.

## 2. Baseball and Bloodshed in Cuba

For the next eight years, I traveled the United States, pitching in the minor leagues, looking for my shot at the big leagues. After Texas, I pitched in Bridgeport, Connecticut; Miami, Deland, and Tallahassee, Florida; Alexander City, Alabama; Dublin, Georgia; Keokuk, Iowa; Portsmouth, Virginia; and New Ulm, Minnesota. During spring training in 1949, after having pitched the previous season for Brooklyn Dodgers affiliate Miami Tourists, I practiced with Jackie Robinson, Roy Campanella, Pee Wee Reese, Duke Snider, and Gil Hodges.

More importantly, I tasted pure freedom. I felt safe. I never feared that a gang of government thugs was lurking around the corner ready to strike if I said the wrong thing. I was free to speak my mind. I would pitch for six months in the United States and then return to Cuba for another six, as I could only obtain a six-month work visa. Shuttling back and forth provided a constant reminder of the difference between the two nations.

Then, in 1949, baseball brought me to Deland, which is approximately 120 miles from Tampa, home to the small immigrant community of Ybor City.

# 3

# Ybor City

Before Miami was the U.S. city most associated with Cuba, the Tampa community of Ybor City was figuratively considered Cuba's northernmost province.

Founded in 1885 by cigar maker Vicente Martinez Ybor (pronounced *eebor* and originally spelled with an "I"), who was born in Spain and raised in Cuba, Ybor City quickly attracted other cigar manufacturers plus immigrants primarily from Spain, Cuba, and Italy looking for work in that industry.

At its peak in the early 1900s, Tampa had more than 150 factories producing more than 500 million hand-rolled stogies annually, with Ybor City being the hub of that activity. With this, Tampa earned the moniker "Cigar City."

Each group of immigrants founded their own social clubs that offered amenities like health care, funeral services, and banking plus preserved traditions of their homeland.

There was the L'Unione Italiana (Italian Club), Circulo Cubano (Cuban Club), Centro Asturiano, and Centro Español—the latter two for those of Spanish blood.

Still, because Cuba was the nation closest in proximity to Ybor, its culture was front and center.

Cuban baseball teams regularly traveled to Ybor for games against local teams and vice versa. The Habana Cubans team was even part of the Florida International League, a minor league circuit that had teams in large Florida cities such as Miami, Tampa, St. Petersburg, Tallahassee, and Habana, Cuba.

The same went for entertainers. Because Tampa was the closest major port to Cuba, musicians from the island started their U.S. tours in Ybor in sold-out theaters. And Ybor performers were regularly booked in Habana, then a nightlife capital of the Caribbean.

Then there was the financial tie—the cigars were rolled using tobacco from Cuba.

## 3. Ybor City

I had known of Ybor for quite some time because it played a significant role in Cuba's history. It was from there that José Martí Pérez—Cuba's equivalent to George Washington—inspired Cuba to fight for its freedom from Spain in the 1890s and fundraised for the cause.

So, before I returned to Cuba, I stopped by Ybor City for a few days in 1950 when my second season with Deland ended.

Ybor was a slice of home through its language, architecture, food, fashion, art, and music. Cuban residents still lived as though they were in their native country.

I loved it there and, throughout the following seasons, returned whenever I had a game within a few hours' drive.

Visiting Ybor also reminded me of the political turmoil occurring back in Cuba. As a baseball player always on the road, I lived in a vacuum. My world was the dirt diamond. World affairs were rarely discussed. But Cuba was a primary topic in Ybor. The Cuban and Spanish residents argued about politics at the cafes and bars and would then listen to Cuban radio stations while sitting on their porches at night. When the music show on the radio ended and news began, broadcasters often spoke of the situation in the island nation's capital. And Spanish-language newspapers such as Ybor's weekly *La Gaceta* kept the Tampa community informed of the tumult in Cuba.

The 1951 season took me to Alexander City, Alabama, and Dublin, Georgia, and I continued in Dublin in 1952.

Since the 1952 baseball season did not start until April, I was in Cuba when I heard the news on March 10 that Batista had forcefully taken back the presidency. He first tried to run for president, but, in most polls, he placed a distant third. So, Batista took power through a coup rather than allowing democracy to run its course.

I was disgusted by the event and his ensuing "presidency." Cuba's constant struggle for a peaceful and stable government was beginning to increasingly concern me.

I returned to Cuba during my baseball off-season from September 1952 to March 1953. In Cuba, baseball season ran from October to February, so, shortly before my heading back to the States for the 1953 season, I went to watch a game at Cerro Stadium, which was close to my house in Habana. Following the game, Fernando "Trompoloco" Rodriguez, Juan Mejido, and Eusebio "Silverio" Pérez—three of my friends who were also baseball players—and I decided to have dinner at a restaurant in the center of the city.

That night, I borrowed my brother Miguel's car. As I drove into the heart of Habana near Parque Central, a police car's siren blared behind me, ordering me to pull over. As soon as my car came to a stop on the side of the road, two policemen leapt from their car with their guns drawn, screaming at us to get out of the car with our hands up or they would shoot us. Shaking, we did as they said. We identified ourselves as baseball players and asked what we had done wrong. This infuriated one of the officers. He began screaming that he did not care that we played baseball because we were also revolutionaries and that he was going to "shove his baton up our asses" and then use it as a baseball bat against our heads. He then lifted his baton to attack.

The other policeman, who had been quiet, held his arm and yelled at him, "Do not hit them! They are baseball players, not revolutionaries." After a brief shouting match between the officers, the angry one calmed down and decided not to beat us. I am certain we would have been murdered if it had not been for the kind officer. And we would have been killed even with the kind officer present if we had indeed been revolutionaries or even just people who were known to have spoken out against Batista.

In March 1953, I obtained full-time residency in the United States. Although I had been contracted to play for Dublin, Georgia, in the 1953 season, there was a salary dispute and the compromise I requested was that I be given a release, making me a free agent able to sign with any baseball club. Not knowing what to do, I decided to go to Tampa, where I had made some friends. I lived in a rooming house at 1505½ Seventh Avenue above the Ritz Theatre, which was a popular Ybor movie theater. The rooming house was run by a Spanish woman named Demetria Suarez.

I stayed in shape by playing for Centro Asturiano and Circulo Cubano in the Intersocial Baseball League, which consisted of teams put together by the social clubs from Ybor City and West Tampa—the city's other Latin District—and I paid the bills through employment at the Corral Wodiska cigar factory. While walking to work every morning along Seventh Avenue, which was also known as Broadway Avenue at that time, a beautiful woman with striking green eyes, Nora Marie Rodriguez, standing at the bus stop on the corner of 18th Street in front of Cuervo's Restaurant caught my attention.

Nora's mother, Noemi "Norma" Concepción, was a nurse who had begun her career with Dr. Juan Silverio, a well-respected Ybor physician, and was at that time working for EENT Dr. Blackburn Lowry in the Citizen's Building on Franklin Street in downtown Tampa. Her father, Richard Callahan Rodriguez, had been manager at the Royal Theatre in West Tampa and the Ritz in Ybor. At the time I met Nora, he had already begun his career as an electrician for the American Can Company. It took me weeks to work up the nerve to talk to her, but when I finally found the courage, she agreed to go on a date with me and we began a relationship.

In July 1953, Charlie Cuellar, a Tampa native and former Tampa

Smokers team member who was playing with Keokuk, Iowa, got me a contract with that team until the end of the season in September. I proposed to Nora before leaving for Keokuk and we were married on November 1. Cuellar's future wife, Dahlia Lopez, was friends with Nora, maid of honor at our wedding, and godmother of our first daughter, Rhonda. Dahlia's father, José, worked with me at Wodiska.

After a week of honeymooning in Miami and a week back in Tampa, I returned to Cuba on November 17 so my bride could meet the rest of my family since only my brothers Miguel and Fernando were able to attend the wedding. While I was glad to be back in my homeland, I was concerned about a harassing encounter with Batista's police. I now had my wife with me and certainly did not want to have her experience anything like what had happened to me the last time I was home.

Fortunately, nothing of this nature occurred.

Still, my spirit remained crushed by this earlier incident. I was a resident of the United States, but my heart never left Cuba. It was my home, and I hated that I had never known it to be anything but in turmoil.

Nora and I remained in Cuba until March 15, 1954. Upon my return to Tampa, I was contracted to play for Portsmouth, Virginia, in the Colonial League, and then Tallahassee, Florida. The Florida International League, of which Tallahassee was a part, was disbanded for lack of public attendance. Once again in Tampa as of June, I got a job as a broom stitcher with Costa Broom Works, 3606 Fourth Avenue in Ybor City.

In December of that year, my first daughter, Rhonda, was born. I decided not to play when baseball season began in the spring of 1955. Being a new father, I put baseball to rest and found a carpentry job with Stone and Webster, the construction firm that was building the expansion of the Tampa Electric Company on Apollo Beach.

But in June 1956, when a baseball friend, Montelongo Lopez, had been offered a contract with a semi-professional team in New Ulm, Minnesota, that he was not able to accept, he offered it to me, and I accepted. Baseball was in my blood, and I longed to play in the professional arena, but the reality that I now had an almost two-year-old daughter for whom I needed to provide put a cap on any future baseball endeavors outside of Tampa. At the end of that season, I got a job maintaining the kiln at the newly opened Tiffany Tile Corp, 500 South Westshore Boulevard.

On December 3, 1957, I began my 30-year career with the City of Tampa Traffic Department, which initially was under the Police Department before coming under Public Works. Playing with the Tampa Tarpons that year was my last professional baseball experience. I continued in the Ybor Intersocial League until 1960.

And that concludes the story of Raul Villamia the baseball player.

Though I played in 1956, the games did not interfere with the next chapter of my life—the story of Raul Villamia the revolutionary activist.

I never thought I would be a revolutionary. But when my brother Mario called me in 1955 and told me that the man who was going to save Cuba needed my help, I remembered the chaos and violence I had seen in my homeland. I thought of the freedom I had experienced in the United States. I wanted all Cubans to taste liberty in their homeland. I told Mario to count me in.

4

# My Revolutionary Brother Mario

While I was not interested in politics as a youth, my brother Mario was the exact opposite. He was as passionate about politics as I was about baseball.

Born Silverio Mario Villamia, but always called by his middle name, Mario began his political career at 16 when he nominated and supported a candidate named Ramon Nande from his Cerro section of Habana in his run for president of the neighborhood. Nande lost the election, but Mario had initiated his first step into the political arena.[1]

Orlando Castro Garcia (no relation to Fidel) moved to San Pablo Street on the corner of Mariano Street, which was a block from our Cerro neighborhood home on Auditor and Mariano. Orlando was one of the leaders of the Juventud Auténtica, the youth division of the Partido Revoluciónario Cubano Auténtico (The Cuban Revolutionary Party—Authentic), the most popular political party of the time. Orlando Castro recruited Mario into the revolutionary scene.[2]

Angel Pérez-Vidal was secretary of the Juvenil Auténtica, and, although he and Mario knew each other back then, they did not become friends until after 1946 when both moved to New York City.[3]

Orlando Castro and Mario worked hard to elect Ramón Grau San Martín president in 1944. They thought he truly cared about Cuba. In that same election, a young politician Eduardo Chibás y Ribas won a Senate seat.[4]

Grau had a good first year as president, but then he turned a blind eye to the corruption of his ministers. He permitted the forming of armed gangster groups who would fight among themselves, and he defended their corrupt activities because in turn they silenced dissidents for him.

Senator Chibás was one of the first in Grau's government to denounce this corruption and gangsterism. Chibás used the radio to speak out against the gangsters who ran Cuba, and he recruited the young men and women of

Cuba, including my brother Mario, to support his efforts. Mario helped lay the groundwork for founding what in 1947 became El Partido del Pueblo Cubano—Ortodoxo (The Party of the Cuban People—Orthodox), also known as the Ortodoxos. He attended gatherings at the home of Cuban Senator Emilio "Millo" Ochoa y Ochoa, who worked with Chibás in establishing the new party.[5]

During World War II, numerous Jewish-owned diamond-cutting workshops operated throughout the island. Mario, our other two brothers, and I found employment in these.

After the war ended, these Jewish owners began closing their workshops and returning to Europe, resulting in a scarcity of jobs, so Mario left Cuba in 1946 for the United States on a V-29 Visa.

**Orlando Castro Garcia and Raul Villamia at Playa Santa Fe in Habana, Cuba, July 1948 (from the collection of Raul Villamia).**

Not even a move to New York City could stop Mario from working for a better Cuba. In New York City, he banded together with like-minded Cubans. Just as they did in their native land, they organized demonstrations and lectures and handed out literature, all about how corrupt Cuba had become. Mario hoped that if he could convince Americans to care about the plight of his homeland, then their elected officials would be forced to care.[6]

Chibás left the Partido Auténtico in 1947 and formed his own political party, the Ortodoxos. With a battle cry of "Vergüenza Contra Dinero" (Honor [Dignity] Versus Money) and "Vamos a Barrer la Corrupción" (Let's Sweep Out Corruption), Chibás was regarded as a future president and as the most honest and idealistic Cuban leader. In New York City, Mario officially left the Auténticos and joined the Ortodoxos, continuing his support of Chibás. Mario and members of El Ateneo Cubano de Nueva York (The Cuban Athenaeum of New York) social club welcomed Chibás when he visited there, and the moment was memorialized in a group photo of 13 men and 13 women.

## 4. My Revolutionary Brother Mario

In the summer of 1951, back in Cuba, Chibás announced that an anonymous Cuban congressman provided him with evidence that the nation's Education Minister, Aureliano Sánchez Arango, was embezzling government money—further confirmation of his claims that the administration was corrupt.

Chibás boasted that he would unveil the evidence on live radio on the evening of August 5. But he never mentioned the Education Minister when he took to the airwaves. Instead, he warned listeners that Batista was planning a coup. He then made a farewell statement and shot himself in the stomach. A few days later, he died.

The definitive reason behind Chibás's suicide has never been established.

Some say that the anonymous congressman got cold feet and never gave Chibás the promised evidence. Chibás thought his good name would be forever tarnished by the embarrassment of not being able to fulfill his promise and could not live with the shame.

Cuban Senator Eduardo "Eddy" Chibás y Ribas, founder of the Partido Ortodoxo political party, visiting New York City, welcomed by a reception of members from the Ateneo Cubano social club. Photograph includes Mario Villamia and Angel Pérez-Vidal (third and fourth from left) in the back row, standing. Chibás sits in the center flanked by seven women, including Carmen Guzman Villamia (Mario's wife, fourth) and Alma Rivera Pérez-Vidal (Angel's wife, sixth). New York, New York, sometime between 1949 and 1950 (photograph by Paul D. Perez, courtesy of Mario Villamia).

Others think he did it to become a martyr and inspire Cuba to rise against corrupt regimes.

Roberto Agramonte y Pichardo assumed the leadership of the Ortodoxos. In 1952, he was the party's candidate and the favorite to win the election for Cuban president.

This was the election that never took place.

Batista, remember, was also running for president, realized he could not win, and took control of the government by military force, just as Chibás predicted. The United States, a country that claims to support democracy, did not care that Cuba's new "president" seized power through a coup d'état. It supported his government through trade, cash, and even military weaponry gifts.

My brother was crushed, but he did not give up hope. He still believed he could change things by speaking his mind.

In April 1952, within one month of Batista's coup, Mario and a group of other Cubans, United States born citizens, and Cuban émigrés from the so-called "29-dayers," named such because without having attained permanent residency they arrived in the United States on 29-day tourist visas and remained in search of a better future, formed the Acción Cívica Cubana (Cuban Civic Action). This was the first U.S.-based anti–Batista organization. It required members to oppose any kind of totalitarianism, whether it be Nazism, Fascism, or Communism, and swear allegiance to the 1940 Cuban Constitution that had been abolished by Batista.[7]

As a founding member of the group, Mario was earmarked to be its president, but he did not feel comfortable with the position's inherent public speaking requirement. And, since he had good organizational skills, he preferred to be secretary. So the group instead named Angel Pérez-Vidal president because he was a great orator with deep revolutionary roots.[8]

The first meeting of the Acción Cívica Cubana (ACC) called Cubans to its newly established clubhouse in the basement of a building at 124 West 96th Street between Columbus and Amsterdam Avenues in Manhattan, where they signed a document confirming their loyalty to the 1940 Cuban Constitution.[9]

Within a few months, the ACC boasted dozens of members in New York City, all of whom swore their loyalty to freeing Cuba. Some of the members included Carlos "Moralito" Morales, Antonio Caceras, Armando Abascal, Luis Ramos, Santiago Pérez-Vidal, Ernesto Pérez-Vidal, José Pico, Raul Delgado, Felix Sardinas, Juan Massana, and Pedro Escalona Gonzalez.[10]

The ACC staged demonstrations at places like the United Nations headquarters and held hunger strikes to bring attention to the Cuban plight. On July 30, 1953, the *New York Times* published a photo of Mario and others picketing in front of the Cuban consulate in protest of Batista's bloody suppression.[11]

Meanwhile, in Cuba, another revolutionary was going above and beyond to free Cuba.

Fidel Castro Ruz's rise to prominence began in 1945 while he was enrolled in the University of Habana and became a member of the Federación Estudiantil Universitaria (University Student Federation), otherwise known as the FEU. This was an organization formed by students in 1922 to defend their rights as scholars. But they also organized demonstrations and protests in matters not related to the university, such as by speaking out against Cuban tyranny. It was during his time with the FEU that I first

Members of Acción Cívica Cubana (ACC), the first U.S. anti–Batista club established, at their clubhouse. Standing: unidentified man, unidentified man, Luis Ramos, Mario Villamia, Carmen Guzman Villamia, Casin Abascal, Santiago Pérez-Vidal, Alma Rivera Pérez-Vidal, unidentified man, unidentified woman, Jose Pico, unidentified man, unidentified man, unidentified woman, Rafael "Felo" Diaz, unidentified man. Sitting: Carlos "Moralito" Morales, Antonio Caceras, Delia Caton with her child, Angel Pérez-Vidal, Mary Delgado, Armando Abascal, unidentified man. New York, New York (courtesy of Mario Villamia).

became aware of Castro. From time to time I would hear his name on the radio when the FEU was discussed.

A type of gangsterism became prevalent between the various political factions, and Castro's life was threatened, so he was assigned a bodyguard named Álvaro Pérez, who was part of a group called Unión Insurreccional Revoluciónaria (Revolutionary Insurrectional Union) of which Emilio Tró Rivero was the leader.

Mario, my brothers, and I had worked with Álvaro in the diamond cutting industry in Cuba.

When Chibás founded the Partido del Pueblo Cubano Ortodoxo on May 15, 1947, Castro affiliated himself with it and soon became one of its top-ranking leaders.

After Batista's coup, Castro began formulating his plan to take Cuba back from the tyrant.

On July 26, 1953, Castro and 160 ill-armed revolutionaries simultaneously stormed the Moncada Barracks in Santiago and the Manuel de Céspedes Barracks in Bayamo. They hoped that by taking the barracks they would set an example for all the people of Cuba by proving that Batista could be defeated and that it was time to take their country back from tyranny. They hoped their boldness would create the uprising for which Chibás had called years earlier.

My eldest brother, Miguel, had been approached about joining the revolutionaries in the attack, but he could not risk anything happening to him. Miguel was our widowed mother's caregiver, the only one of her male children to be living in Cuba at the time, and he was also responsible for our sister Barbara, who had not yet moved to the United States.

Only a half-dozen of Castro's men died in the battle, but many lost their lives after being captured. The prisoners were then beaten and tortured. They were whipped. They were carved. They were bashed with bats. They had teeth pulled from their mouths, nails ripped off their fingers, and eyes plucked from their sockets. The Batista government would later falsely say that these men were killed in battle.

Castro escaped the Moncada Barracks.

Two days later, his brother, Raúl Castro, was detained in San Luis—12 miles north of Santiago—for not having any identification. He was placed in a town prison. His life was only spared because he was not recognized by the military.[12]

Castro and a group of 18 men made their way to the Sierra Maestra mountain range, which they had previously identified as the ideal place for them to wage a guerrilla war.[13]

Hunger and thirst overtook them a week into their journey. Castro began distributing men into small groups. Castro stayed with two men—Oscar Alcalde Valls and José Suárez Blanco. Some filtered through Batista's military lines. Others were captured.[14]

Meanwhile, in an agreement between the Batista government and the archbishop of Santiago de Cuba, Enrique Pérez Serantes, it was guaranteed that, if Castro surrendered, his and his men's lives would be saved. Serantes was a friend of Castro's late father, Angel, and had also performed Castro's father's wedding ceremony to his mother, Lina Ruz.[15]

The archbishop did not trust the army to follow through on their promise. So, he headed for the mountains following the announcement of the agreement. He and his colleagues climbed for hours, shouting the offer of safe conduct to those who surrendered.[16]

Castro and two companions were eventually found on Saturday, August 1 by Lt. Pedro Manuel Sarria Tartabull of Squad 11 of the Rural Police and kept alive as promised.[17]

Though Castro's attack failed, it succeeded in turning him into a cult hero among Cubans all over the world. He was already known by those who followed Cuban politics, but his attempt to take Moncada lifted him to legendary status.

Castro's trial began on September 21, 1953, and ended on October 10. Judge Manuel Urrutia Lleó sentenced Castro and 28 of his compatriots to 15 years in prison on Cuba's Isla de Pinos (Isle of Pines) for his attempt to overthrow Batista. In his court loss, however, Castro came out a winner. In his defense, Castro launched into an epic four-hour speech during which he spoke boldly of 700,000 Cubans who were out of work while Batista lined his pockets. He preached that Cuba needed a better healthcare and education system, reminding the court that 30 percent of the people living in Cuba's rural areas could not even write their own names. He said the land should be taken away from the foreign businessmen who did not care for Cuban people and redistributed to the people so they could better themselves.

Though no oral or written record of the live speech was kept, Castro's supporters, with his help, reconstructed it the best they could and distributed it in booklet form throughout Cuba under the title *La Historia Me Absolverá (History Will Absolve Me)*. It became the rallying cry for a free Cuba. From his cell, Castro became the symbol of Cuban independence.

Antonio "Ñico" López Fernández—leader of the attack on the Manuel de Céspedes barracks—and around 15 others were initially exiled in Guatemala, where he met Ernesto "Che" Guevara de la Serna. López subsequently went to Mexico.

In 1954, during Castro's first year of imprisonment, López then formed a group that planned to storm the Isla de Pinos prison and free Castro.[18]

They needed weapons to carry out the escape plan, and that required money. Fundraising in Cuba would have been too dangerous, so it was decided to approach anti-Batista Cubans in the United States for help. López, already having heard about Mario from Álvaro Pérez, sent Mario a letter dated November 11, 1954, asking for his support in this endeavor to raise funds. Mario agreed.[19]

However, before his fundraising was initiated, Batista shocked his enemies by releasing Castro and his revolutionaries. The amnesty was in part due to the pressure of other countries' governments asking Batista to free his many political prisoners. This was probably done to ease their guilt over supporting such a tyrant. Batista was also planning to attempt to legitimize his government by holding "free" elections. He hoped that liberating one of his most volatile enemies would make it seem like he was a changed leader.[20]

Castro and his men were released at noon on May 15, 1955.

It was during the ferry ride aboard the *El Pinero* from the Isla de Pinos prison to Batabano in the southern part of the province of Habana that the idea was birthed and discussed between Castro and his comrades regarding forming a revolutionary group to continue to fight against and overthrow Batista's dictatorship.[21]

On June 12, less than a month after his release, at a meeting called by Castro that took place in a home located at 62 Factoria Street between Apodaca and Corrales Streets in Old Habana, it was officially agreed that the name of the organization would be Movimiento Revoluciónario 26 de Julio (26th of July Movement), a.k.a. M-26-7, to honor the date of the Moncada attacks that started the revolution.[22]

Castro was named director, and the initial board consisted of 11 members. Present at this meeting were Moncada survivors Castro, Haydée Santamaría Cuadrado (whose brother Abel had been captured at the Moncada, tortured and killed), Melba Hernández Rodríguez del Rey (who married Jesús Montané Oropesa, not present at this meeting because he was in Nueva Gerona visiting family), Ñico López Fernández, Pedro Miret Prieto, José "Pepe" Suárez Blanco, Pedro Celestino Aguilera, Luís Bonito Milian, and non–Moncadistas Armando Hart Dávalos (who married Haydée Santamaría and later became Minister of Education) and Faustino Pérez Hernández.[23]

They relocated to Mexico City to plan their revolution away from the grasp of Batista.

One of Castro's military idols was General Alberto Bayo Giroud, a Cuban-born guerrilla war expert who fought for the defeated Loyalists in the Spanish Civil War and then took refuge in Mexico following the conflict.

## 4. My Revolutionary Brother Mario

In late July 1955, Castro sought a meeting with Bayo to request his assistance in training his men in guerrilla warfare once he recruited them. Bayo in his 1960 book *Mi Aporte a la Revolución Cubana* (*My Contribution to the Cuban Revolution*) reflects on this exchange between them. When Castro asked Bayo to share his tactical expertise, Bayo was amused that the brash young man was seeking his assistance in training a group of rebels that did not yet exist with money that was not yet collected. He told Castro he would help with his revolution once there were soldiers and cash.[24]

So, Castro formulated a plan to raise money by visiting U.S. cities with large Cuban populations: New York City; Bridgeport, Connecticut; Union City, New Jersey; and Miami, Tampa, and Key West in Florida.

Because of my brother Mario's willingness to help fundraise for the planned invasion of the prison on the Isla de Pinos, and his friendship with Álvaro Pérez, he received a letter from Castro confidant Jesús Montané Oropesa, with a postscript from Alvaro. Dated September 6, 1955, it advised him of Castro's intended visit to the United States and asked about the "revolutionary atmosphere" in New York.

It reads, in part:

> Our mutual friend Alvaro gave me, with great demonstration of confidence on his part, the very interesting letter you sent him last August 21st.
>
> Finding my comrade Dr. Fidel Castro absent from the city, I have taken the liberty of answering on his behalf. As soon as he returns, which will be in just a few days, it would be his great pleasure to communicate with you.
>
> On few occasions has there passed through my hands letters as well reasoned as yours. It gladdens my heart to know that there are Cubans across the ocean so concerned for the sacred cause of liberty. I wish all Cubans were like that!
>
> Fidel plans to visit the United States very shortly and surely will have the honor of meeting you and your friends.
>
> My friend Villamia, we would like to know what is the revolutionary atmosphere in the Cuban colony of that city. Any information you could provide us in this respect would be of the greatest interest.
>
> Enclosed I am including thirty copies of the message directed to the Orthodox militants, who met last August 16th at the Martí Theatre in Habana. There, the insurrectional path was unanimously approved and we can say that the bulk of the party is without a doubt, on the true course of sacrifice. I am also including thirty copies of Manifesto #1 addressed to the Cuban people, wherein we declare our irrevocable decision of liberating our fatherland from oppression, and at the same time summarily expound our revolutionary program.
>
> I hope from today forward to count on your esteemed friendship.[25]

That same day, a second letter was sent to Carlos González Seijas, who had been a member of the New York branch of the Ortodoxo party. Concurrently, Angel Pérez-Vidal and Castro confidant Juan Manuel Márquez Rodríguez had been in communication with each other.[26]

Márquez visited New York in early September 1955 and met with Arnaldo Goenaga Barrón, who led the New York branch of the Partido Ortodoxo.[27]

He also met with Pérez-Vidal and Mario. They spent several days reaching out to the Cuban community with the details of this new M-26-7 and discussing possible scenarios for holding a meeting where Castro would address them when he visited the city to formally begin establishing branches of the revolutionary movement. Before his return to Mexico, Pérez-Vidal told Márquez that Castro could expect a letter from him. Castro and Pérez-Vidal had never met, but because of the close friendship he and Márquez shared, and the respect he had for Márquez's ardent sentiments that Castro was the answer to Cuba's freedom, Pérez-Vidal pledged his support.[28]

Castro acknowledged Pérez-Vidal's letter with a nine-page response dated September 19, 1955. He began by praising Acción Cívica Cubana's history of fighting for Cuba's independence and spirit of service to the fatherland and concluded with his expectation of their collaboration with the M-26-7 once established. The final paragraph was a greeting from Castro to nine comrades, of which my brother was the third listed.[29]

In the middle of October 1955, Márquez returned to New York. His task was to prepare and organize Castro's visit and to meet with the various groups in existence there to inform and discuss with them the establishment of the M-26-7.[30]

There were three active organizations in New York: Acción Cívica Cubana (Cuban Civic Action), whose president was Pérez-Vidal; the Comité Ortodoxo (Orthodox Committee), whose president was Barrón; and the Comité Obrero Democratico de Exiliados y Emigrados Cubanos (Democratic Workers' Committee of Cuban Exiles and Emigrants), whose president was Pablo Díaz González. Márquez met with the groups and asked them to unite and combine their efforts under the M-26-7. He made preliminary arrangements and then returned to Mexico. Mario suggested the Palm Garden Hall, located near Eighth Avenue at 306 West 52nd Street in Manhattan, as a place for Castro to address supporters. Mario knew of this facility because it was near his apartment building at 522 West 50th Street.[31]

A telegram sent by Castro to Pérez-Vidal, dated October 6, 1955, advised he would be arriving in New York on Saturday, October 22. A subsequent letter from him, dated October 11, confirmed his arrival aboard the *Silver Meteor* at 10:25 a.m. But another telegram, dated October 14, stated he was instead considering arriving Sunday, October 23, 1955. His October 15 telegram to Pérez-Vidal confirmed that he would definitely arrive Sunday.[32]

Castro and Márquez departed Mexico for the United States at 1 a.m. on Thursday, October 20 and entered San Antonio, Texas, a few hours later, continuing to Washington, D.C. Upon their arrival there, Castro sent a cable to Jesús Montané Oropesa back in Mexico advising him that they had arrived. They reached Philadelphia on October 21 and stayed for two days.[33]

According to Mario, Castro and his men wanted to arrive in New York by train so that a formal greeting could be given to him. If they had come by car, it would have been difficult to gather a large group to welcome him. Castro had researched and confirmed that Pennsylvania Station was the ideal stage for his arrival. It was in the heart of New York City on Eighth Avenue between 31st and 33rd Streets, close to commercial districts, and accessible by many subway and bus lines, making it a well-recognized location that was easy for the Cuban community to reach. Castro was familiar with New York since it was there in 1948 that he and his first wife, Mirta Díaz-Balart, spent their honeymoon. Mirta's brother Rafael was the father of future Florida U.S. Congressmen Mario Díaz-Balart and Lincoln Díaz-Balart, investment banker Rafael Díaz-Balart, and NBC television anchor José Díaz-Balart, making Mario, Lincoln, Rafael, and José nephews to Castro by marriage and cousins to Fidel Jr.[34]

So, Castro, Márquez, and his entourage took the *Silver Meteor* train from Philadelphia, arriving in New York City's Pennsylvania Station on the promised date of Sunday, October 23. A group of about 200 Cubans, including Mario, Pérez-Vidal, Barrón, Antonio González Jaen, Eurice B. Rojas, and Walfrido Moreno were waiting for him at the station. The multitude broke out in cheers and sang the national anthem as Castro was ascending from the track level to the main floor where the group had gathered to welcome him. The first words out of Castro's mouth were "Which one of you is Mario Villamia?" When Mario identified himself, Castro embraced and thanked him. Quite an honor for my brother.[35]

From the train station, Castro and dozens from the group went to Casa Dominicana, the Dominican club of New York, located on Broadway between 137th and 138th Streets. The Dominicans let the Cubans use their hall to have an impromptu meeting for Castro to inform the Cubans of his plans. The club was where Dominican émigrés gathered, and, despite there not having been any prior announcement of the impromptu act, it was well attended by them. They quickly organized a panel with Castro, Márquez, and representatives from New York's three Cuban émigré organizations.[36]

González Jaen made the opening remarks, thanking the Dominicans for the use of their space. Then Pérez-Vidal and Pablo Díaz González spoke, followed by the Bridgeport, Connecticut, representative, Celestino Rodriguez Argemí. Márquez introduced Castro, who made a brief appeal for the Cuban émigrés of New York to support the M-26-7 as the only form of confrontation with the dictatorship.[37]

For the subsequent few days, Castro and the groups held more meetings to prepare for the big one they would be having with the Cuban public at large. One of the first was hosted by the Comité Obrero led by Pablo Díaz González and held at an apartment on 14th Street between Eighth and Ninth Avenues in Manhattan. Castro subsequently met with Acción Cívica Cubana at their clubhouse located at 124 West 96th Street between Columbus and Amsterdam Avenues.[38]

Another task that Castro had to consider upon his arrival in New York was producing a new edition of his *History Will Absolve Me* speech, the original of which was published in Mexico in booklet form. Barrón had a good relationship with the El Azteca printing company, where they had all their materials printed. This initial New York printed edition was accomplished with donations from the three émigré organizations. An order was made for 5,000 copies, but they were short by $300. An emigrant loaned them the money.[39]

At the same time, preparations were being made for the main event.

Acción Cívica Cubana (ACC) clubhouse when Fidel Castro visited. Standing: Carlos "Moralito" Morales, Raul Delgado, Armando Abascal, Pedro Escalona Gonzalez, unidentified man, Santiago Perez-Vidal, unidentified man, Mario Villamia. Sitting: Juan Manuel Marquez, Angel Pérez-Vidal, Castro, Luis Ramos. New York, New York, October 25, 1955 (courtesy of Mario Villamia).

Castro continued meeting with the emigrants, including Carlos Gonzalez Seijas, the brothers Mario and José Fuentes Alfonso, Armando Hidalgo, and Luis Montejo.[40]

On Tuesday, October 25, Cuban journalist Vicente Cubillas Jr. brought Castro and Márquez to the studio of photographer Osvaldo Salas so they could take photos of Castro at Central Park and other locations that José Martí frequented at the end of the prior century.[41]

On Friday, October 28, Castro met with Julio Ramirez Barcega, Celestino Rodríguez Argemí, Abelardo Borjas, Luis Garcia Leal, and other exiles at the Hotel Strathfield in Bridgeport, Connecticut. Ramirez and Rodriguez were the first to speak, followed by Márquez and Castro. Angel Pérez-Vidal and Mario did not speak but were seated at the dais. A group of 20 was captured in a photo, which, aside from Castro and Mario, includes my brother Miguel and Angel's brother Santiago.[42]

Front cover and third page, second edition of the booklet *La Historia Me Absolverá* (*History Will Absolve Me*) containing the defense argument Fidel Castro presented at his court trial for the Moncada Barracks attack.

The following night, a group of exiles gathered in Union City, New Jersey, to meet with Castro, but, shortly after his arrival, police and detectives surrounded the place. The exiles who had invited Castro neglected to get a permit for the gathering. Castro and Márquez slipped out through a side door and were picked up by car a couple of blocks away.[43]

During his 12-day visit, Castro stayed at the Manhattan apartment of Barrón, which was at 208 West 88th Street between Amsterdam and Broadway Avenues. Barrón's wife, Gloria, and two children stayed with relatives while Castro and his traveling companions occupied the

## NOTA ACLARATORIA A LA SEGUNDA EDICION

(20,000 ejemplares)

Este folleto se publicó por primera vez en Cuba el mes de Junio de 1954 cuando todavía sufrían en prisión política los sobrevivientes del heróico ataque al cuartel Moncada el 26 de Julio de 1953.

En plena etapa de terror y represión fueron impresos y distribuídos clandestinamente 20,000 ejemplares que causaron verdadera sensación en el pueblo. La edición se agotó rápidamente y hay ejemplares que pasando de mano en mano han sido leídos y continúan leyéndose por centenares de personas. Ningún documento de esta naturaleza resultó nunca tan apasionado y tan leído en nuestra patria.

Actualmente se están imprimiendo dos nuevas ediciones: una en México que ya está a punto de salir a la calle, y esta que costeamos y suscribimos los emigrados de New York deseosos de que se conozca en el extranjero la hermosa batalla que está librando el pueblo cubano por sus instituciones democráticas.

Los asesinatos de prisioneros indefensos por los esbirros del dictador Batista descritos en este discurso, recuerdan los peores crímenes de guerra cometidos por los nazis en los países ocupados. ...No obstante el mundo los ignora porque las agencias cablegráficas internacionales, sometidas a censuras en el lugar que ocurrieron los hechos no pudieron divulgarlos al exterior. ...Es una verguenza que actos de tan espantoso salvajismo ocurran en nuestro continente y se hayan perpetrado contra ciudadanos de un pueblo noble, cívico, humano y amante de la libertad como el cubano, víctima hoy de un grupo de caínes miserables, merecedores del desprecio universal, que valiéndose de las armas que tienen en sus manos han hecho trizas la carta de derechos humanos suscrita por todas las naciones del mundo y una verguenza todavía mayor, que el resto de la tierra lo ignore cuando es la opinión pública de los pueblos y del mundo el freno más eficaz contra la barbarie. Como una contribución a esa lucha de nuestros compatriotas, para que se conozcan los ideales y sentimientos de nuestro pueblo y recaudar fondos para el movimiento de resistencia con la contribución voluntaria de todos los que adquieran un ejemplar, los emigrados cubanos de New York unidos todos bajo una misma bandera con los valerosos combatientes del cuartel Moncada aportamos a la causa esta edición.

Octubre 30 de 1955.

COMITE OBRERO DEMOCRATICO DE
EXILADOS Y EMIGRADOS CUBANOS

ACCION CIVICA CUBANA

COMITE ORTODOXO DE NEW YORK.

**Integrado hoy en el CLUB 26 de julio de New York**

The third page states the history and purpose of the publication, which initially printed 20,000 copies in June 1954 while Fidel Castro was in prison. The three New York City organizations comprising the leadership of the New York City M-26-7 branch sponsored this edition, and lists their names at the page bottom: Comité Obrero Democratico de Exiliados y Emigrados Cubanos, Acción Cívica Cubana, and Comité Ortodoxo de New York. The booklets were sold as fundraisers. New York, New York, October 30, 1955 (from the collection of Raul Villamia).

## 4. My Revolutionary Brother Mario

Fidel Castro with newly established M-26-7 club members from New York City and Bridgeport, Connecticut. Standing: Mario Villamia, unidentified man, unidentified man, unidentified man, unidentified man, Castro, unidentified man, unidentified man, Moises Crespo, unidentified man, Celestino Rodriguez, Miguel Villamia (Raul and Mario's eldest brother), unidentified man, Carlos "Moralito" Morales, Santiago Pérez-Vidal. Sitting: Felix Sardinas, Luis Castillo, unidentified man, unidentified man. Bridgeport, Connecticut, October 28, 1955 (photograph by Miguel Luis, courtesy of Mario Villamia).

apartment. This became the meeting place for the planning of Castro's activities throughout the time he was in New York City. Angel Pérez-Vidal lived close by at 144 West 91st Street.[44]

Days before the culminating discourse that Castro delivered to the large concentration expected, rumors began to surface. One was that the event was going to be sabotaged. Another was that the U.S. Immigration Department had been tipped off that many illegals would be attending the meeting. And yet another was that Castro was going to be detained by the FBI.[45]

It did not matter.

At 11 a.m. on Sunday, October 30, 1955, Castro spoke to 800 Cubans and other Latin Americans at the Palm Garden Hall during a torrential downpour. It was the most important speech he gave during his seven-week visit to the United States, as it was covered by the press nationally. For those in the United States unaware of the situation in Cuba, it was likely the first time they heard of Castro.[46]

The act commenced with the national anthem. Then the representatives from Acción Cívica Cubana (Pérez-Vidal), Comité Obrero (Diaz Gonzalez), and Comité Ortodoxo (Goenaga Barrón) each gave their opening remarks. This was the first time these three oppositional organizations united in solidarity to make the event a success.[47]

Márquez spoke next and then Castro. Castro began by mentioning the machinations of the enemy in trying to sabotage the event. He shared that the Cuban consul had tried to frustrate their efforts to conduct the meeting, even to the extent of hosting a luncheon for the Cuban community that conflicted with Castro's event, hoping to lure possible attendees away through their stomachs. He referenced the rumor that immigration enforcement was going to raid the meeting and arrest the illegals. He graciously acknowledged the spontaneous support demonstrated to him by the Cuban emigrants.[48]

As he continued, he reiterated many of the points he hit upon in his *History Will Absolve Me* speech, likening the struggle Cubans were facing with that faced by José Martí.

Castro again spoke of freeing Cuba from tyranny and the need for

Fidel Castro speech at Palm Garden Hall. This was the first in a series of events in various U.S. cities where Castro would be addressing Cubans and others who supported the ousting of Batista. At dais: unidentified man, unidentified man, Eurice Rojas, Arnaldo Goenaga Barron, Angel Pérez-Vidal, Juan Manuel Marquez, Ramon Irigoyen, Georgina Eligina Perez, Castro, Luis Garcia Leal, Mario Villamia, Santiago Pérez-Vidal, Carlos "Moralito" Morales, unidentified man, Pablo Diaz Gonzalez, unidentified man. New York, New York, October 30, 1955 (courtesy of Mario Villamia).

the Cuban people from around the world to unite to make it happen, specifically asking the 2,000 Cuban exiles in New York City whom he met during his stay to commit to donating two dollars and two hours of their time per week for six months, reminding them that for the cost of a movie or a whiskey, they could help make Cuba free. He added that in Cuba there were already 40,000 young people who had joined the M-26-7 and committed to a monthly contribution.[49]

It had been previously determined by the M-26-7 National Directorate that the weekly dues for the New York, Connecticut, and New Jersey branches would be two dollars, while in Miami, Tampa, and Key West, where the salaries were less than in their northern counterparts, it would be one dollar.[50]

Summing up his discourse, he said:

> We came to organize the Cubans. We came to do a work that the Apostle taught us in '95. We came to do among many the work that only a giant could do. We came to speak to the Cuban emigrants of New York and of the United States. Because in Cuba, it is happening exactly the same—and we would have to be blind not to see it—it is happening exactly the same as in '68 and '95.[51]
>
> Because in Cuba, ladies and gentlemen, in Cuba a true resurrection miracle is taking place, because they understand that this is a struggle of clean men, sincere men, of honest men, whose soul does not entertain corruption. Because the people have intuition, the people are not deceived as easily as it seems ... the people can perceive who their loyal servants are; the people know with how much love we serve this cause."[52]

When they took a collection, hundreds of dollars were donated to the cause. Copies of the first New York-published *History Will Absolve Me* speech booklet were sold for one dollar. Five thousand five hundred of these had been printed with a foreword signed by each of the three groups whose representative composed the board of the New York M-26-7. Those who did not have money contributed pieces of jewelry.

Castro formally promised and proclaimed for the first time:

> I can inform you with full responsibility that in the year 1956, we will be free or we will be martyrs. This fight began for us on March 10th, it has lasted almost four years, and it will end with the last day of the dictatorship or the last day of our lives.[53]

By this time, my brother Miguel and sister Barbara had moved to the United States because they had brought our mother to live here for a while so she could be near all her children. Miguel and Barbara attended the speech. In a photograph of the audience, Barbara can be seen in the third seat from the right in the fourth row.[54]

My sister Barbara brought a guest, a Dominican friend wishing to meet Castro. Both had an opportunity to do so when they approached Mario as he was speaking with Castro. Barbara always blushingly recalled

**Fidel Castro speech at Palm Garden Hall, audience view. Seated in fourth row, third seat from the right is Barbara Villamia, sister of Mario and Raul, with a Dominican lady who was her guest. New York, New York, October 30, 1955. Note how well dressed the audience is (photograph by Miguel Luis, from the collection of Raul Villamia).**

that moment because when she was introduced to Castro, he nudged Mario, asking him why he never told him that he had such a beautiful sister.[55]

A few days later, on November 3, 1955, his last day in New York City, at a meeting held in Barrón's apartment, Castro signed a proclamation that stated:

> I hereby attest, that the 26th of July Movement is represented in New York by a three-member commission, composed of a representative of each of the organizations that initially adhered to it: Acción Cívica Cubana, Comité Ortodoxo de Nueva York, and Comité Obrero Democrático de Exiliados y Emigrantes Cubanos; that said representative members are, as deemed appropriate by the organizations that designate them, the comrades Angel Pérez-Vidal, Arnaldo Barrón, and Pablo Diaz respectively; that under the responsibility of said comrades, all tasks to be performed on behalf of the Movement remain, showing therefore maximum representation of the same in the city of New York, for all the objectives indicated in the different exchanges of ideas.

These powers are conferred by the national leadership of the Revolutionary Movement of the 26th of July, by the powers that it has conferred on the one who writes this for the work of organization and full preparation of the Cuban people.

New York November 3, 1955
Fidel Castro Ruz[56]

The proclamation served to verify that each individual group would continue to operate independently and that a representative from each would become a member of the board of directors for the newly formed revolutionary club, rather than each of these organizations giving up their autonomy by merging into one group as the M-26-7. Castro knew that asking the leaders to give up their management roles would be too much for their egos to handle. He played his hand perfectly by forming the group the way he did.[57]

In Castro's parting conversations with my brother, he mentioned that Tampa was on his itinerary. Mario told Castro that he had a brother named Raul in Tampa who he was certain would be able to help organize the M-26-7 there.[58]

Castro left for Miami the morning of Thursday, November 3, after signing the M-26-7 proclamation. He and Márquez went in two cars and arrived in Miami on November 5. José M. "Pepin" Gomez Olazabal arranged for their first meeting to be at the home of Luis Canedo Garcia on Ninth Street between Second and Third Avenues in the southwest section of Miami. The meeting was also attended by Félix Elmuza Agaisse, Lino Elías, and Miguel Ángel Sánchez.[59]

They visited former Tampa proprietor José Manuel Paula's restaurant, which many Cubans frequented. They also met Flagler Theater owner Oscar Ramirez and then spoke at the gastronomic labor union of Miami Beach to an audience of Cubans and other Latin Americans who were at that moment on strike. By this time, the board of directors for the Miami branch of the M-26-7 had been established with Juan A. Orta Cordoba as president, Elías general secretary, and Ramirez treasurer.[60]

Another meeting held at the home of *Diario las Américas* journalist Eliseo Riera and attended by about 40 persons was where Castro introduced the board. From this moment, plans began to be put in place to effectuate the large gathering. Lists of the members of the Cuban clubs and all known emigrants were compiled, postcards sent publicizing the planned event. Those who assisted in this handwritten mission were Oscar Rodriguez Delgado, Arturo Chaumont Portocarrero, Orestes Portales, Luis Cañedo Garcia, Pepin Gomez Olazábal, Rodrigo Moreno, Jesús "Chuchu" Reyes García, and Leonardo Muniz, among others.[61]

That Sunday morning, at 10:30 a.m. at the Flagler Theater, 313 West

Flagler Street, northwest of Second Avenue, Castro addressed 1,000 Cuban and non-Cuban supporters. Continuous chants of "Fidel Castro" rang out from the full capacity audience as the event commenced.

Seated with Castro and Márquez at the dais were journalists Guido Garcia Inclán and Luis Conte Agüero, who had arrived that morning to cover the event for the December 4 issue of *Bohemia*. Also seated there were M-26-7 board members Orta and Elías, along with Armando Vasquez, leader of the hotel and food service workers' union, Elmuza, Riera, Orestes Portales, Oscar Rodriguez Delgado, and Alcides Gonzalez. Opening remarks were made by Ramirez, the theater's owner. He was followed by Elías, then Rodriguez Delgado, and Márquez. Chants rang out as Márquez began his speech and interrupted him throughout. At the end of his discourse, he charged listeners to stand with their arms raised, swearing to have Cuba be a free nation in 1956. A thunderous ovation ensued as he returned to his seat.[62]

As the applause diminished, a letter from Pastorita Núñez sent from Cuba was read, as well as a telegram from Carlos Gonzalez Seijas on behalf of the New York M-26-7. Alcides Gonzalez spoke next. It was almost noon, and the audience began to ask that Garcia Inclán and Conte Agüero speak. Both were covering the previous evening's Sociedad de Amigos de la República (SAR) event in Habana and boarded an early plane that morning with barely three hours sleep because they wanted to attend the event at Castro's invitation. Despite being drained, Agüero nonetheless showed himself in his words to be in favor of exhausting all efforts in civic management.[63]

Riera was next to speak, confessing feeling embarrassed by the moral and material support the U.S. government was giving Batista. After greeting some friends of Dr. Rafael García Bárcena y Gomez present at the event, it was announced that the closing words would be delivered by Castro. The multitude jumped to their feet and chanted "revolution" for a long while.[64]

Castro spoke much as he had in New York. In part, he said:

> We want to restore the dignified country, attacked by the "daring sergeant" and the politicians who want to replace the dictatorship that replaced them. These are as much thieves as those, and those as these. The Republic cannot be redeemed with thieves.[65]
>
> Under the pretext of mobilizing public opinion, the great criminals who now want to bathe in the Jordan of anti-Batista-ism cannot be exonerated from guilt. The embezzlers have no public opinion. The criminals cannot be enemies of the dictatorship, because the dictatorship takes care of their bad habits. The embezzlers prefer tyranny to the revolution, as demonstrated on Saturday by arguing from the rostrum with the men of the 26th of July that has already given the revolutionary cause 80 martyrs while they played the game

## 4. My Revolutionary Brother Mario

with the government in a combined electoral process. That is why the criminals want to take the Sociedad de Amigos de la República to a great compromise with the regime, as the only way to survive politically."[66]

Castro insisted that there could be no decent arrangement with those who murdered his fellow Moncada comrades and many other Cubans. And if some still hoped for a peaceful resolution, it had to begin with Batista's immediate resignation and the delivery of power to the rector of the SAR to preside over the general elections.[67]

He added:

Some admire that we set the year of the Revolution. The year is said, but the month is not said, nor the day, nor the hour, or how nor where. We know what should be said and what should not be said. No one can give us lessons about that art.[68]

Conspiring with a group of discontents is not the same as conspiring with the mass of the people who must know their role in the struggle. Martí never denied his revolutionary purposes when he preached in emigration. This tactic cannot be understood by those who have March–10th-style putschist mentality.[69]

Castro's last words were drowned out by a standing ovation and the singing of the national anthem.[70]

Next, he came to Tampa, with his primary focus being Ybor City.

# 5

# Revolutions in Tampa

Fidel Castro Ruz was not the first to bring a revolution to Ybor City. It became a hotbed of such activity over the years.

The first to bring revolution to Ybor City was the most famous of them all—José Martí Pérez, a man whom historians describe as the George Washington of Cuba.

By the 1860s, the Cubans were becoming increasingly volatile toward their occupiers from Spain, but their movement could not become a threat until it was organized under the leadership of one individual whose ideals could compel a singular movement. Enter Martí, a well-educated teacher, writer, and poet who, on two occasions—1871 and 1879—was exiled from Cuba for speaking and writing about the island's need to free itself from Spain's grip. Martí was a powerful speaker and writer, a man whose words could inspire even the most passive Cuban to become part of the movement.

During his exile, he spent much of his time in New York City, where he continued to speak in favor of Cuban freedom via speeches, essays, poems, and newspaper articles. His contributions in New York are memorialized with a statue of his likeness on 59th Street at Central Park in Manhattan.

But Martí also took some 20 trips to Ybor, where he enjoyed immense popularity among members of its large Cuban population who also dreamt of one day seeing a Cuba that was a nation unto itself, not a colony of Spain. It was while in Ybor that he composed the resolutions for the new political party he was endeavoring to establish: El Partido Revoluciónario Cubano (The Cuban Revolutionary Party).

His first speech in Ybor, known as "Con Todos Y Para El Bien De Todos" (With All And For The Good Of All), was delivered on November 26, 1891, at the Cuban social club El Liceo Cubano (The Cuban Lyceum) on the northeast corner of Seventh Avenue and 13th Street. His second equally, if not more famous discourse, known as "Los Pinos Nuevos" (The New Pines), was given at the same location the following night, paying homage to eight medical students in Cuba who were killed by the Spanish on November 27, 1871, during Cuba's struggle for independence from Spain.

When the students were falsely accused of scratching a Spanish journalist's tombstone, the Spanish government murdered them for such a "crime" to teach the Cuban people a lesson: if they disrespected Spaniards they would be put to death because the Spaniards were above the lowly Cubans. This has always been a famous day of mourning among Cubans, as it reminds us of our long history of oppression.

Then, in 1893, from the steps of the Vicente Martinez Ybor cigar factory, Martí delivered the speech historians say led directly to the war. About 100 people gathered at the factory to hear him speak, listening intently and shouting "Cuba Libre" throughout. They carried his message to the more than 10,000 cigar workers—mostly of Cuban descent—who were so moved by Martí's words that they vowed to each donate one day's pay to the cause of Cuban freedom. This money was the first large sum in his fundraising effort needed to supply Cubans with the arms to defeat Spain.[1]

Martí in New York City composed the handwritten order for the battle to begin. It was then brought to Ybor by Gonzalo De Quesada and smuggled to the island inside a cigar rolled at the O'Halloran Cigar Company on North Howard Avenue at Union Street in West Tampa. On February 21, 1895, Quesada delivered it to Miguel Ángel Duque de Estrada, who that same night delivered it to Juan Gualberto Gómez, the insurgent chief of Cuba. The uprising was set for February 24. Ybor played a role in lighting that spark that would come to be known as El Grito de Baire (The Baire Outcry), the battle cry that initiated the war.[2]

Martí died in battle on May 19, just a few weeks after the conflict began.

Still, Tampa remained a hub of pro–Cuba activity throughout the war.

Ybor City residents returned to Cuba to fight in the war, and thousands of U.S. soldiers, including Teddy Roosevelt's famed Rough Riders, departed from Tampa to join the Cuban forces.

Moreover, Clara Barton personally set up a Red Cross base in Tampa that raised money and collected medical supplies and sent volunteers to Cuba to care for the sick and wounded.[3]

Ybor City's next taste of revolution came in the form of the Spanish Civil War from 1936 to 1939, when Spain's tyrant, General Francisco Franco, led the Nationalist Army in a bloody coup against the Popular Front Army. Most Spaniards in Ybor City supported the Popular Front, seeing Franco for what he really was—a dictator who cared nothing for Spain and only wanted to secure himself ultimate power. Residents sent

José Martí Pérez, the Apostle and "George Washington" of Cuba, on the steps of the Vicente Martinez Ybor cigar factory addressing the cigarmakers, urging them to support the independence of Cuba. Tampa (Ybor City), Florida, 1893.

money and supplies to Spain in support of the Popular Front. Ybor City inhabitants also traveled to Spain to fight for the Popular Front under the Abraham Lincoln Brigade, a military unit made up of volunteers from throughout the United States. Unfortunately, in the end, Franco won the war.

Next came Eduardo Chibás y Ribas.

In 1929, along with seven others, Chibás was arrested for plotting to assassinate Cuba's President Machado. For his crime, Chibás was exiled. Wanting to immerse himself in the spirit of Martí, he resided in New York City but also visited Ybor City to meet the community that helped launch the War of Independence.

In time, Chibás was allowed back into Cuba, where he continued his revolutionary ways.

In 1950, due to illness, he temporarily relocated to Canada when doctors advised him to rest in a cold country. His friends in Ybor City learned that he was ill, reached out to him, provided well wishes, and asked that he visit them when healthy.

Chibás returned to Tampa that October. He was met by more than

## 5. Revolutions in Tampa

100 supporters at the airfield and was welcomed like a returning conquering hero.[4]

Throughout his visit:

- He was treated to a feast at the Columbia Restaurant, located on the corner of 22nd Street and Broadway Avenue in Ybor City.
- A rally in his honor was held at Ybor City's Cuscaden Park so he could speak to the public about the atrocities occurring in Cuba.
- He was the guest of honor at parties throughout the city, from private homes to the Afro-Cubans' Martí-Maceo Society's social club building on the corner of Sixth Avenue and 11th Street in Ybor City.
- He was welcomed by a group of 13 in the Hotel Hillsboro lobby, the moment captured in a photo including Victoriano and Roland Manteiga.
- He was a guest on WALT-AM 1110, a local Spanish radio station, so his message could reach those who could not make the rally. There is a photo of Chibás on stage with a large WALT sign behind the group of 18, including Manteiga and WALT's Ruben Fabelo.
- And during a speaking engagement at the municipal stadium in Tampa, he was presented with two very special presents. The first was a ring that belonged to Martí, as it was believed that Chibás would follow in the poet's footsteps and inspire Cuba to rise up and seek freedom from its oppressors. The second present was a revolver that once belonged to General Maximo Gomez. Martí was the inspiration behind Cuba's fight for freedom against Spain, but General Gomez was the military tactician who delivered it.[5]

Ybor City mourned the death of Chibás following his suicide. The community lost more than a revolutionary inspiration. It lost a friend.

Perhaps no one in Ybor City was closer to Chibás than the publisher who praised his life in print for weeks following his death: Victoriano Manteiga, a man who seemed to always be supporting a revolution from Ybor City and who through contacts he made in such ventures became Castro's point man locally.

Manteiga was considered one of the most educated men in all Ybor City. Standing 5'11" with starched salt-and-pepper hair, thick spectacles, and an always stern look upon his face, Manteiga was rarely seen wearing anything but a suit or without a book in hand.[6]

Accompanied by his wife, Ofelia Pedrayes y Madera, Manteiga immigrated from Habana, Cuba to Ybor City in 1914 aboard the SS *Olivette*. He chose Ybor City for two reasons: it was a favorite haunt of Martí's and it

Welcoming Cuban Senator Eduardo "Eddy" Chibás y Ribas at the Hotel Hillsboro lobby. Roland Manteiga, Julio Ferreiro Mora, Buenaventura Dellunde Puyans, Salvador Massip Valdes, Orlando Castro Garcia, unidentified man, Jose Pardo Llada, Luis Orlando Rodriguez Rodriguez, Chibás, Manuel Bisbe Alberni, Juan Amador Rodriguez, Victoriano Manteiga, unidentified man, unidentified man. Two of the unidentified could be Pedro Pablo Llaguno and Pedro Sanchez. Tampa, Florida, October 24, 1950 (courtesy of *La Gaceta*).

was the cigar capital of the world, an industry that could provide him with work.[7]

Manteiga's education positioned him to be employed as a lector (a reader) instead of a cigar roller. Working as a cigar roller made for long and arduous days. This was slightly before radio broadcasts and decades before television. To entertain the employees, the factory owners had lectores read to the workers. The lectores sat in chairs on platforms raised high above the factory floors and, using only their God-given lung capacity and perfect speaking voices, read popular novels, essays, poems, and publications to the workers.[8]

The Ybor City cigar workers went on strike in 1920. They demanded more rights, such as higher wages and safer working conditions. The factory owners blamed the lectores for the unrest, accusing them of reading Communist propaganda to the laborers.[9]

While the literature in question did teach the workers about their rights, it was not Communist. In those days, when laborers asked to be treated better, their cause was sometimes squashed when their employers labeled them as "Communists." The fear of Communism was so great

WALT radio station-sponsored event at El Circulo Cubano (Cuban Club) welcoming Cuban Senator Eduardo "Eddy" Chibás y Ribas, founder of the Partido Ortodoxo political party. Standing: Ruben Fabelo, Pedro Ramirez Moya, unidentified man, Manuel Bisbe Alberni, Aurelio Andres "A. A." Gonzalez. Sitting: unidentified man, Juan Amador Rodriguez, Orlando Castro Garcia, Julio Ferreiro Mora, Eliseo Perez, Jose Pardo Llada, Victoriano Manteiga, Chibás, Luis Orlando Rodriguez Rodriguez, Buenaventura Dellunde Puyans, Emilio "Millo" Ochoa y Ochoa, unidentified man, unidentified man. Tampa (Ybor City), Florida, October 1950 (photograph by Waldo Diaz, courtesy of *La Gaceta*).

that just being categorized as one—even falsely—could end with the accused being ostracized from the community, arrested, or killed. The threat of being a so-called Communist was sometimes enough to silence the strikers.[10]

The factory owners won the strike. But the lectores did not return to work, ever. Factory owners did not want the "Communists" back in their buildings.[11]

Manteiga was among those falsely accused of being a Communist. Without a job and with his name tarnished, he left Ybor City and returned to Cuba. In 1922, however, he moved back to Ybor and decided that the best way to support his family in the United States was to go into business for himself. He founded *La Gaceta* newspaper, a then-daily Spanish publication that continued the cause of which he was a part while a lector—fighting for equality in the cigar factories.[12]

The newspaper regularly published articles about the unsatisfactory conditions in the cigar factories and reported on the tyranny in Cuba and other Latin American countries. During the Spanish Civil War, *La Gaceta* was a vehicle for the Popular Front, helping to promote their message and to raise money and supplies for the cause through its articles.[13]

He was later among the most vocal of Ramón Grau San Martín's critics in the United States, publishing venomous criticisms of his presidency.[14]

I met Manteiga in 1955. By then, the newspaper published weekly, on Fridays, and Manteiga's son Roland Manteiga ran the newspaper with him.

I was working at the Costa Broom Works factory, 3606 East Fourth Avenue in Ybor City, at that time. My young family and I lived in an upstairs efficiency apartment at a house located at 1207 18th Avenue and owned by Victory Bakery proprietors José and Inocencia Santome. Victory Bakery was at 1707 East Broadway Avenue in Ybor, next to the Broadway Bank, where my wife, Nora, began her banking career. While on my way home from work on most Fridays, I would stop at *La Gaceta*'s office at 2015 15th Street on the corner of 10th Avenue (now Palm Avenue) for a copy of the paper.

One day, I told Manteiga that I enjoyed reading his comments in the Spanish editorial called "Chungas y No Chungas" and his son's English column, "As We Heard It." He thanked me, and we spoke for a few minutes. As time passed, we became good friends.

Through his efforts to promote freedom on all fronts, Manteiga became friends with people who were also close to Castro.

First there was Chibás. It was Manteiga who personally invited Chibás to return to Tampa in 1950. And Manteiga was usually by Chibás's side during his visit.

Chibás and Manteiga shared a common friend: Raul Roa Garcia, a former Cuban Secretary of State.

Manteiga also became acquainted with General Alberto Bayo via mail during his Spanish Civil War fundraising efforts. Manteiga thought so highly of the general that he sent him $50, a considerable sum in those days, when he heard Bayo had fallen upon hard economic times in Mexico.

Then there was Cuban sculptor José Manuel Fidalgo.

In 1952, Fidalgo was commissioned by a Tampa organization called the José Martí Memorial Foundation to sculpt a life-size statue of its namesake to be placed in Ybor City, on the steps of the Vicente Martinez Ybor cigar factory, where Martí had delivered a speech in 1893.[15]

An outspoken liberal, Fidalgo had an illegal printing press in the back of one of his Habana studios where he published *La Escoba* (*The Broom*), which may have been a newsletter in support of "sweeping out" government corruption.[16]

And for an inscription on the statuary, Fidalgo went to the words Martí used in the first sentence of his November 26, 1891, speech in Ybor City, "Para Cuba Que Sufre" (For Cuba That Suffers). The statue never did make it to Tampa.[17] I will share more details on this later in the book.

Along with the statue for Tampa, he sculpted miniatures that he circulated throughout Cuba. The phrase "Para Cuba Que Sufre" again became watchwords of Cubans seeking liberty.[18]

This sentiment was not appreciated by Fulgencio Batista y Zaldívar. Fidalgo's studio in Habana was raided and wrecked on January 30, 1953. The Cuban magazine *Bohemia*, in the February 8, 1953, issue, ran pictures showing the studio littered with the symbolic miniatures of the life-sized statue of Martí. The life-size bronze statue was never publicly seen again, although it was reported that it was spirited into hiding by University of Habana students.[19]

There is also an account that indicates Fidalgo made two life-size statues, one of which was requested by Castro, who was then in the FEU, to be placed on the stairs of the University of Habana for the November 27, 1952, commemoration of the eight medical students killed by the Spanish.[20] This statue was reportedly destroyed by Batista's henchmen.

Fidalgo escaped Cuba as a stowaway on the ship *Bahía de Mariel* but later was taken into custody in New York in May 1953. Fidalgo was then exiled to Mexico, where he met up with Fidel Castro and helped his cause.

It was Fidalgo who was asked to reach out to Manteiga on behalf of Castro.

Fidalgo's letter to Manteiga dated October 14, 1955, was as follows:

Very distinguished friend: At the end of the month Dr. Fidel Castro will be arriving in Tampa. His itinerary will be Miami, Tampa, Key West and New York, where the good Cubans are planning to mobilize patriotic acts and they request his presence.

We hope that the trip is of utmost importance for our cause.

It is amazing the transcendence of the work completed for us by Fidel Castro during the last three months that he has been outside Cuba. And if his healthy revolutionary convictions, dynamism and tenacity would make him a standard-bearer in this cause, his power of persuasion makes soon apparent the unfinished debt to Cuba, and feasible joining the blue of youth with grey in the perspective of a good painting. His underlying principles are convincingly realistic.

During his visit a few days ago, when talking about Tampa, of course, you were mentioned, and it was agreed to send you some manifests where you will observe the essence of his revolutionary ideology and his vision of our political problems.

He is very interested, my friend Manteiga, in knowing you personally, since on several occasions—in Cuba as well as here—he has shown the admiration and affection that he feels for your bold writing during the constant and continual battle against the despot of Cuba, as well as your sympathy to orthodoxy and Eddy.

During the historical route that Fidel intends to make, Mr. Manteiga, historic Tampa should not be missed.

You know very well that for Cuban people, Tampa has a deep historical value. Chibás understood that through the magnificent event that you organized and which deeply moved people in Cuba. Fidel also understood this, before and after critical decisions.

We know that there are some newspapers praising the despot; and that their columns are only open to whoever pays the most, ignoring our libertarian ideology; but we also know here in Cuba that Manteiga's Gaceta, is against the despot and its writings serve the supreme ideals of freedom.

In consideration of that ideology, and to mark the journey of Fidel, I am writing these lines.

We believe that before, or after Fidel's trip to New York, you and La Gaceta can conduct a campaign in Tampa to hold an event where Dr. Castro can say very interesting things.

I am sure, my friend Manteiga, that you will be enthused conversing with Dr. Castro.

For the time being, receive with sincere affection a fraternal hug from your friend, José Manuel Fidalgo."[21]

Castro's trip to Tampa was set.

# 6

# Castro Comes to Tampa

At the time that I write this, it has been over six and a half decades since Fidel Castro Ruz strolled the streets of Ybor City, but being a part of that moment remains one of my life's great accomplishments.

Castro's liaison, Juan Manuel Márquez Rodríguez, arrived in Tampa first, on November 13, 1955. His job was the same as it had been in New York and then Miami—to prepare for Castro's arrival.

Márquez was around 40 years old. What stood out the most about him was his pacing. He rarely sat still. I am not sure if that was a regular habit or a temporary one due to the weight placed on his shoulders during Castro's tour of the United States.

I met Márquez at *La Gaceta*'s office shortly after he arrived in Tampa. Victoriano Manteiga and other Tampa Cubans supporting Castro were at the meeting. When prodded for information about Castro's plan, he replied with some of the basics and assured us that Castro would explain everything when he arrived. Márquez said he was only in Tampa to find a location for Castro's Ybor City speech on that symbolic anniversary date of November 27 when the medical students were murdered. His trip was brief as he returned to Miami on November 14 in preparation for Castro's speech on the 20th at the Flagler Theater.

Following the meeting, Márquez and Manteiga visited a few locations around Ybor City, searching for a venue to host Castro's November 27 speech. We thought that would be an easy task, considering Ybor City had a history of supporting revolutionaries such as José Martí Pérez and Eduardo Chibás y Ribas. We thought wrong.

Ybor City also had a history of allowing politics to come between families and friends. At times, political arguments grew violent. To try to quell future confrontations, the social clubs' hierarchies suggested that political events be banned.

So, the Circulo Cubano (Cuban Club), Centro Asturiano, and Centro

Español all denied our request based on a rule that they did not allow any political events to be held on their grounds.

Manteiga then called the president of Los Caballeros Leales de América (The Loyal Knights of America), a society whose membership for the most part was composed of Spaniards and their descendants, many of whom had been born in Cuba and supported the cause of the Republic of Spain in the war against Francisco Franco.

Manteiga told the president that he wanted to rent their salon for a meeting where the situation in Cuba under the dictatorship of Fulgencio Batista y Zaldívar would be discussed. The president responded that they "were not interested in Cuban matters" and refused to rent us the place.

I do not recall who the president of the organization was. However, according to a July 29, 1955, article in *The Tampa Tribune* regarding the Loyal Knights visiting MacDill Air Force Base to honor the retiring base commander, the president as of that month was José Q. Afanador.

In their conversation, Manteiga reminded the president that he was Cuban and that on various previous occasions had been invited by their organization to speak about "Spanish matters." Manteiga recalled that on one of those occasions he spoke about the assassination of the eight students in Cuba by the Spanish government. He also reminded him that he and his newspaper *La Gaceta* always cooperated with them in the aid Los Caballeros Leales gave the Republic of Spain in their struggle against Franco.

The argument fell on deaf ears, however.

Manteiga then recalled that the L'Unione Italiana (Italian Club) held a reception in honor of former Cuban President Ramón Grau San Martín in 1934 after he had been overthrown by Batista in January of that year. He also remembered the strong support they had given the Spanish Republic during the civil war. Manteiga finally shared with us that he had friends in the club's board of directors and thus was confident that they would say yes.

Manteiga called and spoke with the club's president, Joe Maniscalco, and explained that we wanted to rent the theater for a commemorative act on November 27 and that the main speaker would be Castro, leader of the struggle against the dictatorship of Batista in Cuba. Maniscalco's response was that he would allow us the use of the theater gratis because it was a worthy cause. He instructed us to speak with club secretary Vincent Guastella to formalize our request.

The following afternoon, Manteiga and a small group went to L'Unione Italiana to speak with Guastella. I did not go with them because I was working.

That evening, at *La Gaceta*, Manteiga informed us that their conversation with the secretary was positive and that, like Maniscalco, Guastella had been courteous and generous, sympathized with our cause, and agreed that our event could take place on Sunday, November 27 at 3 p.m. in their theater.

Since the location for the meeting was confirmed, flyers announcing it needed to be printed. Manteiga said he would take care of that. We did not know exactly when Castro would be arriving but figured it would be soon after his speech in Miami that Sunday, November 20, at the Flagler Theater.

Castro arrived in Tampa on November 23, 1955. I had taken the week off from my job in anticipation of his arrival at any time. I was doing yard work at my West Tampa home that day when my grandmother-in-law Maria Coniglio Concepción told me that my friend Max Garcia was on the phone. I had known Max from my early baseball days but figured he was not calling me to talk sports. He too was a Castro supporter and spent a lot of his free time hanging out at the *La Gaceta* newspaper office. I suspected his call meant that something big was happening. I was right. Castro was at the newspaper office, he told me, and had asked for me.

I quickly showered and rushed over to *La Gaceta*. But Manteiga informed me that Castro had just left. I had missed him by only a few moments. He provided me with the address at which I could find Castro and said that he was expecting me.

It was around 4 p.m. when I arrived at the house located at 1614 14th Avenue between 16th and 17th Streets. It belonged to a Cuban lady named Dalia Mas Delgado.

I remember Delgado's residence being a wooden, one-family house sitting atop stilts that measured a few feet. Such stilts were the norm in Ybor City to protect the house against flooding during Florida's rainy season. The home also had a large front porch that was connected to the sidewalk by a small set of stairs.

Delgado would later tell me about her time with Castro.

She had a dear childhood friend whom she loved like a sister, Delia Diaz, and who had become acquainted with the M-26-7 through her work in the tourism business in New York City and Miami. I cannot recall if Delia met Castro and his group in New York City and then accompanied the revolutionary leader and three others on the long drive to Miami, or if she met them in Miami and accompanied them to Tampa.

At some point during that trek south, Diaz called Delgado and asked if the revolutionaries could stay at her home.

Delgado agreed. She had heard of Castro through the news and knew that his cause was worthy.

Plus, she surmised, if her friend felt safe as the lone woman in the car full of these men, then she could trust them too.

Delgado and her husband had recently split, and her brother Rolando

Mas and his wife, Migdalia Valdes, lived nearby in a two-story house on the corner of 17th Street and 14th Avenue that had a bakery and poultry store on the first floor. So, Dalia could stay with them while the M-26-7 roomed at her home.

Her first interaction with the M-26-7 when they arrived was one of urgency—they needed to use her bathroom badly.

Castro and his crew were well educated and mannered. If Castro was not in a meeting, he was reading, and when she realized they were smokers and politely asked that they never light up inside her home, they readily agreed. They emptied the trash whenever it was full.

Delgado could not afford to feed these men, so Ybor residents who supported the overthrow of Batista chipped in.

Enrique Someillán, for example, owned a deviled crab cart that sold hundreds of the delicacies throughout the neighborhoods with the help of 10 employees. He dropped off a large bag of deviled crabs each morning at her home for the M-26-7.

Others brought ingredients like rice and potatoes that Delgado would cook.

Then there was her friend Hedda's mother, who lived two homes down. One evening, she brought a large pot of stew for the men. When I spoke with Delgado years later, she recalled that Hedda had dated someone by the last name of Reyes but could not recall his first name. I wonder if it was Jesús "Chuchu" Reyes García.

Throughout the day, Delgado said, she prepared food and served the men.

The young revolutionaries arrived at different times, typically in groups of two or three, for meals, and after they ate, she cleared and cleaned the dishes and then waited for the next group to arrive.

Then, at night, Delgado returned to her brother's home once everyone was fed and ready for bed. But Castro refused to let her go alone, even though it was a short walk, worried that enemies might be lurking and seek to harm the woman who was being so kind to them.

Castro seemed to consider Márquez to be the most responsible of his men, so he charged him with walking her each night to her brother's.

As I climbed Delgado's stairs on that first day I met Castro, the front door was opened by a Cuban stranger who invited me inside.

I was led through the living room, where two or three people sat. I greeted each of them and continued to walk toward the kitchen/dining room. Two women were cooking at the stove while three or four men sat at the kitchen table, one of whom I immediately recognized as Castro.

He did not resemble the man we now know as Castro. He did not

## 6. Castro Comes to Tampa

yet have his trademark beard, nor was he wearing his trademark fatigues. Rather, he was in a buttoned-up comfortable shirt with a loosened tie.

Upon invitation, I joined him at the table. He proceeded to tell me that he was appreciative of the help my brother provided to him in New York City and hoped that he could expect the same assistance from me.

He told me that prior to his scheduled address on November 27 he wanted to have a meeting on November 26 with the most respected Cubans in Tampa to discuss the formation of a Tampa branch of the M-26-7, the reasons for its existence, and its operations and procedures.

We continued speaking for a while about everything from Cuba to his trip to New York to the history of Ybor and its multinational demographic. He then asked my opinion regarding the inflammatory articles in *Bohemia* magazine written after his speech in New York City, which he had rebutted in its recent November 20 issue. I told him it would be good to keep the banter going as it would give more publicity to the movement.

A couple of men then came in, and Castro told me he had to go somewhere. Before he left, however, he told me that I was welcome to visit him at Delgado's house whenever I wanted, and that, if he was not there, the people at the house would be able to tell me where to find him.

It was around 5 p.m. when I left Delgado's house. By this time, Nora and I had moved from our apartment on 18th Avenue and were temporarily living with my in-laws in West Tampa while our home was being built. Rather than going home for dinner I stayed in Ybor City, choosing to visit Manteiga at *La Gaceta*.

We immediately began calling people from *La Gaceta*'s office phones to spread the word about Castro's November 26 meeting and November 27 speech. After an hour or so, I decided I needed to get home to my wife and new baby, Rhonda. Once there, however, I was so stimulated by the day's events that I began calling more people after greeting my family and having a quick dinner.

The following morning, Thursday, November 24, at around 8 a.m., I stopped by *La Gaceta*. Though it was Thanksgiving Day, when families would be gathering to celebrate the holiday, there was much for us to do, so we got an early start. There would be time later in the day to spend with our families. A few people whom I knew were talking outside by the door. We spoke for a few minutes, and I then proceeded inside. Manteiga was busily clacking away on his typewriter. We talked briefly, but I did not want to disturb his work for too long and sat on the couch next to two friends, joining their low-voiced conversation.

About 30 minutes later, Manteiga took a break and came up front. The number of men talking outside had grown, and they rushed inside to join our discussion when they saw Manteiga was breaking. Mostly, we talked about the meeting with Castro on the 26th and the big speech scheduled for the 27th. Flyers for November 27 had already been printed and were distributed among the men to hand out.

When I left *La Gaceta*, I stopped by Delgado's house to visit Castro, but she told me he had just left with a group of people to visit places in Ybor City and West Tampa. I drove around Ybor City in search of the group, finding them in front of the Columbia Music and Appliance store on Seventh Avenue between 14th and 15th Streets, owned by Sam and Molly Ferrara.

Castro's entourage that day included Márquez, Félix Elmuza Agaisse, Leonardo Muniz, "Chuchu" Reyes, Ramon Irigoyen, and Lino Elías. Reyes and Elmuza were Castro's bodyguards. The remaining men were part of

Home of Dalia Mas Delgado, where Fidel Castro stayed while in Tampa during his November 1955 visit to establish an M-26-7 branch in this city. Standing: Dalia Mas Delgado, Hedda (woman), Leonardo Muniz. Sitting: Migdalia Valdes Mas (married to Dalia's brother Rolando), Castro, Raul Villamia. Tampa (Ybor City), Florida, November 26, 1955 (from the collection of Raul Villamia).

Miami's M-26-7, with Lino Elías having the most prominent role as the secretary of the organization.

WALT-AM, 1110, which had the only Spanish-language radio programming in Tampa at the time, transmitted from inside the appliance store. *Fiesta en Tampa*, the program being broadcast, was hosted by Ruben Fabelo and featured Latino music, news, and social commentary.

Muniz informed me that Castro, Márquez, and Elmuza were inside the station asking Fabelo for a few minutes of airtime on his program so that Castro could say a few words to the Cubans in Tampa

I immediately knew that Fabelo would refuse. Fabelo was also a promoter of a group of entertainers who regularly traveled to Habana under

Standing: Hedda (woman), unidentified man, Ramon Irigoyen, Leonardo Muniz. Sitting: Migdalia Valdes Mas (married to Dalia's brother Rolando), Castro, Raul Villamia. Tampa (Ybor City), Florida, November 26, 1955 (from the collection of Raul Villamia).

the name *Fiesta en Tampa* to perform at some of the city's top entertainment venues. Future entertainment opportunities in Cuba would have likely been denied if Batista learned that Fabelo allowed Castro to speak.

Moments after I was informed of the trio's whereabouts, they exited the appliance store and said that Fabelo had unequivocally told them that he would not give them any time on his program. Márquez asserted that they had even offered to pay for their airtime, as if it was a commercial, but Fabelo again denied their request without giving any explanation.

We then walked to the Vicente Martinez Ybor cigar factory at the corner of 14th Street and Ninth Avenue, where Martí gave his speech that spurred the fundraising effort. Castro understood the significance of this location. He did not need a history lesson. He walked around its perimeter, as though wondering if he were retracing any of Martí's footsteps, soaking in the fact that he was stepping on soil that Martí's feet once touched.

He climbed the stairs and stood at the top, on the exact spot where in a famous photo he had seen Martí standing surrounded by Cuban cigar workers. As I watched him, I wondered if he envisioned himself getting the same reaction during his speech—the chants of "Cuba libre." He then spoke to us about Martí and the importance of freeing Cuba. We were all on his side. He did not need to convince us. But he spoke passionately about it anyway, as though reminding himself why he was willing to do what he was doing. He must have known what a tough road lay ahead. His trip to Tampa was just the early miles in a marathon.

The Circulo Cubano, just a block away, was our next stop.

We entered through the ground floor into the cantina. It was full of dominos and card games players. The clickety-clack of dominoes came to a sudden halt when our entourage entered the room. While he was not yet world famous, most Cubans knew the face of Castro. Those in the room who did not immediately recognize him were educated through whispers.

Castro was a rock of confidence. He walked from table to table, shaking hands with everyone, introducing himself as Castro, the man who would liberate Cuba. He then stood front and center and launched into a 15-minute sermon about why he was in Tampa and what he hoped to accomplish. He invited everyone to attend his speech at L'Unione Italiana on November 27. He then bid everyone goodbye, and we walked upstairs, where we were met with humiliation.

We showed Castro the gorgeous theater, and he marveled at the architecture and design. Then, we showed him the library. The wall was adorned with photos of early Cuban leaders such as Martí and former Cuban president Tomás Estrada Palma. There was also a photo of Batista and his wife Marta Fernández. Castro and the members of his group were shocked to see it. They criticized the Circulo Cubano, wondering how a community

## 6. Castro Comes to Tampa

that was so embraced by Martí could honor a tyrant who practiced everything the freedom fighter was against.

The library had a guest book that Castro, some members of his entourage, and I signed. We then went upstairs to the second floor to the grand salon, where all the dances and dinners were held. Castro admired the large chandelier hanging in the center of the ceiling. After a few minutes, we exited the building through the cantina.

We walked to Eighth Avenue and 13th Street, where an old house stood on the southeast corner. This was another historic spot and another embarrassing moment for Tampa. The house was once the home of Ruperto and Paulina Pedroso, who regularly housed Martí during his visits to Tampa. In 1892, during one of Martí's visits, two agents of the Spanish government attempted to assassinate him with poison. The Pedrosos saved Martí's life by nursing him back to health.

Yet the city and its Cuban community had allowed the house to

El Circulo Cubano (Cuban Club) guestbook page signed by Fidel Castro, Juan Manuel Marquez, Lino Elias, Raul Villamia, and Ramon Irigoyen on their visit to the club. Castro writes "A visit to the Marti corner," and Ramon Irigoyen writes "Year of the dictatorship." Tampa (Ybor City), Florida, November 24, 1955 (from the collection of Raul Villamia).

Ruperto and Paulina Pedrosos's boarding house, where they sheltered and nursed Cuban Apostle José Martí back to health after a poisoning attempt by Spanish agents. Martí would stay at their home on most of the 20+ trips he made to Tampa's Ybor City. The home was visited by Fidel Castro and his entourage during his November 1955 visit to establish a Tampa branch of the M-26-7. Rafael Del Pino, Juan Manuel Marquez, Leonardo Muniz, Lino Elias. Tampa (Ybor City), Florida, November 1955 (Photo D-3 File 47 Reg# 4455, courtesy Oficina de Asuntos Históricos [Office of Historic Affairs]. Habana, Cuba).

fall into such disrepair that it appeared the slightest breeze could have knocked it over. Little respect was shown to such an important historic landmark.

The visit to the Pedroso home also reminded us that there might have been men and women in Tampa who were also looking to assassinate Castro on behalf of Batista. The gravity of what I had signed up for began to set in. I was not deterred or frightened, but I was more aware from that point on.

Next on the tour was the Corral Wodiska cigar factory on the corner of 19th Street and Second Avenue. That factory was one of the largest in Tampa and employed a great number of Cubans. It was where I worked in 1953, when, during my baseball off-season, I first moved to Ybor. Across the street on the southeast corner was the Seaboard Cafeteria. Owned by Tony and Grace Russo, it served Cuban, Spanish, and Italian food and was a popular eatery for the factory workers. We thought this would be a great place for Castro to be seen and to meet and talk with the cigar factory employees.

## 6. Castro Comes to Tampa

We arrived at the perfect time. The Corral Wodiska employees had just started their lunch break and were streaming out of the cigar factory for the cafeteria. Castro strolled among the employees and spread the word about November 27, passing out flyers as we talked. We remained at the cafeteria until every employee returned to the cigar factory.

Following the meet-and-greet at the Seaboard, Castro and his men went to Delgado's to have lunch. I returned to *La Gaceta* to briefly discuss the day with Manteiga and then drove home to have Thanksgiving dinner with my family and later call a few friends about the Saturday meeting.

I did not accompany Castro to West Tampa, so the following details are from stories I have heard over the years.

Marcelino Golan's son Ernesto said that Castro stopped by their West Tampa home at 2904 West Chestnut Street off Habana Avenue, where his father and his uncle Carmelo Bueno lived. But no one was home. Ernesto was only 10 years old at the time, and he had only become aware of this via family conversations after Castro was already in the Sierra.[1]

At some point during Castro's visit to West Tampa, a young man by the name of Gilberto Caballero, a student at the University of Tampa, joined the group. At the end of the visit, Gilberto suggested to Castro that they go to the university.[2]

Later that night, Castro visited Ayers Diner on Lafayette Street (now known as Kennedy Boulevard) near the University of Tampa, where he met with a group of Cuban students and spoke to them about the revolution. While there, he also met a University of South Florida professor, Charles Arnade, who was well educated on the history of Latin American revolutions. Accounts of their meeting vary. Some claimed that they spoke about morals and manners over several cups of coffee. Others have said that Arnade blew Castro off, seeing him as just another revolutionary making a promise that was impossible to keep.[3]

What makes Arnade worth mentioning is that he seems to have made a habit out of accidentally meeting famous world leaders. In 1936, Arnade—nine years old and living in Germany—was swimming in a river when a man on a nearby raft yelled out to keep up the hard work and one day he could compete in the Olympics. Arnade was certain that man was Adolf Hitler. Then, in the early 1950s, while in Bolivia researching a book, Arnade frequented a bar known for lively political discussions. Che Guevara de la Serna was among the regulars whom Arnade debated.[4]

The following day, Friday, November 25, Castro and Manteiga, accompanied by others, went to L'Unione Italiana. I did not go with them because I was busy handing out the November 27 notices throughout Ybor City and West Tampa. We also were talking up the pre-meeting planned for the following day and reminding people to come.

I was told that Castro thanked Guastella for allowing us to use the theater and asked him to please extend his gratitude to Maniscalco. Castro invited Guastella to speak at the November 27 meeting, and Guastella accepted the invitation.

Meanwhile, in Mexico, Melba Hernández Rodríguez del Rey was surprised by a visit from Aldo Santamaría Cuadrado, Haydée and Abel's brother. His reason for coming from Cuba was twofold: to share with them certain rumors about assassination plots against Castro and to update them on the progress of the organizational work of the M-26-7 being done in the province of Matanzas and some internal problems of the organization.[5]

They spent most of the afternoon conversing on the matter of the rumored threats on Castro's life. In Cuba it was being said that Batista agents were in Florida, having come to bribe authorities and officials with the purpose of attempts on Castro's life. So, Hernandez and Santamaría sent Maria Antonia González to Miami to warn Castro and Márquez. González was a Cuban living in Mexico City who opened her home to the young revolutionaries, regularly feeding them. When she arrived in Miami, Castro had already left for Tampa, so she came here and reached out to Manteiga. He took her to the house where Castro was staying to inform them of the threats. In particular, the large meeting planned for November 27 was being targeted. Locals were allegedly being threatened with reprisals towards their families in Cuba.[6]

Saturday, November 26 arrived. The *Tampa Daily Times* featured an article titled "Anti-Batista Revolutionist to Talk Here" introducing Castro and reminding the community of his speech the following day at L'Unione Italiana. It was great publicity for the event. I was in high spirits after seeing the article. However, my good mood soon turned sour.[7]

The meeting with Castro to plan his big Ybor City speech was held at Cuatro Caminos Café, located on the east side at 2619 22nd Street near Columbus Drive. The place was named after a restaurant in Habana.

We lined up the chairs in rows and put two tables in the front.

Everything was set. Then, Manteiga arrived with bad news. At 7 a.m. he had received a call from Maniscalco, who told him that the prior evening there had been an "urgent" meeting of L'Unione Italiana's board of directors to discuss Castro's use of their theater for his speech. The board voted contrary to Maniscalco and Guastella and decided against us utilizing the theater for our meeting.

The excuse they gave us for canceling was that one of their rules "prohibited political activities in the club" and that our meeting obviously fell under that category. The Circulo Cubano, Centro Español, and Centro Asturiano denied our request for the same reason, but those three

## 6. Castro Comes to Tampa

clubs let us know this up front, not after we booked and promoted our event.

We decided that Castro should address the audience first to explain his plans for organizing the Club Patriótico 26 de Julio de Tampa, which was the purpose of this meeting, and that, after Castro finished, Manteiga would share the news that L'Unione Italiana had withdrawn their permission. We did not want the bad news to overshadow Castro's vision for our organization and a free Cuba.

The meeting began around 10 a.m. There were about 40 people gathered. Castro and Manteiga sat facing the audience.

Manteiga called the attendees to order so the meeting could commence. He started by introducing Castro, who was received by the people with great enthusiasm. After his introduction, Manteiga gave a brief recap of Castro's revolutionary history and then gave Castro the floor.

Castro announced he was creating a Tampa branch of the M-26-7 and said that the club and its members would oversee public relations efforts and organize protests against Batista and in favor of the revolution, but that the focus of the club would be to raise money to cover the cost of training and arming the rebel forces. He stated that money could be sent to his liaisons in Mexico after he left Tampa.

He said that a board of directors would have to be established, and named Manteiga as president and me as secretary, giving us authority to later name the other board members. He continued that each prospective member would have to complete a formal application and receive an ID card bearing his or her photograph and the signatures of Castro, Manteiga, and myself. They would also receive a booklet with pages designed to have payment stamps attached. Members would receive a stamp that would be glued into the booklet to mark each dues payment made. The club treasurer would be responsible for collecting the one-dollar-per-week dues, handing out the stamps, and making sure everyone was current with their payments. Upon payment, the treasurer would glue into the member's dues booklet a red-and-black postage-like stamp on which was printed "UN PESO" and "M-26-7."

Funds were also to be raised by collecting money in the streets and at functions sponsored by the Tampa social clubs and mutual aid societies and by soliciting donations from Tampa businessmen, especially those in the cigar-making industry.

The first collection for the newly formed club was made while Castro was speaking. In conclusion, Castro said that he expected everyone's cooperation, and that only by working hard would they be able to triumph in the struggle for freeing Cuba.

For Cuba—for Freedom!

## Club Patriotico 26 De Julio De Tampa

Officina: Calle 15 No. 2015    Tampa, Florida, E. U. A.

Solicito ingresar en este Club y contraigo voluntariamente la obligacion de respetar con absoluta lealtad sus postulados democraticos, reglamento y acuerdos.

Nombre  Raúl Villamia Lagos                                        Edad  29

Lugar de nacimiento  Habana, Cuba                                  Estado  Casado

Domicilio                        Tampa, Fla.                        Telefono  R.E. 87067

Empleado por  City of Tampa

Direccion del empleante  Tampa City Hall

Recomendado por  1. Victoriano Manteiga
                 2. Carlos Carbonell

Fecha  Noviembre 27 de 1955

Cuota de ingreso ---------- $2.00

Cuota mensual ------------ $1.00

Firma del Solicitante:  Raúl Villamia Lagos

Por el Club Patriotico 26 de Julio:  Victoriano Manteiga

Por el Club Patriotico 26 de Julio:  Raúl Villamia Lagos

Raul Villamia's M-26-7 membership application form. These were printed on formal M-26-7 letterhead used for all club correspondence, with letterhead envelopes. The top portion states, *"I request to join this club and voluntarily assume the obligation to respect with absolute loyalty its democratic postulates, regulations, and agreements."* The application fee is $2 and the monthly dues are $1. The initial two signatures are the people who are recommending Raul for membership, which were Victoriano Manteiga and Carlos Carbonell. Note on the bottom that Raul had to sign not only as an applicant, but as the secretary of the M-26-7 along with Victoriano as president. Tampa, Florida, November 27, 1955 (from the collection of Raul Villamia).

## 6. Castro Comes to Tampa

Castro gave Manteiga the floor so he could give the audience the bad news about L'Unione Italiana.

Castro then spoke again. He was calm. He spoke as though he had not a care in the world. He was prepared for every obstacle thrown in his path. He was prepared to die for the revolution. A canceled locale was not going to bother him.

He said that the last-minute cancellation of L'Unione Italiana and the other clubs denying us their halls was the result of the pressure put on them by agents of Batista's government in Tampa, by the Cuban consul, and by powerful Tampa people in the real estate and construction businesses associated with the dictator.

Castro continued that we did not have much time, so, if need be, we would have our event anywhere, even in a park or street in Ybor City or West Tampa.

The meeting ended around noon, and a group of us remained to discuss our options.

Castro told us that he would be returning to the house on 14th Avenue and that he would stay in touch with us.

Manteiga, the group, and I went to *La Gaceta*. While there, it occurred to me that there was a hall belonging to a labor union, the CIO Center at 1226 East Broadway Avenue between 12th and 13th Streets, which today houses Sociedad La Union Martí-Maceo Cuban Club (The Martí-Maceo Union Society). I mentioned it to the others, but some thought the place would be too small. I told them I had been inside the building and that the space was larger than it appeared to be from the outside. I emphasized that we could not waste any more time trying to find a place that was larger because there were none we had not already considered.

Pedro Pérez was the president of the local CIO labor union that represented the American Can Company workers of the United Steelworkers of America. He was also Manteiga's friend and someone I knew. Manteiga called him, briefly explained the situation, and asked if we could have the meeting in the steelworkers' union hall. Without hesitation, Pérez told us to come see him.

Manteiga told Pérez in detail what happened with the L'Unione Italiana and explained what the meeting was going to be about. Pérez sympathized with our cause and handed us the keys without charging us for the rental.

After informing Castro of the good news, Manteiga worked on the flyer announcing the new location. His friend Angelo Spoto owned Florida Printing at 2903 East 7th Avenue on the corner of 22nd Street, not far from *La Gaceta*, and promised to print the flyers that afternoon once the shop closed for the day.

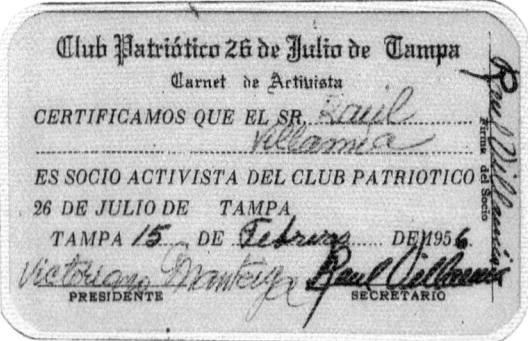

## 6. Castro Comes to Tampa

When the flyers arrived, we sent volunteers to different locations in Ybor City and West Tampa. And we had some of our group drive around with microphones announcing the meeting.

We then called a rental place to order chairs to be delivered the next morning to the union center. The rental place promised to have the chairs delivered before 10 a.m.

More people continued streaming into the newspaper office to volunteer their services. Manteiga and I told them that they had to be at the hall the next morning to receive and put the chairs in place and do whatever was necessary to prepare for the meeting scheduled to start at 3 p.m.

It had been a long day. I decided to head home and relax a bit in preparation for the following day since everything seemed to be working itself out. I stopped at the house where Castro was staying before making my way back to West Tampa. There were some people with him. He and I talked for a while about many things. I asked about the security for the meeting, and he said it had been taken care of. He then said that he was very pleased with our work, appreciated the enthusiasm of the Cubans in Tampa, and was very grateful for the strong support he and his comrades had received. I gave him some cigars my grandfather-in-law Hipólito Concepción had made and took my leave.

Sunday, November 27, was sunny but cool. A *Tampa Sunday Tribune* article titled "Italian Club Bars Theatre to Leader of Cuban Revolt" recounted the story of the last-minute bailout by L'Unione Italiana and the meeting's new location at the CIO Center.[8]

That morning, my wife, Nora, and I woke up before 8 a.m., bathed, dressed, and ate breakfast. Every Sunday she attended the 11 a.m. Mass at Our Lady of Perpetual Help Church (OLPH), and I would sometimes go

*Opposite:* Raul Villamia's M-26-7 dues-payment booklet. Page 1 has date issued—June 16, 1958— and branch "E...No. E-1" designation, signed by Raul Chibás (Eduardo's brother) as treasurer, (illegible) organization, and Gabriel Gil as delegate. Page 2 has member photograph and states *"This card is a credential belonging to the member indicated here, which as such, identifies him in this Organization and will have no value if he is not up to date with all requirements expressed as follows."* It then gives four "responsibilities" and four "rights" of the member listed on pages 3 and 4 (not photographed). M-26-7 membership card front, dated August 14, 1957, signed by Victoriano Manteiga as president and Raul Villamia as secretary, states *"We certify that Mr. Raul Villamia is a contributing member of the 26th of July Patriotic Club of Tampa."* M-26-7 photo ID card front, dated February 15, 1956, signed by Victoriano and Raul, states *"We certify that Mr. Raul Villamia is an active member of the 26th of July Club of Tampa."* Tampa, Florida (from the collection of Raul Villamia).

along with her. I told Nora that on this day, however, she needed to go to the 10 a.m. service and that I could not accompany her. At 9:30 a.m. I drove her to the church, located on the corner of 11th Avenue and 17th Street, a short walk from Delgado's house. I left Nora at church and went to see Castro for a few minutes. From there, I went to the CIO Center on Seventh Avenue to see if I was needed.

At the hall, volunteers were already setting up chairs and preparing the stage where the orators would be seated. Two men came in and told me that Fabelo had been announcing on his radio program that he heard that men were threatening to ignite bombs at a "certain labor hall" that was hosting a meeting held by a group of "irresponsibles." He never mentioned Castro or the M-26-7 by name, but he was obviously alluding to our meeting.

It seems Fabelo was trying to scare people from attending.

We did not worry about the rumors. We had heeded the warning given to us by Maria Antonia González and spoken with the Tampa Police Department, which promised to place officers in the meeting and patrol the area.

I was so involved with all the activities at the hall that I lost track of time and had completely forgotten to pick Nora up from church. I hurried to OLPH, but she was gone.

I decided to stop by Delgado's to see if she might have gone there looking for me. She had. I found Nora conversing with Castro on the porch when I arrived. I apologized to her, spoke with Castro for a few minutes, and then headed home to drop off Nora.

While we drove home, Nora told me that she had walked from the church to the house on 14th Street to see if I was there, and planned, if I was not, to call her parents from the house telephone to ask one of them to come pick her up. But Castro was sitting in a rocking chair on the porch reading when she arrived.

When she had asked him about my whereabouts, Castro answered her somewhat curtly: "Madam, Raul is working, doing things at the union

**Opposite:** M-26-7 dues payment booklet page 5 completes the "rights," and page 6 starts what continues for the remainder of the booklet: pages where the red and black "un peso" ($1) dues stamps are affixed. M-26-7 membership card back side with M-26-7 stamp. M-26-7 photo ID back side with photograph, states *"The person holding this card is a responsible member of the 26th of July Movement, whom he represents in the tasks of organizing, proselytizing and raising patriotic funds to free the people of Cuba. He has a voice and vote in the Club's assemblies, but he also has a greater responsibility in all his actions. For the record, it is signed on behalf of the M.R. 26th of July by its leader. Fidel Castro."* Tampa, Florida (from the collection of Raul Villamia).

## 6. Castro Comes to Tampa

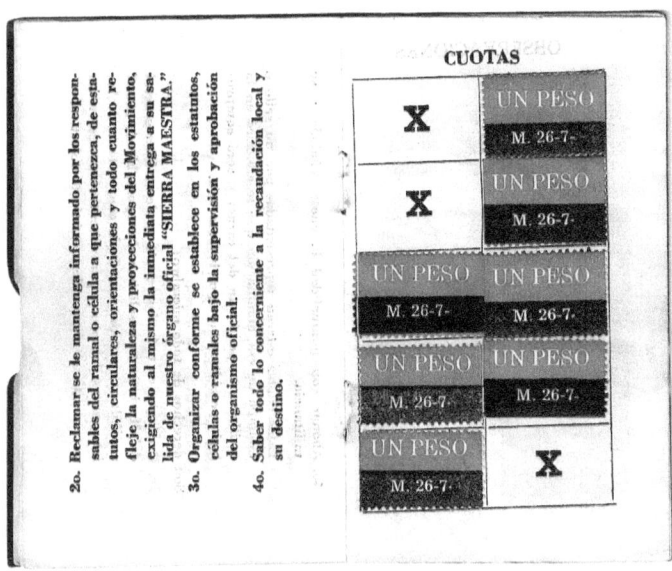

hall for our meeting. But do not worry, Madam, I will get someone to take you home."

Nora thought Castro had seemed a bit irritated with her inquiry and always recalled the only interaction between them with mixed emotions. Perhaps he was beginning to feel the weight of all that had happened in the prior 24 hours. She told me that she had only been there a few minutes when I arrived at the house, so it did not become necessary for Castro to provide a ride for her, nor for her to call her parents.

Nora's grandmother had food waiting for us when we returned home. We had lunch and I then went back to Ybor.

I stopped by *La Gaceta* to see Manteiga, but he was gone. His son Roland told me his father would be going directly from his home to the labor hall, so I proceeded there as well.

I arrived around 2 p.m. People were already there, as were, as promised, police. Two or three policemen stood in front of the building, and a police car was cruising the perimeter.

By 3 p.m., approximately 300 were in attendance. All the seats were occupied, and people were standing in the aisles, in the entrance, and out on the sidewalk, where they could listen via speakers installed on the exterior of the building.

We rented the loudspeakers from a business that was in the same building as *La Gaceta*. Called Radio Center, it was owned by Aurelio

---

**INVITAMOS A TODOS LOS CUBANOS DE TAMPA ....**

Y A TODOS LOS HOMBRES QUE AMAN LA LIBERTAD

Para que asistan, a la Conmemoración del Fusilamiento de los 8 Estudiantes de Medicina de Cuba. Crimen cometido el 27 de Noviembre del año 1871.

Que se Efectuará el **PRÓXIMO DOMINGO 27 de NOVIEMBRE**

En el local de la C. I. O. CENTER 1226 Septima Avenida, Entre 12 y 13 Calle. El resumen estará a cargo del

DR. FIDEL CASTRO
LIDER DE LA REVOLUCION CUBANA
Club Patriotico 26 de
Julio de Tampa

**HORA: 3 P. M.**

Flyer announcing Fidel Castro's speech at 3 p.m. at the CIO Center in honor of the eight medical students murdered by the Spanish government on November 27, 1871. This was the flyer hurriedly made the day before the event when the L'Unione Italiana (Italian Club) withdrew at the eleventh hour their permission to allow the meeting at their facility. Tampa (Ybor City), Florida, November 27, 1955 (from the collection of Raul Villamia).

## 6. Castro Comes to Tampa

"Yeyo" González and his sons, Aurelio Jr. and Guillermo, known as Willie. Guillermo was involved in politics, and Aurelio Jr. was a radio technician and disc jockey. They, along with their father, ran the business, which sold Spanish music and rented out sound equipment and a truck with a loudspeaker to advertise events. A few years later, they sold the business to Billy Delgado, leader of a local band called Riviera Orchestra that often performed at the various mutual aid society dances and other venues.

The time came for the meeting to commence.

Sitting on the stage were those who were addressing the audience: Castro, Márquez, Manteiga, Elías, and Rafael del Pino. The host was a man who was part of the Miami M-26-7. I vaguely recall it might have been Orestes Portales, as his last name rings a bell in my mind, but I cannot be certain. After the national anthem, the gentleman began the meeting by introducing everyone on stage. They each received warm applause, particularly Castro.

Elías was first to address the audience. He spoke briefly, attacking Batista's character and condemning the crimes he had committed against

Dais at the CIO Center for Fidel Castro's speech. Standing: Jesus "Chuchu" Reyes Garcia. Sitting: Lino Elias, Juan Manuel Marquez, Castro, Victoriano Manteiga. Tampa (Ybor City), Florida, November 27, 1955 (courtesy of *La Gaceta*).

the people of Cuba. He spoke highly of Castro, said the Cubans in Miami were very supportive of the cause and that he hoped Tampa's Cuban population would be as supportive.

Next was del Pino. His speech was not well received by the audience. He rarely spoke of Castro or the M-26-7. Instead, he spoke of the Partido Auténtico Revoluciónario Cubano and praised former Cuban president Carlos Prío Socarrás and his desire to free Cuba. The speech was well put together, but considering we were all there to support Castro and not Prío, no one was sure how to react. Del Pino, it is worth noting, was later arrested as a counterrevolutionary after Castro came to power.

Manteiga followed. He thanked United Steelworkers president Pérez for, without hesitation, providing use of the building, and he thanked everyone who came. He then motioned to Castro and the others on stage. "We salute you, in the name of the honest and virile Tampanians who desire today, as in the past century, a truly free Cuba," he said. All throughout his life, he continued, he had been a fighter against dictators, and he would continue to fight them. He asked the people of Tampa to support Castro and his comrades, saying that Tampa's history was united with the glorious history of Cuba.

He briefly attacked Batista for persecuting, torturing, and killing his adversaries, all reasons for justifying his removal. To that end, he explained, Castro and his men needed help in creating an armed force to remove Batista from power. And a branch of the M-26-7 club needed to be started in Tampa, as had been done in New York City, Miami, and other cities. Manteiga invited everyone in attendance to become members, along with their families and friends. Those wishing to do so needed to contact either him or me, he said. He then asked me to stand up so everyone could see who I was.

Márquez was the next speaker. He was a good orator. He first provided a short review of how Batista snatched power, blasting him and his collaborators for the lack of liberty in Cuba and the cruel treatment imposed upon the Cuban people. Márquez shared that he had been mercilessly beaten by Batista's police and told to leave Cuba or be killed. He praised the 1953 Moncada barrack attackers and Castro and then asked for a moment of silence in memory of all who died fighting the Batista regime. He ended his speech by asking the people to join the M-26-7 club and to help bring freedom to Cuba.

A collection was then made by two people, one on each side of the seating area. They passed a straw hat, characteristic of the one worn by the *mambises*, the name given to the Cuban soldiers in their war against Spain. The Mambi hat was also used for the collections in both the New York and Miami gatherings.

Finally, it was Castro's turn to speak. He was welcomed by a long applause. First, he told everyone how grateful he was that they attended the meeting and thanked those in Tampa who helped him organize an opportunity for him to express his ideas. He thanked Pérez for the use of the hall and recounted the problems we had finding a place to hold the meeting. He said there were Batista supporters in Tampa trying to disrupt his attempt to free Cuba, but the large number of people who came to listen to him proved that the sabotage had failed. He continued by mentioning that November 27 was the 84th anniversary of the execution of the eight students by the Spanish government in 1871, a commemoration of a tragic event in the struggle for independence. And he mentioned that on that date in 1891 Martí had also given his famous "Pinos Nuevos" (New Pines) speech in Ybor City.

He then summarized Cuba's history from the time the Spaniards arrived to the present-day Batista regime. From the beginning of the Republic of Cuba in 1902, he said, to the present government of Batista, the island had mostly been governed by corrupt politicians and thieves who looked for power solely to make themselves richer and did nothing to improve the Cuban standard of living. He said Cuba needed an honest government, which is why it was necessary to have a true revolution. They needed to end political corruption and give the Cuban people the work, education, and medical care they deserved.

He reiterated how Batista took power in 1952, not by election, but by coup, and said that force was again needed for Cuba to be free. Money was needed to form the necessary militia, which was why an M-26-7 was required in Tampa. He asked that everyone in attendance donate what they could to the cause. He concluded his speech by stating that he and his comrades were firmly committed to freeing Cuba in 1956, that the fight would be long and hard, but that they were certain that the final triumph would be theirs. He concluded: "We will be free or martyrs! Long live a free Cuba!"

The crowd applauded thunderously.

When the meeting was over, the small group of us who helped organize Castro's activities remained at the hall and spoke with him for a short while. Castro told us he was very appreciative of our cooperation and that he expected that we would continue working with the same enthusiasm when he left.

The next day, at *La Gaceta*, Castro wrote and signed a statement verifying that the amount collected at the meeting was $191.02 and indicated that there was to be a total of $81 deducted from that in expenses for loudspeakers, chair rentals, and printing costs.

More money was collected around the city in the days prior to his big speech, but I do not recall the total. I believe Castro raised a few hundred dollars in all, including the money from the November 27 event.

After signing the statement, Castro and Manteiga went to WTVT Channel 13 to be interviewed.

That day at *La Gaceta* on November 28, 1955, was the last time Castro and I were together. I have since learned that the last person he visited in Tampa was not a Cuban, but an American born Irishman: Tom O'Connor. Once again, my knowledge of this incident is only through third parties and newspaper archives, so I cannot vouch for its authenticity.

O'Connor was a journalist for *The Tampa Tribune*. At some point during Castro's visit to Tampa, the two met on a corner in Ybor City, and O'Connor interviewed him for an article discussing Castro's plans and ideals and announcing his November 27 speech. O'Connor later attended the speech and wrote about it in the *Tribune* on November 28, 1955.[9]

Castro was so grateful for O'Connor's coverage of his trip—especially considering the treatment he received from Tampa's Spanish radio station—that he asked Manteiga for O'Connor's address so he could personally thank him before he left. When he arrived at O'Connor's house, O'Connor's wife initially mistook Castro for the house painter and thought he was there to collect on his bill.[10]

Castro sat down with O'Connor, thanked him for all he had done, and bestowed upon him a personal possession he brought to Tampa—a cigarette lighter engraved with a sketch of the Empire State Building.[11]

Later that day, accompanied by Maria Antonia González and the group with whom he had come, Castro left Tampa for Miami en route to Key West. Though he promised to return following his victory, he never did.

The story of Castro's visit to Tampa is now complete, but the story of Tampa's role in the revolution and its M-26-7 has only just begun.

# 7

# Dark Forces

There were dark forces at work.

On Friday, December 2, 1955, Fidel Castro Ruz departed Miami for Key West. In various cars, he was accompanied by Félix Elmuza, Oscar Ramirez, Pepin Gomez Olazabal, Julio Carrera, Juan Fernandez, Orestes Portales, Rodrigo Moreno, Socartes Alvarez, Leonardo Muniz, Fernando Margolles, and Ortodoxo leaders Abelardo Suero Acosta and Enrique Barroso Dorta.[1]

Juan Manuel Márquez went to Nassau to deflect the attention of those surveilling them, returning to Key West the day before Castro's speech.[2]

In Key West, Castro and some of his companions stayed at the Siboney Motel on Truman and Elizabeth Streets.[3]

A number of emigrants gathered in the afternoon at the Siboney Motel. José Ramon Menendez; Ismael Negrin; and the leader of the MNR (Movimiento Nacionalista Revoluciónario), Rafael García Bárcena y Gomez, who at that moment was exiled in Key West, were among those in attendance. They then made a brief stop at a restaurant on Duval Street, where they met with Candido Moreno, Mario Mato Menocal, and Franklin Varela, who later that evening accompanied Castro on his visit to the home of Julio Cabañas Pazos, one of the prominent figures of the Cuban colony there, and president of the Club San Carlos (later known as the San Carlos Institute), an educational institute located at 516 Duval Street and venerated by the emigrants.

During a meeting at his home, Castro proposed that Cabañas assume the position of president of the M-26-7 about to be established there. But, because of his responsibility as the director of the Club San Carlos, Cabañas felt he would be more useful outside its leadership. He instead recommended Mario Mato Menocal. They decided to formally name Mato as president, Dr. Julio de Poo as treasurer, and Orlando Diaz as secretary. Before departing for the evening, Cabañas and Castro exchanged ideas as to what might be the best location for the rally planned for Wednesday, December 7, to take place.[4]

Castro was hoping to deliver his speech at the San Carlos Institute, where José Martí Pérez had addressed the Cuban emigrants in January 1892. But its regulations prohibited political or religious matters.[5]

Police Chief Bienvenido Pérez was a Fulgencio Batista y Zaldívar loyalist and aligned with the Cuban consul, Rene Morales, and municipal judge Enrique Esquinaldo. Castro hoped to have the use of the Los Venaditos (Elks) club, the American Legion, or the Carpenters' Association, but the police chief pressured the organizations to rebuff the request. Castro's group was denied by another six locations.[6]

It was decided finally to have the event at the home of Dr. Poo, who had a large terrace that could accommodate the number they were expecting. The police chief assured them that he would arrest them all if they did that. They ultimately had to use the Key West Kennel Club's parking lot on Stock Island, outside the jurisdiction of these city officials, to carry out the meeting.[7]

The plan was kept secret, and that evening of December 7, in an almost clandestine manner, they made their way to the Kennel Club. Around 200 people stood in the parking lot as the event began at 8:30 p.m., under the watchful eye of the county sheriff who had helped them obtain the location. Car headlights provided lighting, and the dais was a small table with two young ladies standing beside it holding a Cuban and an American flag.[8]

After a few opening remarks from the Key West M-26-7 board members, Márquez was next to speak. The final speech was delivered by Castro, who began his address mentioning the role of the cigar makers of Key West in the Ten Years' War and the help they gave Martí.[9]

He recalled the significance of December 7 in Cuba's history: it was the day, 59 years earlier in 1896, that General Antonio Maceo y Grajales, "El Titan De Bronce" (the bronze titan) as he was called, died in the War of Independence. Maceo had also visited Key West and was received by the emigrant community with warmth and cooperation.[10]

Castro reiterated the heroic action taken at the Moncada, the plight of the exiles, and the great crisis in Cuba, to again emphasize the help he needed from the Cuban émigrés. At the conclusion of the rally, Márquez insisted that Castro not return to Key West that evening, but rather, just head back to Miami.[11]

The Friday, December 10 issue of *The Key West Citizen* published a small article regarding Castro's speech, accusing its organizers of being Communist for helping the revolutionary leader and his movement.[12]

It is clear why it was so difficult for them to confirm a venue for the Key West speech. The police chief, judges, and other city officials had sold out to Batista and conspired with Key West's Cuban consul to make it impossible for Castro to find a location from which to address the people.

## 7. Dark Forces

All these years later, we must wonder if there was an equally sinister reason for our issues in Tampa.

The Italian Club claimed it canceled because it did not want to support any sort of revolution. I have no reason to doubt that. However, I would be remiss as a historian if I ignored the possibility that there may have been another reason that they did not want Castro to hold a fundraiser there. He was openly against the casinos operating in Habana because he felt they were corrupting the island. Some of these casinos were owned and/or operated by members of the United States mafia. And one of those mafiosos was Santo Trafficante Jr., a native and resident of Tampa and a member of L'Unione Italiana.

When the club's board canceled our reservation, Castro said that they had been pressured by powerful people in Tampa who were in the real estate and construction business with Batista and his family. Some people have translated that to mean "the mafia."

I have never been involved in Tampa's underworld in any capacity. My only connection to it is that I worked with Trafficante's brother Henry at Tiffany Tile in 1956 when it opened, and that I visited Trafficante in a Cuban detention center following Castro's victory, a story that I will tell in greater detail later in this book. Both men were always very cordial to me.

Still, it was no secret at the time of Castro's visit to Tampa that the city had an influential underworld. In 1950, Tampa's mafia problem made national headlines when the Special Committee on Organized Crime in Interstate Commerce, better known as the Kefauver Committee, steamrolled through the nation visiting and investigating through public hearings every city that was believed to have a powerful organized crime syndicate. Tampa was on that list.

For two days in late December 1950, alleged members of Tampa's underworld and allegedly corrupt city and county leaders and law enforcement officials took the stand and were grilled by the Kefauver Committee on the corruption that seemed to permeate every aspect of Tampa government. When the committee's nationwide investigation was complete, it fingered Tampa as one of the most corrupt cities it had visited.

"*Human life in Tampa was almost as cheap as the sands of the beach: in nineteen years there have been fourteen murders and six attempted assassinations in the Tampa underworld—and only one conviction,*" wrote Kefauver in *Crime in America*, a summary of his committee's findings.[13]

Hillsborough County Sheriff Hugh Culbreath was implicated by a number of individuals for being in cahoots with gangsters, and the community's knowledge of one of their lead law enforcement official's illegal ties was spotlighted.[14]

"*The moral of the Tampa story is this: if good citizens of a community shut their eyes to wholesale violation of a law—even if it is a law prohibiting something that a lot of people happen to like—law enforcement and honesty in public office will go to hell in a handcart. It happened in Tampa. It can happen anywhere,"* wrote Kefauver.[15]

Among those who avoided testifying by staying away from Tampa during that time—Trafficante. While Trafficante did not start the corruption, he was allegedly the leader of Tampa's mafia at the time of the hearings.

Though the mafia-owned casino industry was set up by New York gangsters Meyer Lansky and Lucky Luciano, Trafficante was just as important a part of the mafia's plan to turn Cuba into their own gambling empire. Numerous historians have stated that, using riches earned from his illegal empire in Tampa, Trafficante purchased the Sans Souci and was rumored to hold secret interests in the Hotel Habana Riviera, the Tropicana Club, the Sevilla-Biltmore, the Capri Hotel Casino, the Commodoro, the Deauville, and the Habana Hilton.

The casinos are said to have been run legally and earned their gangster owners a wealth of money. These businesses also provided a legitimate reason for them to stay in Cuba, from where they would run their illegal ventures in the United States without interference from American law enforcement, all while providing a business into which to funnel illegally earned money away from the prying eyes of the IRS.

And Batista reportedly allowed this to happen in return for a cut of their earnings.

Trafficante is alleged to have also lined the pockets of elected officials and law enforcement in Tampa, Hillsborough County, and throughout Florida if they ignored wrongdoings locally.

And it is said that Trafficante took good care of hometown friends visiting his casinos.

Perhaps those who enjoyed the spoils of Trafficante's casinos did not want their fun to end. Or perhaps Trafficante just wielded his power in Tampa to force L'Unione Italiana to treat Castro poorly.

Still, the mafia was not Batista's strongest ally in the United States. That title goes to the U.S. government, which was willing to do what was necessary to keep a man in power who American businessmen adored.

The Cuban government protested Castro's use of U.S. territory for revolutionary activities. So, U.S. immigration authorities supported Batista's request and canceled Castro's visa.

On December 10, 1955, Castro returned to Mexico.

He wrote my brother Mario a letter five days later, regarding Mario assuming responsibility for the funds collected in New York City. At the end of that letter he says, *"I had the pleasure of meeting your brother in*

Tampa. I asked him to write you regarding the act. He was designated secretary of the 26th of July Patriotic Club of Tampa. He seems to me a magnificent fellow."[16]

Castro then sent Mario another letter dated December 20, 1955, with instructions to "*deposit in a New York bank the amount to be sent so that it can be collected in Mexico City by Mrs. Orquidea Pino, Calle Fuego #791, Esquina Risco, Jardines del Pedregal de San Angel, Mexico D.F.*"[17]

I have heard that he raised around $9,000 during his tour of the United States, but I have no documented proof to back that up.

Regardless, Castro had enough money to begin his invasion of Cuba.

# 8

# Meet Tampa's M-26-7

Our team was coming together.

Our unofficial headquarters remained *La Gaceta*, and we held our first official meeting a few days after Fidel Castro Ruz left Tampa. It was open to anyone who wanted to join. That gathering is where our core group of members who would stick with the M-26-7 throughout the revolution first came together. Those I recall being there were Victoriano Manteiga, Carlos Carbonell, Marcelino Vila, Max Garcia, Carmelo Bueno, Roque Suarez, Florentino Santos, Juan M. Pérez, Tony Sola, and Marcelino Golan.

Carbonell was a semi-retired cigar factory worker who also worked as a watchman at the V. M. Ybor cigar factory. He later worked at the None Such Bakery in West Tampa.

Vila owned La Crema Bakery at 1702 East Columbus Drive. He was a quiet man who only gave his opinion when needed. His young son, Marc Vila, who would later become director of Tampa Spanish language radio station WQBN-AM 1300, frequently attended the M-26-7 meetings with his father.

Garcia, as I previously mentioned, was a friend from my baseball playing days. He was a city bus driver.

Sola, whom we affectionately called "El Gordito" (the chubby one) because of his girth, was owner of La Casa Loma Restaurant, located at 3209 North Armenia Avenue.

Suarez was a nurse at Gonzalez Clinic located on 14th Street and Ninth Avenue, across from the V. M. Ybor cigar factory.

Santos always wore a hat. Sadly, I do not remember more about him.

Then there were the three family members.

Marcelino was co-owner of Pegol Cabinet Shop on Main Street in West Tampa. He was also a talented actor and singer who performed in several Tampa-based shows over the years, including The Spanish Little Theatre (now known as The Spanish Lyric Theatre) directed by Rene Gonzalez. This is the oldest Hispanic theater group in the nation, founded by Rene in 1959, and performing musicals to this day.

Carmelo Bueno—the brother-in-law of Golan's wife—was a machinist. His young son, Orlando, accompanied him to many meetings and activities.

Juan M. Pérez was a veteran of the U.S. Army who worked at Pegol when in Tampa. His sister Ofelia was the wife of Carmelo Bueno. His other sister, Aida, was the wife of Golan. His third sister, Alicia, was the wife of Juan de la Rosa, who would later join the M-26-7.[1]

Only Golan, Bueno, and Pérez had previous history with revolutions, as far as I know, and their experience was via an attempted coup that was so daring and so inspirational that it is worth recounting in further detail so that you can understand what they brought to the M-26-7.

Decades later, while I was visiting Cuba in the summer of 2010, Pérez related to me that he started his political involvement as friends with Faustino Pérez Hernández after the Fulgencio Batista y Zaldívar takeover. Others in their group were Armando Hart Dávalos, who would become Minister of Education when Castro triumphed; his brother Enrique Hart; José "Pepe" Prieto Rodriguez, who was later savagely tortured and murdered; and brothers Alonso "Bebo" Hidalgo Barrios and Mario Hidalgo. On April 5, 1953, Easter Sunday, he and a group that included Bueno and Golan were planning to take over Camp Columbia in Habana.[2]

The plan, conceived by University of Habana philosophy and sociology professor Rafael García Bárcena y Gomez, was later explained to me by Pérez and García Bárcena's son.

García Bárcena was a beloved professor, poet laureate, and author whose revolutionary seeds took root in opposition to the Gerardo Machado y Morales regime. He became a member of the Federación Estudiantil Universitaria (University Student Federation), otherwise known as the FEU, in 1927.

He was imprisoned several times in his early twenties during the Machado dictatorship. On one occasion, he was imprisoned in a dungeon for 30 days, fed only a daily serving of bread and water, and kept in total darkness.

García Bárcena had been a respected and highly admired revolutionary leader for at least a couple decades by the time Batista carried out his coup. He was an honest, decent man. According to his son Rafael García Bárcena y Valladares he forgave and absolutely had no hatred towards those who mistreated him in prisons during the dictatorships of Machado and Batista. He even prayed for Manuel Ugalde Carrillo, who had him beaten to a pulp by a group of Batista's so-called military intelligence soldiers.[3]

He believed in God and was a Christian, though he professed no formal religion. Because of his many positive character traits, he was esteemed by the students he mentored and the military officers he taught

A visit to Raul and Rhonda Villamia from Rafael García Bárcena y Valladares, son of venerated University of Habana professor Rafael García Bárcena, who founded the Movimiento Nacional Revolucionario (National Revolutionary Movement) on May 20, 1952, the first group in Cuba organized to remove Fulgencio Batista y Zaldívar from power. Tampa, Florida, July 2, 2019 (from the collection of Rhonda Villamia).

at Cuba's National War College. On the morning of Batista's coup, García Bárcena resigned from his position as military psychology professor. But he maintained a discrete relationship with a number of his former students whose respect and loyalty he had earned.[4]

A couple months later, he founded the Movimiento Nacional Revoluciónario (National Revolutionary Movement) on May 20, 1952. The MNR was Cuba's first anti–Batista group, organized to oust the dictator from power, restore democracy, and help transform Cuba into a great nation.[5]

In the early stages of establishing the MNR, García Bárcena did not come home one evening. When word spread, students came out and warned on the radio stations, "Our mothers are going to mourn the blood that will be shed by their children if Professor García Bárcena does not appear in the next 24 hours," and vowed to take to the streets in protest. The television news programs then also covered the kidnapping, and he was released. But he had been brutally beaten. There was not one inch of his face, arms, or visible flesh that did not have either hematomas or lacerations with coagulated blood.[6]

It was determined that Batista's Servicio de Inteligencia Militar (Military Intelligence Service, a.k.a. SIM), headed by Manuel Ugalde Carrillo, was responsible. García Bárcena would likely have been silently made to "disappear" if there had not still been some freedom of the press at that moment.

While the MNR was open to anyone at least 18 years old, García

Bárcena began a process by which the group's members were "tested" as plans for the Camp Columbia assault were made. No one except for García Bárcena and his brother-in-law Alfredo Valladares Abreu knew the date or the location of the future uprising. Valladares was a magistrate in the Court of Accounts, which provided oversight to prevent government corruption. Rehearsals were conducted for almost one year. The MNR members were broken up into cells of about 5 to 10 people, with each cell having a leader.[7]

A call would go out for certain cells to meet at certain locations at certain times, and García Bárcena or Valladares would go to those spots to see who showed up. Each time, the members would think it was for the uprising. They were informed it was a "practice" after they arrived. Those who consistently answered the call and showed up were considered the reliable, committed members. Their mettle had been tested, and they would eventually become part of the 1,242 who would attempt the April 5, 1953, assault on Columbia.[8]

Although some of the group would be armed, it was a civilian uprising. Those comfortable with handling arms were permitted to carry them, and the others did not have to bear arms. García Bárcena did not believe in killing for the sake of killing. In a battle, those on both sides go into it willing to kill or be killed, but simply taking someone's life in cold blood was something he was against.[9]

It was a known fact that García Bárcena was against Batista and planning to do something, but they did not know what, where, or how.

Their target, Camp Columbia, was considered impregnable.

Castro's Moncada attack was not important from a military standpoint for taking Cuba. It was not a place of power. It was simply a barracks. But Camp Columbia was the most powerful military installation in Cuba. It was a fortress that contained all the heavy military equipment and had its own airport. Whoever controlled Columbia controlled Cuba. García Bárcena knew that.[10]

García Bárcena believed it was possible to take Columbia by surprise. If the initial insurrection succeeded, a number of selected former officers were prepared to present themselves at Columbia within 30 minutes once contacted by phone.[11]

Easter Sunday was chosen as the attack date, not only for this element of surprise, but also because, symbolically, it was on this same holiday that the Irish revolted against England in their fight to become a nation, April 24, 1916—Easter Monday. And it also represented the "resurrection" of Cuba, which had been crushed by all the murders of young, decent Cubans.[12]

But the attack never launched.

Juan M. Pérez said the attack had been planned for midday when the changing of the guard occurred. They were to gather at the home of Eva Jimenez Ruiz, on Calle 12, No. 307, Apartmento No. 8 in the Almendares section of Habana at around 10 a.m., not far from where García Bárcena lived at Calle 7, No. 854. But, when he arrived and knocked at the door of the apartment building, a commander of some sort answered the door along with the landlady, who pointed to Pérez and said, "He is one of them." The commander inquired as to why Pérez was there, to which he replied he was there to see his girlfriend, Hilda Aguirre. The commander denied Pérez entry, so he lingered nearby for about 30 minutes and then walked to a clothing warehouse where he worked. Soon after, a heavy police presence—about 10 cars—converged on the building where Jimenez lived.[13]

Pérez wondered if the landlady ratted them out so she could bring in a new tenant paying more than the 15 pesos per month Jimenez paid for her apartment. The landlady may have wanted her out and likely called the police to tell them there was a political gathering at the apartment. When they came, they found the map to Columbia and how they were planning to enter it. They were planning to enter through Post #13. The previous year, Batista entered through Post #6 to carry out his coup.[14]

Or perhaps, Pérez added, the plot was exposed due to the son of Clemente Inclan Costa, the president of the University of Habana. According to Pérez, García Bárcena had instructed them not to have guns on their person until the designated moment, but Rafael Inclan Argudin carried one when he went to Jimenez's apartment. Pérez had hidden his gun in the fence of a home a short distance from Jimenez's on his way to her apartment. Perhaps police found Inclan's gun during a search, which led to a larger search that exposed the plan.[15]

García Bárcena's son adds to the plausibility of that theory. Decades later, he interviewed a fellow who was part of the group. Pedro Julio Martinez Fraga was 16 years old when he joined the MNR. He looked old for his age, so easily passed as being over the minimum 18 years of age. He later confessed to the professor that he had lied about his age because he very fervently wanted to be involved in ousting Batista, and he felt that the plot might have been discovered because of him. Fraga, Inclan, José Hernandez Bacallao, and José Caraballo Orraca arrived at the precise moment the police were raiding Jimenez's apartment. The youths were found to have five revolvers and four pistols with them. Fraga felt culpable of something having been leaked out as they were detained and individually interrogated by the authorities, exposing the plan.[16]

Close to 70 were arrested on conspiracy charges, but only García Bárcena and 12 others were sentenced and imprisoned: Eva Jiménez Ruiz,

Rolando Abay, Gabriel Mancebo, Antonio Valdés Zambrana, Danilo Menendez, Orlando Ventura Reyes, Antonio Saud, Matias Dilio Nunez, José L. Fernandez, José "Pepe" Prieto Rodriguez, José Rodriguez, and Gerardo Lee. His defense attorney was Armando Hart Dávalos, and, on May 21, García Bárcena was sentenced to three years. The sentence was reduced to two years, and García Bárcena was pardoned within one year.

Ruiz was the first woman to be imprisoned as a revolutionary for her part in the April 5, 1953, conspiracy. Accounts may credit Haydée Santamaría Cuadrado and Melba Hernández Rodríguez del Rey with this distinction when they were imprisoned for their role in the Moncada attack, but Jimenez's incarceration precedes theirs.[17]

García Bárcena's son shared with me that he has a tape recording of Lieutenant Colonel Manuel Varela Castro, who was the commanding officer at Columbia that day. In it, the colonel acknowledges that had the assault taken place, they would have succeeded because it had been so perfectly planned. At noon on a Sunday in Cuba, people would have just finished their lunch and been about to begin their siestas. The guards at the various entry posts at Columbia would likely have been relaxing with their weapons lying to their sides. And the fact that it was Easter made it even more improbable that anything would occur since all Cuba would be tranquilly and peacefully celebrating this sacred end to Holy Week.[18]

García Bárcena Jr. said that the insurrection was the topic of discussion everywhere in Cuba and that his father, the man responsible for organizing it, was idolized as a hero.[19]

It bothered Castro that the professor was so popular. He did not like competition. Castro and his followers used to say that García Bárcena was a "dreamer" who did not know what he was doing. But the professor had most of the former military officials working with him, most of whom he had taught at the National War College. And the Easter Sunday plot had been meticulously organized with more than 1,200 participants, all civilians. It was exposed only a couple hours before it was to have taken place.[20]

It is García Bárcena Jr.'s opinion that the Moncada attack happened because everyone was talking about his father's April 5 attempt. He feels that it was simply a strategy to gain notoriety. It was not a military action that could overthrow Batista. It was a massacre. Castro wanted to do something very "loud" to outshout the public outcry at the professor's arrest and imprisonment. García Bárcena Jr. believes Castro was astutely trying to erase his father's memory, and that is actually how it played out. And, with their leader imprisoned, many former MNR members joined the M-26-7; most notable were Armando Hart Dávalos and Faustino Pérez

Hernández. Castro's forces attacked Moncada three months and 21 days after the Easter Sunday uprising.[21]

After García Bárcena's release on June 5, 1954, he would at times secretly leave Cuba during periods when the Batista government would incarcerate or make someone "disappear" preventively. The professor's full name was José Rafael García Bárcena y Gomez, so he would periodically go into exile taking the flight from Cuba as "José Gomez." On May 21, 1955, when he returned from exile, he was met and welcomed back by a group of sympathizers, including Castro, who had just been released from prison on May 15 for the Moncada attack, and Hart. Castro carried García Bárcena on his shoulders. A photo of this appeared in *Bohemia*. Perhaps this was an opportunity for Castro to show he "supported" the beloved professor.[22]

And a little-known fact that García Bárcena Jr. shared with me is that his father saved Batista's life. There was an occasion when the Batista family and other officials were going to attend a Catholic Mass. A priest told García Bárcena that they would be at this service if he "wanted to do something," implying that he could physically eliminate them all. His father thanked the priest for the information but did not do anything. The professor always made it a point of very politely telling people who brought up the theme of killing someone that assassinations were out of the question for him. He always made this known. I wonder if it would have mattered if Batista had known the professor spared his life when his henchmen arrested, tortured, and imprisoned García Bárcena.

None of Pérez, Bueno, or Golan was caught or linked to the Easter Sunday conspiracy. And when I spoke with Golan's son many decades later, he said he was surprised to hear his father was involved in such a plot and stated he believed Pérez erroneously linked him to it. Nonetheless, Pérez very emphatically referenced the three of them being involved in this attempt.

I have included this information about the Easter Sunday uprising not only as part of Pérez, Bueno, and Golan's revolutionary background prior to their joining the Tampa M-26-7, but also to make the point that, although most Cuban revolutionary history accounts credit Castro and the Moncada attack as the start of the revolution, it was actually the MNR under García Bárcena that first galvanized the young people to take action against Batista. The April 5 plot was conceived almost immediately after the coup, and the process of building a core of trustworthy, reliable, committed participants began. Although the plan was unsuccessful, it was the first serious, armed attempt to oppose Batista.[23]

Getting back to that first official meeting we had after Castro left Tampa...

## 8. Meet Tampa's M-26-7

Bursting with excitement following the recent visit from Castro, we got to work the day after that first meeting. We distributed flyers asking for new members and stating that all donations should be dropped off at *La Gaceta*. Those afraid to have their names linked to the cause could contribute anonymously by mailing money to the newspaper's office.

We visited the social clubs and through word of mouth spread the news about future meetings and the need for donations. As we sat in bleachers and watched baseball games, sipped coffee at cafés, slammed dominoes onto tables, or busily worked away at our day jobs, we spoke of the revolution and the importance of supporting it. For those first few weeks, we lived and breathed the revolution.

Our efforts were somewhat stalled, however, as we were missing the fundraising documents that Castro had promised.

Castro sent Manteiga a letter from Mexico, dated December 13, 1955, detailing the issues he and his men faced in Key West. In the letter, he also wrote that the envelope contained our official M-26-7 documents: ID cards signed by Castro for each member, donation logbooks, and donation receipts so we could begin fundraising. Despite Castro's claim, the paraphernalia was not enclosed.[24]

These documents were important for us to possess. Con men are not new to this century. We were worried that some dishonest people would falsely claim to be collecting for Castro to line their own pockets.

Then there was the concern that supporters of Batista would masquerade as M-26-7 members and smear our good name by acting poorly to others in the community in hopes that such actions would prevent us from rallying Tampa behind Castro.

The documents would

### A TODOS LOS CUBANOS DE TAMPA

Todos los cubanos y descendientes de cubanos, que sientan dignamente la causa de la libertad de Cuba, deben unirse al "Club Patriótico 26 de Julio" para contribuir a que desaparezca en breve la tiranía que gobierna nuestra madre patria y que se implante un gobierno democrático.

Para unirse al "Club Patriótico 26 de Julio" deben dirigirse al periódico "La Gaceta", calle 15 y avenida 10, Ybor City, donde serán inscriptos. Si usted quisiera ayudar anónimamente, dirija su contribución por correo o personalmente a esa dirección.

Si usted quiere ayudar a derrocar al dictador Batista; si usted quiere contribuir a que brille la estrella de la libertad en Cuba; si usted quiere hacer que en Cuba gobierne la honradez y la decencia,

¡Unase al "Movimiento 26 de Julio", Asociándose al "Club Patriótico 26 De Julio" De Tampa!

Flyer inviting Cubans in Tampa to join the M-26-7, instructing those interested to go to *La Gaceta* newspaper office to apply for membership. Tampa (Ybor City), Florida, 1955 (from the collection of Raul Villamia).

**M-26-7 members Carlos Carbonell, Raul Villamia, Victoriano Manteiga, Roque Suarez, Manuel Gispert, and Florentino Suarez in front of *La Gaceta* newspaper office. Tampa (Ybor City), Florida, 1955–1960 (courtesy of *La Gaceta*).**

prevent such deceit. If a supposed fundraiser did not have an official donation receipt, the donation was not legitimate. And if someone did not have an ID card, he (or she) was not a member.

We forged ahead with our mission anyway but continuously wondered what happened to our IDs and fundraising books and if we would ever receive them.

Then I received the answer via a January 2, 1956, letter from Castro in Mexico. It read:

> Dear friend:
>
> Since my arrival here, in the course of three weeks, I have mailed two letters to our comrade Manteiga, without having received any response even as I am wording these lines. For this reason, I am sending these few lines, requesting that you speak with him to find out if he has received my letters, or if the delay is the result of excess mail due to these Christmas holidays, or on the contrary, he has written me and I have not yet received his letter.
>
> I earnestly implore you, write me as quickly as possible, giving me news about yourselves and the club. I hope that in my absence, you have continued to work and that no manner of obstacle or skepticism has delayed you. These are fitting circumstances for judging the quality of the men we find in our path. An undertaking as great and difficult as this cannot be accomplished without the collaboration of upright men who are responsible and conscientious. It is these that I believe I have

found in our trip to the United States, when we deposit our confidence in those who have been left in charge of organizing the clubs. I await the outcome.

You may direct the envelope to the following address:

> Sra. Hilda Gadea
> Napoles #40 Apto. 16
> Colonia Juarez
> Mexico, D.F.
> Receive fond regards from
> Fidel[25]

I wrote Castro via Gadea explaining such to him. I said that even without the proper documents we were working hard and making progress but that we would welcome any identification that proved our relationship to the revolution. (It is worth mentioning that Gadea had just recently become Ernesto "Che" Guevara de la Serna's first wife.)

In early February I received a letter from Mexico dated January 31, 1956, that was sent by Jesús Montané Oropesa, one of Castro's right-hand men and a veteran of the Moncada attack. It read:

> Dear Raul,
>
> We acknowledge the receipt of your letter dated 5 January 1956, which I am answering in absence of our comrade Fidel.
>
> In your letter you said that you had not received the paraphernalia (models/forms) for the functioning of the Club, but comrade Manteiga communicated with us, dated 31 December, as having received them, in spite of which we expect that you have been continuing to intensely labor in the recruitment of new members and the collection of necessary funds.
>
> According to the information we have received regarding the work of the other patriotic clubs in that country, we are satisfied and content. We hope that the results of the work for which you are responsible will equally bring us such pleasure.
>
> In appreciation of your letter, receive a revolutionary embrace from,
>
> Jesús Montané[26]

I was unaware that Manteiga had also contacted Castro, and I never found out where he had located the documents. I also am not sure why Montané indicated in his January 31 response that the documents had been received. After receiving Castro's January 2 letter, I had spoken to Manteiga about the matter of the missing documents, so if he wrote a December 31 letter saying they had been received, why would he have told me they had not, prompting me to write the January 5 letter? There obviously was some miscommunication and confusion in the sequence or dating of the letters, but ultimately, all was clarified.

With everything in hand, Manteiga called a meeting at *La Gaceta* for the board members and others interested in supporting the revolution to make their membership official. Approximately 25 people signed up that day. Others preferred to give donations and help in the demonstrations without formally joining.

Besides the stamped booklets documenting member dues, members were given a numbered receipt booklet with perforated stubs. Each time the member received a donation, they had to record the amount on the permanent (bound) section of the booklet and give a perforated stub to the contributor as a receipt.

From the beginning, we knew that supporting the revolution was going be hard. We knew Batista's followers would want to thwart our attempt to help Castro free Cuba, but those of us in charge of the club's leadership always maintained devotion and enthusiasm, knowing that doing so would rub off on our members. Also, we knew that many men and women in Cuba would be dying for the cause. How could we complain about our work when blood would soon be spilling?

Letter from Fidel Castro to Raul Villamia, inquiring about two letters he had sent Victoriano Manteiga without getting a response, asking Raul to speak with Manteiga to confirm that he received them.

There was still one major obstacle in our way in the first few months of our activity that worried us: news from and about Castro grew rare. All was quiet on the southern front. In retrospect, we now know that was because he was carefully planning his journey back to Cuba from Mexico and was collecting the necessary arms, but at the time no one knew what was going on. This was decades before email and cell phones made the world smaller. There was not even a landline at which Castro could be reached. Our only form of communication was through snail mail or telegram.

We kept working, and things went well for a while. Then, many

In this two-page letter, Castro also wanted "news about the club." Tampa, Florida, January 2, 1956 (from the collection of Raul Villamia).

members lost interest. They no longer came to our meetings, nor were they involved in any of the club activities. We were not sure if this was due to not hearing much about Castro in the news or other reasons.

Our membership dropped to about a dozen people, and that made it difficult for us who kept up the task of raising money and doing the other activities to enable the club to thrive. As time passed, the small group that remained continued to keep the club alive.

Back in Cuba, on April 29, 100 revolutionaries attacked the Goicuria Barracks in Matanzas, 60 miles from Habana. A bloody battle ensued, the rebels were defeated, and their leader, Reynold Garcia Garcia, was killed. Batista ascertained that the attack had been funded by Cuba's former president Carlos Prío Socarrás, so he had him arrested and deported to Miami.

Then, in late June, news broke that, under pressure from Batista, Mexican authorities rounded up and arrested Castro and his revolutionaries. They were charged with violations of immigration laws, illegal possession of military weapons, and conspiring to mount a revolution against a foreign government. Authorities also seized the revolutionaries' weapons, supplies, and cash. Of note is that Mexican authorities stated that Castro and his companions did not maintain relations with Communists.[27]

My brothers Mario and Miguel, along with Angel Pérez-Vidal, his brother Santiago Pérez-Vidal, and cousin Ernesto Pérez-Vidal were part of a commission from Acción Cívica Cubana that met on June 24 with the Mexican consul in New York City in protest of Castro's arrest.[28]

Trying to turn a negative into a positive, Manteiga used the arrest to drum up support for the revolution, hoping it would remind the Tampa Cubans that Castro was sacrificing his own wellbeing for the betterment of Cuba.

On June 29, 1956, Manteiga published the following in *La Gaceta*:

Fidel Castro, who is our friend just as Eduardo Chibás was, has been arrested in Mexico and is accused of conspiring against Fulgencio Batista, the man who stole the presidency through use of the military force on the fateful morning of March 10, 1952.

Perforated M-26-7 receipt booklet for the collection of donations. The stub bound into the left side of the booklet would remain there and the perforated right side would be detached and given to the donor. The M-26-7's address of 2015 15th Street was the office of *La Gaceta*, where the M-26-7 was headquartered until they obtained their own space in the El Pasaje Hotel building at the beginning of 1960 (from the collection of Raul Villamia).

We feel deep sympathy for Fidel and his friends because they are honest, educated, modest and want to restore glorious freedom to the people of Cuba who have lived under a dictator for years who has become a millionaire with the money from the Cuban Treasury.
 This dictator is also an accomplice in a number of crimes and is supported by killers who torture and exploit the people and destroy Cuba's industrial life and international prestige.
 Fidel Castro is poor and worthy. Batista and his accomplices are rich and without dignity.
 Fidel Castro is brave and honest.
 Those who help Batista are gangsters....
 Cuba needs a lot of men like Fidel Castro.[29]

In late July, Castro and his men were freed after former Mexican president Lázaro Cárdenas intervened on their behalf.

In November 1956, through the press, Castro then commanded that Batista step down as president of Cuba and leave the country. *La Gaceta* published the demands on November 23.

One portion of it reads: "*Hand over the presidency of the Republic to a person that inspires confidence to all Cubans and who is appointed in consultation with the revolutionary organizations and political parties that oppose the government.*"[30]

War was on the horizon.

Back in Mexico in September 1956, Castro, accompanied by Antonio del Conde, whom the Cubans referred to as "El Cuate" and who had a legal business for buying and selling weapons, was in the province of Veracruz by the Tuxpan River, near a little town bearing the same name. They had been exploring various areas for the purpose of finding a locale where they might test some arms. He trusted El Cuate and had often utilized him when purchasing and testing arms.[31]

Castro noticed a yacht anchored in the river that was for sale. He purchased it, and the *Granma*, as the boat was named, made its entry into the revolution's history.[32]

The *Granma*'s owner was Robert B. Erickson, an American who lived in Mexico City. Erickson agreed to sell the yacht, but, as part of the deal, there was a house he owned near the riverbank in the city of Santiago de la Peña that Castro would have to also agree to buy. This condition was acceptable to Castro because the house could serve as a place to store arms, uniforms, and supplies for the excursion plus serve as a meeting point for the rebels.[33]

Del Conde negotiated the purchase for Castro and paid Erickson $15,000 for the yacht, using money that had come from Prío. The former Cuban president also purchased the house by means of a $10,000 mortgage.[34]

The *Granma* was in bad shape and required a great amount of work. The repairs continued through October and November, and by the end of the month it was ready to sail. The men going on the expedition began to arrive in Tuxpan, and by November 24, they were all there.[35]

That day there was inclement weather—strong wind and rain. At nightfall, the men began to load the weapons, fuel, and the few rations they had obtained. Castro oversaw all the details as they prepared to embark. When all was ready, 82 men boarded the yacht, which had a maximum capacity of 25 persons.[36]

Around 1:30 a.m. on November 25, 1956, the *Granma*, with its lights off, made its way down river to the coast. The 82 passengers kept absolute silence so that they would not draw the attention of the Mexican authorities. The rain continued. Radio communication indicated that all navigation was being suspended by the port authorities due to the bad weather. The unlikelihood of being found traveling at a time when it was expected that no boats would be allowed to navigate was an added assurance that they could leave the area undetected.[37]

It was two miles to get to the coast, from which point forward it would be open sea until reaching their destination—the southern coast of the Oriente Province in Cuba.[38]

According to their calculations, the *Granma* would arrive in Cuba at daybreak on November 30, the fifth day after having set sail. Its delay in arriving by this targeted date was caused by a variety of reasons. There were mechanical problems and other issues resulting from the extremely overweight cargo of persons and munitions aboard a vessel designed to withstand a much lighter load. The extra weight resulted in the boat moving at a much slower pace. One of its engines became disabled for days. One of its pilots was thrown overboard, and time was spent rescuing him.[39]

Other accounts indicate that the arrival was purposely delayed. The plan had been that, on November 30, a group of M-26-7 revolutionaries led by Frank País García was to carry out an uprising in Santiago de Cuba, to support the landing of the *Granma* as a distraction to occupy the attention of Batista's army, having them think the *Granma* was to land in the vicinity. It was in this uprising that the rebels first wore the olive-green fatigues and red and black M-26-7 armbands.[40]

However, anti–Castro sentiment suggests that the landing was purposely late, and the uprising was a set up to put País at risk of being eliminated. He did not die on this occasion, but there were three casualties: José "Pepito" Tey Saint-Blancard, Otto Parellada Echevarria, and Tony Aloma. País was a very popular leader, and it has been said that anyone who was a strong leader was a possible threat to Castro, and therefore was eliminated.[41]

Finally, on December 2, they caught sight of the lighthouse at Cabo Cruz in the southern coast of Oriente, and Castro directed the pilot to navigate in that direction. As they neared the coast, they ran aground in the muddy mangroves a short distance from land. It was around 6 a.m. when the group began to disembark in an area called Los Cayuelos, a couple of kilometers from the Las Coloradas beach to the northeast of Cabo Cruz and south of Niquero. This was the moment the war between Castro's rebel forces and Batista's dictatorship commenced.[42]

The shipwreck forced them to abandon most of their weapons, food, and a large radio transmitter. Jumping overboard, the rebels found themselves chest deep in water. Making their way through the swamp, Castro led them—arms raised, holding their rifles over their heads—as they navigated the mile-long stretch towards shore. It took them over two hours to reach dry land.[43]

They took a headcount upon reaching shore and noticed eight of their men were missing, one of whom was Juan Manuel Márquez Rodríguez. It was later learned that he and his companions had unknowingly deviated from the group and reached shore slightly more north than where the balance of them had.[44]

While heading east towards the Sierra Maestra, Castro and his men came across a man named Angel Pérez Rosabal, who was a charcoal maker. Castro shared with him who he was and what he was intending to do. Pérez invited the group to his home and prepared them something to eat. Suddenly, a government patrol boat appeared offshore and started firing in their direction. Moments later, a plane strafed the area. Castro ordered everyone to go to a small forest near there in which to find refuge and wait for Márquez and his men.[45]

After being there a while, the order was made to keep moving towards their destination, with Pérez guiding them in the direction of the mountains. Shortly after noon, the rebels arrived at an area known as El Ranchon (Big Ranch). There, Pérez indicated to them the course they should take, and he returned to his home. Castro and his men continued to advance marching at night and sleeping hidden among the trees during the day.[46]

Of course, back in Tampa we had no knowledge of any of this. We were not privy to top-secret details. As far as we knew, Castro and his men were still in Mexico.

The other branches had also been experiencing issues.

Mario received a February 14, 1956, letter from Castro expressing disappointment at the slow progress being made in New York due to the infighting between the groups. Acción Cívica Cubana was endeavoring to carry out Castro's instructions, but the other two clubs' egos distracted from the objective.[47]

Even so, more of a forward movement was happening with the New York club than in Miami, which Márquez notes as "dismal" in an undated letter to Angel Pérez-Vidal, while praising the efforts of Acción Cívica Cubana.

My brother Mario had moved to Miami at the end of November to provide help.

On December 2, 1956, as we had done every Sunday since founding the M-26-7 in Tampa, the remaining dozen or so members gathered at *La Gaceta*. Shortly after midday, Manteiga received a phone call from a friend who informed him that he had just heard an unconfirmed bulletin on an English-speaking station that rebel forces under the command of Castro had disembarked from Mexico and were heading for the Oriente Province of Cuba. We raced to *La Gaceta*'s workshop where the radio was kept and heard the same report.

A few hours later, another unconfirmed bulletin came in from Mexico via radio. It said that Castro and his fellow revolutionaries had vanished from Mexico. For over a week, they had not been seen at any of the places they had been frequenting in Mexico City. It was further rumored that they had launched their boat from somewhere in Veracruz en route to Cuba.

After months of simply going through the actions of supporting the revolution, we were again energized! Castro was true to his word! He was invading Cuba! The revolution had begun!

Our excitement soon turned to concern, however. We hoped everyone onboard that boat was safe. It was a treacherous journey by sea, and surely Batista knew they were coming and was ready. We hoped the revolution would not come to a swift end. We hoped our friends were well.

When no update on their whereabouts was broadcast over the next few hours, we all returned home to continue our radio listening vigilance with our families.

On December 3, the Cuban government released a statement to the national and foreign press that the news regarding the rebels landing in Cuba had been a complete fabrication and that the situation in Cuba was normal. That same day, the *New York Times* ran an article with the headline "Cuba Planes, Troops Annihilate 40 Invaders." Cuban radio then broadcast the same bulletin.[48]

We had no way of knowing the truth in Tampa. We could only pray for the best.

On December 4, Márquez and his comrades reunited with Castro's group and continued advancing, their every step challenged by low brush growing amid jagged volcanic rock. Having had no food or water, they fortuitously happened upon an area where sugarcane was growing; they were sustained by chewing some of it.[49]

The morning of December 5, they set up camp near a sugar field at the edge of the woods in a place called Alegría de Pío. Unbeknownst to them, the Batista army had cordoned off the region in which they had been walking after having been tipped off by a local guide named Laureano Noa Yang. The troops found their trail and were slowly closing in. They were suddenly awakened by bullets as they were sleeping at around 4 p.m. Three men were killed in the ensuing crossfire: Humberto Lamothe, Israel Cabrera, and Oscar Rodríguez Delgado, but the rest escaped in different directions, either alone or in small groups. Some, including Márquez, were captured and executed. A total of 21 were killed. Others, such as Montané, were captured and imprisoned. And still others managed to escape and make it into the towns.[50]

Before nightfall on December 5, the Batista government issued another bulletin on Cuban radio stations, saying that a group of "bandits" headed by Castro had landed in Cuban territory during the early morning. It further asserted that the Cuban military forces had gone in pursuit of these bandits and contacted them a few hours later and engaged them in battle. The skirmish resulted in many of them being killed. The bulletin reported that among the dead were Castro and his brother Raúl Castro. Others, they claimed, were captured, and the small group that escaped was being pursued by the forces.[51]

Castro, of course, was not dead. He had escaped. During the subsequent days, survivors began finding one another. Soon they numbered 14, among them Raúl Castro, Ernesto "Che" Guevara de la Serna, Camilo Cienfuegos Gorriarán, Faustino Pérez Hernández, Ramiro Valdes Menendez, Universo Sanchez Alvarez, and Juan Almeida Bosque.

But still, none of this news was reaching the United States.

Stories were conflicting. We wondered what the truth was.

We did not know whether Castro was alive or dead, whether the revolution had begun or ended.

We questioned if Cuba would ever be free or always be enslaved.

We wondered. And we waited for the truth to come out.

# 9

# The Media's Role in the Revolution

Ernesto "Che" Guevara de la Serna once said, "The presence of a foreign journalist was more important for us than a military victory."

Following the initial conflicting reports, it was finally confirmed by the Cuban government and journalists that Fidel Castro Ruz and the rebels had indeed landed in Cuba and that a fierce battle between them and Fulgencio Batista y Zaldívar's army had occurred. That was all that was confirmed. The rest was a mystery.

It was reported by the media that some M-26-7 members had been killed, some had been captured, and some had escaped and made their way to the Sierra Maestra, a mountainous region of Cuba with heavy jungles, a perfect place from which to wage a guerrilla war. Into which category Castro fell was the great unknown. The Cuban government kept its stance that Castro was dead, but some of his supporters claimed that he was alive and well in the Sierra Maestra.

It was decided to suspend all club activities in Tampa until we could confirm the status of Castro and his revolutionaries.

It was hard enough to fundraise when there was no news of Castro's whereabouts in Mexico. When news hit that he could be dead, it became an impossible feat.

Victoriano Manteiga, however, continued the fight through *La Gaceta*. He reported on the revolution in Cuba and unapologetically did so from a pro–Castro standpoint. He wrote that Batista was arresting or killing anyone he deemed to be in cahoots with Castro and printed the names of the victims. He stated that he heard that 400 revolutionaries had made their way to the Sierra Maestra to join with those of Castro's men who had made their way there. And he wrote that Batista temporarily shut down the University of Habana because he believed that many of the students were pro–Castro. Manteiga painted a picture with words of a worried Batista.

## 9. The Media's Role in the Revolution

Then, on December 14, 1956, Manteiga reported the sad news that our friends Juan Manuel Márquez and Félix Elmuza had been slain during the battle that had occurred after the boat had landed in Cuba. I had only spent a few days with them, but we bonded over our common desire to free Cuba of tyranny. They were great men, men willing to die for their beliefs. As I write this, it has been over 64 years since their deaths, and I continue to remember them for the sacrifice they made.

To honor them, Manteiga wrote:

> Juan Manuel was cultured, honest and proclaimed, "I struggle and fight for the freedom of Cuba and if necessary shall die. Batista is a monster … and has become the enemy of Cuba."
>
> Elmuza was a journalist who knew the difference between decency and false impeccable moral values. He also condemned Batista and kept his promise to win the war or die like the warriors of Yara and Baire.
>
> We pay our humble tribute to those friends, our brothers in defending the rights of the Cuban people. We are deeply sorry to hear of the revolutionaries who have perished or are injured.[1]

We continued to wait for news of Castro's condition. The Batista government prohibited the press from getting close to the Sierra Maestra. The only news he wanted coming out of Cuba was that which he approved. While he could not storm the jungles of the Sierra Maestra and defeat the revolutionaries in combat, he had his men surround the perimeter to keep revolutionary communications from escaping the jungle.

Meanwhile, my brother Mario traveled to Mexico and, on January 20, 1957, met with the leaders of the M-26-7 National Directorate: Pedro Miret Prieto, Gustavo Arcos Bergnes, and Melba Hernández Rodríguez del Rey, who was one of the two women involved in the Moncada attack along with Haydée Santamaría Cuadrado. Hernandez's husband was Jesús Montané Oropesa, the Moncadista who, having been on the *Granma*, was subsequently captured and imprisoned.[2]

At this meeting, Mario was named head of arms acquisition in the United States, responsible for obtaining weapons to be sent to the rebels in the Sierra.[3]

Also, because there had been no communication between the expeditionaries and the leadership in Mexico, Mario was immediately asked to go on a secret mission to Cuba with letters to Montané and Faustino Pérez Hernández, a Moncadista and former member of Rafael García Bárcena's MNR, who had also been a *Granma* expeditionary making it to the Sierra Maestra. It was customary to insert secret messages in letters by writing these hidden portions in lemon juice, in between the lines of the visible script. The letters would then be ironed, the heat revealing the portions written in lemon juice by turning it brown.[4]

**Mario Villamia's visit to the M-26-7 Directorate in Exile, headquartered in Mexico City. Gustavo Arcos Bergues, Melba Hernandez Rodriguez de Rey (the other woman besides Haydée Santamaría that took part in the Moncada Barracks attack), Melba Ortega Gainza (Miret's wife), Pedro Miret Prieto, and Mario Villamia. Mexico City, January 20, 1957 (courtesy of Mario Villamia)**

By this time, unbeknownst to those outside Cuba, Pérez Hernández was heading up the revolutionary movement in the "llano," which was the name given to those in the M-26-7 in Cuba who were not in the Sierra. Mario was likely the first link of communication between Cuba and the exiles after the *Granma* landed.[5]

Mario was given a matchbook with a piece of its cover ripped off. While sitting on a bench in the Vedado section of Habana, he was approached by a couple of men asking for a light for their cigarettes. Mario produced the matchbook, and the men produced the missing piece of the cover, indicating they were his contacts. He was instructed to go to a dentist, Virgilio Jacas Quintana, at Calle 78, No. 8907, to be treated for a "toothache."[6]

Jacas became a proponent of the anti–Batista sentiment after the coup d'état of March 10, 1952, and, subsequently, joined the M-26-7. He later became involved with the national organization through Pérez Hernández and Haydée Santamaría, considered the most respected female in the M-26-7. His dental office was used for secret meetings by the national leaders during Castro's imprisonment and his exile in Mexico.[7]

As soon as Mario was in the examining room, he learned he needed to give Jacas the two letters. Although Mario had initially been instructed by Miret to hand deliver the letters to Pérez Hernández personally, this alternate plan was put in place due to Pérez Hernández being highly sought by the Batista forces. Attempting to deliver the letters personally would have possibly jeopardized his underground cover and might have gotten Mario killed in the process.[8]

Miret's letter to Faustino advised him that Mario would oversee collecting arms stateside, and asked they identify someone from Cuba to work with him. Miret sent Pablo Fernandez Alegre from Mexico, and Frank País García sent Lester Rodriguez Pérez and Jorge Sotus Romero from Cuba.[9]

This meant Mario was now part of the M-26-7 National Directorate in Exile.[10]

The local Miami M-26-7 branch was presided over by Jacinto Vásquez, but Miami soon also became the seat of the National Directorate in Exile that had been previously headquartered in Mexico.[11]

Thus, Mario's new role in the business of collecting arms commenced, with Miami as his base of operations. Through that secret mission, he was privileged to learn that Castro was alive and well before any news was made public.[12]

And then entered the foreign journalist of whom Che spoke.

In late January 1957 a revolutionary was sent on a daring mission to slip past Batista's troops and get word to an American journalist that Castro was alive and wanted to speak with him. The M-26-7 chose Herbert Matthews, a 56-year-old senior editor with the *New York Times* who was known in Cuba for having been a reporter in Spain during their civil war of the 1930s. The newspaper's Habana correspondent Ruby Hart Phillips communicated Castro's request to Matthews, and he accepted the offer. Matthews arrived in Habana, days later, accompanied by his wife so as to appear like a tourist. Pérez Hernández was the person who made contact with the journalist. Along with Pérez, a banker named Javier Pazos Vea joined them.[13]

Pazos, who served as their interpreter, was the son of Felipe Pazos Rodriguez, who had been head of the Banco Nacional de Cuba (National Bank of Cuba). Matthews, his wife, and the two members of the M-26-7 traveled together to the city of Manzanillo, where the wife remained. The three men drove in a jeep for six hours, and then walked an additional two hours to arrive at the designated meeting point. On the morning of February 17, 1957, Castro and Matthews met and spoke for the next couple of hours. Photographs were taken.[14]

When the article was published on February 24, 1957, in the *New York Times*, the world was aware that Castro was alive and taking the fight to Batista.[15]

A month and a half later, CBS reporter Bob Taber also interviewed Castro, and that broadcast further excited us because it included the presence of Americans within his troops. At the time, those Americans had no connection to my city of Tampa. But decades later, one of them—Mike Garvey—would move to and later retire in Clearwater, Florida, from where he would share his amazing tale with me.[16]

Garvey was 13 when his father, a petty officer in the Navy, was transferred to the Guantánamo Bay Naval Base in Cuba. There, Garvey attended William T. Sampson High School and befriended Victor Buehlman and Charles Ryan, two and four years older than he was, respectively.[17]

Garvey described them as a wild bunch that would often leave the base to visit the nearby town of Caimanera, which the men stationed at Guantánamo Bay frequented because it hosted a red-light district.[18]

Garvey was never questioned by the establishment owners because he looked much older than his actual age (or perhaps they just didn't care?).[19]

During these trips off the base, the three young men developed relationships with Cubans who would tell them of the atrocities that Batista committed so that he could remain in power.[20]

By the time Garvey was 15, he and his two friends decided it was their duty as decent human beings and temporary residents of the island to help the people of Cuba.[21]

They joined the underground movement sometime in mid–1956, Garvey recalled, and helped the anti–Batista soldiers acquire weapons from the naval base. But they never stole a thing.[22]

Instead, they would befriend the naval base's new arrivals and serve as tour guides, taking them for their first good time in Caimanera. They would let them know where the best bars were and, more importantly to those men, introduce them to the women of the red-light district.[23]

Then, in return, Garvey, Buehlman, and Ryan would ask one of the new arrivals to purchase them a hunting rifle on base with money that—unknown to the men—was provided by the Cuban underground.[24]

There was nothing suspicious about the request. Who would suspect that three teenagers living in a U.S. naval base were supporting a movement to remove the Cuban dictator from power? And the well-weaponized American military men could never have imagined that hunting rifles could be used in war.[25]

They would only each buy one gun at a time, hide it in foliage on the base, and then sneak it to the edge of the base and hand it over the fence to the underground soldiers. Let me write that again: they handed the guns over the fence of a naval base to men and women involved in the revolution.[26]

Garvey estimated that he did that three times over a five-month period, though he did not know if his older partners did so more times without him.[27]

They then heard that Castro was seeking reinforcement for his army in the Sierra Maestra. So, the three American teenagers decided it was time to do more for the revolution.[28]

They walked off the base as they normally did when they wanted to go into Caimanera, only this time they got into a cab driven by a supporter of the underground who was expecting them. He took them to a farmhouse about 60 miles away, Garvey estimated, where a secret staging area was set up as a recruiting base for Castro.[29]

They stayed there for maybe a week, and then he, his friends, and a little more than another 50 recruits, all Cubans, were loaded onto flatbed trucks and taken to meet up with Castro's men in the mountains.[30]

Garvey recalled being shocked at what he found. Castro did not have an army. He had fewer than 20 men with him.[31]

With Castro was Che, and Camilo Cienfuegos Gorriarán, and all three were surprised to find that the new recruits included American teenagers.[32]

Still, he said, they were not treated differently from the other soldiers.[33]

It was not easy, Garvey told me. One time, dinner was a horse's heart, and, despite being repulsed by it, he ate every morsel because food was so scarce.[34]

They were mostly being trained in guerrilla warfare and drumming up support from those who resided in the area.[35]

On one occasion, Garvey said, a group of Castro's men dressed as members of the Cuban Army, patrolled the mountains, and met a local who bragged of killing a farmer who supported the revolution.[36]

Castro's patrol captured the man and brought him back to camp, where the revolutionaries demanded that he be killed immediately. Castro first wanted to make sure that the local had not made the story up to impress what he at first thought were Batista supporters. So, Castro sent a patrol to the farmhouse to investigate. It turned out to be true, so Castro held a trial, and the man was convicted.[37]

Castro asked his troops what should be done with the murderer. All of them, including the three American teens, voted for execution via firing squad.[38]

At some point, Garvey and his friends wrote letters to their parents, President Dwight Eisenhower, and the U.S. embassy in Habana explaining that they were alive and supporting the revolution and that the United States should do the same because Batista was a monster.[39]

Word began to spread around the United States of the American teens supporting Castro. They were nicknamed "The Guantánamo Boys."[40]

Then, in April 1957, CBS reporter Taber reached Castro in the mountains and part of his report included Garvey and his friends. The interview broadcast on May 19, and I remember watching it with shock, amazement, excitement, and fear: they were only teenagers, and I wondered if they knew what they had gotten themselves into.[41]

Not long after the broadcast, the U.S. embassy in Habana reached out to Taber and requested that he ask Castro if he could bring the boys home.[42]

Perhaps realizing that having American teenagers killed in battle would be terrible public relations, Castro agreed and told Garvey and Buehlman to leave with Taber. Ryan, being the oldest, was allowed to stay. He was involved in combat a few weeks later, and he too then left.[43]

Though they were only with the revolution for a short period, those three American teenagers had a major impact on it.[44]

They became international news and shone a brighter spotlight than ever on the revolution. The world had been reminded that Castro was alive, and the news reports reiterated that the people of Cuba stood behind him.[45]

It is worth noting that, on July 18, 1996, the "GTMO Boys" were featured in a CBS Dan Rather special titled *The Last Revolutionary*. They subsequently visited Cuba at Castro's invitation and were treated like VIPs.[46]

In Tampa, the combination of Matthews's article and Taber's report rejuvenated us. It lifted our spirits and gave us the motivation to continue working for the triumph of the revolution and the liberty it would provide Cuba. Our membership began to increase. We collected funds and staged protests in and outside of places such as Tampa's Cuban consulate, the airport, the courthouse, the post offices, the cigar factories, the social clubs, and anywhere many people would congregate. We began meeting once a week again. All was going well.

Miami replaced Mexico City as the location of the M-26-7 National Directorate in Exile, and we made regular trips to the city to meet with their club. We supported their activities and vice versa. Key West's group did the same. Florida was a bustling hub of pro-Castro activities.

Support for Castro grew in Cuba too. Threatened, Batista increased his persecution of opponents: he arrested, tortured, and assassinated them. More Cubans fled their homeland, and many came to Tampa. Some became members of the M-26-7.

Revolutionaries who remained in Cuba would not be deterred by Batista's acts of barbarism. Some groups took it upon themselves to overthrow Batista rather than acting in unison with Castro.

On March 13, 1957, the Directorio Revoluciónario (Revolutionary Directorate) attacked the presidential palace to assassinate Batista. Forty of the revolutionaries were killed in the failed attempt and its aftermath, including FEU leader José Antonio Echeverría Bianchi and former Auténtico party congressman Menelao Mora Morales.

The attackers made it into Batista's office, but the dictator had left minutes earlier to check on his sick son in his palace bedroom. The revolutionaries tried to fight their way into the palace's residential area, but after a long gun battle all but a few were killed. While this battle was raging, Echeverria led an attack on Radio Reloj. They overtook the station and erroneously broadcast that Batista was dead. As the revolutionaries fled the station, police gunned them down, killing five.

That evening, angered by the attempt on his life, Batista ordered his police to arrest and murder a great number of known revolutionaries. It was considered one of the bloodiest days in the history of the revolution.

On April 20, four of the Directorio Revoluciónario members who had taken part in the presidential palace attack were killed in their Habana hideout, Apartment #21 at 7 Humboldt Street by Colonel Esteban Ventura Novo and his men. The Humboldt 7 Massacre, as it was called, took the lives of Fructuoso Rodríguez Pérez, Joe Westbrook Rosales, José Machado Rodriguez, and Juan Pedro Carbó Serviá.

I traveled with Manteiga and other members of the Tampa branch of the M-26-7 on May 18, 1957, to Miami's M-26-7 meeting commemorating the death of José Martí, who died on May 19, 1895. The meeting also honored those who had recently fallen in the name of Cuban freedom, specifically those who died in the Humboldt No. 7 and the presidential palace massacre, as well as the Goicuria barracks attack, the battles in the Sierra Maestra, and the Moncada attack.

Because he lost friends in the Goicuria, Carlos Prío Socarrás was one of the two keynote speakers at the Miami meeting that honored the fallen. The other keynote speaker was Manteiga. That was quite an honor for our Tampa leader.

On May 19, 1957, Castro's sisters, Lydia and Emma, spoke at a fundraiser in Miami. M-26-7 members from New York, Key West, and the newly formed Chicago branch joined Miami at this historic rally. The Castro sisters had promised to later stop in our city for a similar rally. Unfortunately, the visit never materialized.

On that same day, 27 followers of Prío, led by Calixto Sánchez White, embarked on a revolutionary expedition aboard the *Corinthia*, a U.S.-registered small ship that left from Biscayne Bay and landed in Cuba on May 23. This second Prío-financed expedition was to launch an additional front against Batista from the Sierra Cristal, a pine-tree-heavy mountain region of Cuba. Batista's army was waiting for them. One of the 16 rebels killed in this battle was Jorge Prieto Ibarra, brother of Tampa resident Mario Prieto.[47]

On June 23, 1957, a Mass at Our Lady of Perpetual Help Church in Ybor City was offered in memory of Jorge. In a show of support for the family of this young revolutionary martyr, some of us from the club as well as representatives from the Miami group were in attendance.

Flyers and notices were distributed and publicized in newspapers for the event one week later, on June 30. Revolutionaries from throughout Florida again gathered in Tampa, but this time for a joyous occasion—the first organized event hosted by Tampa's M-26-7 since Castro had visited. More than 200 individuals attended the event held at El Boulevard Restaurant owned by Jaime Fernandez Pendas and Amable de la Torre, on the northeast corner of 9th Avenue, at 2101 Nebraska Avenue, across from the Centro Asturiano. The Miami M-26-7 contingency in attendance included the president of the Miami M-26-7, Jacinto Vazquez; the treasurer, Edilberto Serrano; and my brother Mario.

Other distinguished Miami guests included Carlos G. Peraza, a well-known revolutionary journalist, and José Manuel Paula, a former Tampa resident who operated a restaurant in Miami. We paid tribute to those who died fighting to free Cuba, as we had at the Miami event a few weeks earlier. The event was a success, as it raised $124 for the cause. The event also succeeded in getting the word to

**CONTRA LA TIRANIA**
A los Cubanos y sus Amigos de Tampa:

Para reiterar nuestra adhesión a Fidel Castro y sus compañeros, héroes de la Libertad de Cuba, les invitamos a que concurran el domingo próximo, Junio 30, a las 2:30 de la tarde, a un acto que se celebrará en el que era salón de banquetes del Restaurant Boulevard, 9a Avenida casi esquina a Nebraska.

Miami mandará una brillante representación al frente de la cual vendrán José Manuel Paula, Jacinto Vázquez, Alberto Mora, Edelberto Serrano, y Carlos G. Peraza y otros "activistas" del 26 de Julio de esa ciudad.

También invitamos a todos los miembros y amigos de las agrupaciones que luchan por la libertad de Cuba y que acaban de realizar un hermoso acto de unidad contra la tiranía en Miami.

Recordaremos a los caídos en el Moncada, en el Goicuría, en el Palacio Presidencial; a los asesinados expedicionarios del Corintia; a los asesinados en Holguín, en Humbold No. 7, en las calles de Santiago de Cuba, de la Habana y otras ciudades y pueblos de Cuba.

La causa de la libertad ultrajada en Cuba requiere el esfuerzo de los cubanos de ideales martianos y de todos los hombres de sentimientos democráticos, no importa donde hayan nacido. No olvide el día, la hora y el lugar: Junio 30, 2:30 p. m., esquina de la 9a y Avenida y Nebraska.

Por el Comité Organizador,
**Victoriano Manteiga, Pdte.**
**Raúl Villamía, Secretario**

M-26-7 flyer inviting Tampa Cubans to a banquet at the El Boulevard Restaurant on 9th and Nebraska Avenues, in memory of those who died in the attacks on the Moncada Barracks (July 26, 1953), the Goicuria Garrison (April 29, 1956), the city of Holguin (December 23-26, 1956), the presidential palace (March 13, 1957), Humboldt No. 7 (April 20, 1957), and the *Corinthia* expedition (May 19, 1957). The Miami M-26-7 sent representatives Jose Manuel Paula (former Tampan who owned a Miami restaurant), Jacinto Vasquez (Miami M-26-7 president), Alberto Mora, Edelberto Serrano, and Carlos G. Peraza (journalist). Mario Villamia was among those in the 30-car caravan from Miami who attended the event. Tampa (Ybor City), Florida, June 30, 1957 (from the collection of Raul Villamia).

## 9. The Media's Role in the Revolution

Mario Villamia, Oscar Asencio Duque de Heredia, and Roberto Garcia Serrano on the sidewalk in front of *La Gaceta* newspaper office, in town via a 30-car caravan from Miami to attend the memorial banquet at El Boulevard Restaurant on 9th and Nebraska Avenues. Tampa (Ybor City), Florida, June 30, 1957 (Photo D-3 File 47, Reg# 4453, courtesy Oficina de Asuntos Históricos [Office of Historic Affairs]. Habana, Cuba).

the community about our cause; *The Tampa Tribune*, WFLA Channel 8, and WTVT Channel 13 covered the meeting.[48]

But, prior to the 3 p.m. start of our meeting, the portrait of Batista that hung in the Circulo Cubano's library had been removed and torn in half. Cuban Club President Angel Gomez asserted that it was not one of their club members, so the eyes fell upon our organization. I can positively write that it was not one of us. We detested a portrait of a tyrant and murderer hanging in the club, but we did not believe in or condone vandalism.

Then, other trouble began to brew.

Another revolutionary group that had no formal name and was not sanctioned by Castro had formed in Tampa. The group met at the home of Enrique Someillán, the crab cake vendor who delivered food to Castro while he was in Ybor.

Decades later, Someillán's nephew Felix Someillán detailed his uncle's life.

As a little boy of four or five years old, Someillán grabbed a frying pan full of hot grease off the stove and spilled it all over his face. At the hospital, doctors were impressed that, despite the great pain the boy must have been in, he never shed one tear. They told Enrique that he "portrayed the part of a *capitan*," or "captain" in English. "Capitan" became Someillán's nickname for life.[49]

Still, the grease left scars in the form of light-colored skin around his eyes, so, to hide the marks, Someillán typically wore dark shaded sunglasses in public, even when inside or at night.[50]

Someillán was involved in another coup plot while residing in Cuba before Castro's revolution. His nephew said he believed it took place in the 1940s and involved overthrowing Batista but could not say for certain. Someillán fled Cuba when the government was tipped of his active role in the coup plan. It is unclear if that occurred before or after the attempt. It was then he came to Tampa along with his three brothers—Carlos, Alfredo, and Evaristo, who was the nephew Felix Someillán's father.[51]

Castro, according to the nephew, asked Someillán to help the revolution, and he agreed to assist in running guns and other needed supplies to Cuba, though it remains unclear why he did not immediately join the M-26-7 in Tampa.[52]

It also remains odd that despite being on the same side of the revolution as we were, on at least one occasion, some from their group started a fist fight with M-26-7 members and we had heard they had been bad-mouthing us around the community.[53]

It became a distraction.

## 10

# The Radicals

It felt like we were being infiltrated by the enemy disguised as allies.

At our meeting on July 16, 1957, a group of these radicals from the nameless pro–Fidel Castro Ruz group showed up with a written solicitation bearing 16 signatures requesting their membership into Tampa's M-26-7. The names on the petition were Miguel Roche, Mario Iglesias, Miguel Alamo, Raul Cartaya, David Torre, Rafael Duran, Conrado Castillo, Ernesto Ponce, Enrique Someillán, Guillermo Hermida, Alberto Rojas, Ramon Rodriguez, Victor Ferrer, Sergio Garcia, Anibal Velaz, and Rafael Alvarez.[1]

We asked the group to step outside while we discussed the matter since there had been issues such as the fistfight with some of them in recent weeks. We initially thought to deny the petition, but ultimately, in the interest of fostering harmony among all in Tampa fighting for liberty and democracy in Cuba, decided to grant membership to them all. Perhaps they would cease to fight against us if they fought alongside us, we rationalized.

We invited them back inside and told them the good news.

Victoriano Manteiga welcomed them. Velaz then proposed that various committees, each consisting of three persons, be made to deal with various duties: a Treasury Committee to work with and assist the club treasurer, a Propaganda Committee to prepare and disseminate information relating to important revolutionary issues, and a Public Relations Committee to promote interactions with the community.[2]

The original M-26-7 members readily agreed with Velaz's idea and approved of the logical plan. The Treasury Committee consisted of Gilberto Rodriguez, Miguel Roche, and Conrado Castillo. The Propaganda Committee consisted of Victor Ferrer, Guillermo Hermida, and Ernesto Ponce. The Public Relations Committee consisted of Roque Suarez, Marcelino Vila, and Roland Manteiga. And a fourth committee was then created and charged with holding demonstrations at Tampa's Cuban consulate and airport. It consisted of Anibal Velaz, Miguel Roche, Ernesto

Ponce, Raul Viana, David Torre, Miguel Alamo, Mario Iglesias, Luis Riestra, and me.[3]

The final order of business at that meeting was organizing a commemorative event on the fourth anniversary of the Moncada attack. It was decided that we would picket the Cuban consulate, collect money throughout the city during the day, and then hold a fundraising event in West Tampa at night.[4]

Still, not all of Tampa was on our side. In the July 19, 1957, edition of *La Gaceta* newspaper, Manteiga reported on an incident that had occurred during a weekend dance at the Cuban Club. According to the report, a woman was sitting with several friends at a table on the Cuban Club's patio when she yelled, "Viva Fidel Castro! Viva Fidel Castro!" This comment angered one of the other patrons, who told her that she would be asked to leave if she shouted those words again. The two exchanged angry words, and the police had to be called in to calm the situation. The police agreed with the anti–Castro patron and told the woman she had to leave.[5]

"Why is it wrong to scream 'Viva Fidel Castro,' the hero of the Sierra Maestra and five and a half million Cubans who yearn for the fall of the dictator, Fulgencio Batista?" asked Manteiga in the article.[6]

The following Sunday, July 21, a delegation of the Tampa club that included Manteiga, Santos, Carbonell, Someillán, and me attended a meeting in Miami jointly sponsored by the various revolutionary organizations there. It took place at the Flagler Theater and was attended by more than 1,000 people. Some of the speakers were Lino Elías, Edelberto Serrano, Alcides Gonzalez, Carlos G. Peraza, Felix Martinez, Rene Viera, Alberto Mora, and Cuba's ex-president Carlos Prío Socarrás, who continued to personally fund many of the pro-revolutionary efforts.[7]

It was amazing and inspiring to see so many come together in the name of Cuban freedom.

A few days later, on Wednesday, July 24, we met in Tampa. There was a moment of silence in remembrance of the lives lost on July 26, 1953, and the ensuing days in the Moncada attack. Manteiga shared that a tribute would take place that Friday at the American Legion Post #248 at 2105 North Jamaica Street between Spruce and Pine Streets in West Tampa. Its president, Manuel Fernandez, was a friend of Manteiga's and mine, and he allowed us the use of the hall. Someillán oversaw the committee to prepare the salon for the function, and he did a great job.[8]

Thursday, July 25, 1957, began at 10 a.m. with picketing outside the Cuban consulate in Tampa, which supported Batista's tyranny. Other members of the M-26-7 collected donations throughout Tampa. But rain ended both efforts early when it stormed around 3 p.m.[9]

We held our tribute to the Moncada attack at the American Legion on Friday evening at around 8 p.m. Representatives from the clubs in New York and Miami attended, along with several Tampa supporters. We raised a good amount of money.[10]

Then at some point during the next few days, two of the new members—Ferrer and Alvarez—were arrested for public intoxication. We could not allow our members to act in such an inappropriate manner. They represented not just our group but the ideals of the revolution as a whole. So, at the following meeting on July 29, we voted to expel them from our ranks. There was no argument on their behalf from their friends. But, at that same meeting, we also voted to form a committee consisting solely of members of their group—Roche, Someillán, Ponce, and Velaz—to make door-to-door solicitations for donations. Because of the recent influx of donations, we also voted to procure a bank safety deposit box in which to keep the organization's funds.

Our next meeting was held on August 7, at which we named Someillán to the Propaganda Committee to make up for the loss of Ferrer.

Despite Someillán's good work, the original M-26-7 members began questioning the decision to bring him and his friends into the fold. There were rumors that they were still bad-mouthing us around the city, questioning how we conduct our business and saying they could do things better if in charge.

While our group was experiencing growing pains, the New York City–based M-26-7 was celebrating a great success. In the August 9, 1957, edition of *La Gaceta*, Manteiga reported that New York members raised a 60-by-40-foot M-26-7 flag outside the crown of the Statue of Liberty. Police confiscated the flag a few hours later, around 10:30 a.m., according to Manteiga, but the statement was made: the M-26-7 was for liberty in Cuba on the same level as the United States enjoyed.[11]

At our August 14 meeting, Manteiga proposed organizing a symbolic celebration of our own honoring the death of Eduardo Chibás y Ribas by placing a wreath at the José Martí bust located in front of the Circulo Cubano. At that same meeting, Sergio Garcia was named to the Propaganda Committee in replacement of Ponce. The meeting notes do not indicate why Ponce left.[12]

It was also decided that, to avoid future problems with members, a committee consisting of Luis Riestra, Roche, Velaz, and Miguel Alamo would interview the members of our organization who had been rumored to express statements contrary to our ideology. They would have to leave the club if they truly had different opinions on how the M-26-7 should be operated. It was not up to them or even us to determine how the club had to function. We followed the orders of the M-26-7 National Directorate in Exile.[13]

During our August 20 meeting, the new members seemed determined to take over the club, requesting that we designate vice chairs to our various committees, then pushing for themselves to be named to the new positions. We surmised their idea was that if the chair vacated the position, their men would assume the leadership role and in time they would be heading up every committee. Again, in the spirit of unity, we passed their motion, naming Someillán vice-president, Velaz vice-secretary, and Domingo Diaz vice-treasurer, keeping in the back of our minds to make sure the chairs did not step down and allow a coup to occur. We hoped that perhaps there was not a secret agenda behind the vice-chair idea and that the radicals did indeed care more about the cause than themselves.[14]

The September 4 meeting brought the control issue to a head. Velaz, seconded by Cartaya, Alamo, Someillán, Rojas, Ramon Rodriguez, Conrado Castillo, and Domingo Diaz, proposed that Tampa's M-26-7 cease to exist, unite with the Organizacion Auténtica (Authentics Organization) and the Directorio Revoluciónario (Revolutionary Directorate) and form one united group that would be called El Comité Pro Unidad Revoluciónario de Tampa (The Pro Unity Revolutionary Committee of Tampa) to make Tampa an example of a united revolutionary effort.[15]

Velaz further proposed the immediate creation of a manifesto to inform Cubans everywhere that the revolutionary groups in Tampa were a united force and to disseminate this manifesto to all exile communities in the United States, inviting them to follow Tampa's example in having one revolutionary organization unified for the cause. He claimed that he hoped for Tampa to be a symbol for the rest of the exile community.[16]

While this idea seemed logical in theory, in practice it could not work because:

1. Tampa M-26-7 could not make any changes, especially ceasing to exist as an organization to unify and become part of another organization, without having the authorization of the M-26-7 National Directorate in Exile. Manteiga explained that we could cooperate with other groups as far as propaganda and civic actions, but always with each organization maintaining their distinct personalities.

2. The M-26-7 was the largest patriotic organization in Cuba, and its leader, Castro, the most popular. The members of the Directorio Revoluciónario were predominantly university students. The Organizacion Auténtica was made up of members of Prío's Partido Auténtico (Authentic Party) and it was not very popular in Cuba.

3. These two organizations had no official representation in Tampa. No one claiming to be associated with them was ever able to provide credentials proving their membership. It had been well

documented that Castro came to Tampa and founded the M-26-7 and our official IDs proved we supported the organization. No leaders from the other two groups had been known to have come to Tampa to form local branches, and no one had IDs to prove their membership. How could we have merged with these groups without proof that their leaders wanted to do so or that the locals claiming to be part of the groups were granted the power to make such decisions?

4. Our job in Tampa was to raise funds for the M-26-7 in Cuba, stage protests, and disseminate information relating to Castro's ideas and plans. Finding unity among these various groups was the responsibility of the M-26-7 in Cuba.

Manteiga explained that, for these reasons, we could not carry out such an action and denied the request. He was seconded by Carbonell, Roque Suarez, Vila, Santos, Duran, Iglesias, Max Garcia, Bueno, and me—mostly M-26-7 originals. Manteiga then emphasized that it would be required that representatives from any other revolutionary groups coming into the city to work with or meet with us to present credentials proving their membership in these groups. Velaz retorted that we should at least meet with representatives, which we agreed to do, but only as a venue for exchanging ideas and not for entertaining the notion of uniting groups.

Velaz was furious and embarrassed by the denial. His group of eight began shouting in protest as they abruptly left the meeting.

Not long after that explosive meeting, Velaz and Someillán formed a new group, calling it by the name Velaz proposed at our meeting. They even printed a booklet outlining their plans for unifying the Tampa anti-Batista sympathizers, naming us as one of the entities that would join them even though we told them we never would.[17]

But the unification they sought never materialized.

Throughout Tampa in late August, English language placards warned tourists to stay out of Cuba for as long as Batista was in power. Though I do not recall whether these were the work of the M-26-7, they were also reported to have been seen in Miami and New York as well, so it is possible.

In late September, Manteiga and I traveled to Miami to meet with Dr. Roberto Agramonte y Pichardo in his apartment. Dr. Agramonte, remember, was running for and was set to win the presidency of Cuba when Fulgencio Batista y Zaldívar seized control of the government. Also present at the meeting was Dr. Manuel Bisbe Alberni, a professor at the University of Habana and friend of Manteiga's dating back to Chibás's last visit to Tampa. Agramonte and Bisbe informed us that Castro was aware of and concerned about the divisions in exile, explaining that Castro felt Batista was spending huge amounts of money to divide the opposition, hoping to weaken the revolution from within.

September passed, and the problems with the radical group returned. They had been meeting at the Trelles Clinic, an Ybor City medical facility, and their top agenda seemed to be to spread false rumors about the M-26-7.

They claimed prior to Castro's arrival in Tampa that he had emissaries contact two people in Tampa about leading his M-26-7—Manteiga and Jorge A. Trelles, owner of the medical clinic.

Front cover of *Comité Central Pro Unidad Revolucionaria* booklet that was created by the oppositionist group that wanted to unite all the Tampa revolutionary organizations under one banner, as the booklet title suggests (from the collection of Raul Villamia).

> Manifiesto del Comité Pro-Unidad Revolucionaria de Tampa, integrado por Delegados y dirigentes del Directorio Revolucionario, Club Patriótico 26 de Julio y Organización Auténtica (O.A.), que radican en Tampa, Florida, y que fué aprobado en asamblea general conjunta. de estas, las únicas organizaciones revolucionarias existentes en Tampa, a los dos días del mes de Octubre de 1957.
>
> Se han omitido las firmas de los que componen dicho Comité, con el deliberado propósito de evitar suspicacias, en cuanto a que no nos mueve, al dar este paso transcendental, personalismo de ninguna especie y que solo nos alienta una ambición: la de llegar a ser imitados para bien de Cuba.

> Aclaración al emblema de la portada: Al escudo cubano lo rodea una cadena cuyos eslabones representan a cada uno de los sectores revolucionarios estrechamente unidos. Solo es simbólico, ya que no todos esos sectores tienen representación en Tampa y por ende en el Comité Pro-Unidad Revolucionaria, No obstante es una invitación a los mismos para que integren la UNIDAD.

Page 2 of *Comité Central Pro Unidad Revolucionaria* booklet. The M-26-7 never agreed to this, but despite their rejecting the idea, the opposition included the M-26-7 in this publication as being in favor of it. Of all the organizations listed, the only one in existence in Tampa was the M-26-7. Tampa, Florida, October 2, 1957 (from the collection of Raul Villamia).

But Trelles, they said, refused the post because he was already head of another political organization, Organizacion Auténtica, a militant division of the Authentic Party. Trelles did in fact support Prío, and Castro may have contacted him about helping his cause as well, but Castro was an Ortodoxo, and it was highly improbable that he would have considered an Auténtico as head of the M-26-7.

It is apparent that Manteiga was the first and only choice to lead Tampa's M-26-7, as proven by the wording of the letters written to Manteiga by José Fidalgo and Jesús Montané.

In late September, according to a September 21, 1957, *Tampa Tribune* article, Someillán and Alamo were arrested for showing up at *La Gaceta* and threatening to kill Manteiga and Roque Suarez, who was also at the office. Someillán later told police the altercation began because they charged Manteiga with publishing "conservative" news stories about Castro—a laughable claim. Police said that the two men threatened to blow up *La Gaceta* if Manteiga did not agree to their demands.[18]

Manteiga, per the article, grabbed for his gun, but office bystanders held him back and police were called to the scene.[19]

Police are quoted in the article as saying that Someillán had other men standing as lookouts outside of *La Gaceta*. By the time law enforcement arrived, the radicals had fled *La Gaceta*, but Someillán and about 10 other men were later found at his home. Someillán and Alamo—who told police they both lived at 1515 10th Avenue—were arrested for threatening the lives of Manteiga and Suarez and later released on $500 bond. Charges, from what I remember, were subsequently dismissed.[20]

When later asked why his uncle may have acted out against the M-26-7, Felix Someillán surmised that Someillán simply had a different view on how to help Castro.[21]

In New York on September 15, Angel Pérez-Vidal was arrested. There had been an uprising by some of Batista's Navy about 10 days earlier in Cienfuegos, Cuba. One of the men who had participated in the conspiracy, Sgt. Miranda, escaped Cuba aboard the cargo vessel *Bahia de Nipe*, hoping to seek political asylum once they docked in New York City.[22]

The stowaway was discovered while the ship was en route. Cuba was notified, and Batista ordered the captain to arrest and return Miranda to Cuba.

A few days before the ship arrived, Pérez-Vidal learned of the situation and determined that some action was needed to ensure Miranda was able to receive the asylum sought by stepping on American soil. A group composed of members from Acción Cívica Cubana, which had been one of the three groups designated as the New York City branch of the M-26-7, and the Directorio Revoluciónario organized a protest demonstration at the dock, with a plan of boarding the ship to rescue Miranda and give him safe passage.[23]

Pérez-Vidal and the group arrived at 1:30 a.m. in torrential rain and were mere feet from the ship when they were met by members of the New York Police Department, who scuffled with them and prohibited them from gaining access. He and Luis Blanca Fernandez, the leader of the New York City Directorio Revoluciónario group, were both arrested and taken to the Manhattan Detention Center called "The Tombs."[24]

According to Pérez-Vidal, the M-26-7 Directorate in Exile was not supportive of this action and refused to pay his bail since the action was carried out in unison with another revolutionary group. Ultimately, the Acción Cívica Cubana paid it. An attorney well known in the mafia community was retained to defend him, and the case was dismissed. Unfortunately, Sgt. Miranda was executed upon arriving in Cuba.[25]

On November 1, 1957, we learned that perhaps Manteiga's anti-unification stance was wrong when the Cuban Liberation Junta Unity Pact was approved in Miami by the exile community. This agreement was signed by representatives from six Cuban political groups: the Auténticos, the FEU, the Directorio Revoluciónario, the Directorio Obrero Revoluciónario (Revolutionary Workers' Directorate), Partido Revoluciónario Cubano, and the M-26-7. It stated that they would work together under the Junta de Liberación Cubana (Cuban Liberation Junta) to overthrow Batista. This was like the idea pitched to us by the eight radicals.[26]

Meanwhile, in Cuba, one of the revolutionaries' tactics against Batista was to burn the sugar plantations, so the Tampa M-26-7 coined a slogan "There will be no sugar crops in Cuba until dictator Batista is ousted."

The club rented a truck and placed signs denouncing the tyranny, with sugarcane stalks between each sign. Manuel Fuentes and I drove the truck throughout Ybor City and West Tampa over a two-day period, November 5 and 6.[27]

Then, in the following week's edition on November 15, 1957, a photograph of me with the truck was featured on page two.[28]

On November 29, 1957, to quiet his doubters, Manteiga published in *La Gaceta* the letters from Castro's men sent in 1955 asking him to lead the M-26-7. The radicals' ploy was working, however, as we continued to have to spend time putting out fires that we could have spent supporting the revolution.[29]

Our meetings were open to all members, and they were all welcome to share their opinions. This was an example of free speech sometimes being a burden. Occasions began to arise where we had to expel some for speaking negatively about Castro and the M-26-7. Denouncers had infiltrated the club with some of their friends whom we did not know. They were causing unnecessary and sometimes violent discussions with the sole objective being to disrupt our work and harmony among members.

We continued as best we could.

In December, Manteiga's anti-unification stance was vindicated when, via a letter Castro wrote to the exile community dated December 14, 1957, we learned that the Miami Unity Pact was not endorsed by our revolutionary leader. Excerpts include:

> We were informed that the pact was endorsed in Miami by the 26th of July Movement and these other organizations I now address.
> The 26th of July Movement did not designate or authorize any delegation to discuss said negotiations...

Raul Villamia with sugarcane truck in support of Fidel Castro's rebels burning Cuba's sugarcane crops in protest of dictator Fulgencio Batista y Zaldívar. The truck was driven on November 5 and 6, 1957, by Raul and Manuel Fuentes, throughout the streets of Ybor City and West Tampa, garnering support via a loudspeaker. Tampa, Florida (photograph by *La Gaceta*, appearing in their November 15, 1957, issue; from the collection of Raul Villamia).

While the leaders of the other organizations who endorsed the pact are abroad fighting an imaginary revolution, the leaders of the 26th of July Movement are in Cuba, making a real revolution.

...Because after all is said and done, it has been the 26th of July Movement alone that has been and is carrying out actions all over the country. Only the militants of the 26th of July have brought rebellion from the wild mountains of Oriente to the western provinces. Only the militants of the 26th of July have committed sabotage, executed Batista's thugs, burned sugarcane plantations, and carried out other revolutionary actions. Only the 26th of July Movement has been able to organize the workers all over the country for revolutionary action. It is also only the 26th of July that has today been able to undertake the strategy of strike committees. The 26th of July is the only sector that cooperates with organizations of the Civilian Resistance Movement, in which the civilian sectors of almost all the localities of Cuba are united.

Let it be understood that although we relinquish any claim to position or power in the government, it must also be understood that the militants of the 26th of July do not relinquish and will never relinquish orientation and leadership of the people—from the underground, from the Sierra Maestra, or from the tombs to which they are sending our dead. And we do not relinquish our role because it is not merely we

## 10. The Radicals 125

New York City sidewalk with Juan Jaraica (who would, on July 17, 1959, help Angel Pérez-Vidal give President Manuel Urrutia Lleó safe passage out of the presidential palace when Fidel Castro was deposing him), Armando Abascal, Julio Perez, Angel Pérez-Vidal, Manuel Urrutia Lleó, Mario Villamia, unidentified man. Urrutia went into exile in New York City in November 1957. New York, New York, 1957–58 (photo courtesy of Mario Villamia).

ourselves, but an entire generation that has a moral duty to the people of Cuba to provide substantive solutions for their great problems....
...To die with dignity, one has no need of company.[30]

Shortly after releasing that letter, Castro announced that Judge Manuel Urrutia Lleó would assume the presidency of Cuba when Batista was overthrown. This was welcome news. Urrutia was a popular choice, as he was a liberal politician and lawyer. Urrutia had been exiled to New York City in November 1957 after having been forced by Batista to resign from the bench for having rendered an opinion, as chairman of a three-judge panel in Santiago de Cuba, that 150 youths brought to court on charges of rebellious action be released since there was no peaceful means left to Cuban citizens to defend their constitutional rights. This shocked the government and brought rejoicing throughout a rebellious Cuba. Mario, while on a visit to New York, had occasion to spend time with Urrutia, as captured in a photograph of the two of them in a group of six, including Angel Pérez-Vidal.[31]

While the exile community celebrated the news of Urrutia being chosen as president, in Tampa we mourned the loss of our leader. Near the end of December 1957, Manteiga resigned as president of Tampa's M-26-7. He told us he was stepping down because he needed more time to attend to the demands of running his newspaper and because divisive meetings were becoming an exercise in futility. He just could not afford to expend more effort than he already invested.

It felt like the intruders had won.

# 11

# New Leadership

We did not have to wait long for a new leader.

We were originally flustered when we lost Victoriano Manteiga as our leader, but quickly realized that it was for the best. Manteiga was then able to concentrate on other affairs that could support the club, and his replacements were qualified to lead us.

The members proposed that I assume the presidency position, but I did not accept. That position inherently required more oratory demands in both languages, and, at that time, I preferred to remain in the office I occupied, which involved less public speaking. Plus, I had just begun my employment with the City of Tampa Traffic Planning Department, so did not think it was wise to take on additional responsibility while starting a new job.

So, we elected Eduardo Mijares Pujals as president.

I remember little about Mijares's background except that he was a well-respected attorney in Cuba who had to flee into exile for speaking out against Fulgencio Batista y Zaldívar and that in Tampa he worked in some capacity at a law firm. I also recall that I would sometimes visit him at his home on the upper floor of a house between 13th and 14th Streets on the north side of 14th Avenue. He had a young son at the time who was about six years old.

One of his first acts as our new leader was to positively respond to Fidel Castro Ruz's anti–Miami Unity Pact letter. This was done via a letter published in the January 17, 1958, edition of *La Gaceta*:

> The July 26th Movement of Tampa dutifully endorses the document addressed to all the revolutionary groups in Miami that was signed by our leader Fidel Castro Ruz in the Sierra Maestra on December 14, 1957 on behalf of the National Directorate of our organization.
>
> Considering that we are part of a revolutionary organization and that we constitute the rear of the army, we estimate that orders are met, not discussed and we understand that it is the National Directorate of the July 26 Movement that ultimately makes decisions and that we need only to continue to fulfill our duties and raison d'etre (reason for existence).

At the same time we ask that all members of our organization and their supporters, and connecting lines, now more than ever, up the task of raising funds through bond sales with the aim of helping the Liberation Army of the Revolutionary Cuban fighter....

> Liberty or Death
> July 26th Movement
> By the Executive Committee of Tampa
> Dr. Eduardo V. Mijares Pujals, President
> Dr. Virgilio Jacas Quintana, Secretary General of Organization[1]

Jacas's signature still baffles me.

I had not resigned from my position as secretary of the club when Manteiga left the presidency, yet Jacas's name was mentioned in the *Gaceta* letter with a title of secretary general. I can only guess this was done to assign a title to him so that he would be the one replacing Mijares if it came to that, since, as already stated, I did not want the role of president.

Jacas was the dentist with whom Mario met on his secret mission to Cuba the previous year.

He must have left Cuba and moved to Tampa shortly after he met with my brother.

When Manteiga stepped down, Jacas was working as a cashier at the Columbia Restaurant. I recall that I used to visit him there when visiting my wife, Nora, who worked in Stephen Demmi's dental office across the street from the restaurant. Stephen Demmi was brother of John Demmi, Nora's godfather, who, decades later, was proprietor of JD's Sandwich Shop, next to the Columbia Restaurant, in the building that now houses the Columbia Centennial Museum.

Manteiga, in the meantime, with more time to dedicate to helping the organization in ways besides calming tension, used his significant pull with the media community to bring more attention to the plight of the Cuban people. At that juncture, he had been publishing *La Gaceta* for 36 years. His circle of influence rippled outside the Tampa Bay area by virtue of his longevity and respect for his professionalism.

This became evident on February 14 when the NBC television network filmed portions of an M-26-7 meeting held at his newspaper office, to be included as a five-minute clip in a broadcast of *The Today Show*. The news program was one of the most popular morning shows in the nation, broadcast every day from 7 to 9 a.m. on 126 stations to millions of people throughout the country.[2]

The segment featured the show's well-known host, David Garroway, interviewing Manteiga and his son Roland Manteiga about Batista's

## 11. New Leadership

crimes, Castro's revolution, and what U.S. citizens could do to help, such as donate funds and petition the federal government to stop arming Batista's troops. Reporter Paul Cunningham narrated the clips being presided over by Mijares.

The story was broadcast on February 27 at 7:40 a.m.

It was also around this time that Jacas had to leave us.

When he fled Cuba, his wife, Gloria Sanchez, was gravely sick and had to stay behind at the Miramar Clinic. She died there in mid–February 1958. A notice of her death appeared in the February 21 *La Gaceta*.

Jacas succeeded in reentering Cuba in a clandestine manner to see her prior to her death and told her he came back because the revolution had succeeded, which was a cover so as not to upset her. Although he was sought by Batista's henchmen, he attended her funeral and then went to Mexico, where he continued working for the revolution. I have a letter from him dated March 30, 1958, from Mexico where he asks me to give his regards to Mijares.[3]

Meanwhile, *The Today Show* returned to Tampa to film a follow-up to the story for a March 18 broadcast. The subsequent show aired from in front of the Columbia Restaurant.

This was a major victory for our organization. I am unaware of any other U.S.-based M-26-7 gaining such national exposure. It was hard for me to celebrate, however, as I had received bad news.

My brother Mario had been arrested for illegal arms possession.

# 12

# Mario's Missions

My brother Mario's star was on the rise among those endeavoring to liberate Cuba.

He; his wife, Carmen Guzman Villamia; and his two daughters, Natacha and Arlene, had been living in a two-story home at 1443 Northeast Miami Place in Miami that they rented from my wife's uncle Johnny Rodriguez. Part of the house was used to accommodate my mother and siblings whenever they were in town.[1]

But after he returned to Miami from his secret mission to Cuba at the end of January 1957, Mario also needed a house where arms could be prepared, stored, and smuggled. So, he found another two-story home that was hidden from street view by trees. He had always referred to it as "la casa de piedra" (the stone house). My recollection when visiting was that it was made from shaved stones, flat-surfaced, like cinder blocks. An FBI report lists an address of 60 S.W. 18th Road in Miami from which 5 large trunks were picked up and sent to Houston, Texas, so this could be the location of the arms-prepping home.[2] This is not the same building as another structure similarly designated and located on N.W. 22nd Street and Seventh Avenue in what is now the Little Havana section of Miami and where supposedly Fidel Castro Ruz had a meeting with Luis Conte Agüero in November 1955 when there to establish the M-26-7.[3]

The first floor was where the arms cleaning and prepping took place. The upstairs is where my sister Barbara and brother Miguel lived. Although they technically resided at Johnny's house that Mario rented, they often stayed at the stone house, where they assumed the role of lookouts from their second-floor perch.[4]

Remember, the letter Mario took to Faustino Pérez Hernández via Virgilio Jacas Quintana was letting the M-26-7 in Cuba know that Mario was heading up U.S. arms acquisition and asking them to send someone from Cuba to help him. So, Pedro Miret Prieto sent Pablo Fernandez Alegre from Mexico and Frank País García sent Lester Rodriguez Pérez from Oriente to help Mario. Jorge Sotus Romero came later. The four were responsible for soliciting weapons from any and every possible geographic location and venue, including the military and mafia. And since none of Fernandez, Rodriguez, and Sotus knew the language or culture, Mario was the one who helped them navigate in a country unfamiliar to them.[5]

My sister Barbara would often recount the day she took up residence in the house of stone and still had her set of suitcases packed. Sotus went upstairs and, seeing the pair of suitcases, took them and dumped the contents out, telling her he needed them. Barbara was very upset about it and told Mario she wanted those suitcases back. Eventually, one of them was returned to her. It always became a topic of conversation at family gatherings, and we still have the suitcase.

My brother and his crew were joined by Howard K. Davis, a young U.S. veteran living in Miami. He was not Cuban but was also interested in helping the Cuban people in their fight against Fulgencio Batista y Zaldívar.[6]

Davis joined the U. S. Army in 1947 and graduated from pathfinder training in 1948. The following year he graduated from ranger training and from there went as part of a unit into combat in Korea. In 1952 he got out of the active army and joined the National Guard. When he left the National Guard, he joined the Air Force Reserves until 1954. In the air force, Davis was a NCOIC (Non-Commissioned Officer in Charge) of the pararescue section of an air rescue unit. He was a parachutist, an expert in aerial delivery. Because of his pathfinder, ranger and special operations training, he knew "unconventional warfare."[7]

Davis had experience with airborne operations, but, when he and Mario met, he had not yet become a pilot. That license would come later with Sotus picking up the tab for the training since they needed pilots to fly munitions to Raúl Castro in the Sierra Cristal Mountains in Oriente.[8]

Mario and Davis met when a friend of Mario's, Dario Ochoa, who went to school with Davis introduced them after Davis asked Ochoa how he could get involved in the Cuban cause. Davis had just gotten out of the service and was getting his GED.[9]

One of the first missions in which Mario involved Davis was utilizing Davis's car to transport arms to Cuba. Castro's sister, Juanita Castro, lived in Miami Beach at the time. Mario brought Davis over to her residence to introduce them. She and Pablo Fernandez Alegre explained the details of the operation and had Davis hand over the keys to his four-door Rambler station wagon. The following day, his car was returned, and he was instructed to take the ferry from Key West to Habana. Davis did not witness the process of having the arms put in the car, but was told that the door panels, except for those on the rear passenger side door, had been removed and the cavities filled with weapons.[10]

Interestingly, when the car was inspected by the customs agents upon reaching Habana, the only part of the car looked at was the rear right passenger door. It begs the question whether this occurred due to foreknowledge gained from others who often made the trip, or whether certain customs workers were cooperating with the revolutionaries and knew what door would not be hiding arms. Davis went to a hotel and had a knock at the door within two hours. He surrendered his keys and was told to take it easy for the day, so he went sightseeing. His car was returned the following day and he went back to Miami. The mission had been a great success, and all involved were very pleased with the outcome. He was then sent on another mission to New Orleans with Mario and Rene Rayneri. When the revolution triumphed, Rayneri was named Cuban ambassador to El Salvador, and Mario is the one who recommended him for that position.[11]

Mario then introduced Davis to Sotus, a man he referred to as "Raúl Castro's most trusted captain" and who went by the war name of "Caballo Blanco" (White Horse). Remember, Sotus was sent to work with Mario in arms acquisition around the same time as Rodriguez Pérez and Pablo Fernandez Alegre. Most of the supplies had been going to Castro's camp in the Sierra Maestra. He was, after all, top dog, and most wanted to be in good with him rather than younger brother Raúl, who had a rebel camp in the Sierra Cristal. But munitions were needed by Raúl Castro nonetheless.[12]

So, Mario and Davis discussed options for getting arms support to Raúl Castro. They came up with the idea of making aerial containers that would be used to transport weapons via parachute into the Sierra. It was considered efficient and relatively cheap as compared to taking things by boat, which was pricey and easier for the Cuban military to detect. And, because of Davis's background, he knew how to deliver items by air.[13]

Mario and Davis rented a second-floor space in a two-story warehouse near Northwest 36th Street and Eighth Avenue in an industrial area of Miami. They bought two specialized sewing machines and all the needed raw materials: nylon webbing and the hardware for connecting the parachutes and fastening things together, the same materials used by the U.S. Army and Air Force manufactured by the Pioneer Parachute Company. The cargo parachutes were bought ready-made. Mario and Davis crafted the containers to attach to the parachutes.[14]

The weapon would be placed on a nylon sheet lined with an inner layer of paper, rolled up like a cigar and inserted into the container. Then, a cap would be put on each end and attached to the parachute. When the apparatus was dropped, the rebel on the ground would just pick it up, take it to wherever it was needed, unsnap a couple snaps, roll it out, and have the weapons and ammo available.[15]

In a letter Mario wrote to Fidel Castro Ruz dated May 22, 1958, he mentioned that he made about 50 of these containers. They closed the shop once they accomplished making these.[16]

They also continued with the other, more conventional method of moving the arms via cars, which would be pulled apart and stuffed with ammo in whatever hiding place they could fit them, including the gas tank. These would then be driven to various port locations where expeditions were being prepared.[17]

On December 15, 1957, Mario temporarily moved his family to Houston so he could complete a mission sponsored by Carlos Prío Socarrás, whose Organizacion Auténticos political party followers were also working to overthrow Batista. Although Mario had been a founding member of the first M-26-7 in exile established in New York City, he was willing to support Prío because he did not feel that Castro should have a monopoly on the revolution. He wanted others involved. Prío had substantial money and gave them funds to organize buying weapons to send to Cuba. Prío, remember, had also funded the purchase of the *Granma* and the house in Mexico to store the arms and shelter the men who would be bringing them to Cuba aboard the small yacht berthed near the property.[18]

In Houston, a home rented by Robert McKeown as of December 1957 was used to store arms for an expedition planned on a yacht called *Buddy Dee*.[19]

Prior to this, after weeks of secret negotiations, in October 1957, the Junta de Liberación Cubana (Cuban Liberation Junta), which called for all the anti–Batista groups to unite, was created in Miami. Reference to this has already been made in Chapter 9. The M-26-7 did not want to be part of it, but Lester Rodriguez Pérez and Felipe Pazos Rodriguez unwittingly signed the Unity Pact on behalf of the M-26-7. According to Mario, Rodriguez Pérez thought this unity would provide much-needed funding for the badly needed munitions, since by joining the Junta, material, financial, and human resources would be shared among the political and revolutionary Cuban opposition.[20]

This created a problem for Rodriguez Pérez, and he was removed from his position as the M-26-7's military affairs coordinator in exile by January 1958 and replaced by Alonso "Bebo" Hidalgo Barrios. Because he was in Houston, Mario was out of the loop of what was happening in Miami with the Junta. It was difficult for news to reach him where he was. He just continued doing what he was commissioned to do: obtaining and storing arms.[21]

In February 1958, Mario called Davis. The house where the arms were being stored was in Seabrook on Galveston Bay. The yacht *Buddy Dee*, owned by Manuel Arques, one of the six involved in this mission, was docked in Kemah. Mario wanted Davis to help prepare and package the munitions to be sent to Cuba.[22]

On February 18, Mario and Davis were at the hotel discussing strategy. Then, Mario took Davis to the house to have an initial look at the arms. They picked up an M-1 and brought it back to the hotel so Davis could show Mario how it was dismantled, cleaned, and re-assembled. But shortly after they arrived at the hotel, a bizarre thing happened. A call came to Davis's room from a reporter asking for him by name and posing questions about Cuban revolutionary activity going on in the area. Davis acted as if he had gotten the wrong number, saying he was obviously calling him by mistake as he had no idea what he was talking about. But Mario and Davis were spooked. Mario wanted to immediately go back to the arms house to see if they could remove as many arms as possible for safekeeping. Davis did not think it was a good idea, but, since Mario was insisting, he complied.[23]

When they got there, they realized it might be under surveillance, so instead of trying to remove arms, they quickly dropped off the M-1. It was already evening. They had only made that second brief trip to the house when the situation got bad.[24]

After driving on the dark highway for just a few miles, they noticed headlights in the distance behind them. Mario had a handgun he kept in the car. So, he threw the gun out the window into the river as they drove around a bend and were out of view for a few minutes while crossing over a bridge.[25]

They continued driving a bit. But soon it was apparent that the car was steadily speeding towards them. Davis was driving and initially thought the car was going to try passing them since they were approaching at such a velocity. That thought was dispelled when red lights started flashing and they were pulled over by police who questioned them about arms. Of course, they responded they did not know anything about any of that. Nevertheless, they were taken into custody at the police headquarters and placed in cells with five others: Francisco Obregon, Manuel Arques, Abelardo Pujol Barrera, and Angel Banos, and Evelyn Eleanor Archer. Mario and Davis did not recall seeing Archer there, but she would not have been in the same cell as the men. These others were implicated with working with Prío on the planned expedition, of which Mario was a part. Because Davis was the new kid in town and they probably had not gotten a good handle on him, police believed his excuse that he was in town visiting Mario and his wife, who were friends of his. But the others were not believed because they had been under surveillance for some time.[26]

Police released Davis and Banos. I am not sure why Banos was let go.[27]

Davis returned to Miami, while Mario and the others went through the legal process. Mario was charged with "conspiracy to violate the National Firearms Act, failing to register firearms, unlawful possession of transferred firearms, and possession of firearms on which identification numbers had been obliterated." He was freed on bond and allowed to go back to Miami until the sentencing.[28]

Mario shared his sentiments regarding the Houston expedition in his May 22, 1958, letter to Castro, which reads in part:

> It was agreed that the first part of the plan should be to take to Cuba all the men who wanted to fight with arms in hand. We did not like the idea, but we had to cede because the truth of the matter was that we could not count on the resources needed to carry out the original plan in a short time. The provisions by air would be done later.
>
> In accordance with that agreement, I was sent to Houston, Texas (chosen as the place from which the expedition would leave) the 15th of December '57 to begin undertaking my responsibilities for the work to be done there. It was planned that all would be ready by the end of December 1957, or at the latest, within the first fifteen days of January 1958. The plan was fairly advanced in its course when the dissolving of the Liberation Junta occurred. I learned of this later on because in the place I was, news from neither Miami nor Cuba would reach me. I have no knowledge of what was discussed in Miami concerning this matter, I only know much time was lost.
>
> Even though I wanted to return to Miami, my obligation was to remain in Houston taking care of what was under my responsibility until some other decision was made. I later learned that at a meeting that had taken place in New York, a decision was made to change the plan, but by then, it was too late. Through informants in Miami, the plan had been exposed and the police in Houston had been alerted and were investigating. In an attempt to salvage some of the equipment, I went to the house where we were storing it, accompanied by the American who was helping me, but when I got there, we noticed the house was already under surveillance. We hurriedly left in the car and were arrested on the highway about three miles from the house. I was imprisoned a number of days and accused of "conspiring against a friendly government, illegal possession and transport of firearms, etc.," finding myself free on bail at the moment.[29]

Mario was instructed by the courts to not participate in revolutionary activities.

He did not listen.

In early April 1958, barely two months after his February 18 arrest, Mario was asked by José Llanusa Gobel, one of the leaders of the M-26-7 National Directorate in Exile, to accompany him on a trip to Haiti. The trip almost cost Mario his life.[30]

Angel Pérez-Vidal and a Canadian were working on a plan to broker an arms deal with Haiti. Andrew Robert Leslie McNaughton had been a test pilot during World War II, the son of General Andrew George Latta McNaughton, a Canadian scientist, army officer, cabinet minister, and diplomat. The general was commander of the Canadian Armed Forces during World War II. The son had a scientific research company and was later to become known as the "Godfather" of Laetrile, a purported anti-cancer drug. He had started gun running to Israel in the 1950s.[31]

Pérez-Vidal had received an introductory call from McNaughton sharing that he sympathized with the Cuban revolutionary cause and was wishing to meet to discuss ways he could be of service. They arranged to meet in Montréal, Canada.[32]

He informed Pérez-Vidal that there was a man by the name of Hubert Fauntleroy Julian in the Bronx who had connections with Haiti's president François "Papa Doc" Duvalier. Born in Trinidad, Julian studied in England and finished school in Canada before becoming the first licensed Black pilot in America, earning him the nickname "The Black Eagle."[33]

The plan was to have the arms shipped to Haiti and from there to Cuba.[34]

McNaughton would provide the initial $10,000 investment to begin putting the plan in place.[35]

After having these basic details, Mario informed Llanusa, who then decided he wanted to go to Haiti as a backup to Pérez-Vidal to make sure all would be in order. If a deal was made, Llanusa had the authority to have the payment arranged. He asked Mario to go with him.[36]

Pérez-Vidal and McNaughton traveled from New York, and Llanusa and Mario from Miami. They met up in Montego Bay, Jamaica and then went to Haiti, staying at the Hotel Castle D' Haiti. Llanusa and Mario did not take part in the meetings with Duvalier, which transpired over a three-day period, with Julian joining them on day three.[37]

Since Haiti was in dire need of arms for their own forces, the provision laid on the table by Duvalier was that Haiti would either receive $200,000 worth of military equipment or $100,000 in cash once the Revolutionary Government was in place in Cuba. It seemed reasonable, given that he was allowing them to warehouse our arms in his country in the hopes of giving them safe passage to the Sierra.[38]

While that meeting was taking place, Mario and Llanusa walked around the city and stumbled upon a voodoo demonstration. There, Llanusa happened to spot someone he recognized—a ruthless Batista henchmen, Rolando Masferrer Rojas, head of a group of assassins who were known as "los tigres de Masferrer" (Masferrer's tigers). They thought it strange that he was in Haiti, so they returned to their hotel room.[39]

When all four were back at the hotel at the end of the day, the desk clerk called Pérez-Vidal, informing him someone was requesting to see and speak with them. Pérez-Vidal asked he be sent to their room. A young man who spoke English with a slight accent introduced himself as a Haitian Air Force captain and provided all the credentials to prove his identity. He would be piloting the airplane taking the arms to Cuba.[40]

He informed them that, from the moment they had arrived in Haiti, Duvalier had communicated with Batista all the plans discussed and a conspiracy was in the works. Masferrer had brought Haiti a loan of $4 million with the agreement between the two dictators that, in addition to that sum, Batista would soon be giving them an additional $20 million for Duvalier to reveal all Cuban revolutionary activities there and keep the coasts of Cuba under surveillance. That very morning in the early hours, a Cuban plane with military personnel had arrived with orders to bring them to Cuba. Hearing this shed light on why Masferrer was in town.[41]

The Haitian captain urged them to contact the Canadian consulate immediately and arrange to leave the country early the following morning if possible. He also shared that he would like to join the rebel army in the Sierra. McNaughton reached out to the Canadian consul and was instructed to go the following morning to the consular office, where the situation would be resolved as promptly as possible.[42]

Not satisfied with the swiftness of that plan, they contacted a pilot recommended to them by the Haitian captain. The pilot owned a four-seat Cessna that could fly them out before daybreak. But the sun had not yet risen when law enforcement agents were pounding at the door demanding they go with them under orders from Duvalier. McNaughton immediately called the consul, who told the agents that McNaughton and the group were to report to the consulate so the situation could be addressed. After this exchange, and once authorized by their supervisors, the agents left, with the understanding they would be going to the consulate.[43]

Instead of heading to the consulate, they went to pick up the captain, who accompanied them as they went to get the pilot, all making their way to the Port-au-Prince airport. They left all their suitcases and personal belongings at the hotel since the Cessna had barely enough room for them, and they were flown to Jamaica. As soon as they arrived, they directed themselves to the Canadian authorities, with Pérez-Vidal and McNaughton staying in the country a couple of days before returning to New York.[44]

Upon their return, they unsuccessfully tried to reach Julian, who they subsequently learned had stayed in Haiti for an extended period as a "special assistant" per Duvalier's request.[45]

These above details are included in Pérez-Vidal's book *Historia Intima de la Revolución Cubana* (*An Intimate History of the Cuban Revolution*), and this is how he described what happened. I can see how questions would be raised as to why the authorities were permitting them to go to the Canadian consulate versus following through with Duvalier and Batista's plan to send them to Cuba. But I have Pérez-Vidal's book and memories, Mario's recollections, and Llanusa's April 16, 1958, "Report in Reference to Trip to Haiti" that he submitted to the M-26-7 as the source of this information.[46]

Llanusa's report, however, gives a slightly different account, as follows:

Given the impossibility of resolving anything in that country, since according to the captain himself who gave us the previously mentioned tip, there weren't even 2,000 machine guns in the entire Haitian army, we had resolved to return the following day, but late that same night to the hotel came the president of the Senate who had vowed to obtain the permit in exchange for the necessary armament for his country, utilizing Mr. McN's credit at the place known to us.

He said that he himself would take or send with Julian to NY the legal permission from the Haitian government to purchase the weapons at the designated point and that it was an indispensable conclusion for carrying out any operation; to guarantee his word, he gave us a document where he was attesting that shortly, the permission from the government would be obtained, signed and authorized by him (Senate-President). They insisted that McN should promptly go to NY to be putting into place the deals, and the next day two of us left for Miami and two for NY.[47]

So, the accounts may differ in some of the details, but the bottom line is their lives were in jeopardy if they remained any longer than they did.[48]

As for Mario, he was back in Miami, grateful for his life and waiting to learn his fate in terms of the prison sentence.

Sometime in late February, shortly after being free on bail and just prior to this Haiti trip materializing, Mario brought Davis over to Prío's house to introduce them. He and Mario then sent Davis to Mexico to train under General Alberto Bayo Giroud. Davis was with Bayo for about three weeks. It may have appeared that the trip was for the Cuban rebel leader to train Davis, but it was actually for Davis to evaluate the training and critique it for improvements. Davis concluded that Bayo had done an excellent job. His training technique was very similar to what he had undergone in ranger training at Fort Benning, Georgia.[49]

The training with Bayo took place at his home in Mexico City and was carried out in groups of about eight. They would train from 10 a.m. until late afternoon. Another American, Jay Allen Kilgore, who had no military training, was part of this group. At the end of the training, they were told to go to Merida, Mexico, to take part in a mission, with Davis serving as their military chief. Dr. Heliodoro Martínez Junco was the political chief. Another of the men on the mission was the M-26-7 Pinar del Río Province military coordinator Jesús Suárez Gayol. It is worth noting that, on April 10, 1967, Gayol would be the first Cuban rebel to die under Ernesto "Che" Guevara de la Serna's command in Bolivia's guerrilla war.[50]

After a few days in Merida, when they got word that the mission was to begin, a half-dozen police squad cars came to pick up Davis and the 11 men. They transported them about 45 minutes to an area where there were several boats. Apparently, the organizers of the mission had a deal with the local Mexican police, who wanted to help the Cubans overthrow Batista.[51]

Davis and his men took seven large motorized boats loaded with military equipment down a river that became narrower and narrower until it ended under a tunnel-like canopy of overgrown trees near a deserted island. Through knee-deep water, the men took the equipment off the boats and carried it to an area of dry land about 100 yards away. They concealed themselves and the cargo because the Mexican Coast Guard patrolled the area from its station just north of it. Davis believed the island is what later became known as Cozumel. He recalls he and Kilgore commenting to each other that if they ever came back there, they could set up a hotel and make it a spot for tourists. They were there about two weeks. Food was so scarce that they ate snails off the beach.[52]

Then a big Cuban fishing vessel named *El Corojo* anchored about 50 feet offshore. All the equipment had to be put on this boat. The yacht, owned by Cuban doctor and former Cuban House of Representatives member Diego Cesar Rodriguez, departed on April 5, 1958, and sailed for three days. The cargo it carried included 74 Czech rifles that Lester Rodriguez Pérez had purchased about one year earlier, 2,000 pounds of dynamite, 45,000 bullets, 31 pistols, four machine guns, and one anti-tank rifle.[53]

They arrived on April 8 in Punta de Palma, Cuba, one day before the dismal "general strike" of April 9—called for by Castro as the final blow to the Batista dictatorship—was to have taken place. But there was a problem. Authorities knew *El Corojo* was coming, and they were looking for it. Someone from another fishing boat told the *El Corojo* captain they were being sought. So, the crew took the boat and anchored it between two small islands, hiding it under trees and chopping down the mast so it would not be seen above the height of the trees. They evacuated the boat and unloaded as many of the munitions as they could, hiding them in trees. They trudged through three feet of water to a ranch being used to store equipment to be taken to the mountains in Pinar del Río, where they would be establishing a rebel camp. The abandoned yacht was discovered on May 14 by the Sixth Rural Guard Regiment "Rios Rivera," and the remaining supplies were confiscated by the authorities.[54]

They spent several days at the ranch and managed to get the munitions and men through the towns via flatbed trucks covered with hay. They were taken to a valley area with a small stream running through it and told that this was going to be the jumping-off point to go into the mountains. So, they set up a staging area and waited to get the go-ahead to proceed up the mountain. But, after they had been there a couple days, a nine-year-old local *guajiro* (country) boy came into the camp and informed them that there was a company of Batista soldiers moving towards an area where they could cut the group off from going up the mountain.[55]

That was the first indication they had a problem. The second indication was that there was a light Cuban airplane that periodically flew overhead. That plane began circling over the camp on the day the boy warned them of the Batista troops moving in to cut them off. Davis and the men moved quickly to start ascending the mountain. They had no time to bring the thousands of pounds of arms and ammo they had brought from the ranch. These were all lost. They had to escape with only what was on their bodies, and successfully made it into the mountains.[56]

However, someone who was later discovered to be an agent of Batista led five of the men away from the group, telling them Davis was an SOB gringo who was going to get them killed. Instead, the agent led them to an area where they were captured, tortured, and hanged from trees where their bodies were left for days. Although Davis knew the agent by the name "Guillermo," his real name may have been Evaristo Venereo. Even from the start as they underwent Bayo's training together, Guillermo was very critical of Davis's input, perhaps because as a former Cuban military officer, he felt he should have been in the position of authority given to Davis. That is what Davis surmised at that point in time, but, in hindsight, he believes "Guillermo" was a spy from the very beginning, seeking to undermine any revolutionary effort regardless of who was in charge.[57]

Moments after he had led the five to desert, locals informed Davis's group that Guillermo/Venereo was a Batista agent, and a "court martial in absentee" hearing was convened with Davis as one of the judges. The unanimous vote was "death."[58]

Davis later learned that Guillermo had gone to the Sierra Maestra to do the same thing there as he had done with the men in Davis's group, but they had already been informed he was a Batista agent, so they tied him to a tree and executed him on the spot.[59]

Only half of the original group of 12 men that commenced the mission made it into the mountains. But many locals and other recruits were joining them, so they soon numbered about 50.[60]

To this present day, Davis does not know the name of the mountain range that was the destination of his mission. He was at a disadvantage because he could neither speak nor understand Spanish, so completed the mission not knowing most of the particulars. But, based on research, the conclusion is it would have been either the Sierra de los Órganos or the Sierra del Rosario.[61]

After Davis successfully established the mountain campsite of about 50 rebels, he spent some two months there doing intelligence gathering, training in weapons, small unit formations, ambushes, guard posts, etc. During this time, he was known by his nom de guerre "Davy." Then, he and Kilgore were detached from the group and instructed to go to Habana to train the underground in sabotage and other formations. That did not end up taking place because the contact that was supposed to meet them with further instructions never showed up.[62]

Davis managed to keep in his possession a tourist ID with the name David Cummings that he had used in the past. But, unfortunately, Kilgore had no form of ID since all their belongings had been left at the ranch they occupied prior to going up the mountain. Upon arriving in Miami from Habana, Davis immediately went to Frank Fiorini's house to ask for his help in getting Kilgore out of Cuba. Fiorini, later known as Frank Sturgis, one of the Watergate burglars, was involved with the Cuban revolutionary operations in Miami.[63]

When Davis returned to Miami, Mario was still awaiting sentencing and possible incarceration. Mario had to be on his best behavior, so he kept a low profile. That impromptu trip to Haiti with Llanusa was not something he should have done, and he realized this after the fact. He was sentenced in July and out on parole, more reason for him to lie low with involvement in revolutionary activities—until January 1, 1959.[64]

When Batista fled on December 31, 1958, Mario was on one of the first planes to Cuba with Davis, but we will get to that later in the book.[65]

## 13

# A Revolutionary Hero Leads Us

There was work to be done.

Though I was very worried for my brother's wellbeing, I could not allow myself to dwell on that. I still had a family to look after and a revolution to support. My brother, unfortunately, was a casualty of war and I had to consider him lucky, as others paid with their lives.

The friction and controversy caused by those who had infiltrated the M-26-7 grew worse. The problem came to the attention of the National Directorate in Exile, so they designated Roberto Agramonte y Pichardo Jr. to resolve the difficulties that were interrupting the Tampa club.

Eduardo Mijares Pujals was relieved of his duties when Agramonte sent Guillermo León to Tampa on April 3, 1958. He came with a notice to the directors and members stating that all previous club bylaws were henceforth being annulled, and that the board of directors was dissolved, along with all previous factions. It stipulated that León would assume the title of "delegate" of the M-26-7 of Tampa, having maximum and sole responsibility with the full power and backing of the National Directorate in Exile.

After the arrival of León, the way the money was collected changed. Before, we had used the perforated booklet method, where half the numbered receipt would remain in the bound portion and the other half was given to the donor. Then, in July 1957, we had small cards with Tampa M-26-7 printed across the top, in 25 cents to $10 denominations, with a line on which to write the donor's name. The lesser values were on a yellow card and the greater on a light blue card. Each was numbered and had a stamped signature of Fidel Castro and Manteiga's and my names as president and secretary. Once León came, the new method became the sale of numbered pre-printed "bonos" (bonds) issued by the National Directorate, each also bearing a denomination from 25 cents to $10. Though the bonds resembled currency, they served only as a receipt for the amount purchased. They would not have any future redemption value.[1]

## 13. A Revolutionary Hero Leads Us

León remained in Tampa until mid–May, when he was called back to Miami because the National Directorate needed him. León named Rodolfo Vasquez as temporary delegate. Vasquez was a physician at the Gonzalez Clinic at the intersection of Ninth Avenue and 14th Street in Ybor City. Until such time that a permanent delegate was named, we, the vested members of the club, temporarily suspended all formal meetings where plans would be discussed and decisions made but continued collecting money in the manner designated by the M-26-7 National Directorate in Exile. Vasquez served as delegate a short time since the National Directorate wanted the position to be occupied by someone not from Tampa.

Then, in the early part of June, a small group of our members were at *La Gaceta* when Vasquez came by to introduce us to Gabriel Gil Alfonso,

Tampa M-26-7 donation bonds in denominations from $.25 to $10, bearing the names of Victoriano Manteiga as president and Raul Villamia as secretary. Yellow bonds were for $.25 and $.50, and blue for $1, $5, and $10. This was an alternate fundraising method, aside from the perforated booklet in image on page 98. Tampa, Florida, July 1957 (from the collection of Raul Villamia).

the new Tampa delegate sent from Miami. This was quite an honor. Gil was a true revolutionary hero whose story was well known by us.

Gil had been involved with the revolution since the planning of the Moncada attack. A 30-year-old café chef at the time, he was a former Cuban soldier who Fidel Castro Ruz placed in charge of the revolution's cell in Lawton, a neighborhood in Habana. Gil had 23 men from Lawton ready to take part in the Moncada attack, but, due to lack of arms, was told to bring only nine of them.

When it became evident that the mission was a failure and they were all doomed to be slaughtered or captured, Gil retreated and found refuge in a nearby barbershop with fellow revolutionary Ismael Ricondo Fernández, whose hand was mangled by a bullet. Gil changed into a *guayabera* (a traditional Cuban shirt) in hopes that he could mask his identity as a Castro soldier by dressing the part of a missionary on a pilgrimage to the nearby Virgin of Charity shrine. He could not bring Ricondo with him, unfortunately. His hand needed immediate medical attention. Gil did bring part of Ricondo with him, however. Unbeknownst to Gil, his guayabera was stained with blood from Ricondo's hand.[2]

After meeting up with two other revolutionaries who fled Moncada, Gil tried to pass through an army roadblock by using his pilgrimage story

### A LOS OBREROS DE LAS FABRICAS DE TABACOS

Ustedes ayudaron noblemente a José Martí con centenares de miles de pesos.

Ustedes ayudaron a obreros huelguistas en esta nación y en el extranjero.

Ustedes socorrieron a ciudades y países perjudicados por ciclones, inundaciones, incendios y terremotos.

Ustedes ayudaron a la República Española cuando la agrediera el Fascismo internacional.

Ahora pedimos vuestra generosa aportación monetaria, en la proporción que cada uno pueda, para ayudar a la juventud cubana, encabezada por el heróico Fidel Castro, a devolverle a Cuba su Libertad.

Las tarjetas de donativos, con la firma de Fidel Castro estampada por medio de un cuño, son de 25c, 55c, $1.00, $5.00 y $10.00.

Por el Club 26 de Julio de Tampa
Victoriano Manteiga, Presidente
Raúl Villamia, Secretario
Julio de 1957

M-26-7 flyer to the cigar makers asking them to donate to the M-26-7. They are reminded that, in the past, they helped raise funds for: José Martí Pérez's War of Independence; the cigar industry's striking workers in the United States; cities and countries that were ravaged by hurricanes, floods, fires, and earthquakes; and the Spanish Republic's struggle against Fascism. Now they were being asked to support Fidel Castro in his quest to liberate Cuba. Tampa, Florida, July 1957 (from the collection of Raul Villamia).

### 13. A Revolutionary Hero Leads Us

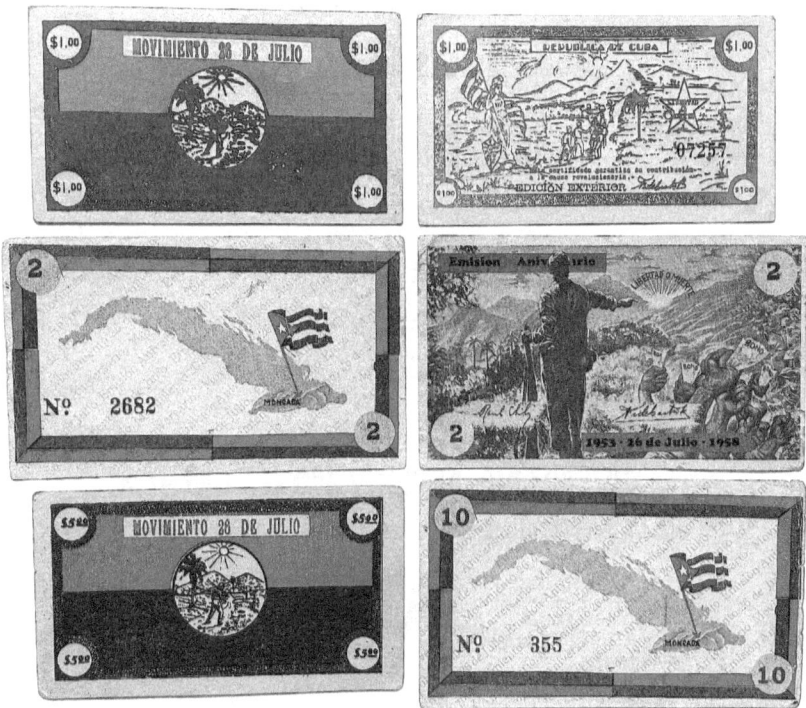

Donation bonds from the M-26-7 National Directorate in Exile in denominations of $1 to $10. These were used from 1958 forward for the M-26-7 branches outside Cuba. Note the designation that these were "exterior editions." Though they resemble currency, there was no face value to them; they only served as "receipts" for the denomination amount purchased. These replaced the local Tampa donation bonds in image on page 143. Tampa, Florida, 1958 (from the collection of Raul Villamia).

for the trio. But the Fulgencio Batista y Zaldívar soldiers noticed the blood on Gil's shirt, and the rebel threesome was arrested and sent back to Moncada for questioning. Gil was locked in a guard corps cell with 20 other suspects waiting to be interrogated.[3]

Gil was then taken outside to the roof of the Officer's Club building and pushed to the ledge. He was shown bodies of other revolutionaries lying dead on the sidewalk below. They had been tossed from the roof for not talking, and he was threatened with a similar fate if he did not tell the guards everything he knew. Gil maintained his innocence, still claiming he was a tourist. For some reason, he was among those chosen to live. Others who refused to talk were executed. Unfortunately, Ricondo was found while seeking medical assistance and executed.[4]

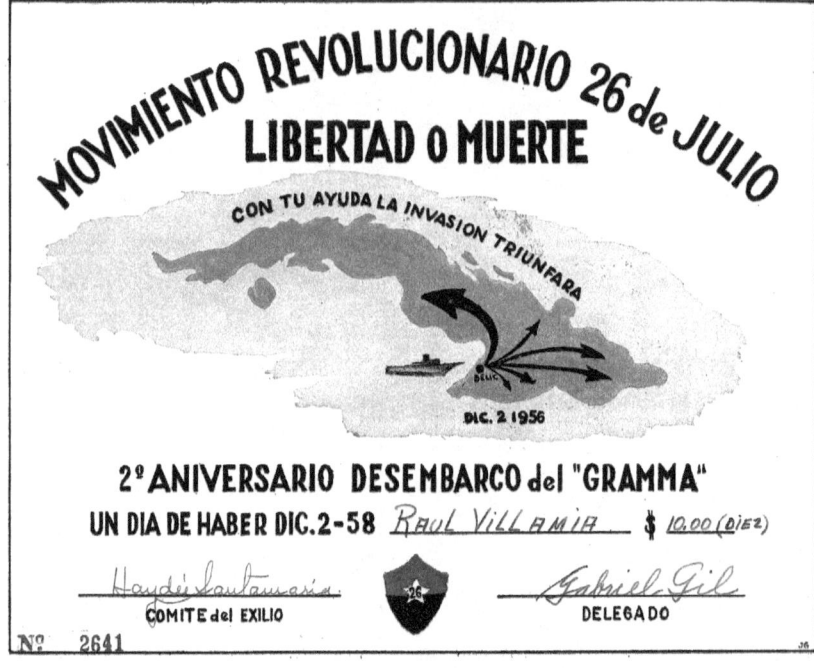

M-26-7 Committee in Exile (title used alternately with M-26-7 National Directorate in Exile) donation bond commemorating the second anniversary of the *Granma* landing. Note Haydée Santamaría Cuadrado and Gabriel Gil Alfonso's signatures. By this time, the M-26-7 Committee in Exile was headquartered in Miami, Florida. It is not known whether this bond could be used as a receipt for any denomination, since the amount could be written in. Perhaps it can be assumed it was only used for a minimum of $10 and up due to it commemorating the *Granma*'s arrival. Tampa, Florida, December 2, 1958 (from the collection of Raul Villamia).

Later, in court, other revolutionaries admitted that Gil was indeed one of the leaders of their battalion. He confessed to his participation but never implicated anyone else. He was among those imprisoned with Castro and freed as part of the pardon.[5]

When Castro was exiled to Mexico, Gil went with him and later took part in the *Granma* expedition, one of 20 Moncada veterans to do so. He survived the *Granma* landing and fought alongside Castro in the mountains until he grew ill in late 1957. He was then asked to go to the United States to support the revolution in other ways, such as by serving as a delegate to branches of the M-26-7.[6]

Upon meeting him on that June afternoon, we introduced ourselves and made small talk as we all got to know one another. Gil stated that he wanted to meet with all the active members as soon as possible so he could get to know everyone and discuss what needed to be done moving forward.

It was agreed that the next gathering would take place two days later at member Tony Sola's La Casa Loma Cafe.

Those I recall being at that meeting are Carlos Carbonell, Juan M. Pérez, Carmelo Bueno and his son Orlando, Max Garcia, Mario Iglesias, Marcelino Vila, Rafael Duran, Juan de la Rosa, Alberto Nunez, Marcelino Golan, Pedro Pérez Nunez, and Florentino Santos.

Gil began the meeting by explaining that the National Directorate in Exile told him that we in Tampa, despite the past problems, had done a good job of supporting the revolution in terms of fundraising and propagandizing the cause. He instructed us to continue collecting funds in the manner designated by the directorate and informed us that, in addition, we could also sell flags, pins, ties, armbands, key chains, and more items with the M-26-7 insignia on them that we could obtain from Miami.

Gil then asked us to give an account of our activities from the time Castro visited Tampa to the present. Everyone participated in that lengthy conversation, and we left nothing out—the good or the bad. We detailed our meetings with Castro and our fundraising and public relations efforts to that point: our picketing of federal buildings; the memorials we held in honor of the fallen; and our collection of donations at picnics, ballgames, and social club events. We said that most of our support came from the blue-collar cigar workers. We told him that *La Gaceta* provided us with a well-respected outlet for our propaganda but that we received no support from the local Spanish radio station. We explained how Ruben Fabelo had

M-26-7 tie, flag, pennant, and armband, used for fundraising. Also, M-26-7 shield-shaped emblem and circular seal rubber stamps used for confirming donation payments. The large shield is the prototype for the stamp. Tampa, Florida, 1956–1960 (from the collection of Raul Villamia).

even turned down Castro's request for time. We told him that we had several meeting spaces: La Casa Loma, Vila's La Crema Bakery, and, of course, *La Gaceta*. We finally told him everything that had happened with the radical group, though they had fallen silent in recent months. One of our members then mentioned that he had just heard that Anibal Velaz had left Tampa and that his group had dissolved, which was welcome news to all of us who were tired of dealing with those faux revolutionaries. We left the meeting that day feeling positive about our organization's future and about the future of Cuba.

We commemorated the fifth anniversary of the Moncada attack at the Union Center on Palm and Nebraska Avenues. A flyer had been distributed, so the event was well attended.[7]

As had seemed to be the norm, the good news—

> **A LA COLONIA CUBANA Y AL PUEBLO DE TAMPA**
>
> Mañana sábado se cumplirá otro año del ataque al Cuartel Moncada de Santiago de Cuba por un grupo de valientes cubanos mandados por FIDEL CASTRO.
>
> Los tampeños, los cubanos y el mundo todo saben de las atrocidades que los verdugos de Batista cometieron después de que las armas dejaron de funcionar.
>
> Allí se escribió uno de los más horrendos capítulos de la historia de Cuba.
>
> Para recordar y honrar a los que allí combatieron y murieron, mañana celebraremos una velada, a las 8:00 de la noche, en el local de Palm y Nebraska, cedido por las uniones obreras . . .
>
> Venga y únase a nosotros si de veras ama la Libertad y la Justicia.
>
> Por el MOVIMIENTO 26 DE JULIO
> GABRIEL GIL,
> Delegado
>
> Nebraska & Palm Avenues
> UNION CENTER
> Tampa

M-26-7 flyer inviting the Tampa public and Cuban colony to an 8 p.m. commemoration of the fifth anniversary of the Moncada attack, to take place the following day at a hall on Palm and Nebraska Avenues in Ybor City, lent to them by the labor unions. Tampa (Ybor City), Florida, July 25, 1958 (from the collection of Raul Villamia).

our new strong leader and the fall of the radicals—was followed by bad news. On July 11, 1958, my brother Mario was sentenced to two years in prison and a $500 fine. When Mario heard this, he felt as if the blood was draining from his head, and he collapsed. He had to receive medical attention.[8]

On August 12, however, I was finally brought good news concerning Mario. A federal judge in Houston, Justice Allen Burroughs Hannay, released him and his companions, placing them on probation for the remainder of their sentence provided they remain on good behavior, i.e., not get involved in the revolution again. Mario's release was an example of the benefit of knowing people in high places. He had been close with Manuel Urrutia Lleó since the magistrate's exile in New York. Urrutia had been the presiding judge who sentenced Castro to prison for the Moncada attack in 1953. He was also designated by Castro to be Cuba's first president under the new Revolutionary Government. In an open court on July 25, Urrutia stated, "They are Cuban patriots, not criminals," and pleaded for clemency.[9]

Mario immediately returned to Miami, where, on August 14, a large crowd gave him and the others a hero's welcome. Cuba's ex-president Carlos Prío Socarrás and his wife, Mary Tarrero, were among those present to celebrate their release.[10]

Having to live a normal, non-revolutionary life must have been a tough transition for Mario, considering he had spent a significant number of years working to free Cuba. What may have made it easier on him, however, was that the news coming out of Cuba continued to be positive.

And in New York that same month, Angel Pérez-Vidal was again arrested, this time for complicity in transporting weapons. In the middle of 1958, José Sanjenís Perdomo approached Pérez-Vidal about an expedition that Justo Carrillo Hernández wanted to organize. Sanjenís had been chief of police under the Prío regime. Interestingly, Sanjenís would later be the doorman at the Dakota apartment building in New York City the night its famous resident John Lennon of the Beatles was killed on December 8, 1980, and the one who identified Mark David Chapman as the assassin.[11]

Although Sanjenís and Carrillo possessed the necessary economic resources, they lacked the ability to gather enough men and weapons for the expedition. Pérez-Vidal agreed to help, and the military training began in the Catskill Mountains in New York.[12]

This undertaking was done without the knowledge of the M-26-7 Directorate in Exile for fear of them being denounced since this was not M-26-7 authorized.[13]

At the end of August, a group including Pérez-Vidal's brother Santiago and friend Francisco Garcia were arrested in relation to confiscated weapons. He was again sent to "The Tombs," tried in a Brooklyn court, and found not guilty. The M-26-7 directorate, learning that Pérez-Vidal was continuing to carry out activities without their approval, removed him from his position as official delegate of the New York M-26-7 that September. He was then considered just a member. Committee leader José Llanusa Gobel named Heriberto Gonzalez to replace him.[14]

While this was a blow to Pérez-Vidal, it was only more proof that

Castro strongly disapproved of M-26-7 members' involvement in any activities with other revolutionary groups.[15]

Meanwhile, in Tampa, each night I would sit on my porch and listen to Radio Rebelde, a station set up by Ernesto "Che" Guevara de la Serna in the Sierra Mountains to transmit reports out of Cuba about Castro's mounting victories. On a clear night, the broadcasts were as crisp as those coming out of Tampa. I recall the station had a refrain that went "Aqui, Radio Rebelde, transmitiendo desde las montañas de la Sierra Maestra … territorio libre de Cuba" (Here, Rebel Radio, transmitting from the mountains of the Sierra Maestra…. Cuba's free territory). Its announcers were the actress Violeta Casals and the professional radio announcer Jorge Enrique Mendoza. And each week, Victoriano Manteiga would publish the highlights of Radio Rebelde's broadcasts for those who may have missed the reports or in case bad weather blocked the radio waves.

We learned through Radio Rebelde that Fidel Castro Ruz opened two fronts in the province of Oriente, one in the northeast in the Sierra Cristal under the command of Raúl Castro, and the other in the mountains surrounding the city of Santiago de Cuba under the command of Juan Almeida Bosque.

Concurrently as these two new fronts were opening in Oriente, in the center of Cuba in the province of Las Villas, the Directorio Revoluciónario under the command of Faure Chomón Mediavilla was operating a front with some of the survivors of the attack on the presidential palace that had taken place on March 13, 1957. There was another group that had collaborated with the Directorio Revoluciónario but had separated from them to form a second group calling itself El Segundo Frente del Escambray under the command of Eloy Gutiérrez Menoyo.[16]

In Miami, Howard K. Davis had become a pilot, with his flight training funded largely by Jorge Sotus Romero, who needed reliable, trustworthy persons to fly arms to Raúl Castro's camp in the Sierra Cristal. Most of the munitions had been going to Castro in the Sierra Maestra, many of which were delivered by Pedro Luis Díaz Lanz and Frank Fiorini (a.k.a. Sturgis) via big DC-3 airplanes.[17]

Davis already had a flight school at Miami International and Tamiami Airport. Sotus was more loyal to Raúl than Fidel Castro and was always looking for ways to get arms to him. He had Davis purchase a Staggerwing Beechcraft airplane, which was a high-performance aircraft. A Cuban pilot was going to be initiating its first trip to the Sierra Cristal. But he lost control upon landing and crashed. The pilot was fine, but the airplane was so badly damaged that it had to be chopped up, burned, and buried so as not to be seen by Batista's air control.[18]

It was painful to see their shiny, new, costly plane literally go up in

## 13. A Revolutionary Hero Leads Us

smoke. Now they had no plane and no way to get into the mountains. Sotus figured a small plane is better than no plane, so he asked Davis to fly a Cessna 175 with as much ammo and arms as it could safely hold. He then told Davis he wanted him to meet Raúl Castro Ruz.[19]

They flew at night. There were no lights anywhere, only the stars. Davis had no visual horizon to cue him. It was like being in a big black hole not knowing up from down. At a certain point, Sotus instructed Davis to circle around a few times flashing his landing lights. Suddenly, runway lights appeared on the ground—electric lights! Davis was amazed and very surprised.[20]

As Davis was landing, Sotus suddenly jumped out of the plane before it had come to a stop and hid because he thought it might be a trap. He was not sure if it was Raúl Castro's campsite. After Davis brought the plane to a stop, it became apparent that the airstrip was controlled by Raúl Castro's people. Sotus came out of hiding and spoke to someone. At that point, he told Davis they had to go to another airstrip and had to have one of the men there come in the plane with them to direct them to that airstrip.[21]

They took off and flew the heading provided by the man. They landed around 10 minutes later when another electric runway appeared. Sotus walked Davis to where Raúl Castro was waiting and introduced them. While the munitions were being unloaded and the plane was being prepped and fueled up for the return flight, Davis and Raúl Castro had a four-hour conversation about everything under the sun. Raúl Castro spoke very good English.[22]

The most memorable portion of dialogue that Davis recalls is when he asked Raúl Castro about the five Russian submarines that were rumored to have been spotted off the coast of Oriente Province bringing arms to the rebels. This was being circulated among the revolutionary circles in Miami. Raúl Castro's response confirmed that it was true, prompting Davis to inquire whether he was concerned that involving the Russians in any revolutionary activity might cause them to want to take over later. Raúl Castro responded, "When there is a great need, sometimes you have to do business with the devil." He stated to Davis that they were literally down to their last rounds of ammunition. When I asked Davis years later if he detected any sense of sibling rivalry during their conversation, Davis described it best by saying Raúl Castro did not think it fair the majority of support was going to his big brother, making him feel like he was "sucking hind teat."[23]

Another topic that Davis found memorable was when Raúl Castro mentioned that he was interested in Davis bringing him some tape recorders and surveillance equipment because he was concerned about some of the people in his camp. He wanted to use the recorders to determine whether he had unreliable people working with him. He wanted to check on the people he had on his team and find out what they were talking about when he was not around. He told Davis that he was not confident that everyone was on his side. But the part that really floored Davis was when Raúl Castro stated that he was not sure about Vilma Espin Guillios (who would later become his wife). Davis surmises he said that just to see if Davis would repeat it when he returned to Miami. He figured Raúl Castro had said that to feed him some false information and see whether it got back to him through another source. Davis never saw Raúl Castro again, so he had no opportunity to question him about it.[24]

Over the subsequent months, the rebel forces that operated in the mountains of Oriente began to spread out to the plains. They would occupy small towns without much resistance from the Batista forces, which began to retreat. In August, Castro ordered Majors Camilo Cienfuegos Gorriarán and Ernesto "Che" Guevara de la Serna with a platoon of about 150 men to advance towards the western destination city of Santa Clara in Las Villas. Castro's purpose was to divide the island in half and cut off government communications and transportation from the center of the country to the east. Castro would stay in Oriente, intending to have his troops surround the city of Santiago in preparation for an attack.

In the advancing of their forces towards Santa Clara, Che and Camilo Cienfuegos Gorriarán again found little resistance. Batista's government army was becoming demoralized, losing interest in the fight. Many of them deserted, surrendered, or joined forces with the rebels, whose numbers continued increasing as men from the occupied villages enlisted with them.

Unfortunately, the United States also stepped up its efforts to prevent support from making it to Cuba, specifically arms. Regular reports made the newspapers about U.S. law enforcement raiding boats stocked with arms destined for Cuba, similar to the one Mario was assisting. And a few of the arms shipments they stopped had ties to Tampa.

14

# Gun Smuggling from Tampa

Decades after the M-26-7 in Tampa dissolved, I—a former founding member and president—learned something new while researching for this book.

I honestly had no idea that weapons were going to Cuba through Tampa.

Perhaps it is because it was done on a need-to-know basis and there was no reason for me to know since, unlike my brother, I would likely have declined if asked to assist in such a venture.

Perhaps these arms shipments had no official attachment to the M-26-7 even when our members were involved.

In November 1957, the *Philomar III*, a yacht loaded with arms and military uniforms that were to be delivered to Fidel Castro Ruz's revolutionary army, was seized by U.S. agents off the Florida Keys. *Philomar III* was owned by Belarmino Fernandez of Tampa. Fernandez said he leased it to Gilbert L. Visbal of Miami but thought it was to be used for fishing. Visbal was one of those listed as arrested in the raid.[1]

In March 1958 *El Orion*, a small vessel packed with arms, was seized off the lower Texas Gulf Coast. Among the 36 arrested were three Cubans from Tampa.[2]

And in September 1958, another yacht, *The Harpoon*, loaded with arms, was seized at Port Everglades, Florida. Four Cubans who lived in Tampa were among the 33 arrested. One of them was our M-26-7's former delegate Dr. Rodolfo Vazquez. Law enforcement officials claimed that those caught wore armbands identifying themselves as soldiers in the rebel army of Castro and members of Organizacion Auténtica, Prío's revolutionary group.[3]

Following the revolution, Tom Dunkin, who covered the revolution from Cuba as a photojournalist for the *St. Petersburg Times* and *La Gaceta*, wrote an article detailing Tampa's role in arms smuggling to Cuba and used those three cases as evidence. *"One U.S. sympathizer even offered to provide the rebels a small submarine for sneaking weapons to Castro,"* wrote Dunkin. *"His offer was rejected by the cautious Ybor group 'because we didn't know where it came from.' ... Admitted by Ybor Castro supporters, but anonymously, is the fact that 150 machine guns seized in Miami last year, packed in oil drums, passed through Tampa."*[4]

Further adding to the lure of Tampa as a hub of arms deals during the revolution was Ellis Clifton. In the 1950s and '60s, Clifton was the head of Hillsborough County's Vice Squad, the department charged with breaking up Tampa's organized crime ring. Clifton alleged he made a deal with Castro to help get guns to the revolutionaries in Cuba. When or where this deal was made, he never did say.[5]

Clifton's primary goal was to arrest Santo Trafficante Jr. However, because the mafioso was operating his illegal empire from the safety of Cuba, there was too much water and too many people in between Trafficante and the crimes for there to be any direct evidence linking him to the illegal activities. If Clifton was ever going to build a case against Trafficante, he needed him out of Cuba. Castro also wanted Trafficante out of Cuba, as he did all the mafia leaders. Castro felt the mafia-operated casinos were denigrating the nation.[6]

A deal between the two men made sense. Clifton said the agreement he made with Castro was that he would help run guns to Cuba if Castro handed him Trafficante following his victory. Clifton, however, never did provide further details, coyly saying that some of his secrets would go to his grave.[7]

Again, I was not involved in any of these deals.

But in July and August of 2010, when my daughter Rhonda and grandsons Wynter and Javan Galindez and I visited Cuba, we had an opportunity to visit Gabriel Gil Alfonso, whom I had not seen since our visit in 1980 when he occupied the position of Dirigente del Municipio de la Habana (Director of the Municipality of Habana). Rhonda had many questions for him, one of which was the matter of gunrunning in Tampa. Gil said that Mario Triana and Juan M. Pérez were the ones he knew of who had a hand in arms acquisition, adding that both these men "did much for the revolution."

When we spoke with Pérez during that trip and asked about his gunrunning, he detailed that Faustino Pérez Hernández had instructed him to go to Miami and start working in arms acquisition under Alonso "Bebo" Hidalgo Barrios. Juan Pérez had initially come to Tampa on March 19, 1955, although shortly afterwards he went into U.S. Army training at Fort Jackson, South Carolina, and then was subsequently stationed in other states during his military commitment. Hidalgo replaced Lester Rodriguez

## 14. Gun Smuggling from Tampa

Raul Villamia sharing with Gabriel Gil Alfonso a copy of their photograph together on January 1, 1959, when a large group of Tampa M-26-7 members and sympathizers congregated in celebration of dictator Fulgencio Batista y Zaldívar fleeing Cuba. Habana, Cuba, August 4, 2010 (from the collection of Rhonda Villamia).

Pérez early 1958 after the Liberation Junta Pact meeting in Miami taking place November 1, 1957, when Rodriguez unknowingly signed the document on behalf of the M-26-7 without Castro's authorization. So, I will deduce that Pérez's involvement in arms acquisition began early 1958.[8]

Pérez told us that he transported the weapons in cars or in a truck owned by Mario Triana, a carpenter who had been living in Tampa since the 1930s. Pérez's being in the U.S. Army possibly facilitated his getting some weapons from there, but he told us that he "went all through the U.S. buying arms" and would take the guns to Miami.[9]

Pérez claimed to be the only one who collected arms in Tampa. But others in Tampa helped him collect and make weapons.[10]

Pérez shared that well prior to his death on April 10, 1958, José "Pepe" Prieto Rodriguez had been given a grenade by Manuel Carbonell

Raul Villamia visiting with Juan M. Perez and reminiscing about their M-26-7 days. Habana, Cuba, August 3, 2010 (from the collection of Rhonda Villamia).

Alfonso to take apart so he and Carmelo Bueno could learn how to make grenades.[11]

Prieto was a member of the Movimiento Nacional Revoluciónario (MNR) and part of Rafael García Bárcena's April 5, 1953, plan to assault Camp Columbia. He was one of the 13 sentenced to prison because of it. After that, he joined the M-26-7. He was again arrested in 1954 in relation to a stash of weapons warehoused at a Presbyterian medical laboratory located at No. 222 Calle Salud in Habana, of which Faustino Pérez Hernández was director. Prieto had organized the domestic manufacture of grenades, and part of these and other weapons were stored by Pérez Hernández in the lab. Also arrested with Prieto were Pérez Hernández, Armando and Enrique Hart Dávalos, and Alonso "Bebo" and Mario Hidalgo Barrios.[12]

Once free and undeterred, Prieto continued his dedication to conspiratorial activities and was arrested yet more times.

By now Fulgencio Batista y Zaldívar's henchmen knew him well and exacted more tortuous methods in dealing with him. Ultimately, on April 2, 1958, he was accidentally discovered making his way to his hiding place and taken into custody. Despite brutally torturing him, Batista's men were

## 14. Gun Smuggling from Tampa

unable to make him divulge sensitive information, so they viciously finished him off by castrating him, gouging his eyes, severing his tongue, and giving him 17 fractures before shooting him. His cadaver was found on April 10. He was so mutilated that it was difficult for his father to identify him.[13]

Marcelino Golan's son Ernesto would later recall Prieto as a good-sized fellow with dark black hair and a big black mustache who lived in the same Habana neighborhood as his family, and who visited Golan's family in Tampa sometime in 1956. He remembers Prieto being involved in planting bombs in Habana, but always with the promise he was certain to place them in areas without civilians.[14]

While I was researching for this book, Rafael García Bárcena Jr. shared that Manuel Carbonell Sr.'s son Manuel "Manolito" Carbonell Duque was a member of the Federación Estudiantil Universitaria (Federation of University Students) or FEU. He was a very jovial young man who liked arms. He was one of the conspirators in the Easter Sunday plot. After Castro came to power, he became his lead bodyguard ... at least in Brazil. García Bárcena Jr. discovered this when Manolito Carbonell stepped out of Castro's airplane while in Rio de Janeiro during the time his father was Cuban ambassador to Brazil, a position in which he served from 1959 until shortly before his death on June 13, 1961.[15]

Manolito Carbonell's father was also a conspirator against Batista. I do not remember a Carbonell other than Tampa M-26-7 member Carlos Carbonell, whose son George Carbonell later said that during the revolution his father kept grenades in a closet.[16]

Ernesto Golan confirmed that his uncle Carmelo Bueno made grenades in Tampa. Since Bueno knew Prieto and once operated a Habana foundry with a machine shop, Ernesto Golan's recollection substantiates Juan's account that both Bueno and Prieto were provided a grenade so they could learn to make the weapon.[17]

Finally, there was Felix Someillán's claim that his uncle Enrique Someillán transported weapons to Miami, though he was not sure if this was during his short stint with the M-26-7 or before or after. Felix Someillán said his father, Evaristo Someillán, assisted Someillán with this venture by transporting weapons along with clothes, food, and medicine to Miami and Key West in an 18-wheeler.[18]

On one occasion, Felix Someillán recalled, his father was pulled over and the truck was confiscated, but Someillán had connections that could get both his father and the truck with all its supplies released. Felix Someillán, however, could not recall why his father was arrested or whom his uncle contacted.[19]

And although I was never involved with any weapons smuggling, I did almost play a role in shipping one gun to Cuba for use in the revolution.

On December 29, 1958, Max Garcia and I ran into one another at the Centro Asturiano's cantina, which we both frequented. As we quietly discussed the revolution, Garcia leaned in close and whispered that someone had offered to sell him an M-2 rifle for $100. Garcia explained that the M-2 could be both semi-automatic and automatic. It would fire a bullet each time the trigger was engaged but, when a button at the top portion of the rifle was pressed, it would fire like a machine gun if the trigger remained engaged. Garcia added that it was a small rifle that did not weigh much; he said he had tested it and that it was in good condition. It also came with two cartridges. I reminded Garcia that I was not involved in anything having to do with arms, but we could speak with Gil to see if he might be interested.

I called Gil from the cantina payphone and put him on the line with Garcia. They spoke for a few minutes, and then Garcia handed me the phone. Gil asked me if I could front him the $100, which I did. He asked me to give the money to Garcia so he could purchase the M-2 and said I would be reimbursed by the M-26-7 later. He also asked me to keep the rifle for him for a few days because he lived in a boarding house on Columbus Drive, and he was concerned someone might steal it. I agreed to the plan and provided Garcia with the $100. We decided to meet at the cantina the following day so he could give me the rifle.

The next day, December 30, I got off work at 3:30 p.m. I was working for the City of Tampa's Traffic Department at the time, and our workshop was located on the corner of Sixth Avenue and Ninth Street, across the street from the Martí-Maceo Society and a short distance from the Centro Asturiano. When I arrived at the Centro, Garcia was already there. We exchanged pleasantries and then proceeded to the parking lot to make the deal.

I said that we should make sure it worked before Garcia gave me the rifle.

We got into Garcia's car and drove to a desolate area on East Hillsborough Avenue past 56th Street, where we fired a few shots. Convinced it functioned, we headed back to Centro Asturiano. Garcia gave me the rifle, and I placed it in the trunk of my car. We remained there talking for a while, and then I went home.

I phoned Gil later that evening and told him Garcia had given me the rifle. We then discussed the possibility of rain ruining a demonstration we had planned for the following day in front of the U.S. Post Office downtown on Florida Avenue between Madison and Twiggs Streets. It was a protest against Batista's bombing of cities that resulted in the killing of innocent women and children. Our conversation concluded with him telling me that he would take the M-2 off my hands as soon as he could.

The next day in Tampa a group of eight picketers paraded back and

## 14. Gun Smuggling from Tampa

forth on the sidewalk of the U.S. Post Office in downtown as planned. The rain came down hard that morning, so we postponed the picketing until the weather cleared. It ceased raining around 3 p.m. I arrived at 3:30 p.m. after I got off work. We decided to commence the picketing at 4:30 p.m. when the federal employees got off work and would be exiting the building. Shortly after we began picketing, *The Tampa Tribune* and TV reporters arrived to cover the event, each media outlet interviewing Gil through an interpreter. The demonstration ended at 6 p.m., and we then all returned to our homes to ring in the new year. By morning, our little demonstration was forgotten by the local news outlets. Bigger news had occurred.

As we watched the final seconds of 1958 tick away, my family ate our traditional 12 grapes—one for each month for good luck in the coming year. On the TV, the ball atop the Allied Building in New York City's Times Square descended and disappeared, marking the start of a new year and soon a new chapter in the history of Cuba.

Growing up in Cuba, it had been a custom for those who owned a gun to go outside at midnight and fire it into the sky, symbolizing shooting the old year to make way for the new one. That year, I fired the M-2 into the air.

It was never used in the actual revolution. It was never needed.

Throughout the previous few days in Cuba, unbeknownst to us, Ernesto "Che" Guevara de la Serna had received word that a train full of troops and weapons had departed Habana headed for Santa Clara. He moved part of his troops west, near the train tracks entering the city, using a bulldozer to move the tracks out of alignment, preparing to ambush the train. When it arrived at daybreak on December 29, the train derailed, and the rebels attacked "el tren blindado" (the armored train).

The rebel forces outnumbered the government army, so Batista's men surrendered. By the afternoon, rebel forces had totally occupied the city. Camilo Cienfuegos Gorriarán had already occupied other cities in the eastern part of Las Villas.

When I woke the morning of January 1, I learned that Batista had fled. Castro had won.

# 15

# Victory

I went to bed around 2 a.m. as a man born in a controlled country. I woke up a triumphant man whose homeland was free.

Shortly before 6 a.m. on Thursday, January 1, 1959, I was awoken by a loud knock on my front door. It was Hipolito Concepción, my wife's Cuban grandfather. He and his wife, Maria Coniglio, lived next door. He was a cigar maker and accustomed to getting up just as the sun rose, but rarely knocked on our door that early.

I wondered if there was an emergency. It was the only reason I could think he would be at my door at that time of morning. The excitement I saw on his face upon opening my door told me that nothing was wrong. He came with good news. But what type of good news called for such an early morning visit?

I immediately learned it was the best news.

Concepción told me they were broadcasting on Cuban radio stations that Fulgencio Batista y Zaldívar had fled Cuba. I rushed into my living room and turned on the radio. I was elated at what I heard. We had won! Cuba was free!

However, I did not have time to celebrate. I was sure that as a member of the M-26-7 I would have duties to perform.

I quickly dressed, had breakfast, and was out the door by 7 a.m., my destination being *La Gaceta*.

The trip by car would normally only have taken 10 to 15 minutes. This morning, however, it took much longer. Caravans of cars adorned with Cuban flags formed an impromptu parade, traveling from Ybor City to West Tampa, vice versa, and then back again, all the while honking their horns and blaring celebratory Cuban music from their car radios. I had never been happier to be stuck in traffic in my life.

When I finally made it to *La Gaceta*, I met with Gabriel Gil Alfonso and a host of other members of the M-26-7. After exchanging congratulations, we decided to ease our way through the throng of celebrators to the Cuban Club, where a crowd had congregated around the building's

## 15. Victory

exterior bust of José Martí. We spoke with quite a few people about how bright Cuba's future looked, and we soaked in praise and thank-yous from those who knew we had helped the revolution in our own way.

We then decided to head to Seventh Avenue, where the largest mass of people had formed, dancing and singing and shouting, "Viva Cuba libre!" and "Viva Castro!" as loud as they could. The more subdued filed into Our Lady of Perpetual Help to light candles and thank the Lord for allowing them to live to see the day Cuba was free.

The bulk of the crowd on Seventh Avenue congregated in front of Sam and Molly Ferrara's "Columbia Music and Appliance" store, where exterior loudspeakers broadcast the news directly from Cuba. Photographer Henry Rodriguez took a photo of the moment. It was magical.

Ironically, Ruben Fabelo was front and center, one of the stars of the show. His radio program, *Fiesta en Tampa*, was set up to broadcast from the shop's porch. Sitting alongside him were station announcers Ramon Bermudez and Pedro Ramírez Moya.

Bermudez, a friend of ours who had always cooperated with the M-26-7, asked us if we wanted to say anything on the program. We readily agreed. Gil, members of the M-26-7, and I took our turns stating what a wonderful occasion it was while reminding the people that they needed to demonstrate good behavior. We did not want the first day of Cuban freedom to be marred by poor decisions in Ybor City and West Tampa. When we were done, Victoriano Manteiga arrived, and Bermudez eagerly asked Tampa's greatest orator to share a few words. He reiterated what we said. However, his version was more powerful than ours. Manteiga had a way about him.

By this time, it was 11 a.m., and Gil asked the M-26-7 members to return to *La Gaceta* so he could speak with us in private. There, he told us that he had received orders that he was to return to Cuba immediately and that I was to become the new delegate of the Tampa M-26-7.

This time I accepted the position. The first time I had been asked to assume the club's presidency, when Manteiga resigned in December 1957, I was reluctant because I had just begun working for the City of Tampa—a government position. Aside from my not being comfortable with public speaking, I felt being president would have me too much in the public eye, which could cause me problems with my job.

Although I was already a U.S. citizen, I was supporting and representing another country. As secretary, I would not be as noticed as I would be as president. But by January 1959, I had already been at my job for 13 months. The triumph happened so suddenly, and since I had been the only other individual personally named by Fidel Castro Ruz to a leadership position besides Manteiga, I accepted the role of delegate. Gil gave

Tampa M-26-7 members and Fidel Castro supporters gathered in front of Ybor City's Columbia Music and Appliance store at 1416 East Broadway (7th Avenue), owned by Molly Ferrara, in celebration of dictator Fulgencio Batista y Zaldívar fleeing Cuba. Raul Villamia and Gabriel Gil Alfonso are in the center holding the flag. Standing: (woman) Morales, unidentified man, (man) Morales, unidentified man, unidentified woman, unidentified man, Pedro Ramirez Moya, Mario Iglesias, Homero Olmedo, Villamia, unidentified man, Gil, Carlos Sureda, Marcelino Vila Jr., unidentified man, unidentified man, unidentified man, Juan M. Perez, Carmen Marill, unidentified woman, unidentified man, Benny Cuellar, unidentified woman, unidentified woman, Francisco Fernandez de la Nuez (Circulo Cubano president). Kneeling: Ramon Bermudez, (man) Pineiro, seven children, Ruben Fabelo (Spanish radio host), Rodolfo Vasquez. Tampa (Ybor City), Florida, January 1, 1959 (photograph by Henry "Rod" Rodriguez, courtesy of *La Gaceta*).

me a signed, handwritten note verifying this edict. All these years later, it remains one of my greatest honors. An emotional Gil then told us how grateful he was for all we had done. His departing words were: "We will see each other in a free Cuba."

We wanted to return to the streets and rejoin the celebration, but we knew that there were still pressing matters to which we needed to attend. We decided that as our first order of business we needed to occupy the

Cuban consulate. The consul was Guillermo Bolivar y Morales del Castillo. He was not a bad man, but he was appointed by Batista and represented a regime that ruled Cuba through fear. The tyrant was no longer in power, so a Castro representative, someone representing the new Cuba, needed to take over that position. We considered it our duty to occupy the consulate as Castro's Tampa revolutionary branch until the Revolutionary Government named a new permanent consul.

It was New Year's Day and the consulate was closed, so we agreed to occupy it first thing in the morning. But minutes later a friend rushed into *La Gaceta* saying that a group of pro-Castro Cubans were on their way to the consul's residence—109 West Lambright—to stage a protest. A couple of club members and I hurried from *La Gaceta*, hoping to intercept the group, worried that they might act in a way that would result in violence. We did not agree with Consul Bolivar's decision to support the Batista regime, but he had not directly done anything to the Tampa community to warrant harm against him or his family.

We arrived at Consul Bolivar's residence to find about a dozen people shouting anti-Batista sentiments and slurs toward his house. There were not any M-26-7 members in the crowd, but I recognized a few men who had been supportive of our cause as non-members. As I asked them to please leave the consul and his family alone, the police arrived to do the same. I introduced myself to the police and explained that I was calming the situation. They were appreciative and left, trusting everyone would respect my wishes. Thankfully, everyone did.

We returned to *La Gaceta* to discuss our plan for occupying the consulate and learned that we were on the same page as the M-26-7 National Directorate in Miami. While we were gone, National Directorate Secretary José Llanusa Gobel (the Llanusa from the Haiti trip with my brother Mario) sent a signed telegram instructing us to peacefully occupy the consulate. A short time later, we received a phone call from Ernesto Betancourt, a representative of the Cuban Revolutionary Government in Washington, D.C. He reiterated to me what the telegram stated and elaborated that we should occupy the consulate for as long as it took for a permanent consul to be selected. He said we needed to consult with Gerardo Pérez Puelles, who had been named the coordinator of the M-26-7 in Miami, if there was a problem.

I informed the other members of my conversation with Betancourt and warned them that we were not allowed to use any sort of physical force to remove Consul Bolivar. I chose six men to go to the consulate with me in the morning; among them were Juan M. Pérez, Mario Iglesias, and Carlos Sureda, all of whom had been involved with the M-26-7 either since or within a short time after its inception in Tampa. It seemed fitting that those who devoted so much time to the cause should be on hand to declare that the consulate was under the Revolutionary Government's jurisdiction. I told them to wear a suit and tie, as we were officially representatives of the Cuban government and needed to act and dress in a way that would make our native land proud.

However, while we were acting on orders from the Revolutionary Government, we were still bound by the City of Tampa's laws. I did not want to enter the Cuban consulate before consulting with local law enforcement. I told my select group of men that we would meet across the street from the consulate rather than directly in front of it—to avoid confrontation with any potential remaining Batista supporters—and then walk to the nearby police station together to inform the chief of our plan.

The remaining members were instructed to dress as they wished and gather across the street from the consulate until we returned.

The following morning, I informed my boss that I would be using a vacation day and then, at the appointed time, we took our position across from the consulate, which was in the Flagler Building at 416 Tampa Street, room 207. There was already a group of people I did not recognize standing in front of it, waiting to learn of Bolivar's fate. Two police officers stood at the doorway to make sure the situation stayed calm. The police presence confirmed my decision to meet across the street because too many pro-Castro supporters may have worried the officers and we did not want to appear anything but peaceful.

One of the non-M-26-7 Cuban men in front of the consulate saw us arrive and crossed the street to introduce himself as Gus Radcliff, a Cuban native who spoke fluent English. He offered to accompany us to the police station to act as interpreter. I was not sure how he knew of our destination, but I knew that we needed someone with his linguistic ability and thus took him up on his proposal.

At police headquarters, we told the officer at the front desk why we were there and asked if we could speak with the chief of police. The officer informed the chief of our presence, and, a few moments later, a man wearing civilian clothes walked from one of the offices and introduced himself as Deputy Chief Norman Brown. He thanked us for involving the police department rather than acting as rogues and then took us to meet with Police Chief James P. Mullins. The chief explained that if we acted peacefully the police department would not interfere in our matters, but if anyone got out of line on our part or acted out against us, the department would act swiftly.

We returned to the Flagler Building and, accompanied by the two officers who had been at the door, I went upstairs into the consulate office.

## 15. Victory

Radcliff wanted to come with me, but I saw no need for him since the consul and I both spoke Spanish.

The consulate's office was one of several offices located along a narrow hallway. Its outer door opened from the hall into a small waiting area. A second door then led into the consul's chamber. The outer door was open, but the chamber door was locked.

I knocked on the chamber door, and someone I would later learn was the consul's son, Rene, let us in. Consul Bolivar was sitting at his desk. I introduced myself, stating, "As delegate of the M-26-7 of Tampa, I am here with my fellow members to occupy the consulate by order of the Cuban Revolutionary Government." I presented him with the telegram I had received from Cuba.

Bolivar responded that he could not hand over the consulate until he was officially ordered to do so by the Cuban State Department, explaining that he needed evidence that those who signed my telegram had the authority to make such an order. We peacefully discussed the matter for a few minutes and then hoped to settle it with a phone call to Habana. However, we could not reach anyone in Cuba since the new government was still trying to organize itself. I decided to return to *La Gaceta* to contact the National Directorate in Miami and told my companions to remain outside the consul's office until I returned. I did not want them discussing official matters with the consul in my absence.

Back at *La Gaceta*, I was informed that a telegram had been sent to Gil from the National Directorate. It read:

> The struggle is not over until Dr. Urrutia takes possession of the provisional government. Maintain organization, take inventory and send money to Miami.
>
> José Llanusa[1]

Llanusa must not have known that Gil had already been called back to Cuba.

I tried to contact Haydée Santamaría Cuadrado, to inform her that I was the new delegate and to ask how to proceed at the consulate, but I was told she had left for Habana. I then asked to speak with Gerardo Pérez Puelles but was told that he could not be located.

I next called Betancourt in D.C. and, luckily, he was available. He informed me that Emilio Pando, who worked with him at the Cuban embassy in Washington, D.C., sent Bolivar a telegram earlier that day telling him to either cooperate with me as the delegate of Tampa's M-26-7 until a permanent consul was named or to turn the consulate over to me. Bolivar had not informed me of this telegram when I had initially conferred with him.

It seemed subordinate to the new government, but I figured he was

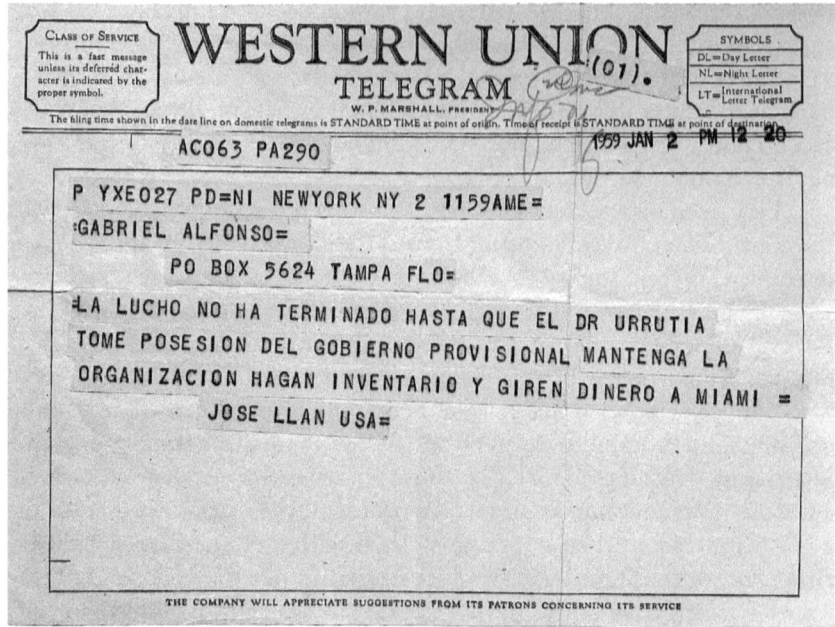

Western Union telegram from Jose Llanusa Gobel of the M-26-7 Committee in Exile to Gabriel Gil Alfonso, advising that "the struggle is not over until Dr. Urrutia takes possession of the provisional government. Maintain organization, take inventory, and send money to Miami." Tampa, Florida, January 2, 1959 (from the collection of Raul Villamia).

probably trying to come to terms with the events of the past 24 hours. We decided to allow him to remain in the consulate until a new consul was named. He was experienced while I was not. However, Betancourt informed me that I needed to occupy the consulate as well. The Cuban government could not have a former Batista-appointee acting as sole representative of Cuba in Tampa.

I never mentioned the telegram to Bolivar when I returned to the consulate. There was no need for confrontation, and pointing out that he purposely did not tell me of it could have escalated a war of words. Instead, I reiterated the telegram's stance as though it was my idea and offered for him to remain in the consulate, explaining that I would understand if he wanted to leave. After pondering the options for a few moments, he agreed to share the consulate with me and provided me with a set of keys.

He then informed me that there was a vice consul—Eliseo Pérez—who had been sick for the past few days and asked what I would like to do with him. I decided he too should continue to perform his duties until a new consul was named.

## 15. Victory

My companions and I remained at the consulate until closing time. I told those with me that, when the consulate opened for business on Monday, I wanted two men posted there from that point forward and that I would occupy the office when I got off work at 3:30 p.m. The men selected were either self-employed or had flexible work hours, so they were easily available.

I picked up a copy of the afternoon edition of *The Tampa Times* on my way home and noticed a peculiar article detailing that morning's activities. The headline read, "Tampans Make Bid to Seize Consulate" adorned by a photo of Radcliff and two of my companions in front of the building.

The article read:

> Ten Cuban rebel sympathizers tried to take over the Cuban consulate in the Flagler Building in downtown Tampa by peaceful means today. They were unsuccessful immediately but the full result of their efforts still was uncertain this afternoon.
>
> Cuban Consul Guillermo Bolivar refused their demand to install Raul Villamia as the new consul for the Cuban revolutionary forces.
>
> Most of the group identified themselves as members of the 26th of July faction. They reported Villamia is in charge of all Tampa operations for the revolutionary forces.
>
> Two Tampa policemen were on the scene despite it being peaceful.
>
> An hour-long debate ended in a deadlock. Spokesmen for the rebels said the office would be closed. Bolivar himself said he has no authority to close the office.
>
> "Everyone wants to go home," Gus Radcliff, spokesman for the rebel group said.
>
> When asked how many rebel refugees they expect to fly to Cuba, some of the demonstrators said "thousands" and others reported it was "secret information."[2]

Most of the article was correct. It was only the last two paragraphs that astounded me. Radcliff had been labeled as a "spokesman for the rebel group." The article did not have a byline, so I do not know who wrote it and have no factual proof of how the writer received such bad information.

I would guess that the press arrived when I left the building to go to *La Gaceta* and, knowing my companions spoke broken English, Radcliff took that opportunity to identify himself as our spokesperson to exaggerate his importance. As for "thousands of rebel refugees returning to Cuba"—that was news to me. I would surmise that Radcliff made that up so that he sounded more informed than he really was.

An even more error-filled article was published following morning. This one was in *The Tampa Tribune*. The headline read, "Rebels Here Fail in Bid for Consulate" and the reporter, Cecil Mann, identified Radcliff as one of the leaders of the M-26-7. Almost the entire article was based on

M-26-7 members and Raul Villamia as newly appointed M-26-7 delegate and interim Cuban consul visit Police Chief James P. Mullins before occupying the consulate. Carlos Sureda, unidentified man, Leoncio Coutin, Villamia, Mario Iglesias, Gus Radcliff, and Police Chief James P. Mullins. Tampa, Florida, January 3, 1959 (photograph accompanying article by Cecil Mann titled "Rebels Here Fail in Bid to Seize Consulate," courtesy of *The Tampa Tribune*).

Mann's interview with Radcliff. Everything Radcliff told the reporter was wrong, and for an obvious reason. Radcliff had no idea what the M-26-7 was doing because he had no affiliation with it then or at any point during the revolution. In fact, no member of the M-26-7 had ever seen Radcliff prior to his offer to act as our interpreter on January 2, 1959.[3]

Radcliff was quoted as saying that the rebel forces deemed it most important to gain access to the consulate's records and that we should simply walk in and take over if the consul would not hand the office over to the M-26-7. He further stated that, if we were arrested, *"It will not matter ... we have been ordered to take the records."* No one had ever ordered us to take any records from the consulate. He finally again falsely asserted that rebel refugees in Tampa would soon be flown back to Cuba.[4]

I was frustrated with the numerous errors in the article but cannot place the blame on the reporter. The transference of leadership of the M-26-7 from Gil to me had been done internally, and the official telegrams had not been made public. The local English-speaking publication would have

## 15. Victory

no knowledge of those events. The reporter then met an English-speaking Cuban looking for his 15 minutes of fame who had no qualms about taking advantage of the reporter in order to attain it. The reporter was a victim.

That same afternoon, *The Tampa Times* finally got it right when they published an article written by Tom Inglis headlined, "Rivals Share Office, Castro's Men Get Foot in Consulate."[5]

Villamia was *"armed with a telegram from Castro's forces authorizing him to take control, and backed by several members of the 26th of July Movement,"* it read.

> Bolivar firmly refused to turn his office over to Villamia but agreed to share it with him until a new Cuban government formed and can clear up the situation. Until a permanent appointment is made it appears there will be two men in the saddle at the consul's office here.
>
> Villamia and Juan Pérez, another leader in the 26th of July group, visited Police Inspector Norman Brown this morning before making his move on the consul's office.
>
> In the interview with Brown he explained it was his intention to take the

Raul Villamia conversing with soon-to-be-replaced Cuban Consul Guillermo Bolivar y Morales del Castillo, sharing new consulate protocol under the nascent revolutionary regime. Tampa, Florida, January 3, 1959 (photograph accompanying article by Tom Inglis titled "Castro's Men Get Foot in Consulate," courtesy of *The Tampa Times*).

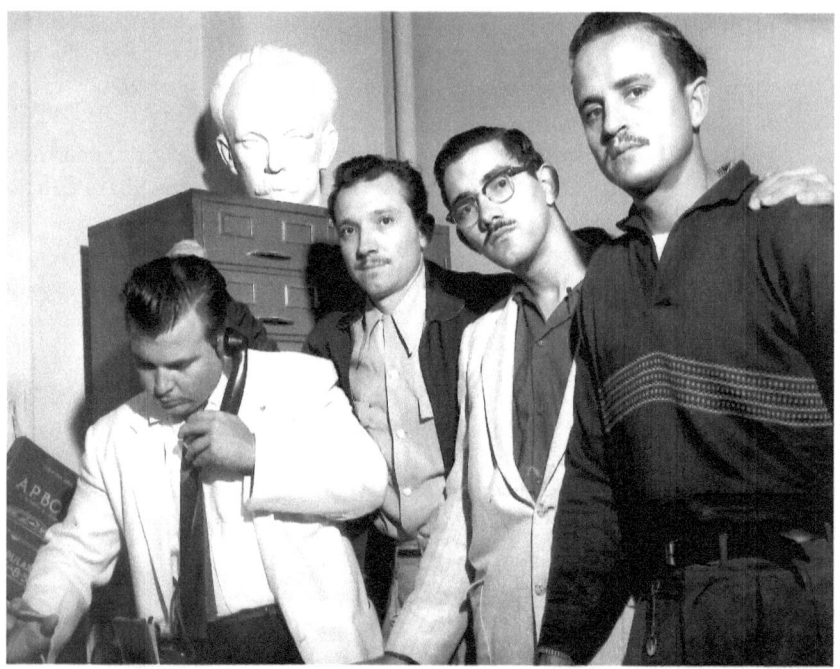

M-26-7 occupying the Cuban consulate. Juan M. Perez, interim Cuban Consul Raul Villamia, Carlos Sureda, and Juan Torres. Tampa, Florida, January 4, 1959 (photograph by Charles Hendrick, accompanying Hendrick's article titled "Tampa Followers of Castro Make Peaceful Invasion of Cuban Consulate Here," courtesy of *The Tampa Tribune*).

office peacefully—but to assume full possession. He displayed his Spanish language telegram authorizing him to take quick, but peaceful, possession of the office.

"We are representatives of the Cubans in Tampa," Villamia said. "We are the Castro forces represented here by the 26th of July Movement."

Pérez said that Villamia's tenure in the consul's office will be a provisional one. He will stay on until the new government appoints a new consul.

Bolivar declined to turn over his office to Villamia on the grounds that the telegram was not signed by anyone of authority that he recognized. Throughout the debate over control of the local office Bolivar has maintained he has no authority to turn over his funds and his papers to anyone. He maintained he has been entrusted with the office and will stay in his position until he is officially relieved.

Pérez said action of the new Cuban government clarifying the situation in the Tampa office is expected in the next week.

As the debate over the consul's office waxed hot, hundreds of other Cubans, refugees from the revolution and the Batista government awaited a chance to return to their homeland.[6]

## 15. Victory

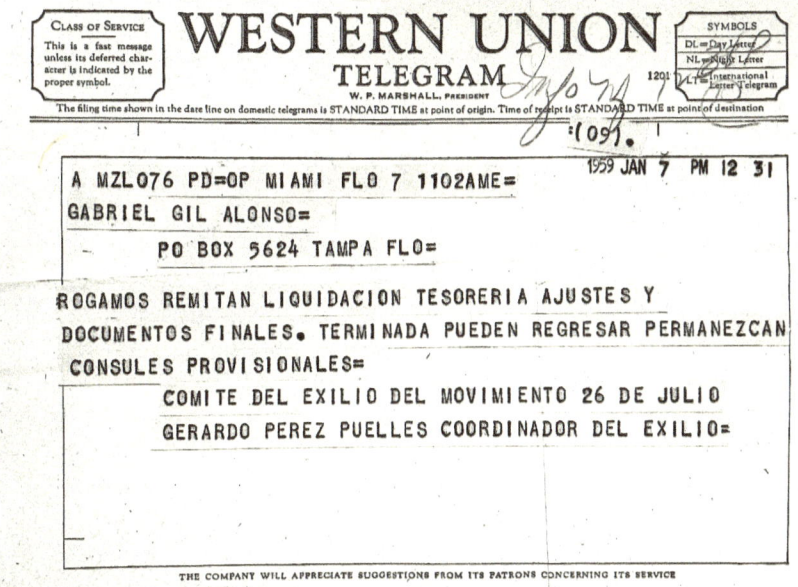

Western Union telegram from Gerardo Perez Puelles of the M-26-7 Committee in Exile to Gabriel Gil Alfonso, advising: *"Please send cash clearance adjustments and final documents ... once finished, you can return ... provisional consuls remain."* Tampa, Florida, January 7, 1959 (from the collection of Raul Villamia).

Then, the following day, another accurate article penned by Charles Hendrick was published in *The Tampa Tribune* under the headline "Tampa Followers of Castro Make Peaceful Invasión of Cuban Consulate Here."[7]

After those early January publications, Radcliff was never mentioned again in any of the newspapers, nor was he ever seen again in Tampa by any of us. It was our opinion that he likely left for Cuba with the newspapers that placed him in the limelight, perhaps hoping to obtain some position of prominence in the new regime based on his "involvement" in the Tampa club.

Interestingly, on January 7, another telegram was sent to Gil's attention. This one was sent by Gerardo Pérez Puelles, coordinator of the M-26-7 Committee in Exile. This may have been instructing Gil to wrap up some financial matters, and once having completed that task, to return to Miami, leaving interim consul—i.e., me—in place.[8]

Again, it is baffling that even by this date, the committee in Miami did not seem to know that Gil had returned to Cuba and was no longer in Tampa.

# 16

# Fallout

I am not sure the newspaper has ever been such a pleasure to read as it was in the weeks immediately following the victorious revolution.

On January 9, 1959, an excellent article written by journalist and photographer Tom Dunkin was published in *La Gaceta*. "Another Gun—Another Soldier" it was called:

> An amazed world awoke January 1 to find Cuban dictator Fulgencio Batista overthrown. The manner in which youthful Fidel Castro and 11 survivors of an 82-man military expedition persevered to defeat an army of 42,000 soldiers under Batista still is incomprehensible to many.
>
> Deposed Dictator Batista was quoted January 2 as saying his downfall came because the revolutionaries were better armed. Batista said a U.S. halt to further arms shipment imposed last March was partly responsible—that he could not obtain adequate weapons and munitions. I cannot agree.
>
> The rebels did possess a superior weapon Batista lacked, which defeated the dictator. This was a stubborn, unquenchable, and at times, pathetic belief in freedom and democracy, plus faith in Fidel Castro's leadership. Torture and death were all Batista had to fight this faith and urge to be free. These were not enough, and truly were inferior weapons.
>
> Rebel faith was badly shaken by drastic reverses suffered by the rebels in Castro's "all-out war" declared last April—but only in the hearts of those hoping for a quick and easy victory. The rebellious spirit never faltered among those dedicated to a free Cuba.
>
> Foremost among objections to the Batista regime, voiced by Cubans from all strata of society from simple workers to highly educated professional men, was Batista's unconstitutional seizure of government March 10, 1952. This was diametrically opposite the Cuban democratic principle. This belief was sufficient basis for a successful revolution, but required the leadership of a man of Fidel Castro's stature.
>
> This belief was strong enough to withstand fear of torture and death. It is easy to state principles, not so simple to die for them. The average Anglo-Saxon finds it difficult to believe the horrors to which the Cuban patriots were subjected.
>
> An American, Mervin Cummings, a professor at the University of Oriente,

## 16. Fallout

in Santiago, aided in escorting safely to jail January 3—two days after Batista fell—a Santiago woman in whose home were found arms and instruments of torture. "Among them," Cummings told me, "was an implement for gouging out eyes."

Cummings and two rebels safely conducted the Batista "chivato" to prison, although crowds in the streets howled for her blood. The long-suffering Cuban people would have killed her immediately, without rebel protection.

Cuba's 26th of July rebels have greatly surprised many Americans with their courtesy and discipline—exactly the opposite of the Batista soldiers' conduct.

Rebels rounded up an estimated 1,000 persons in Santiago January 8 and jailed them as suspected of having tortured and caused the death of many patriots. Huge throngs of citizens lined the streets to jeer their hated enemies, and to shout for their blood.

Yet I saw no mistreatment of the accused traitors, other than a push now and then to move a reluctant and fearful prisoner. Although many times outnumbered by the mobs, the rebel soldiers were in complete control of the situation, and followed to the letter their orders for no killing or mistreatment of prisoners. This protection of the rights of an accused person is another democratic principle ignored by the dictator.

Batista's complaint of inability to get arms is not true. Rebels showed me many carbines made in the Dominican Republic, where the dictator now hides. He got helicopters and aircraft from Great Britain, and recently a shipment of tanks from the latter source.

On the other hand, the rebels were severely handicapped in this respect. Their arms supply routes via the U.S. were illegal, according to U.S. law. Many persons were arrested, hundreds of thousands of dollars in weapons seized, which hampered the rebel cause.

But, the indomitable rebel spirit prevailed. The arms shipment continued through the U.S., Mexico and Venezuela, to supplement the rusty shotguns and rifles owned by citizens, and military weapons seized from the Batista army. And, as one rebel put it, "when we get another gun we have another soldier to use it."

Guns, tanks and planes are a necessity for warfare. The rebels were poorly equipped in comparison to Batista's troops in this respect. But the unpaid rebel soldiers' decisive weapon was his unfaltering belief—and the similar belief by a majority of the Cuban people that "our cause must prevail because it is just."

What the future holds for Cuba is speculative. Fears of communistic influence among the rebel groups have been expressed by many in the U.S. From personal experience with the rebels, I can report no evidence of communistic tendencies observed—unless unity of purpose is considered collectivism.

However, many diverse groups had a hand in Batista's defeat. How their demands for a share in the spoils of war affect the new government remains to be determined. But I firmly believe that if Fidel Castro's intentions previously stated—with many already accomplished—are carried out, a democratic "Cuba Libre" will become a reality.[1]

Dunkin was not the only Tampa journalist to visit Cuba following the fall of Batista. Manteiga traveled to the island with his son Roland Manteiga to see old friends, cover the victory, and bask in the newfound freedom of his homeland. Accompanied by Gabriel Gil Alfonso, he was taken to meet Castro to have a firsthand look at history. Not just anyone could meet with Castro. He was a busy man, placed in charge of the Revolutionary Army and working hard to help President Manuel Urrutia Lleó bring order to the island. The fact that Manteiga was provided such access speaks volumes for how well he was respected.

The following, published on January 16, 1959, in *La Gaceta*, is Roland Manteiga's account of the meeting:

> We journeyed to Cuba last weekend and had the pleasure of talking to Fidel Castro once again. We last met in November 1955.
> 
> This amazing young man of 32 years performed a feat thought to be impossible by defeating the armed forces of Dictator Batista. He began with only a handful of men. He has now set out to fulfill the second seemingly impossible task, to give Cuba an efficient and honest government. We believe that this tireless warrior will also be successful in this tremendous project.
> 
> He has surrounded himself with some of Cuba's best minds and men who have never had their hands stained with the smear of corruption and greed.
> 
> We met Dr. Castro in Camp Columbia, the large military installation located in Habana, which he now calls Camp Rebel. We heard him discuss some of his intentions in the same room once occupied by General Tabernilla, Batista's military chief, now in exile in the United States.
> 
> Here, for the first time in print, are some of the future plans of Castro for Cuba.
> 
> He plans to convert Camp Rebel, formerly Camp Columbia, from the large installation that it is into a school for 10,000 children.
> 
> He plans to do away with the traffic corps in Habana and will replace them with 2,000 Boy Scouts. They will be trained, fed, clothed and educated. This will be the first time in history that such a project has ever been attempted in the world.
> 
> He plans to reorganize the Cuban army, navy and air force. Many of his top rebel chieftains will command military units.
> 
> He will open a school for paratroopers and the Cuban soldiers will undergo the toughest and most rigorous training possible.
> 
> He will completely separate the relationships between the military and civil units. The military forces of Cuba will no longer be used for civil purposes, such as acting as police and civil guards, but will be used only for the protection of Cuba itself against any outside forces and interests.
> 
> Dr. Castro plans to strengthen and enlarge the school system throughout the whole island.
> 
> He plans to reorganize the rural police and provide modern police facilities and equipment for them.
> 
> Finally, Dr. Castro plans to rid Cuba of corrupt officials and give honest

government which in time will bring prosperity and enlightenment to the citizens of that island.²

In that edition of *La Gaceta*, Manteiga also sought to right the lies being spread about Cuba's new government. He wrote:

Much has been said in the American press during the last three or four days about the executions in Cuba.

Congressmen, newspaper columnists and newspapers have all been shouting for Castro to stop the "mass executions" of the multi-murderers of the Batista regime. To one who has been close to the situation, we are surprised at the reaction of the Congressmen and the newspapers, but we realize that this reaction is based on the lack of knowledge.

Very briefly, we are going to give you an insight on the executions based on facts and truths.

1. All persons so far executed have confessed to being or have been proven multi-murderers.
2. While the verdicts in most cases have been swift and to the point, the state has offered undeniable proof and, in many cases, produced eye witnesses to the assassinations (soldiers testifying against former officers). Most of the assassins were men of authority such as army captains and colonels and police sergeants and captains.
3. No one has been executed for political reasons only.
4. The majority of the assassins used torture as a prerequisite to murder.
5. It is estimated that 21,000 Cubans died on both sides during the Batista five-year regime. But 10,000 of these were murdered by Batista's professional assassins. These were victims of murder, not warfare.
6. There are many cases where the assassin has confessed to or has been accused of many murders. As an example, one captain, 32 tortured victims; another captain, 68; another officer, 108 victims slain by his own hands; one negro police officer in Habana when accused of 28 murders openly boasted that the correct number was 32; and so on.
7. The Cuban magazine, "Bohemia," this week published one million copies showing many photos and printed many descriptions of some of the atrocities committed by "mad-man" Batista and his savage horde.
8. In all the large police stations throughout Cuba were found implements of torture. Tools for pulling out fingernails, instruments for gouging out eyes, whips, knives, etc. Most of the large police stations also have private cemeteries where the victims were buried secretly.
9. Graves are now being found where tortured victims were buried alive.
10. There is a small lagoon near the Tropicana nightclub outside of Habana. While it is small, it is believed to be very deep, some people say it is without bottom. Countless victims were drowned in this "lagunita" by Batista's "savages" when they were thrown in with weights tied to their feet.

11. The forces of Fidel Castro have not tortured any of these assassins.
12. Whereas most of the murders committed by Batista's "dogs" were done secretly and hidden from the press, Castro is permitting the press to attend the trials and executions. But this democratic method is going against him ... he is getting bad press in the United States.
13. Some 3,500 persons associated with the Batista regime are in jails and prisons throughout the island. Most of these will be released within 60 days.
14. The American Embassy was aware of many of the atrocities committed by the Batista government, yet no protest was made.
15. Many American newspapers and U.S. Congressmen were told of these atrocities, yet no voice was loud in protest of this primitive savagery.
16. Batista and his henchmen depleted the Cuban treasury by stealing hundreds of millions of dollars.... How much of this money is now behind the loud protest in the United States?
17. The foreign policy of the United States continues to be "helpful to dictatorships and tough on democracies," at least in Latin America. Let's help Castro bring peace, prosperity and democracy to Cuba.[3]

Another misperception he was able to correct was that of the status of Santo Trafficante Jr.

Following Batista's flight, some Cubans were finally allowed to display their animosity toward the casinos. Before Castro's troops could effectively occupy the capital and bring order to the island, rioters stormed into six of the 13 Habana casinos and smashed slot machines, dice, blackjack tables, and other gambling paraphernalia with sledgehammers. Among those casinos left in ruins were Capri, Deauville, and Sevilla Biltmore. Comodoro and Sans Souci were spared.

But, shortly after Manuel Urrutia Leo was named president, Castro, as head of the Revolutionary Army, shut down the casinos, impounded the cash found in them, and froze bank assets of establishments owned by those with ties to the American mafia.

There were whispers that Castro had plans for the casino owners who moonlighted as American mafia leaders—prison or death. Most casino owners with ties to organized crime fled Cuba immediately following Castro's victory, taking as much money with them as they could and leaving much behind, choosing life over dollar signs.

Trafficante was stubborn, however. He refused to leave. There were rumors that he gave money and/or guns to Castro during the revolution, playing both sides in order to secure his future no matter the outcome of the war. Other rumors stated that he thought Castro would realize how much money the casinos brought to Cuba and change his mind about closing them or that Batista would return to power.

## 16. Fallout 177

"Castro is a complete nut," Trafficante's attorney, Frank Ragano, quoted his client as saying in his book, *Mob Lawyer*. "He's not going to be in office or power for long. Either Batista will return or someone else will replace this guy because there's no way the economy can continue without tourists, and this guy is closing the hotels and casinos. This is a temporary storm. It'll blow over."[4]

Gossip about the whereabouts of Tampa's most infamous son were rampant in Tampa during the days following the revolution. Some claimed he was in hiding in Cuba. Others said he fled, was imprisoned or assassinated.

Manteiga learned that Trafficante was still in Cuba and living out in the open as though he had not a care in the world.

In the January 16, 1959, edition of *La Gaceta* that detailed his trip to Cuba, Roland Manteiga wrote about their visit with Tampa's don:

Much has been said about gambling and gamblers in Cuba. We have read many times since the overthrow of Batista that the gamblers fled Cuba and that the new Cuban government was going to prohibit future gambling. We now bring you the facts on the gambling situation and a story about Santo Trafficante, the former Tampan who operates several gambling casinos in Habana.

We scoop all the newspapers in the country with this exclusive interview.

We met Santo in a Habana restaurant and exchanged cordialities, having known him for a number of years.

We told him that we wanted the real story about the gambling situation in Cuba and he agreed to tell us. However, he pointed out that he had to introduce us to other gamblers in Habana so that they could tell their story, for each gambler had his own story and version.

Santo told us that he now knew as many people in Cuba as he did in the United States and has decided to make Cuba his home.

He pointed out that the gambling racket in Cuba was not what it was cracked up to be. For instance, some of the following statements are a composite of what Santo and the other gamblers told us.

Few tears were shed by American gamblers when Batista was overthrown. Not only did many government and police officials extort huge sums of money from them but used abusive tactics when present in the casinos.

For instance, when police colonel Ventura would enter a casino, 20 bodyguards with submachine guns would come in also. The sight of so many guns would drive the regular customers home.

The son of Habana's second assassin, Pilar Garcia, would go to the casinos, play on credit and of course never paid his debts.

This was the usual practice for many of the officials. Garcia's son once won three thousand dollars in a casino and placed the winnings in his pockets. He then had a drink and proceeded to gamble again. This time he lost $40,000.

He signed an IOU and left with his original three thousand winnings. Needless to say, he never did pay back the $40,000.

When they wanted to borrow money, which was not to be paid back, and the gambler would hesitate, guns would be whipped out. The gambler would always lend the money under these conditions.

Santo told us that 1958 was a poor year for the gamblers in Habana. With many tourists staying away from Habana because of the Civil War, the casinos were taking a beating because of the large overhead. Expensive floor shows and hundreds of employees in contrast to few tourists produced losses. He told us that the Sans Souci Club was losing $3,000 per week and this included the revenue from the gambling casino.

The restaurant of the Hotel Deauville which was also part of the gambling casino was losing $3,000 per week. However, the casino provided profits enough to take care of the deficit in the restaurant.

It is Santo's belief that Habana will become one of the most prosperous cities of the world under the new government of Fidel Castro providing Habana keeps open its gambling casinos to the American tourists. However, he quickly pointed out that unless the rich Cubans are permitted to gamble, the casinos would probably have to close.

Contrary to the much publicized supposed flight of all the American gamblers from Cuba, none left the island except Meyer Lansky, operator of the Habana Riviera, who went to Miami last week and another operator, whose name escapes us at this moment.

The "notorious" Santo Trafficante is a well-known and well-liked man in Habana. Proof of this was seen wherever we went.

Both Cubans and Americans would call out to him when he walked by and many would walk up to shake his hands and greet him.

We told him that he was one of the most publicized gamblers as far as the American press was concerned. He laughed and said he was not worthy of that distinction.

We believe that the Castro government will permit the gambling casinos to open for the American tourists and the wealthy Cubans.

Many of the gamblers in Cuba believe that the reason they have been so much in the news is because American newspapers are being influenced by Miami Beach and Las Vegas hotel interests which lost a lot of business to the Habana Hotels which have gambling casinos as an additional tourist attraction.[5]

In the following week's edition of *La Gaceta*, Manteiga wrote about one last fascinating meeting in Cuba he had with an old friend, Rogelio Pujol, an employee of the American Embassy. Pujol told Manteiga that, during the revolution, he was approached by members of Batista's dreaded military intelligence police, Servicio de Intelligencia Militar (Military Intelligence Service) or SIM, who inquired about Manteiga. According to Manteiga's January 23, 1959, article in *La Gaceta*:

> While Pujol was walking one day near the Embassy, he was stopped by agents of SIM who were apparently waiting for him.

"Mr. Pujol, the chief would like to ask you a few questions."

"Gentleman, I am an American citizen in the service of the Embassy of the United States and if your chief wants to interrogate me he can come to the Embassy."

"This is not a serious matter and we would appreciate you accompanying us."

He went with the secret military police. Mr. Pujol was questioned by the Chief Advocate of the Army.

"Mr. Pujol, are you the correspondent for La Gaceta of Tampa in the United States?"

"I am not a correspondent for any newspaper. I am serving the United States in the press attaché's office of the American Embassy."

"Do you know Victoriano Manteiga personally?"

"I have known him for many years. I worked for him in Tampa."

"Do you know if he belongs to the Communist Party as we have been told?"

"Victoriano Manteiga is a man of liberal ideas and for that reason he has been fought by the Communists."

Mr. Pujol explained his friendship with Manteiga in detail and then the hard-eyed brute of the SIM said in soft tones:

"Mr. Pujol, we ask you not to tell the American Ambassador about this conversation as we do not wish to be involved in a discussion with the Embassy."

Mr. Pujol was then invited to drink coffee.

Ed. Note—Mr. Pujol is lucky that he is an American citizen, for had he been a Cuban we shudder to think of the beating and torture which might have been his fate.[6]

## 17

# My Return to a Free Cuba

For the first time in my life, I walked Cuban soil owned by the Cuban people. I felt great satisfaction that I had devoted the past four years of my life to an effort that ultimately helped topple one of the most ruthless dictators Cuba had ever known. I was euphoric that the oppressed Cuba I had lived in for the better part of my life was finally free! Although I had already made my life in the United States and had no intention of returning to live in my beloved homeland, it was gratifying that my family who still lived there would now enjoy new hope in a liberated Cuba.

February 2–8, 1959, was my first time back to Cuba since I had spent an extended honeymoon there from November 17, 1953, to March 15, 1954.

For this trip, Victoriano Manteiga provided a signed letter dated January 19, 1959, attesting that I was a representative of *La Gaceta* in case I might need it. If my status as director of Tampa's M-26-7 was not enough to provide me with carte blanche access throughout the nation, adding press credentials to my revolutionary position surely would. However, my brother Mario's new position with the Cuban government outdid both my M-26-7 position and Manteiga's letter.

Mario arrived in Cuba within 24 hours of Fulgencio Batista y Zaldívar fleeing. He and Howard K. Davis flew there from Miami International Airport on a Cessna 175 plane piloted by Davis and his flying school business partner Paul Lazar. They were bringing newly minted President Manuel Urrutia Lleó to assume his position at the presidential palace. They landed at the Columbia Barracks airfield and were met by a group from the M-26-7 who were not able to escort Urrutia to the palace immediately because it was in the possession of the other revolutionary group, the Directorio Revolucionario (DR), which had overseen one of the other rebel strongholds in the mountains, El Segundo Frente del Escambray (the Second Front of the Escambray). The DR had been formed in 1955 as an "armed" branch of the Federación Estudiantil Universitario (FEU). The students who were members of the DR were trained to use weapons. The M-26-7 had not yet occupied the palace. So, after landing, Mario, Davis, and Lazar were taken to someone's residence while Urrutia was meeting with the revolutionary entities mapping out his assumption of power, a process that lasted a couple days and was carried out in Oriente Province.[1]

Davis cannot recall whose residence they stayed in those next few days, but he does remember walking around a jubilant Habana and at one point hearing gunshots. He was told that it was Rolando Masferrer Rojas's "Tigres," Batista's notorious group of assassins, who were not willing to submit to the rebel government. At the designated time within those subsequent couple of days, on January 5, Davis, Mario, and Lazar were notified that Urrutia had returned to Habana, and they would be accompanying him to the palace. They were picked up and reunited with the new president, and the group was given access to the palace.[2]

Davis recalls that it was early evening just after sunset when they arrived and the palace staff offered them something to eat and drink. They were very apologetic that unfortunately there was not much food there so the best they could offer were sandwiches. As the four were sitting around the linen-dressed dining table in the opulent dining room, they joked about feeling like they were "barbarians taking over Rome." Davis and Lazar were dressed in their flight suits, and Mario was in casual attire, so it was almost comical as they pictured themselves in this regal scenario.[3]

After their meal, Mario, Davis, and Lazar were assigned sleeping areas. They passed a bedroom with a large built-in glass refrigerator as they made their way to the rooms. In it were about a dozen fur coats that had belonged to Batista's wife, Marta. Cigars with Batista's name on the cigar ring were on a table. Davis took a couple for his Cuban father-in-law. They had a quiet night, retiring at a reasonable hour since the following day was going to be quite busy.[4]

The international news networks were at the palace that next morning. Howard recalls being interviewed and asked if it was worth it to have been involved in the revolution. Of course, they all gave glowing comments. It was already six days into the new year and the new regime, but the rebel leaders had not yet arrived in Habana. Mario and Davis had been told that Fidel Castro Ruz; his brother, Raúl; and Ernesto "Che" Guevara de la Serna were reluctant to immediately come to Habana because they were suspicious it might be a trap to kill them. So their triumphal arrival did not take place until January 8.[5]

In the meantime, Urrutia and the new staff were getting settled into the palace. Davis decided to go to Camp Columbia accompanied by Lazar to see if they could borrow a Jeep since they were without transportation at the palace. Davis ran into Pedro Luis Díaz Lanz, who was chief of the

Revolutionary Air Force, when they arrived at Columbia. Davis greeted him warmly, but Díaz Lanz reacted nastily when he saw Davis, and angrily said to him, "You are not needed here. You are being detained and are going to be thrown out of the country." He gave Davis no reason for this, so Davis can only guess that it was due to a situation that had occurred the prior year.[6]

At one point that previous year, Díaz Lanz was going to Mexico to try and set up the transportation of arms and ammo to Castro, and he wanted Davis to go with him and help with this. Davis was having health issues at that moment and told Díaz Lanz that he was not able to travel, which greatly upset Díaz Lanz. He offered to go to Mexico at a future time that Díaz Lanz might want him there, but he never heard back from him. After that is when Davis and Jorge Sotus Romero flew to Raúl Castro's camp to deliver arms. So, Davis assumed Díaz Lanz was still angry that he had not helped him get arms to Castro but did help Sotus.[7]

Díaz Lanz put Davis and Lazar on a Piper Cub, which dropped them off in Key West. From there they departed back to Miami. Davis never again saw Díaz Lanz, so that was their last exchange, which left a very bad taste. Davis does not recall notifying Mario about this. However, according to Mario, Davis contacted him from Columbia to advise him of the situation that Díaz Lanz was detaining him. Mario recalls that Díaz Lanz wanted to arrest Davis and keep him detained at Columbia. But Mario says he spoke to Díaz Lanz and requested he let Davis go. That would coincide with his being put on a plane to Key West. While Davis and Mario's recollections of the event differ slightly, I am reflecting what each of them recounted to me concerning the occurrence.[8]

Of note is that a few months into his post as chief of the Revolutionary Air Force, Díaz Lanz became very vocal in his opposition to the Communist influence on the new regime. On June 29, 1959, Castro removed him from his position and Díaz Lanz left for Florida. He dropped anti-Communist leaflets over Habana on October 21, 1959, and, by April 1960, he was recruited by the CIA.[9]

Since Mario had been a pillar in the revolutionary movement from shortly after Batista's coup in 1952 and responsible for arms acquisition in exile, Mario merited a high leadership position in the new regime. Urrutia asked Mario what position he wanted, and he replied, "Minister of Tourism." Mario, Davis, and Lazar had already taken steps to start a private air service for executives who did not want to travel in commercial flights. On December 30, 1958, they formed a corporation called Executive Air Service, Inc., each having 33,000 stock shares apiece. Theirs was to be an exclusive service that had already been authorized by Urrutia. Had all turned out well in Cuba, it would have been the pioneer in what today is known as corporate air services.[10]

## 17. My Return to a Free Cuba

Urrutia instructed Minister of the Presidency Luis Buch Rodríguez to draw up the paperwork naming Mario the tourism minister. But, a couple days later, Urrutia called Mario into his office and very apologetically said that he could not be named to this position. Apparently, Buch communicated to Haydée Santamaría Cuadrado about Mario's naming and she went to see Urrutia to say there was someone she wanted in that position. With Santamaría being such a respected and recognized revolutionary, Urrutia could not deny her request.[11]

Mario was not certain but seemed to recall Oscar Ramirez as the name of the person Santamaría wanted. Remember, he was the owner of the Flagler Theater in Miami where Fidel Castro Ruz spoke on November 20, 1955, and where many M-26-7 activities were hosted. He was someone with whom she had worked in Miami while she and Buch oversaw the M-26-7 National Directorate in Exile. If it was Ramirez, he did not occupy the position for long because Jesús Montané Oropesa then assumed it.[12]

But, for his many contributions to the revolution, Urrutia placed Mario in command of the president's secret service as chief of security at the presidential palace and promoted him to the rank of captain in the Revolutionary Army.[13]

Angel Pérez-Vidal had also arrived within those initial 24 hours and was named palace financial administrator and chief of staff. He oversaw all non-military personnel and functions, as well as duties that fell within the role of vice president, although there was no formal title as such. Pérez-Vidal and his wife, Alma Rivera, lived in the third-floor residential portion of the palace, in a room between the president's quarters and the quarters reserved for Castro when he stayed at the palace. My sister Marta was hired by Pérez-Vidal for a supervisory position in the payroll department. One of her responsibilities was processing the payment of Castro's wages and that of all the palace staff and services.[14]

As previously stated, President Urrutia arrived at the palace on January 5 and Castro on January 8 after a long parade from the Sierra into Habana. A photograph of Raúl Castro ascending the stairs with his wife, Vilma Espín Guillois, and a group of 24 that included Lester Rodriguez Pérez, Juan Almeida Bosque, and Mario may mark the moment Raúl Castro first arrived at the palace. Rodriguez dedicated the photo to Mario on January 20, 1959.

So, by the time I visited Mario in February, he had been in his position as chief of security for about a month.

I spent my first day in Cuba with my family in the Cerro. The next day, I visited my brother at the presidential palace. I arrived at the palace entrance around noon and identified myself to the guards, telling them I was there to see my brother. A guard left to get word to Mario and returned

Lester Rodriguez Perez, Juan Almeida Bosque, Raúl Castro Ruz, wife Vilma Espin Guillois, and Mario Villamia in a group of 24 ascending the presidential palace stairs, possibly on the day the rebels arrived to take possession of the palace. Lester dedicated the photograph to Mario by writing "To comrade Mario Villamia, who always was one of the good ones in the bad moments." Habana, Cuba, January 20, 1959 (photograph by Dirección de Publicidad Palacio Presidencial [Presidential Palace Advertising Department], courtesy Mario Villamia).

a few minutes later to tell me that my brother was in his second-floor office.

I was led up a large marble staircase that was about 12 feet wide. Mario was waiting for me in the doorway of his office and invited me inside. After speaking for a few minutes, we made our way to the palace dining hall for lunch.

The future chief of palace police, Captain José Luis Cuza Téllez de Girón, joined us. He would be named to this position in March. He was in the palace that day, but not yet in his official charge.

Cuza had been commander of Company B in the Segundo Frente del Escambray. After the revolution triumphed, he and his troops lived in the Camp Columbia barracks where Raúl Castro was commander in chief of the military.

## 17. My Return to a Free Cuba

At Cuba's presidential palace when Mario Villamia was chief of security. Unidentified man, unidentified man, Virgilio Jacas Quintana (dentist to whom Mario delivered letters for Faustino Perez Hernandez and Jesus Montane Oropesa via February 1957 secret mission), Jose Suarez Gayol (first Cuban to die under Che Guevara de la Serna's command in Bolivia), Pablo Fernandez Alegre (who helped Mario with arms acquisition in the United States and was Mario's daughter Arlene's godfather), Julio Perez, Lester Rodriguez Perez (who helped Mario with arms acquisition in the United States), Miguel Villamia (Mario and Raul's brother), Mario Villamia, Rene Rayneri, unidentified man. Habana, Cuba, early 1959 (photo by Dirección de Publicidad Palacio Presidencial [Presidential Palace Publicity Department], courtesy of Mario Villamia).

Cuza would later tell me that an incident occurred at the palace in early March involving Urrutia's wife, Esperanza Llaguno Aguirre. One of Urrutia's wife's staff members was fired, and the woman's husband confronted the president wanting to know the reason for her dismissal, making threats. The situation was diffused by the guards, but Palace Military Guard Chief Gilberto Cervantes went to Columbia to discuss the situation with Raúl Castro, who then named Cuza the palace police chief on the spot and charged him with establishing a palace police force composed of by a portion of his troops. The written order naming him to the position is dated March 4, 1959.[15]

During our conversation, I shared with Mario the story of the M-2 I had purchased in Tampa the day before Batista fled.

Since Gabriel Gil Alfonso and I had not had an opportunity to coordinate the handing over of the M-2 to him prior to his spontaneous departure, it ended up staying in Tampa. I did not know what to do with it but did not want it in my house. By this time, my daughter Rhonda was a very active four-year-old. My handgun had been easy to safeguard, but this was not as simple to hide. I had it wrapped up in fabric and kept in the closet of our bedroom, of course with the cartridges and bullets separate. Nonetheless, I was uneasy about having it in our home.

Captain Cuza volunteered to take the rifle, telling me that if I had an opportunity to bring it to Cuba to seek him out. I readily agreed, although I had no idea how I would carry such a weapon onto a boat or airplane in Tampa.

Following lunch, Mario gave me a tour of the palace that ended in my witnessing a Castro speech.

Urrutia may have been president, but Castro was the face of the country. He was the one who delivered freedom to the island, so he was the one the people looked to for reassurance that all would be OK.

He gave many speeches, sometimes multiple speeches per week at venues throughout Cuba.

Fidel Castro Ruz speaking from crowded balcony at the presidential palace. Mario Villamia and Angel Pérez-Vidal are at the top of the photograph near the concrete pillar. It is not known whether this may have been Castro's first address to the people upon arriving at the palace. Note the four photographers with their cameras. Habana, Cuba, January 1959 (photograph by Dirección de Publicidad Palacio Presidencial [Presidential Palace Advertising Department], courtesy Mario Villamia).

I do not recall the substance of his speech. It was so long ago. I remember he was on the palace balcony addressing a large gathering of people as I stood with a group that included Ernesto "Che" Guevara de la Serna and Camilo Cienfuegos Gorriarán in the Grand Ballroom adjoining the balcony. Though I stood only a few feet from the revolutionary hero, both the room and the balcony were so crowded I could barely catch a glimpse of him. I could, however, feel his presence. His passion permeated the atmosphere.

I have a photo Mario gave me of Castro on the balcony giving a speech. In the packed crowd surrounding him are Mario and Pérez-Vidal. Whether this photo is one taken on the occasion I was there, I have no way of knowing.

Before I left Cuba, I visited the Hilton Hotel, which was Castro's permanent residence at the time. I saw him from a distance in the hotel but was again not able to get up close to him.

That was the last time I would ever see him in person.

## 18

# Signs of Trouble

With victory came more responsibility.

The Cuban treasury had been robbed by Fulgencio Batista y Zaldívar. The treasury totaled around $500 million when he stole the presidency in March 1952. Only $70 million remained when he fled Cuba.

We knew we could not replace the $430 million that was stolen, but every little bit helped while the government sought ways to financially stabilize itself.

However, although our goal had changed, our job had not—we raised money, collected goods, and launched a public relations campaign to get others to support Cuba.

Even Tampa's highest official showed his support. Mayor Nick Nuccio formally extended Fidel Castro Ruz an invitation to visit Tampa. His February 11, 1959, letter stated in part:

> As you know, a large portion of the population of Tampa is composed of Cuban citizens from your country, who have a deep affection for you. They have followed your accomplishments with great interest and they have a sincere desire to see the people of Cuba enjoy peace and happiness under your able leadership.

Other M-26-7 members—usually Juan M. Pérez and Mario Iglesias—went to the consulate every day during those weeks that I shared it with Guillermo Bolivar y Morales del Castillo. We had a good relationship with Bolivar and the vice consul, Eliseo Pérez. All was going well.

On February 10, 1959, the Cuban Secretary of State announced that Bolivar had officially been relieved of his duties and his vice consul was named the temporary consul until a permanent one could be chosen. Just as I believed I did good work as head of Tampa's M-26-7 but thought that Victoriano Manteiga was a more natural choice as leader, I thought the same about Pérez taking over as temporary consul. He was a veteran of the Cuban War of Independence, and, at 87 years old, he was experienced yet full of energy.[1]

## 18. Signs of Trouble 189

```
COPY                                                    COPY


NICK NUCCIO              CITY OF TAMPA         AMERICAN MUNICIPAL ASSOCIATION
  MAYOR                EXECUTIVE OFFICES        FLORIDA LEAGUE OF MUNICIPALITIES


                          February 11th
                            1 9 5 9



       Honorable Fidel Castro
       Commander of the Armed Forces of the
       Republic of Cuba
       Havana, Cuba

       Dear Senor Castro:

       As Mayor of the City of Tampa, it is my pleasure to extend
       a most cordial invitation to you to visit our wonderful city
       again as soon as it is expedient for you to leave your country.

       As you know, a large portion of the population of Tampa is
       composed of Cuban citizens from your country, who have a deep
       affection for you.  They have followed your accomplishments
       with great interest and they have a sincere desire to see the
       people of Cuba enjoy peace and happiness under your able
       leadership.

       It would be an honor for all of the citizens of Tampa to
       welcome you.  I hope that you will accept our invitation and
       avail yourself of the opportunity to enjoy the warm hospitali-
       ty which is our pleasure to extend to our visitors from Cuba.


                                       Very cordially yours,



           NN/aw                           Mayor
```

Tampa Mayor Nick Nuccio's letter to Fidel Castro Ruz, inviting him to visit Tampa. Tampa, Florida, February 11, 1959 (from the collection of Raul Villamia).

While my time in the consulate was short, I did make one large impact.

In 1956, the home belonging to Ruperto and Paulina Pedroso—the married couple who saved Martí when he was poisoned—was demolished. And the land, owned by Cuban citizens Manuel Quevedo Jaureguízar and his wife, Mercedes Carillo La Guardia, was deeded to the Cuban government on December 5, 1956, for a Martí memorial. Original plans were to make the Pedroso home a museum. But the structure was too deteriorated to be salvaged. Batista donated some $18,000 to turn it into a park, and the effort was spearheaded by local historian Tony Pizzo, who was the executive vice president of the Pan American Commission, an organization founded to promote trade, commerce, tourism, and cultural relations with Latin America, particularly Cuba.

Architects Ivo A. De Menecis and Frank P. Patterson designed the park, which, according to their sketch, was to have a bronze replica of the Pedroso house in its center, a shrine under a gazebo type structure. Their design was approved by Cuba's Ministry of Public Works, and its unveiling was planned for April 11, 1957, a date commemorating Martí's return to Cuba to fight in the Cuban War of Independence. Domingo Ranon and Maximo Jimenez were the contractors. The City of Tampa under the administration of Mayor Nick Nuccio made the sidewalks around the park. An October 21, 1956, newspaper article titled "Cuba to Raze Martí House to Build Garden Sanctuary" included a photo of the proposed architectural sketch, but the sanctuary was never made.[2]

A concrete wall with wrought iron rails enclosed the property with a double-door iron gate facing Eighth Avenue. Engraved in the concrete entryway over the door were the words "Parque Amigos de José Martí" (Friends of José Martí Park). And this was all that had been done ... there was no shrine or gardens as indicated in the sketch. It was nothing but an open vacant space, surrounded by an iron fence.

Unfortunately, the park was not being well tended. Weeds grew, and garbage accumulated. No one cleaned or maintained the grounds, and there was a large padlock on the entrance doors.

So, I obtained the key to the park's entrance during that time I occupied the Cuban consulate. Club members volunteered to periodically mow the grass and clean the grounds. In a July weekly meeting of the M-26-7, we voted to become official caretakers of the park. No longer was the park kept locked during daylight hours. Subsequently, member volunteers took charge of regularly maintaining the park. We planted white rose bushes, white roses being Martí's favorite flower, featured in his poem "Cultivo Una Rosa Blanca" ("I Have a White Rose to Tend") from his *Versos Sencillos* (*Simple Verses*).[3] The rose bushes were planted for the commemorative event we had there on October 10 in honor of El Grito de Yara (The Yara Outcry), which signaled Cuba's declaration of independence from Spain in 1868, the beginning of the Ten Years' War.

I welcomed a return to normalcy and supported the Revolutionary Government by working hard as a fundraiser.

Membership increased, and the board met once a week to discuss and plan fundraising activities, including forming a Tampa Aid to Cuba committee. The committee in charge of these activities was comprised of

## 18. Signs of Trouble

M-26-7 members planted white rose bushes on October 10, 1959, to celebrate El Grito de Yara (The Yara Outcry), the anniversary of the 1868 start to the Ten Years' War. Cristo Perez, Raul Villamia, Victoriano Manteiga, unidentified man, unidentified man, Carmelo Bueno, and Carlos Carbonell. Photograph appeared in the February 19, 1960, *La Gaceta*, to make the point that the M-26-7 had been caretakers of the Parque Amigos de José Martí (Friends of Jose Marti Park) for eight months prior to the new Cuban consul, Rene Dechard, locking them out of the park to prevent them from hosting the Martí statue's unveiling on February 24, 1960. Tampa (Ybor City), Florida (courtesy of *La Gaceta*).

Carlos Carbonell, Israel Garcia, Ramon Cruz, Juan M. Pérez, José Rodriguez, Carmelo Bueno, José A. Cabrera, Pedro Pérez Nunez, Benigno Garcia, Julio Herrera, Cristo Pérez, Ray Delgado, Max Garcia, Ursula Cruz, Julia Gavilla, Celida Pérez, Violeta Pérez Triana, Marcelino Vila, Mario Triana, Marcelino Pérez, and me. José A. de Cardenas was named to a special committee, along with Roland Manteiga, responsible for collecting from doctors and medical clinics.[4]

We were much more successful in raising money after Batista was ousted than we were during the revolution. With Batista gone, Tampa Cubans no longer had to fear violent retribution for supporting a free Cuba.

In late March we proudly raised $890.82 over a two-week period, a number unheard of during the revolution. We had a fundraiser at the

M-26-7 fundraiser for Cuba's "Aid to The Agrarian Reform" as a participant in the annual West Tampa Sheriff's Association Festival held on Howard Avenue in West Tampa. Standing: Ray Delgado, Carlos Bueno, (man) Quinones (cook at Casa Loma Restaurant), Raul Villamia, unidentified man. Sitting: Juan M. Perez. Tampa, Florida, March 28, 1959 (photograph courtesy of *La Gaceta*, appeared in the April 3, 1959, edition).

Centro Español of West Tampa and at the Sheriff's Festival, both on Howard Avenue in West Tampa.

April 1959 had a few successful fundraising events.

A mid–April fundraiser was held at the Casino Theatre in the Centro Español in Ybor City, managed by Ramon Bermudez. It was supported by Angelo Spoto, our old friend and owner of Florida Printing. He partnered with Tony Frisco of Frisco Printing to provide contributors with ribbons denoting that they gave to the cause. Over the course of two days, we raised $120 at the theater while Spanish movies played.

In late April, I attended a picnic at the Centro Asturiano that totaled 700 people in attendance dining on yellow rice and chicken. Along with Juan M. Pérez and Ray Delgado, I collected $50 in a short period of time.

Also in late April, we welcomed Virgilio Jacas Quintana back to Tampa for a visit. He had been named Deputy Director of Public Works Taxes in Cuba.

The highpoint of our fundraising was raising $2,080 at an event in late May. It was held at the Cuban Club and was attended by Cuban

## 18. Signs of Trouble 193

governmental dignitaries, representatives from the Cuban magazine *Bohemia*, and Dr. Roberto Agramonte y Pichardo. Tampa dignitaries included Mayor Nick Nuccio and Cesar Gonzmart, son-in-law of Columbia Restaurant owner Casimiro Hernandez and renowned violinist, who performed at the event.

May was a special month in terms of collections of supplies too. In mid–May, we shipped 500 boxes of clothes to Cuba. Pedro Aguilera, director of the Department of Assistance to War Victims and Their Families, sent me a letter on May 19, instructing us to send these boxes to them and explaining that they had already requested the Habana customs department to receive them exempt from taxes.[5]

We continued to accept all kinds of donations—money, clothing, food, medical supplies, and so on. When enough donations accumulated, they would be sent to Habana in a small ship operated by Delfa Lines, which made regular trips to Cuba.

However, on August 4, we received a letter from Juan M. Leon Planas, personal delegate from Oriente Province to Minister of Social Welfare Dr. Raquel Pérez Gonzalez, and learned that some of our efforts were for naught. A three-carton, 461-pound shipment of baby food that we had sent to Gabriel Gil Alfonso on January 21 never arrived, and neither had the large boxes of clothing sent in May.[6]

Juan Almeida Bosque, chief of western tactical combat forces, sent me a June 18 response to a mid–April inquiry I had made regarding the status of the baby food shipment, asking for more details so he could determine where it could be. He instructed that further shipments be sent to the attention of 1st Lt. Eugenio Rodriguez, under his command for such matters. But of course, we had already sent the May shipment by then, based on the instructions in Aguilera's May 19 letter. We ascertained they had been stolen—that much cargo does not simply go missing. The cargo may have been taken before it left Tampa, somewhere between the port and its destination in Cuba, or at the destination before it could be accounted for.[7]

It became evident that defeating Batista was not the revolution's finale. There was still a lot to do, and there were still enemies of the revolution looking to return Cuba to the form of government we had worked to oust. The prime reason was that many were worried that Cuba's new laws would hurt their "bottom line."

In his first 100 days in office, President Manuel Urrutia Lleó made changes to the government that helped the peasants but hurt the rich. He cut rents by 50 percent for low-wage earners, properties owned by Batista and his ministers were confiscated, the telephone company was nationalized and the rates were reduced by 50 percent, laws demanding separate facilities for blacks and whites were abolished, and land was redistributed

Cuba's Director of Immigration Ruben Acosta and Deputy Director of Public Works Taxes Virgilio Jacas (the dentist to whom Mario Villamia delivered the letters for Faustino Perez and Jesus Montane in that February 1957 secret mission) visit Tampa's *La Gaceta* office on April 26, 1959. On the sidewalk in front of the newspaper office are: Ray Delgado, Jose de Cardenas, Cristo Perez, Acosta, Juan Contreras, Raul Villamia, Jacas, Manuel Fuentes, Victoriano Manteiga, Roland Manteiga, Juan M. Perez, Gilberto Rodriguez, Jose A. Cabrera, and Carmelo Bueno. Tampa (Ybor City), Florida (photograph courtesy *La Gaceta*, appeared in the May 1, 1959, edition).

among the peasants (this included land owned by Castro's family) to be used for farming.

In support of the new farmers, in January 1959 El Movimiento Patriótico de Tampa de Ayuda al Campesino Cubano (The Tampa Patriotic Movement for Aid to the Cuban Farmers) was founded by Roberto de los Rios. Their clubhouse was in Ybor City on 14th Street between 9th and 10th Avenues, in the same El Pasaje Hotel building that would within the year be housing the M-26-7 headquarters. Members of this group included Joséph A. Casanova, Roberto de los Rios, Felipe "Indio" Jimenez, Abelardo Arteaga (who would, up until his death in 2016, be the official custodian of the keys to the José Martí Park in Ybor), Carlos "Bigote" Nuñez, and

## 18. Signs of Trouble 195

Enrique Mendoza (whose sister was married to Ray T. Williers, secretary of another post–revolution group called Fair Play for Cuba, which I will detail later in the book).

These men raised money and obtained farm equipment for Cuban peasants who acquired land through the agrarian reform program. Part of their fundraising included a pageant to select "Tampa's Queen of the Cuban Agrarian Reform," who would be crowned at the festival taking place on February 11, 1960. A December 10, 1959, letter signed by Cassanova and De los Rios was sent to Carbonell inviting the M-26-7 to submit candidates. This contest was not only done for the financial benefit, but for fostering the bonds of friendship between our two countries.[8]

Still, the U.S. government was not happy about these changes in Cuba. For instance, much of the land given to the peasants was owned by corporations—the telephone company, for example—in the United States. In response, the United States announced that it would no longer supply the technology and technicians needed to run Cuba's economy and later reduced sugar orders. These decisions were made in hope that the new government would fail and the old one could be ushered back in.

The United States also waged an all-out public relations war against Cuba, telling Americans that Cuba was destined to fail and that its government was made up of thieves.

In Tampa, we hoped to negate such statements with our own public relations efforts. Taking up that charge were Victoriano and Roland Manteiga.

Both made public appearances throughout the city, sharing about what they saw in Cuba as opposed to what the U.S. government was preaching. For example, Roland Manteiga spoke at a Lions Club meeting in January and reminded everyone of the atrocities Cuba suffered under Batista, explaining that the people of Cuba saw Castro as an equal to Martí and that they supported the new laws being passed under President Urrutia rather than opposed them as some in the United States claimed.

But mostly, the Manteigas supported the PR efforts through their *La Gaceta* newspaper, using it as a vehicle to print the truth through editorials written by others and themselves.

They also regularly published editorials written by sculptor Juan M. Fidalgo Rodriguez that shared interesting happenings within the Cuban government. One of the more fascinating pieces he sent to *La Gaceta* was published on April 10, 1959, and informed readers that Batista had men in the Cuban government who were regularly plotting the assassination of Fidel Castro Ruz. While Castro was not the president, he was the symbol of the revolution, and murdering him would have been the biggest possible blow against the new government, even larger than assassinating President Urrutia.[9]

On April 7, 1959, at the Church of the Angels in Habana, Victoria Esperanza Lydia Urrutia, eight-month-old daughter of President Urrutia, was baptized by Monsignor Bishop Martin Villaverde. Her godparents were Castro and Graciela Frances Castane, as it states in her baptismal program. Whether Castro did this as a public relations gesture to appeal to the religious sector, we will never know. But a mere three months later, Urrutia was skewered by him and forced out of office. So, it makes one wonder why he would have gone through such a charade.[10]

Excitement built toward the middle of April when Castro visited the United States as a keynote speaker before the Society of Newspaper Editors in Washington, D.C. It was hoped he would also meet with President Dwight Eisenhower while in D.C. It was hoped Castro could help the president to see the truth about the new Cuban government. It was hoped that the two men could agree on how the United States could support the new Cuban government, enabling Cuba to begin to fortify its economy. It was hoped a new era of Cuban/United States relations would be born.

Angel Pérez-Vidal made the arrangements for the trip. Victor Formerio de Yurre Clayton, who at the time was Mayor of Habana, was designated by Urrutia to join Pérez-Vidal and assist him in organizing the trip activities. Coincidentally, decades later while attending Duke University, my grandson Wynter met and became lifelong friends with De Yurre's grandson Anthony De Yurre. Pérez-Vidal and De Yurre traveled to D.C. first and then New York City, where Castro made a speech at Manhattan's Central Park on April 24. This was considered an unprecedented event because Central Park did not allow gatherings for political purposes.[11]

Castro was initially authorized by New York City to conduct his speaking event at the Polo Grounds, a stadium in the Bronx that had hosted polo teams, and, later, numerous baseball, football, and soccer teams. But, after that location was confirmed, Castro asked Cuban journalist Luis Conte Agüero his opinion of the arrangements that had been made for the speech. Agüero said he would have preferred the speech be given in an open public space like Central Park, where it would be difficult to calculate the number of people in attendance. Castro liked the idea and asked Pérez-Vidal to effectuate the change.[12]

At the meeting with the mayor's office, Pérez-Vidal shared Castro's desire to speak at Central Park. He was told the reasons why this was not possible, so he thanked them for all the municipal efforts already expended in obtaining the Polo Grounds. In the same breath, he then said that unfortunately, if Castro could not speak at Central Park, he would regrettably consider not holding any speaking event in New York City. He would only be present for the banquet offered him by the journalists, then immediately depart afterwards, canceling all other scheduled activities,

## 18. Signs of Trouble

including the official welcome planned by the mayor. After a short deliberation, they allowed him to speak at Central Park.[13]

On April 17, 1959, Manteiga, believing the trip could bring progress to Cuba, wrote (note: Manteiga wrote this before Castro departed, but it was published after):

> Castro and His Visit to the United States
> Fidel Castro, Prime Minister of Cuba, will leave Havana for Washington, D.C. this coming Wednesday, this April 15th. In the capital of the United States he will speak before the Society of Newspaper Editors and will express his ideas in such a manner that no one will be able to twist the profound meaning of his words.
> Cuba is carrying out the program of the Revolution which started at the Cuartel Moncada in Santiago de Cuba the 26th of July 1953 and which continued with warfare in the mountains of the Sierra Maestra, Sierra Cristal, Sierra Escambray, etc., and finally ended with the flight of Batista last January 1st.
> The Cuban Revolution is a revolution which is trying to help the people, it is not like other revolutions in other countries, which serve only to replace one "selfish interest" with another.
> And because this is a real revolution that is dedicating the energies and intelligence of its leaders for the good of most Cubans, great obstacles have been placed in the straight path which it follows.
> The Revolution found $70,000,000 in the treasury which had been ransacked by the thieves and thugs of Fulgencio Batista, $430,000,000 less than was there when the ex-sergeant, the "monster," supported by the militarists stole the government on the 10th of March of 1952. Seventy million ... and the price of sugar is at 2.9 cents per pound, when the price was 3.50 and 4.07 and more cents per pound during the years the "Beast" ruled.
> Seventy million, with 500,000 unemployed citizens and this in spite of the fact that the sugar crop is being harvested. Seventy million, and the honest Revolution is being attacked unfairly by important newspapers in both Americas, influenced by news agencies which cry out against the executions of criminals. Seventy million ... with the sugar quota considerably reduced and with the sugar crop expected to exceed 5,800,000 tons.
> Cuba needs economic aid, that is to say, a loan which will foster rapid industrial development to help her rise out of the pits of poverty.
> The news agencies, mentioned by Fidel Castro, would do Cuba a great service if they would cease their slander. Cuba wants and asks the cooperation of the honest press in the United States and in the Latin Americas, the press which does not accept subsidies and which cannot be bribed.
> Cuba now has an honest government, where high government officials in serving their country have accepted smaller salaries than provided by law. They await happier days. Cuba has left "infamy" to enter into "decency" and to deny her help is to "play the game" of the bandits who fled Cuba on the 1st of January and their "friends" in this country.
> Will the task undertaken by the Revolution which is trying to drive away the

"misery" from the fertile Cuban soil be understood by the newspaper publishers? Will the Eisenhower administration help the Government "of the people and for the people" headed by Dr. Manuel Urrutia and Prime Minister Fidel Castro without strict conditions?

The people who intend malice or have little knowledge would place the "red" label, the communist stain, upon the new government of Cuba; but the Cubans and well-informed foreigners know that the Revolution is democratic and that its mission is to create a life of less hardship for the 6 million children, women and men of Cuba.[14]

Unfortunately, the trip was an utter catastrophe in terms of diplomatic relations between Cuba and the United States. On the day Castro arrived, President Eisenhower went to Georgia to play golf and left Vice President Richard Nixon as his representative.

Nixon's meeting with Castro was not productive and, coupled with the Cuban government's decisions that were unpopular among American leaders, the road for diplomatic failure had been paved.

I felt it was a slap in Castro's face to have chosen a golf game over meeting with the new leader of a country 90 miles from our shores and whose history was so intertwined with ours. Our respective nations were distinct threads in one mutual tapestry. I was very disappointed at the reception Castro was given by our government's highest official. I began to feel great concern that this was not the way to start a good relationship with an emerging foreign government. Things tend to end poorly that start poorly. I believed the United States demonstrated great disrespect to Castro. And I feel that this initial act of disrespect is what laid the groundwork for the distancing and eventual diplomatic divorce between our two nations.

I felt bad. I felt very disillusioned. I began to wonder if I had invested all my years of revolutionary involvement in vain. I had had high hopes and great expectations that once Castro came into power our countries would have a good relationship. And when that did not happen, I felt very let down by my adopted country of which I had become a citizen.

A few months later, Habana's La Cabana fortress was hosting nuptials. On June 2, Ernesto "Che" Guevara de la Serna married his second wife, Aleida March. Mario attended the ceremony, appearing in photos of the newlyweds cutting their wedding cake and toasting to their happiness.

And on June 20, Mario's second daughter, Arlene, who was just a couple months shy of her third birthday, was baptized by Father Angel Villaronga at the Corpus Christi Church in Marianao, Habana. Her godfather

## 18. Signs of Trouble

Baptism of Mario Villamia's second daughter, Arlene, at the Iglesia Parroquial del S. Corpus Christi en Marianao church. In center: Mario's wife Carmen Guzman Villamia holding Arlene, Juanita Castro (Fidel Castro's sister) as godmother, Pablo Fernandez Alegre as godfather, and Father Angel Villaronga officiating. Behind them: Irene Villamia (Mario and Raul's sister), Mario, three friends of Juanita, Marta Villamia (Mario and Raul's sister). Habana, Cuba, June 20, 1959 (courtesy of Mario Villamia).

was Pablo Fernandez Alegre, who had assisted Mario with arms acquisition in the United States and was now Sub-minister of Agriculture. Her godmother was Juanita Castro, Fidel's sister.

In early June, Manteiga and his son once again traveled to Cuba to meet with Castro and other friends. During their meeting with Castro, they presented him with the check for $2,080 we had raised at our May fundraiser and inquired about the possibility of him returning to Tampa. Castro explained that he wanted to personally thank the people of Tampa for their assistance and was trying to find the time, but his countless duties were making such a venture difficult.

Roland Manteiga wrote of their visit to Cuba in his *La Gaceta* column on June 12, 1959:

Brief news of our 3-day visit to Cuba:
Cuba ... bella Cuba, a land of plenty is still a land of want. The government of Fidel Castro has ruled 5 months and while much has been accomplished, there still remains much to do.
We talked with Fidel Castro on the afternoon of our return (Monday, 5 p.m.). We found him about 10 pounds heavier than in January, most of it

collected around the waist, we also found him still fighting strong to fulfill the needs of the Cuban people.

He asked us (Victoriano Manteiga and yours truly) to continue helping his and the Cuban people's cause because powerful forces were working against him.

During our short visit with Fidel (45 minutes), we acted as a translator for him in a discussion with an American tomato grower. He was meeting with a group of unemployed Cuban farmers and an American who has much experience in the mass growing of tomatoes in Cuba. It was finally agreed that the man would receive $600 per month and 10 percent of gross sales delivered in the United States.

On Saturday night we found thousands of Cubans "paseando" (strolling) in "El Prado" and on the "Malecon." On Sunday we found many Cubans returning from a day at the beach ... from the Tarara Beach area where we spent Sunday at General Alberto Bayo's home. We found the road back to Habana at dusk loaded with buses and automobiles bumper to bumper for miles. We also found inefficiency in some of the government offices, inefficiency brought about because of the firing of thousands of experienced but corrupt help and hiring honest but inexperienced personnel. However, time will take care of this handicap.

We had lunch with Dr. Faustino Pérez, the young and quiet Minister of the Recovery of Stolen Money and Properties. He told us that his department had already recovered more than $30,000,000 from Batista and his henchmen, not counting furniture and real estate which when sold will add millions more to this amount. Dr. Pérez also told of difficulties confronting him but spoke optimistically about the future.

We saw less bearded soldiers than in January. We took movies (close-ups) of Fidel Castro, Camilo Cienfuegos, "Che" Guevara, Commandante Miret, Mancilo Fernandez, Minister of Labor; General Bayo and his family, and many other well-known Cuban figures. We found our good friend, the well-known sculptor J.M. Fidalgo, who is the secretary of General Bayo, sick in the infirmary of La Cabana.

We spoke briefly with Conte Aguero, famous Cuban TV and Radio news broadcaster of CMQ. He is also a well-known writer. A recent book by him about the life of Eddie Chibás mentions the editor of this newspaper, Victoriano Manteiga, several times as a real friend of Chibás.

We met again our friend of many years, now Ambassador and private secretary to Fidel Castro, the enchanting woman politician Conchita Fernandez. We talked with many happy and not so happy Cubans.

We shall discuss our visit to Cuba in more detail in the weeks to come, including the possibility of a counter-revolution.[15]

*La Gaceta* never did follow up on a report of the assessment of a counter-revolution based on what Roland and Victoriano Manteiga saw and heard while in Cuba in June. However, while they were in Cuba, the *New York Times* reported on June 5, 1959, that Cubans in the United

## 18. Signs of Trouble

States had been planning a counter-revolution and that a Tampa man was involved.

7 Indicted in Miami in Arms Smuggling
The Dominican Consul, a Miami policeman, a Tampa flier and four others were indicted by the Federal Government today for conspiracy to smuggle arms to the Dominican Republic. Prosecutors said they hoped to arraign all next Friday.
The charges stemmed from seizure May 22 at Miami International Airport of a plane laden with guns and ammunition reportedly destined to help Gen. Fulgencio Batista dislodge Premier Fidel Castro of Cuba. General Batista, living in exile in the Dominican Republic, has denied planning such a coup.[16]

The article later listed the plane's pilot as Samuel Poole Jr., a Tampa resident. Charges against Poole were later dismissed.[17]

As Castro told the Manteigas, dark forces were indeed working against Cuba, trying to undo all for which many had fought. We were concerned about Tampa's link and, as Castro asked, we agreed to be more vigilant.

Seeking out counterrevolutionaries was one of many concerns with which Manteiga was burdened. He was also worried about the wellbeing of his friend, Santo Trafficante Jr., who had been arrested and imprisoned in Cuba since they last met.

Manteiga backed most of the decisions made in Cuba since the Revolutionary Government was installed, but he was against what he believed was the unfair incarceration of Santo Trafficante Jr. Further disturbing Manteiga, the United States was pushing for Cuba to deport Trafficante, accusing the infamous Tampa resident of selling narcotics.

On July 3, 1959, Roland Manteiga wrote in *La Gaceta*: "*Santo Trafficante, to our knowledge, has never been accused in Tampa of selling drugs. How can these (U.S.) officers ask for his extradition if they do not have evidence against the Tampa resident who has been living in Havana for the past five years ... if the Cuban authorities have no evidence against Trafficante, it does not seem fair to deport him.*"[18]

Manteiga wrote such defenses of Trafficante knowing that Castro and other Cuban government officials regularly read *La Gaceta*. In the June 12 edition, there was an article reporting that Trafficante and fellow Tampan Henry Saavedra, along with Oscar Reguera Martinez, had been arrested for deportation as "undesireables." The June 19 issue stated that Trafficante had been incarcerated in Triscornia, preventing him from attending his daughter's imminent wedding, and questioned why this was done with no evidence of wrongdoing. It has been rumored that, while never mentioned in *La Gaceta*, Manteiga also spoke one-on-one with Castro about Trafficante's imprisonment and was a major factor in the Cuban government's decision to temporarily release Trafficante, albeit under heavy guard, so he could attend his daughter Mary Joséphine's wedding that was held in Cuba on June 21, 1959.[19]

On July 10, *La Gaceta* published photos of that wedding. In the same edition, Roland Manteiga wrote of his trip with his father to Cuba over the Fourth of July weekend that included a visit with Trafficante in Triscornia:

> We spent the 4th of July weekend in Habana, Cuba. Lovely Habana, with the very rich and the very poor.
> 
> We interviewed Santo Trafficante in Triscornia (Cuba's Ellis Island). The Tampan, who is facing deportation, appeared to be in the best of health. In fact, he looked better than we had ever seen him before.
> 
> Triscornia, which lies at the top of a hill overlooking the harbor, is really quite lovely and peaceful.
> 
> Santo is permitted to have all the visitors he wants and there are no strict regulations.
> 
> Santo's lovely and gentle wife spends many hours of the day with him in the gardens of Triscornia.
> 
> He told us that the Cuban authorities treated him very nice and were very generous in their attention. He is permitted a radio and a T.V. set. There are no cells at Triscornia.
> 
> Santo is a great admirer of Fidel Castro and will faithfully watch and hear Castro every time he speaks over T.V. None of Castro's speeches are shorter than two hours.
> 
> We talked with Ruben Miro at Triscornia. Miro was the leader of the "invaders" of Panama several months ago. The Pan-American was deported to Miami this week.
> 
> We stayed at the Hotel Comodoro on beautiful Miramar Beach this trip. The Comodoro is also a "yacht club" for the moderately wealthy Cubans of the Habana area and we can guarantee you that many of Cuba's loveliest girls spend the weekend at the Comodoro Club with their families.
> 
> Real beauties can be found frequently in abundance at the Comodoro.
> 
> We talked with Commandante Camilio Cienfuegos and his aide, who was in Tampa recently, in Sammy Paxton's restaurant, right across from the Habana Hilton. The Cuban hero can be seen at Sammy Paxton's several times each week, even though it might be for only a few minutes.

[Author's note: Sammy Paxton was a native of Tampa who opened clubs throughout the Gulf Coast. In the early 1950s, he moved to Cuba and opened his restaurant.]

> We were accompanied by the famed Cuban sculptor and revolutionist J.M. Fidalgo during our stay in Habana. He is the man who wrote to us in 1955 from Mexico saying that he was sending a young man named Fidel Castro to us because Castro needed help in his fight against the tyrant of Cuba, Fulgencio Batista.
> 
> We enjoyed an early morning visit with Dr. Juan Orta, secretary of the

Prime Minister's office, at his home in the Miramar sector and later saw the white haired Orta at the Prime Minister's office. He and the much-admired Conchita Fernandez, personal and political secretary to Castro, tried to get us an appointment with Castro on Monday, but they could not locate him.

We took movies of and with Dr. Faustino Pérez, the gentle and soft-spoken Minister of Recuperation of Stolen Properties. We enjoyed several telephone conversations with the dynamic General Alberto Bayo at his home in Tarara, but because of the tight schedule we could not arrange a personal interview. His charming wife was in Mexico for a few days. We also visited Carlos Franqui, the editor of Cuba's most influential newspaper today, "Revolución." This newspaper is the official organ of Castro's party, the 26th of July.

Cuba's most famous TV and radio news commentator, Conte Aguero of CMQ-TV, was extremely kind to us and "La Gaceta" during a five minute interview he did of us on his one-hour program. He conducted one similar to Dave Garroway's Today Show.

His program begins at 1 p.m. and since this is during the siesta hour it is the most viewed news program in Cuba today. Saw the fabulous show at the Capri but missed the others for lack of time.

We got a peek at Cesar Romero, who was staying at the Habana Riviera. Romero will start acting in a movie to be filmed on the Isle of Pines.

While the newspapers here were full of news about shootings and bombings in Habana, we traveled nearly four hundred miles in Habana during our three days there and we heard and saw no shootings or bombings.[20]

And then I prepared for another visit to Cuba that was set to begin July 10 and was indeed a busy one.

## 19

# Visiting Santo Trafficante Jr.

I was about to become a gun smuggler.

My brother Fernando, who had lived in Cincinnati since 1946, sold an apartment building that he owned and returned to Cuba. He asked if I would come to Ohio to help him move and drive one of his two station wagons back.

He wanted to come to Tampa and then go to Cuba via the Key West ferry, taking one of the cars on the ferry.

Fernando had everything ready for the move, so all that needed to be done was load up the cars with his belongings.

During the trip the thought of taking the M-2 rifle to Cuba in Fernando's car entered my mind. Fernando did not like my idea. But I told him that the United States was not going to search his car when it left for Cuba. I further said that I would call Captain José Luis Cuza Téllez de Girón, the chief of the palace police, if they searched the car and found the rifle when entering Cuba. After I explained this to Fernando, he agreed with my plan. We arrived in Tampa tired, so I went to bed a little before 11 p.m. since I had to work the next day.

We decided to drive the green Pontiac station wagon to Cuba, so I began to study the car and consider the best place to hide the rifle. Under the seat? Inside the door panels? In the motor? I figured these would be the places most likely searched. Then I raised the car a little and got underneath it to observe what the frame looked like. There, I found a place where I could hide the rifle. I took the M-2 apart, separated the metal trigger barrel from the wooden butt, and for some reason marked in ink my initials RV inside the butt.

I wrapped the two pieces individually in a thick plastic. Then, using wire, I attached them to the beam of the auto frame and painted the plastic covering with a color matching the beam. I waited a few minutes, mixed soil and water to make mud, and, with a brush, spread it all over the area where the rifle was to give it better camouflage.

## 19. Visiting Santo Trafficante Jr.

A couple of days later, at around 9 a.m., we headed out to Key West down Highway 91, also known as the Tamiami Trail. The weather was good, and we arrived in Key West about 4 p.m.

After settling at our small hotel room, I went to the car and had a look underneath it. Everything was just as it was when we left Tampa.

The next morning, July 10, we woke up around 6 a.m., took a shower, and went to have some breakfast at a nearby restaurant. Back at the hotel, we packed up the few belongings from our overnight stay, checked out, and made our way to the ferry dock. We waited for about 20 minutes before our car was loaded aboard. I was a little worried, but by 9 a.m. I could relax when the ferry started to move. The trip was pleasant. Neither Fernando nor I had anything about which to be concerned.

We arrived in Habana sometime around 2 p.m. Shortly afterwards, they began unloading the vehicles. It was our turn to go through Customs and Immigration. We had no problem with immigration, but, when I moved the car forward to be inspected by Customs, an agent ordered us to get out of the car, opened all the doors, and looked inside. He asked me to open the hood and inspected the motor. Then he searched our luggage. In mine, he found one of the two cartridges that I had forgotten to put with the other parts of the rifle underneath the car. Instead, I had stuck it in my suitcase without thinking. Before the agent said anything, I told him that it was for Captain Cuza, chief of police at the presidential palace. The agent told me that it was not permitted to bring arms into Cuba. He said he would have to confiscate the cartridge and that I should tell Captain Cuza to come claim it at the Customs Office. He gave us his name so we could relay it to Cuza.

They never looked beneath the car.

When we left the disembarking area and were on the street next to it, we found a pay phone so I could call the palace and speak with Mario. He came to the phone after a few minutes, and I told him I was at the docks, having come with Fernando in his car on the ferry, and that I had brought the M-2 for Cuza. I said I wanted to deliver it to him. He was very happy to hear the news and told me to come to the palace garage.

We parked the car near the entrance to the garage on Monserrate Street and asked the attendant to let Cuza and Mario know we were there. They came out to meet us.

After greeting one another and talking for a few minutes, Cuza asked me where the rifle was.

He was surprised when I started to go underneath the car.

I came out with the two plastic covered packages within about 10 minutes. He was astounded at the gumption we had to bring this from Tampa underneath the car on the ferry.

He brought the packages into the garage, unwrapped the pieces, and began to assemble the rifle. I told Cuza that Customs had confiscated the other cartridge, but the agent told me not to worry because he could go pick it up. I gave him the agent's name. Cuza was very pleased and thanked me.

In my 2015 visit to Cuba with daughters Rhonda and Denise, we fortuitously were able to see Cuza at his home and had a chance to talk about the rifle. He used that rifle for quite a while, even taking it with him on certain missions to Moa in the Holguin Province of Cuba. I would have loved to have seen that rifle once again and had a look at my initials that I had inscribed inside it. Cuza turned it in at the completion of his deployments. Since M-2s were rather rare at the time, I had often wondered if that might have been the M-2 that Ernesto "Che" Guevara de la Serna used and that was by his side when he was killed in Bolivia on October 9, 1967. And though the M-26-7 was supposed to have reimbursed me the $100 I paid Max Garcia for that rifle, they never did. So, I guess that technically makes me its owner.

During this July 1959 visit to Cuba, I had an opportunity to spend time with some of the old comrades from the Tampa M-26-7, among them Juan M. Pérez, who had left Tampa a few months earlier to assume a position with the Ministry of Education. I went a couple of times to watch a baseball game at Cerro Stadium and visited with buddies from my playing days.

And I also saw Santo Trafficante Jr., a visit set up through Mario, who, shortly after the revolutionary triumph, became acquainted with the alleged Tampa don.

There was a fellow who worked in Palace Security under Mario who had been in the M-26-7 in Habana and knew many of the people having to do with the casinos because he used to frequent them. And at the request of the mafioso, he set up a dinner meeting with Mario and Trafficante.

Mario was unsure why Trafficante was wishing to meet him but went ahead and agreed to go. The meeting occurred at some point after Mario was named chief of security for President Urrutia but before Trafficante had been arrested.

The dinner meeting was at the Plaza Hotel restaurant. While the exact details of the conversation have faded with time, Mario recalled that the purpose of the meeting possibly had to do with Trafficante getting an idea what might be coming down the pike regarding the status of the casinos. He probably figured Mario was privy to information that would be of benefit in determining their fate as the new government took steps to make changes. This must obviously have taken place during the period when the decision to shut down the casinos had not yet been made and the clubs'

## 19. Visiting Santo Trafficante Jr.

proprietors had not yet been sent to Triscornia to be detained and eventually deported.[1]

When I asked for a meeting with Trafficante, Mario used his government connections to set it up.

Mario drove me to the Port of Habana. We parked near the wharf and boarded the ferry to Triscornia, which was located on the northern side of the Habana Port between the town of Cojimar and the Cabana Fortress, an eighteenth-century complex that remains the largest such in the Americas.

The detention center was adorned by a collection of around 50 homes and a grocery store. It was a short walk from where the ferry docked. We entered the detention center's administrative office, explained our intentions, and were led to the center's patio, where we were told to wait. I saw Trafficante approaching us within a few minutes.

As I stated earlier, I had never met Trafficante. I would occasionally see him in Ybor City, but we were never introduced and had no reason to speak. I knew his brother, Henry, with whom I worked at Tiffany Tile, but not well enough to call him a friend.

I introduced myself to Trafficante and explained that I was there on behalf of Victoriano Manteiga, who had asked me to stop by and see him. Although Manteiga had visited with him earlier that month, he had requested I check in on him during my trip. After so many years, I do not recall the details of the reason why Manteiga had charged me with making sure I saw Trafficante, but it could possibly be that Manteiga asked me to see if Mario could intervene in getting him released.

Triscornia was not a regular prison. Trafficante was not locked in a cell, and he could move about in this immigrant detention center as he wished. He was also dressed and fed well.

We walked the yard for about 15 minutes and made small talk, mostly about Tampa, never broaching the topic of politics.

Trafficante, however, did ask Mario if he could do anything to help him get back home to the United States.

Mario agreed that he would see what could be done. We wished him well and said goodbye, my first and only conversation with the famed gangster.

When Mario returned to the palace, he asked for Urrutia to release Trafficante and send him back to the Unites States, noting that they just had him detained there with no plan on what to do with the Tampa man.[2]

Mario later shared that he did not like exchanging favors with these underworld people, but did him this courtesy as he would have for any American citizen who was in an immigration difficulty.[3]

Urrutia called Triscornia and ordered Trafficante to be released, but the president was ousted before the alleged gangster was freed.

On July 17, 1959, Fidel Castro Ruz went on national Cuban television and, during a three-and-a-half-hour speech, declared President Urrutia to be treasonous and unfit to serve in office because he was hampering reforms and his anti–Communist stance could hurt the nation.[4]

In response, Cubans staged rallies demanding that Urrutia resign.

I have no recollection of watching this televised speech or the public uprising that occurred afterwards where the palace was surrounded by people demanding his resignation. I surmise there was little visible protest occurring in my Cerro neighborhood, which was far from the palace.

Urrutia gave up the presidency later that day. Angel Pérez-Vidal is the one who typed up his letter of resignation and handled all the logistics for getting him; his wife, Esperanza; and their sons, Alejandro and Jorge, safely out of the palace through a somewhat hidden entrance out of the view of the bloodthirsty throng. Pérez-Vidal's wife, Alma Rivera, remained at the palace with Urrutia's 11-month-old daughter, Victoria Esperanza, and partially blind elderly mother, Herminia Lleó, who were not fit to travel in the abrupt and dangerous manner in which they had to depart. Safe passage for them was provided in subsequent days.[5]

Obviously, Urrutia's departure directly affected Mario's position at the palace. A new president would be bringing in a new staff.

Days later, Osvaldo Dorticós Torrado was appointed president by Castro. Mario was able to remain in the palace at the United Press International office, but, with his friend Urrutia now gone, he no longer served in a position of power.[6]

I do not recall Mario and I having much conversation about it during those initial few days the presidency changed hands. After all, I was staying at our family home in the Cerro and Mario was living with his wife and daughters in Vedado, so it was not like we were all around the dinner table each night.

But certainly, in the many years after he returned to the United States, we often spoke of the great disillusionment he felt not only by having his Minister of Tourism position yanked from him, but also having Urrutia forced to resign due to false charges made by Castro.

Mario was beginning to see a different side of Castro, and the encroaching tentacles of Communist ideology were concerning to him. He often recounted that, whenever Castro would see him, he would put his arm around Mario's shoulder and ask him how things were going. Mario always responded that all was well. Of course, he had his very strong opinions regarding the trajectory of things, but knew better than to share his thoughts with Castro.

19. Visiting Santo Trafficante Jr.

M-26-7 members welcoming Raul Villamia at the airport on July 28, 1959, upon his return from a July 10–28 visit to Cuba. Standing: Carmelo Bueno, Alberto Nunez Bordon, Cristo Perez, Raul, Victoriano Manteiga, Pedro Perez Nunez, Ray Delgado, Julio Herrera. Kneeling: unidentified man, Mario Iglesias, Benigno Garcia, Jose A. Cabrera. Tampa, Florida (photograph by Eddie Hernandez, courtesy of *La Gaceta*, appeared in the July 31, 1959, edition).

Nevertheless, at least for those almost three weeks I was in Cuba to witness these key historical events, we tried to make the best of it and keep a positive outlook in support of the long-sought Cuban renaissance we had worked so hard to put in place.

On July 26, the country celebrated the sixth anniversary of the Moncada attack. There was a great assembly in the Plaza Civica commemorating this historic first blow of the revolution. Hundreds of thousands of farmers from all over the island, who for the first time owned the land they were tilling, came to Habana for the event.

My family and I went to the gathering.

The streets were adorned with brightly colored banners hanging on and between buildings. Farm machines and equipment and electromechanical projects made by students of Belen, the prestigious Jesuit school Fidel and Raúl Castro had attended, were on display for an agricultural expo at the Capitolio (capitol).

I was relishing this fresh start my beloved homeland had been given, and already noticed the positive impact the new regime had made, particularly within the agricultural and educational spheres.

The plaza—about a 10-minute walk from our home—had been built after I had moved to the States, and it was a very large area. This was the first and only time I had ever seen such a large group of people in one location. I was awestruck. We were there for about an hour, and then decided to go back home to watch it on television.

The following day I spent around the house with my family and with my mother. I remember that in her living room an M-26-7 flag hung in the window.

When I returned to Tampa on July 28, Manteiga and 10 members of the M-26-7 welcomed me at the airport. A photo of the group appeared in the July 31, 1959, edition of *La Gaceta* with an article titled "Recibimiento Al Compañero Raul Villamia."[7]

## 20

# New and Old Enemies

Suddenly, those once against Fidel Castro Ruz were for him.

While I was in Cuba as a true representative of Tampa's M-26-7, there was another Tampa Cuban masquerading as such—Ruben Fabelo. The same Ruben Fabelo who once denied Castro a few minutes on his radio program to promote his Ybor City fundraiser was in Cuba as an "ambassador" from Tampa. Fabelo, remember, regularly brought a group of entertainers under the name *Fiesta en Tampa* to Cuba to perform.

Fulgencio Batista y Zaldívar would continue to support *Fiesta en Tampa* as long as Fabelo said good things about Batista and his rule on his radio program. Batista was so supportive of Fabelo that he awarded him the Carlos de Céspedes Medal of Honor, which was given to people or entities for their cultural, social, political, or other contributions to the Cuban government.

Tampa's M-26-7 would not allow such a lie to become the truth. He never helped us. He instead tried to hinder us. We learned that Fabelo was traveling to the city of Camaguey in Cuba in July with a group he was calling "Embajada Fiesta En Tampa" (Fiesta in Tampa Ambassadors) and his fellow "ambassadors" included Enrique Someillán and other members of the radical group that caused us so many problems. It was incredible that these men were going to Cuba as Tampa's representatives.

So, we sent a letter to the municipality informing them of Fabelo's conduct against the revolution to expose him for the fraud he truly was.

Juan M. Pérez, who had relocated to Cuba and been given a high-ranking position in the nation's Ministry of Education, then wrote an article about Fabelo for the Cuban newspaper, *Revolución*, detailing Fabelo's lack of support for the revolution prior to victory. Via the article, Pérez requested that no official support be given to Fabelo's group when they traveled to Cuba for their cultural exchange trip.

I do not know specifically what happened while Fabelo was in Cuba in July 1959, but he must have been either embarrassed or treated poorly due to our letter and the article, because he sought revenge upon us when he returned to Tampa. He did so by publishing a one-time edition of a small, 16-page newspaper called *Ecos* that was circulated throughout Tampa's Latin communities. This newspaper's sole purpose was to smear the true supporters of the revolution and to prop himself up through a series of lies.[1]

For instance, Fabelo published a letter dated June 17, 1958, that was allegedly sent to him by Gabriel Gil Alfonso just days after Gil arrived in Tampa. The signature on the letter looked like Gil's, but his was simple and easy to forge. More importantly, the message gave us reason to doubt the letter's authenticity.[2]

The letter began with the words, "*In the name of the 26th of July Committee in Tampa, we thank you for the cooperation you have given to the cause of the liberation of Cuba.*" It is strange that Gil would have used the word "Committee" in the title of the club rather than "Movement," which was our official name and the name by which we were known. Still, it could be argued that he used "Committee" because the National Directorate in Miami used the term "Committee in Exile" as part of their title. If this were the only issue we had with the letter, an argument could be made that we in fact did not have an argument against the letter's legitimacy. However, we had further proof.[3]

Gil arrived in Tampa on June 6, 1958. Two days later, at our meeting at La Casa Loma Restaurant we told Gil about Fabelo's refusal to support the revolution. It would therefore be incredible if, nine days later, Gil sent Fabelo a letter thanking him for his support. Gil had no reason to doubt our word. Fabelo had neither invited Gil on his radio show nor spoken out against Batista. Finally, Gil never told us that he wrote a letter to Fabelo, which he would have done at a meeting per protocol. We believed that Fabelo wrote or had someone write the letter when he returned from his first trip to Cuba following the revolution's victory. Ultimately, I had occasion to personally ask Gil about this letter when I visited him in Cuba in 2010, and, as we had suspected, he confirmed not having written it.

This letter was not the only questionable item published in *Ecos*. The newspaper also included a telegram from Cuba dated July 13, 1959, that Fabelo claimed to have received from Gil thanking him for his support and for sympathizing with the revolution. Any person could have sent him that telegram and typed Gil's name. No identification was needed to send a telegram, and it did not need to bear the signature of the sender. We believed this was another fraudulent attempt to put words in Gil's mouth. And when later inquiring with Gil about it, he also denied sending it.[4]

In another section of the newspaper, Fabelo discussed the letter we sent to Camaguey and then printed a list of 23 M-26-7 members who signed it, referring to us as his "accusers." To discredit us, he said that Pérez and

# "Le Partimos La Siquitrilla" - R. Fabelo
—Vea Página 8

TAMPA, FLORIDA, JULIO 1959

## La Mejor Embajada De FET

A juzgar por el recibimiento oficial de la Embajada de EE. UU.A. en La Habana, las cortesías de Aduana, la publicidad, en la prensa, radio y televisión de Cuba; así como el hecho que en Tampa el Tribune, Times y Canal 13 cedieron amplio espacio y tiempo a la Sexta Embajada de F.E.T., puede decirse que ha sido la mejor hasta la fecha. Ni un solo incidente desagradable entre el grupo; cumpliéndose el programa al pie de la letra y viéndonos obligados a cancelar o no poder aceptar otras invitaciones por falta material de tiempo. Qué más se puede pedir?

Visitamos La Habana, Camagüey y Varadero (Matanzas)—3 provincias y ¿quién sabe cuántos pueblos?

**IMPORTANTE CABLE DEL COMANDANTE GABRIEL GIL**
(Vea Página 9)

LOS QUE FIRMARON LA CARTA ENVIADA AL COMISIONADO DE CAMAGUEY

He aquí la relación de los nombres de los que aparecen como firmantes de la carta dirigida al Comisionado de Camagüey: Raúl Villamía, Juan M. Pérez, Carmelo Buenobonell, Marcelino Golán, Orlando Bueno, Marcelino Vila, Israel García, Rafael Durán, Ray Delgado, Mario Iglesias, Benigno García, Julio Herrera, Ramón Somoano, Pedro Pérez Núñez, Zenaida García, Célida Pérez, José Luis Mirranda, Juan de la Rosa, Ramón Cruz, Benny Cuéllar y Cristo Pérez.

El refrán dice: "el que calla otorga". Si alguien de los que aparecen aquí, no firmaron la citada carta, quedan invitados a negarlo por escrito. Acusaremos recibo de tu negativa y le daremos la publicidad necesaria.

El Municipio de Camagüey

*Por Resolución del Señor Comisionado Municipal...*

**Huésped Distinguido**

*[seal/signature]*

Camagüey, Junio 13 de 1959

DOBLE HONOR — El Comisionado de Camagüey, Sr. José Aguero Ferrin, al conocer bien la actuación de Fabelo para con los revolucionarios en Tampa, rompió el Diploma que ya tenía Fabelo con su nombre pintado por un dibujante, para que no sólo llevara la firma del Comisionado Municipal, sino que con su propio puño y letra escribió el de Fabelo.

RECIBIMIENTO — Por primera vez, a la llegada de la Embajada F. E. T. al Aeropuerto de Rancho Boyeros, se encontraba esperando, para recibir oficialmente a los tampeños, el Sr. Kilday, oficial de la Embajada de EE.UU.A., en La Habana. Aquí lo vemos estrechando la mano de Rubén Fabelo. Solicitó el Sr. Kilday la cooperación del Departamento de Aduana y el delegado Sr. Oteiza Setién extendió toda clase de cortesías al grupo de Tampa.

**Niega Pastorita Núñez El Uso De Su Nombre**

Cuando se inició una colecta por F.E.T., personas mal intencionadas publicaron una hojita avisando que el dinero para la Reforma Agraria sólo debía remitírsele a Fidel Castro o Pastorita Núñez. En carta al Sr. Florentino Santos, que indagó este asunto, Pastorita Núñez niega autorización del uso de su nombre para colecta de ninguna clase.

**Acusa miembro del 26 instituciones tampeñas**

Afirma que negaron su apoyo al Dr. Castro en el viaje que realizara en 1955 a esa ciudad y que hoy critican a los verdaderos revolucionarios

**Fotos Del Acusador De Fabelo**
(Vea Páginas 8 y 9)

Nos visita el señor Juan Manuel Pérez, miembro del 26 de Julio de Tampa, que además integra la organización «Tampa Aid to Cuba», creada para recabar fondos para la Reforma Agraria, quien desea poner de manifiesto la actitud de distintas organizaciones tampeñas.

Según el señor Pérez algunas instituciones como el Círculo Cubano de Tampa, la sociedad Martí-Maceo y el programa radial La Hora Latinoamericana, que dirige el señor Rubén Fabelo, hoy se autodenominan revolucionarias, cuando en realidad negaron su apoyo al doctor Fidel Castro durante la visita que éste hiciera a esa ciudad en el mes de noviembre de 1955.

Continúa manifestando nuestro visitante que a título de revolucionarias esas organizaciones fomentan intercambios de relaciones y tienen anunciada una embajada artística que se proyectan traer en el próximo mes de Julio, acto este al que él considera no debe dársele apoyo oficial de ninguna clase, por su anterior comportamiento, el cual según afirma...

Pérez, puede dar fe el propio doctor Fidel Castro.

Termina sus planteamientos el señor Pérez manifestando que le apoyan en su declaraciones miembros del 26 de Julio de Tampa de probada ejecutoria, entre los que cita a Raúl Villamía, Carmelo Bueno, Max García, Mario Triana, y Benigno García.

**ACUSACION HECHA POR JUAN M. PEREZ EN CUBA**

(Vea Pag. 3)

---

Front page of *Ecos* newsletter, a one-time 16-page publication by Ruben Fabelo, Spanish radio station host of the *Fiesta En Tampa* program. Apparently published to discredit the Tampa M-26-7 and self-adulate Fabelo's role in and support of the revolutionary movement. Tampa, Florida, July 1959 (from the collection of Raul Villamia).

I fomented a disturbance at the Tampa International Airport when two captains of the Rebel Army—Rene Gonzalez and Carlos Borjas—arrived in Tampa for a visit. He claimed that, because of the disturbance, parents of the girls who were part of the F.E.T. Ambassadors, on the day of their departure, requested police protection from Mayor Nick Nuccio. According to Fabelo, Mayor Nick Nuccio assigned two policemen, Reinaldo

Abreu and George Rodriguez, indicating that if Pérez and I showed up at the airport we would have been asked to leave. This was a total lie. Why would we protest two officials of the Rebel Army we supported?[5]

Besides such an act being out of character for Pérez and me, it was logistically impossible. I was visiting Cuba at the time of these supposed episodes. I was not in Tampa. Nor was Pérez. He had been living in Cuba since May.

These distractions were becoming tiresome.

## 21

# A Dead Revolutionary in Tampa

A ghost was seen in Ybor City in November 1959.

On October 28, 1959, a small plane taking Camilo Cienfuegos Gorriarán from Camaguey to Habana disappeared. Presumed lost at sea, Cienfuegos was pronounced dead.

Those working against the revolution then began spreading two conspiracy theories. The first was that Fidel Castro Ruz, fearing Cienfuegos's popularity was approaching his own, was behind the deadly crash. The second was that Cienfuegos was unhappy that Cuba was moving toward Communism. Knowing such an opinion meant Castro would want him dead, Cienfuegos escaped the island nation. Castro was willing to pretend Cienfuegos was dead because he was too embarrassed to admit that a leader of the revolution had fled, went the theory.

Both sound ridiculous to me. A plane crashed. A hero died. End of story.

Still, some in Tampa wanted so badly to believe the second conspiracy theory that they thought they spotted Cienfuegos in our city. Or they wanted people to believe it so badly that they lied that they saw him there.

It began with a *Tampa Tribune* article on November 18, 1959, quoting an anonymous source who claimed to have personally spoken with Cienfuegos. *"The informant, who asked that his identity be withheld, said he has talked with Cienfuegos recently,"* read the article. *"He said the officer, a right-hand man of Cuban Prime Minister Castro, has shaved his beard and is living in Ybor City."*[1]

According to a November 19, 1959, *Tampa Tribune* article, Cienfuegos allegedly arrived in Tampa in the following way: He and three other Cubans flew their plane from Camaguey to an abandoned World War II airstrip on Cayo Largo, a small island off Cuba's southern coast. They then filled the gas tank and flew to a deserted strip of highway north of Naples where automobiles flashing high beams created a makeshift landing strip.

From there, they went to Ybor, where anti-Castro Cubans were willing to help him change his identity and forever hide in safety in the United States. Chief of the Tampa Police Department Neil Brown was quoted in that November 19 article saying the claims were "ridiculous."[2]

Still, according to a November 19 article in the *St. Petersburg Times*, the U.S. Border Patrol took the tale seriously enough to send agents to Tampa. *"We are heading down all leads, but we have had no success,"* John Bradford, head of the Border Patrol, told the press.[3]

One tip led the Border Patrol to the home of Tampa doctor José R. Suarez, according to news archives. Instead of Cienfuegos, they discovered Radio Cremata Valdes, a Cuban senator who served under Fulgencio Batista y Zaldívar, the president overthrown by Castro. He was there legally as an alien resident of Tampa visiting Suarez.

Then a November 20, 1959, *Tampa Tribune* article told of Lawrence G. Gifford, a Bradenton mailman moonlighting as a private investigator. After he had spent the evening in the Latin District asking questions about Cienfuegos, Gifford said, he was assaulted in the dark near the Ybor railroad tracks by a Spanish-speaking man. He could not further identify his attacker.[4]

Neither the press, nor law enforcement, nor private investigators ever found proof that Cienfuegos was in Ybor.

The reason being, of course, that he was tragically killed.

## 22

# Who Freed the Gangster?

The gangster was free.

On August 19, 1959, Santo Trafficante Jr. was released from Triscornia.

Then, on November 11, 1959, he boarded a National Airlines flight, leaving the nation of Cuba forever.

However, while this signified an end to his relationship with the island nation, his story has never really ended. For decades, theories have abounded as to why and how he was freed.

My brother Mario contended that his talk with Manuel Urrutia Lleó is what led to Trafficante's release, even if it occurred after he left the presidential office.

Some believe that a secret deal was brokered by Jack Ruby between an imprisoned Trafficante and Fidel Castro Ruz. Supposedly, he would work as a Castro agent in the United States in return for Trafficante's release. This supposed deal would one day link him to President John F. Kennedy's assassination.

That Kennedy theory has never been backed by anything but hearsay and circumstantial evidence, with the story first being reported in the book *Mob Lawyer* written by Trafficante's attorney, Frank Ragano. But historians have found countless inaccuracies in Ragano's story, the most telling being that Trafficante was not even in Tampa on the day Ragano claimed that the infamous gangster confessed to him there that he was involved in Kennedy's murder.[1]

Then there is the theory that Trafficante paid to be released. The Cuban government was broke, and a monetary offer would surely have been welcomed. This theory was supported by Ellis Clifton, the head of Hillsborough County's Vice Squad, who picked Trafficante up at the airport in Tampa. According to Clifton's account, told to journalist Paul Guzzo, this was all part of his secret deal with Castro. I must again stress that I have no proof that the deal was made. However, Clifton, armed with a subpoena that linked Trafficante to the 1957 murder of famed New York gangster Albert Anastasia, met Trafficante when he arrived in

Tampa. This is the only firsthand account of Trafficante's arrival of which I know.²

Years later, Clifton would tell Guzzo: *"I cut a deal with a Cuban official from National Airlines and another with the Immigration Department. [The Sheriff's Office] had [contact with] a man who was chief of the Cuban Air Force, and the sergeant in my department talked to him at least once a week to find out Santo's status and when he was getting out. So, one night, around 12:30 a.m., I got a phone call from National Airlines and the Immigration Department saying they had put Trafficante on a plane and he would be landing in Florida soon."*³

Clifton instructed the Cubans to detain Trafficante until he arrived, armed with a New York County District Attorney Office subpoena from the Albert Anastasia murder case.⁴

Clifton said that, when he arrived, Trafficante *"wasn't dressed all natty like he normally was. His pants were short to the top of his shoes. His cuffs were also short, and he had on a real ratty shirt and shoes."* It looked, he remembered, like they dressed him in *"something they found in the corner."*

> It looked like they dressed him as poor as they could to make him look bad. I barely recognized him. I looked him up and down and said, "I am Captain Clifton with the Hillsborough County Sheriff's Office," and he said, "Clifton, you son of a bitch, you've been hounding my ass ever since I first saw you as a reporter." I let him rave on and on, but I said, "The bottom line is, if you show your face on the street, we have a court order to arrest you every time we see you." Well, he raved on for a bit again and we chatted back and forth and I said, "I won't arrest you today. I'll let you go." ... So as I started out the door, I looked back to Santo and asked him, "How'd you get out?" And he said, "I gave him $3 million, and they let me save $600,000. That's all they left me with."⁵

In the morning, Clifton said he learned that the New York County District Attorney's Office had canceled the subpoena from the Anastasia investigation. Ragano then went down to the Hillsborough County Courthouse and filed a writ of habeas corpus, claiming Clifton and the Hillsborough County Sheriff's Office were harassing Trafficante. Clifton said the court order meant he could not arrest Trafficante.⁶

Whether this is all true or just partially will unfortunately never be known.

## 23

# Creating José Martí Park

We were creating drama of our own in Tampa while the Santo Trafficante Jr. story was playing out.

As the United States government began to sour on forging a relationship with Fidel Castro Ruz, we decided we needed to remind Tampa why we supported him back in 1955.

We planned a series of public demonstrations that we believed would fuel feelings of pride among Tampa's Cuban American population, pride for the fact that Cuba had finally obtained independence after years of being an official colony of Spain and then an unofficial colony of the United States.

In mid–August 1959 we paid homage to Eduardo Chibás y Ribas with a short and eloquent ceremony in front of the Cuban Club's exterior bust of José Martí Pérez. We laid a wreath in his memory at the foot of the bust's pedestal and then listened to a few speakers who boasted of Chibás' dedication to cleaning up the Cuban government. These orators reminded those in attendance that previous regimes only cared for money and would do anything at the expense of the Cuban people to fatten their wallets. Throughout the event, Chibás's famous slogan, "vergüenza contra dinero," was reiterated. *Vergüenza* means "shame," but the slogan is usually translated to mean "Honor Versus Money." And that was what we wanted Tampa's Cuban population to remember: While Batista shamed Cuba in the name of dollar signs, Castro was working to restore honor to the nation.[1]

On September 12, we organized a caravan at 3 p.m. in support of the Cuban government. It began at José Martí Park located on Eighth Avenue and 13th Street in Ybor City at 3:30 p.m. and ended on Columbus Drive in West Tampa. A flyer had been distributed, inviting everyone to participate. It literally rained on our parade that day, but that did not stop 150 cars from making the trek from the park to Nebraska Avenue to Cass Street to Howard Avenue and finally to Columbus Drive. As was the case following Batista's flight from Cuba, cars were adorned with signs celebrating Cuba's freedom.[2]

Then, on November 27, we honored the eight medical students who were executed in Cuba on that day in 1871 by the Spanish. The ceremony began at the Martí bust in front of the Circulo Cubano, where we placed flowers, and concluded in José Martí Park with speeches about Cuba's long history of slavery to foreign governments as well as its own. To accentuate the point that Castro brought Cuba freedom, those in attendance were reminded that November 27 was also the date that our revolutionary leader had spoken in Ybor City.

Other events were sprinkled in between the aforementioned, and each was a success. We could not shake the feeling, however, that these demonstrations would have been more visually powerful if we had an

¡AL PUEBLO DE TAMPA!
En Defensa Del Honrado Gobierno De Cuba

El Movimiento 26 de Julio de Tampa, que conoce a fondo la obra honrada del actual Gobierno de Cuba, solicita la cooperación de todos los cubanos de limpia historia y de todos los latinos y anglo-sajones que aprecian la democracia en su exacto valor, para que se agreguen con sus automóviles, a la Cabalgata que se celebrará el sábado 12 de Septiembre, a las 3:30 de la tarde, partiendo del Parque José Martí a recorrer algunas calles de nuestra ciudad.

El Gobierno que tiene de Presidente al Dr. Osvaldo Dorticós y de primer ministro al héroe y Líder Dr. Fidel Castro, es casi diariamente calumniado por periodistas mal informados o sobornados que ultrajan la verdad y engañan al noble pueblo americano.

Los cubanos de Tampa, incluyendo a todos los grupos que han ayudado a la causa de Cuba Libre, tenemos la obligación de protestar ordenadamente contra los difamadores y pedir se comprenda la obra que realiza la Revolución en beneficio de 6,000,000 de cubanos.

¡No se olvide, Parque José Martí, Octava y Calle 13, 3:30, Sábado 12 de Septiembre!

CLUB PATRIOTICO 26 DE JULIO DE TAMPA

M-26-7 flyer inviting the people of Tampa to participate in a caravan "in defense of Cuba's honest government," from the calumnious accounts by mal-informed American journalists. Event taking place on September 12, 1959, leaving from Friends of José Martí Park at 3:30 p.m. Tampa (Ybor City), Florida (from the collection of Raul Villamia).

appropriate locale at which to hold them. We wanted José Martí Park to become such a destination but knew it needed work before it could be an inspirational place to visit.

On occasion, José Martí Park would become the topic of conversation between Victoriano Manteiga and me. We wanted a statue of Martí placed there.

This would not be Manteiga's first Martí statue venture.

In May 1945 at a meeting in the Circulo Cubano, Manteiga proposed the idea of erecting a bust or a statue of José Martí at the social club since the Apostle of Cuba had left many fingerprints in the city of Tampa.[3]

It was not until May 1949 that a committee called The José Martí Memorial Foundation, which may have in 1952 become El Comité Pro-Monumento a José Martí (The José Martí Pro-Monument Committee),

## 23. Creating José Martí Park

was formed to establish a permanent memorial in Martí's honor. It was founded in response to a situation that happened during the Gasparilla festivities of 1948, a Tampa Mardi-Gras type tradition founded in 1904, where a fictitious pirate named José Gaspar invades the city. Maria Teresa de Cardenas, queen of the Habana Carnival, when presented flowers by Tampa mayor Curtis Hixon, asked to be taken to the monument of José Martí. Having been told there was no such monument here, she welled up in tears, so she and her maids were taken to the steps of the V. M. Ybor factory, where she placed the flowers at the door entrance.

The embarrassing situation made all the Cuban newspapers, so the Habana chapter of Los Caballeros Orden de la Luz (Order of the Knights of Light), a Masonic lodge, raised funds for a bronze bust of Martí to be made in Cuba. It was installed on August 7, 1949, at El Circulo Cubano. Cuban officials, lodge members, and a Cuban warship participated in the unveiling.

This was the first and only tribute to Martí until March 18, 1950, when the Ybor City Rotary Club dedicated a stone marker at the base of the stairs of the Vicente Martinez Ybor cigar factory in honor of the 1893 speech given there by Martí to the cigar makers. A photo capturing this moment includes my wife, Nora, as she was a maid in that year's Latin American Fiesta Queen's court, which took part in the unveiling ceremony.

Then, as mentioned earlier, in 1952, Manteiga reached out to his friend José Manuel Fidalgo in Cuba to create a bronze Martí statue to be on those same steps. But Fulgencio Batista y Zaldívar thugs made sure that statue was never seen by the public. The life-size statue was thought to have been destroyed when the studio was raided. Though Manteiga had originally proposed in that 1945 meeting that a statue or bust be made, and ultimately, Cuba provided the bust, Aurelio Andres (A. A.) Gonzalez and Jorge A. Trelles, physicians who each owned an Ybor medical clinic, again brought up the subject in 1952 of erecting a life-size statue. Tony Pizzo was named president of the Comité Pro-Monumento a José Martí (José Martí Pro-Monument Committee), with Gonzalez as vice president and Trelles as treasurer. Manteiga, having a friendship with Fidalgo and being a member of the committee, solicited the sculptor to erect the statue. But ... the bronze statue never made it to Tampa.

When again considering a life-size statue in the autumn of 1959, Manteiga and I reached out to the office of Foreign Minister Raúl Roa García to inquire about financial help from the Cuban government towards the project.

We knew such assistance would be tough due to Batista pillaging the nation's treasury, but we thought we would at least ask.

Unveiling of José Martí marker at Vicente Martinez Ybor Cigar Factory. In 1893, Martí addressed cigarmakers from the factory steps, encouraging them to support Cuba's independence from the Spanish. Rotary Club members, civic leaders, and the queen and court of the Latin American Fiesta Association took part in the ceremony. Court maids Elaine Quesada and Nora Rodriguez (Raul Villamia's future wife) stand behind the flowers, with Queen Helen Setticasi on the steps behind the marker. Tampa historian and Rotary Club of Ybor City President Tony Pizzo is at the podium at the top of the stairs. Tampa (Ybor City), Florida, March 18, 1950 (photograph by Vicari's, from the collection of Rhonda Villamia).

The next day Manteiga was able to speak with Minister Roa's chief of staff, Leovigildo Fernández. Manteiga explained the nature of the project we were planning. Fernández said that he would inform the minister of our project and the financial assistance we were seeking, asking Manteiga to call him back in three days to get the minister's response.

Manteiga did so, and Fernández told him that the minister sympathized with our plans, but that the Revolutionary Government did not have the funds available to help. So, the Tampa M-26-7 decided to proceed with the plans to erect the statue on its own.

To make the Martí statue, Manteiga thought of Cuban sculptor Alberto Sabas Muguercia, who was living in Tampa and had previously erected the statue of Christopher Columbus at the entry of Bayshore Boulevard and a bust of Garibaldi at L'Unione Italiana. Sabas came to the newspaper office to discuss the matter with Manteiga, saying he had actually begun making a model for a statue of the Apostle and welcomed the M-26-7 commissioning him to erect it. I imagine that, with the triumph of the revolution, Sabas may have been inspired to begin creating a likeness of the man who first brought liberty to Cuba, the man Castro emulated.

Manteiga recalled that the José Martí Memorial Foundation, of which he had been a committee member when established in 1949, had $270 on deposit in an Ybor bank. He contacted Armando Dorta and Rogelio Berdeal, who had been committee president and treasurer, respectively, to inform them of Sabas's desire to erect the Martí statue and discuss the matter of funding it. They concurred with Manteiga's proposal to have Sabas complete the statue.

Berdeal and Dorta placed a November 20 notice in *La Gaceta* asking former members of the 1949 José Martí Memorial Foundation to attend a meeting at the Circulo Cubano on the 25th because, as they stated, "There is now the possibility that Tampa can have a statue of the Apostle Martí, made by the Cuban sculptor Sabas."

In the November 27 edition of *La Gaceta*, the substance of the meeting was reported. It was agreed that, by way of Dorta, Berdeal, Manteiga, and Tony Pizzo, fundraising efforts be made. As representatives of the M-26-7, Ray Delgado and I attended the meeting.

I will confidently state here that the funds were raised by the M-26-7, and we were the ones who initially reached out to Sabas about the project and discussed it with him before the José Martí Memorial Foundation was resurrected for entering into this conversation.

Some accounts claim the statue was paid for with the funds left over from the foundation's failed project in 1952 when endeavoring to have Fidalgo make a statue for the Ybor factory stairway, but I have found no proof that any part of that supposed $270 was used for erecting the statue. What I do offer is my eyewitness account of meetings and discussions Manteiga and I had with Sabas. And I can also attest to the fact that M-26-7 masons cleared and dug the space for the foundation and actually constructed the base.

We called for a general assembly of the M-26-7 members so we could propose the idea and discuss the strategy for building the statue.

Manteiga opened by explaining what was being planned regarding the statue. He mentioned that we had asked for assistance from the Cuban government, but that it could not help, so it was necessary to have the club members fundraise to erect the statue. I then briefly addressed the audience and answered questions raised by the members. When I finished speaking, I asked Manteiga to stand next to me. He as the former president and I as the current president asked the assembly for a vote on whether to approve or reject the proposal we had presented. The members unanimously approved the plan. Manteiga said a few words, and then introduced Sabas, giving him the floor.

Sabas began by saying that he appreciated the M-26-7 commissioning him to erect the statue. He continued that he wanted to make the statue out of bronze, but that it would be very costly and he understood there was not enough money available to make it of this material. So, it would be made of a mixture of concrete and plaster of paris.

Sabas showed us a sketch so we could see how he was going to make

M-26-7 members with José Martí statue sculptor Alberto Sabas Muguercia at the M-26-7 clubhouse for a meeting after the Martí statue was unveiled on February 28. Standing: Manuel Lozano, Maria Luisa Gervac, Ricardo Bravo, Ofelia Perez Bueno (sister of Juan M. Perez, wife of Carmelo Bueno), Armando Diaz (whose wife, Josie Liccio, worked with Raul Villamia's wife, Nora Rodriguez, at Broadway Bank in Ybor City), Billy Lima, Enrique Perez (father of Juan M. and Ofelia). Sitting: Raul Villamia, Sabas, Carlos Carbonell, Victoriano Manteiga, Carmelo Bueno, Ray Delgado, Alberto Nunez Bordon. Tampa (Ybor City), Florida, March 1960 (from the collection of Raul Villamia).

the statue. He said that it would be like the Martí statue in Habana's Parque Central. The statue itself would be eight feet tall and facing forward with its right arm extended level to its shoulder and its hand opened. Its left arm would be resting alongside the body. The statue would be wearing a bow tie, a vest, and a long coat almost to his knees, unbuttoned. The feet would be separate, with the right one more towards the front than the left one. There would be a small wall behind his feet from the pedestal base up to about where his coat hem was.

The base of the statue would be about four feet high, so that the entire statue would stand about 12 feet tall. The inscription at the base would be taken from Martí's poem *I Have a White Rose to Tend*. The portion of the statue that was the body would be made at his studio and the foundation and base would be made in the park itself. Masons would be needed for the construction of the base and foundation. Several masons at the meeting volunteered to do the job.

After Sabas finished his explanation of how the statue would look and answered some questions posed by the members, we ended the meeting. The board members and Sabas were asked to remain.

Once the assembly left, we asked Sabas to expound on what the estimated cost of erecting and installing the statue would be. Sabas answered that he would do it for free since he, as a Cuban had great admiration for Martí, understood the lack of money available and the great desire of Tampa Cubans to pay homage to Martí. The masons were not going to be paid for making the base, so we would only have to pay for the cost of the materials, which would not be any more than $450. He said he was ready to begin the project when so requested.

The board approved the making of the statue and the commissioning of the sculptor. We asked our finance secretary to work with Sabas to make the necessary arrangements for ordering and paying for the materials. We then asked Sabas to begin the work at his earliest convenience.

From November when the M-26-7 commissioned Sabas to start working on the project, he had told us it would take about three months to complete. The club, in agreement with Cuban consul Eliseo Pérez, planned for the unveiling to take place on February 24, the day commemorating El Grito de Baire (The Baire Outcry), which was the beginning of the Second War for Cuban Independence, following the Ten Years' War.

Weeks after the start of this very special project sponsored by the club, I received a call from my brother Miguel in Habana the morning of Saturday, December 5, informing me that my mother Balbina was in a coma and that, according to the doctors, had suffered a cerebral hemorrhage. I immediately made my reservations and was on the next flight out to Cuba. When I arrived at the house, my mother's condition was the same, and it remained that way until the following day, December 6, when she died. We held her funeral and burial the next day.

By this time, my brother Mario had been out of his position as chief of security for almost five months. When Manuel Urrutia Lleó was forced to resign the presidency on July 17, new president Osvaldo Dorticós later brought staff of his own choosing. Mario continued working in the palace at the United Press International office.

I stayed in Habana until December 13 and then returned to Tampa. Keeping busy with the club activities was a good distraction in mitigating the pain of my mother's loss.

Unfortunately, good news on the Cuban front was becoming hard to find.

## 24

# Battling the Consul

We went from heroes to enemies in less than a year.

Many of those who once cheered us for assisting Fidel Castro Ruz quickly changed their attitude as United States-Cuba relations continued to sour.

Fulgencio Batista y Zaldívar supporters who fled Cuba were coming to Tampa and then sought revenge on those who supported the revolution.

And while it seemed the whole city was once on our side in early 1959, it felt like the majority of Tampa was against us by the end of that year.

It began in December 1959 when we learned one of our own had already turned against Castro.

My baseball friend Max Garcia was arrested for attempting to fly to Santo Domingo with a planeload of aeronautical parts valued at $40,000. He was immediately expelled from the M-26-7. We had heard he was using a plane he supposedly owned for counterrevolutionary activities. Curious about whether my friend had indeed changed sides, I visited the St. Petersburg–Clearwater International Airport where the plane was said to be parked. It was, and I took pictures, but I was not able to look inside. I never confronted Max about it.

Then, in early January 1960, Carlos Carbonell was fired from his job at the None Such Bakery. Customers demanded Carbonell be let go for being a Communist or they would cease frequenting the bakery. Carbonell was not a Communist. He believed in democracy and freedom and wanted both for Cuba. However, no matter the truth, the bakery owner could not risk losing business and had to get rid of Carbonell. Following this incident, due to the accusations, Carbonell could not find steady work, so I stepped in to help.[1]

From the time I moved to Tampa in 1953, the Cuban magazine *Bohemia* was published weekly and distributed by Melchor De La Parte, who had a sundries store on 15th Street between Seventh and Eighth Avenues. After the triumph of the revolution, the Cuban newspaper *Revolución* was also distributed in Tampa, although I believe it was Felipe "Indio" Jimenez

227

from the Patriotic Movement of Tampa for Aid to the Cuban Farmer instead of Melchor that was selling them.[2]

In November 1960 it occurred to me to have someone from the M-26-7 distribute *Bohemia*. It made sense to funnel the profits of this widely read magazine to someone who had invested time in the revolutionary cause. I approached Carbonell with the idea of him being the distributor. He agreed.

So, I sent a letter to *Bohemia* dated November 20, 1960, in which I requested they consider having Carbonell be their distributor in Tampa instead of Melchor for all the reasons mentioned. I received a response dated November 24 from Rafael Rodriguez Luloaga, head of circulation, in which he stated that they were very pleased to inform me they have been in contact with Carbonell, acknowledging that he had been designated by me to assume the distributorship in Tampa, and letting him know that he would be commencing his position with issue #49 dated December 4. His responsibilities would include going to the airport on a weekly basis since it was circulated every Sunday in Cuba. Being that there were frequent flights between Tampa and Habana, the magazines would just be put on the flight.

But he earned only a few cents per copy, and his wife also could not find work. It was a tough time for their family.

Things only worsened as the relationship between the United States and Cuba became more strained and the relationship between Cuba and the USSR strengthened.

When the Revolutionary Government first came to power, it confiscated properties owned by Batista and his collaborators. Later, Castro began to appropriate the properties of other Cubans and some Americans to institute his agrarian reform program that redistributed the land owned by a few to the peasants for farming. He was giving Cuba back to Cuba. Those who had land nationalized were to be paid back with bonds over a 20-year period with an interest rate of 4.5 percent.

The U.S. government would not accept this deal and, weeks before the end of 1959, American airplanes dropped incendiary devices to burn Cuba's sugarcane fields, reducing the harvest of the crop most needed for the island to sustain its economy.[3]

Early in 1960, there began to be a war of words and accusations between the two governments. Acting Secretary of State Charlie Herter sent a note to Cuba protesting the illegal expropriation of some U.S. properties in Cuba without paying any type of compensation.[4]

Cuba responded by expropriating all the large cattle ranches and sugar plantations, accusing the CIA of sending the planes that bombarded and burned the sugarcane fields. Castro also accused them of training Cuban exiles as a force to invade Cuba.[5]

## 24. Battling the Consul

Vice President Richard Nixon in a speech made during his presidential campaign declared that measures would be taken to punish Castro for his actions, including reducing the quota of sugar sold to the United States.

On January 19, Castro responded by announcing the immediate confiscation of all the large Cuban and U.S. estates (latifundias). He then had an altercation with Spanish Ambassador Juan Pablo de Lojendio e Irure while speaking on television. In his speech, Castro accused the ambassador and the Spanish Embassy of being involved in some covert operation with the United States to get anti–Castro Cubans out of the country in a clandestine manner. Hearing this, the ambassador barged into the television station, confronted Castro while on the air, called him a liar, and demanded a retraction. Castro then gave Lojendio 24 hours to leave Cuba.[6]

After the last accusations against the United States, Herter appeared before Congress to ask that President Dwight Eisenhower be given power to change the law regarding the Cuban sugar quota. He also called for the U.S. ambassador in Cuba, Philip Bonsal, to indefinitely return to Washington, D.C.

On January 21, 1960, Eisenhower made a declaration asking for the initiation of negotiations between the two countries, and the Argentinian ambassador acted as mediator. U.S. Ambassador Bonsal returned to Habana and said America would consider extending economic assistance to Cuba. But in a speech made by Castro on January 28, he made no mention at all of the United States.

The Cuban government on January 31 then announced the imminent arrival of Anastas Mikoyan, Deputy Prime Minister of the Soviet Union. On February 4, Mikoyan arrived in Cuba to open a Soviet exposition in Habana, and Castro took advantage of that opportunity to speak with him. Among things they discussed was an attempt to come to a trade agreement, and possible Soviet economic aid to Cuba.

*La Coubre*, a ship from Belgium carrying a cargo of weapons bought by Cuba, arrived in the Habana port on March 4. When the cargo was being unloaded, there were two explosions, one following the other in a manner of seconds. More than 100 people died, and hundreds of others were wounded. My brother Miguel, who worked at the customs area of the port, was there the day it happened. Castro immediately accused the CIA of sabotaging the ship, even though those close to the event believed it was the improper handling of the cargo that sparked the explosions. Castro announced on May 8 that Cuba was going to be establishing diplomatic relations with the Soviet Union. The two countries signed various trade agreements, including one concerning the export of Soviet oil to Cuba.

The Revolutionary Government continued confiscating Cuba's foreign-owned properties, the majority of which were owned by

Americans. Upper-level Revolutionary Government officials who were not in agreement with the direction Castro was heading, including many original department heads, began leaving Cuba. Owners of newspapers, radio, TV, and other businesses followed suit.

Castro passed a law that prohibited Cubans owning more than one house. They took possession of homes that were being rented out by their owners. This affected many United States-owned companies as well.

Our family had two houses next to each other. The original house was a wooden structure built in the Cerro section of Habana in 1922. The family originally lived in the Vedado section of Habana on Zapata Street. It was where my parents lived after marrying and where my four oldest siblings—Miguel, Fernando, Barbara, and Irene—were born. We then moved to the wooden house on Auditor Street, where older brother Mario, me, and my youngest sister, Marta, were born. The concrete block home was built in 1952. Both homes were being occupied by my family, with a portion of the wooden one being rented out. When this law went into effect, the people living there no longer had to pay rent, and this part of the wooden house became theirs to use for the remainder of their lives.

Many years later, Enrique Someillán would learn he had a rich uncle he had never met who was also affected by this law.

According to Someillán's nephew Felix Someillán, his uncle Guillermo Someillán was a one-time Cuban Air Force pilot who later made riches in the development industry and became known as one of the island's more eccentric characters for his penchant to drive through Habana in a pink Cadillac with a lioness in the passenger seat.[7]

In 1957, Guillermo Someillán erected a 30-story high-rise in Habana that he aptly named The Someillán. According to Felix Someillán, as the story goes, Guillermo Someillán was approached by either Castro or high-ranking government officials, told the property now belonged to the country, and asked whether he was with or against the revolution. Guillermo Someillán supposedly replied that he was in favor of himself and would never be a bother to anyone if they let him remain in the penthouse, to which the government agreed. Even though his riches had been nationalized, because he was allowed to continue to live this lavish lifestyle, Guillermo Someillán was for decades after that referred to as Cuba's last millionaire.[8]

Back in the United States, the winds of change were becoming more and more evident throughout 1960.

In Tampa, we were concerned, but we had to believe that everything would work out and that Cuba would maintain a free society rather than turning to the Soviet Union's form of Communism. We could not believe that all we had labored so hard for would be for naught.

## 24. Battling the Consul 231

Up until then, we had been having our meetings at *La Gaceta* and cafes or bakeries owned by members. We needed something official to mirror the fact that we supported an official government. We rented a space at 1318 Ninth Avenue in Ybor City at the old El Pasaje Hotel building off 14th Street that had once been the Cherokee Club. The building was owned by Concepción Jimenez, widow of José Ramon Avellanal. I happened to have kept one of the rent receipts listing a $40 payment for the period November 15 to December 14, 1960, signed by Concepción Avellanal.

Some historians claim that José Martí Pérez slept in the Cherokee on November 25, 1891, during the first of many nights he would spend in Ybor City, but he could not have. The building was finished in late 1895 and Martí was already dead by then.

On January 28, 1960, in commemoration of the 107th birthday of the illustrious Cuban patriot, the M-26-7 inaugurated its clubhouse. An article about its launching appeared in the *La Gaceta*'s January 29 edition. The master of ceremonies was Ray Delgado, and the speakers were Manteiga; Carlos Carbonell; Roberto de los Rios, representing the Patriotic Movement of Tampa for Aid to the Cuban Farmers; and Odelio Garcia, a former instructor in the Sierra Maestra.

Victoriano Manteiga agreed to resume as president. I willingly stepped down and took on my former role as general secretary. I believe I did a good job as leader, but Manteiga's oratorical ability, name recognition, and long history of fighting for equality all made him a better choice.

The rest of the new board of directors was composed of Marcelino Vila as vice president, Mario Iglesias as general vice secretary, Luis Duenas as finance secretary, Tony Sola as finance vice secretary, Ray Delgado as propaganda secretary, Orlando Bueno as propaganda vice secretary, Carlos Carbonell as recording secretary, Humberto Baez as recording vice secretary, Carmelo Bueno as organization secretary, Mario Garcia Montalvo as organization vice secretary, Cristo Pérez as order/discipline secretary, and Alberto Nunez Bordon as order/discipline vice secretary.

In late January 1960, the opaque white José Martí statue was completed. Alberto Sabas Muguercia instructed the volunteer masons to begin constructing the statue's base and attach the bas-relief of adults and children representing the Cuban people to its front. Within one week, the base was complete, the statue was mounted, and a commemorative plaque was added to the base. We covered the statue and planned an unveiling on February 24, which was the anniversary of El Grito de Baire (The Baire Outcry) in the village near Santiago de Cuba that launched the Cuban War of Independence in 1895. After the unveiling, a dinner was to be held at our headquarters.[9]

A few days after we announced the plans for the event, the *Tampa*

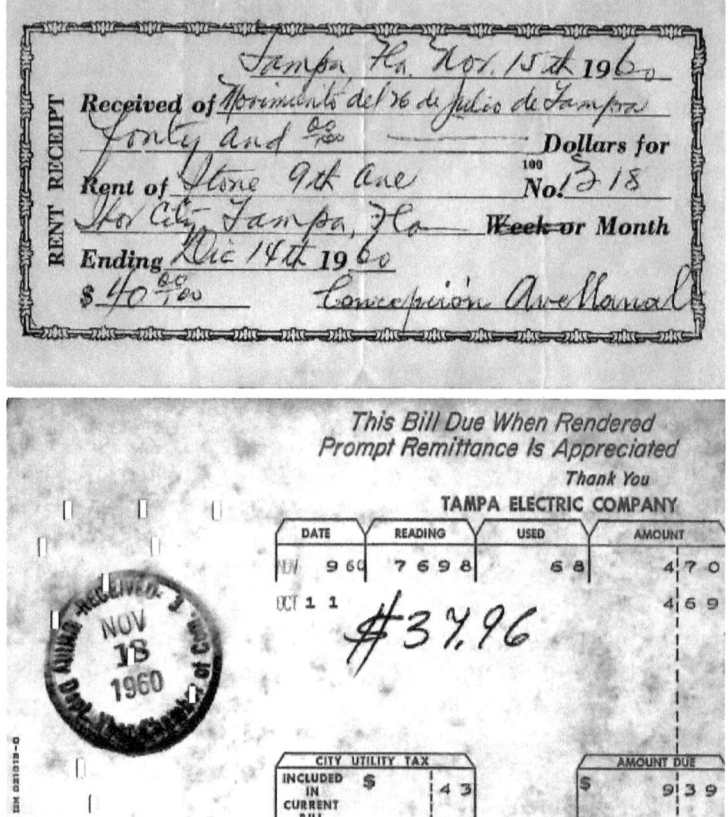

Forty-dollar rent receipt for M-26-7 clubhouse storefront space at 1318 9th Avenue for period between November 15 to December 14, 1960, signed by Concepcion Avellanal, owner of El Pasaje Hotel. Note she correctly spells "Ibor" with an "I" on the receipt. Tampa (Ybor City), Florida (from the collection of Raul Villamia). Back side of TECO (Tampa Electric Company) receipt for November 9, 1960, and paid on November 18. Though the balance is $9.39, it seems that $37.96 was paid.

*Times* on February 4 published an article titled "Martí Statue Erected" that detailed the unveiling slated for the 24th and included an interview with the sculptor, Sabas. The article stated: "*The local 26th of July Movement commissioned him to do the work, the sculptor said…'with money raised in the neighborhood.'*" All was set. However, the plan was soon changed by Tampa's new Cuban consul, Rene Dechard y de la Torriente.[10]

Dechard was named to replace Eliseo Pérez in late January, with Cesar Rivero Mas as his vice-consul. Tampa's M-26-7 found it to be a curious choice. Dechard was once close with Batista. Also worrisome from a

## 24. Battling the Consul

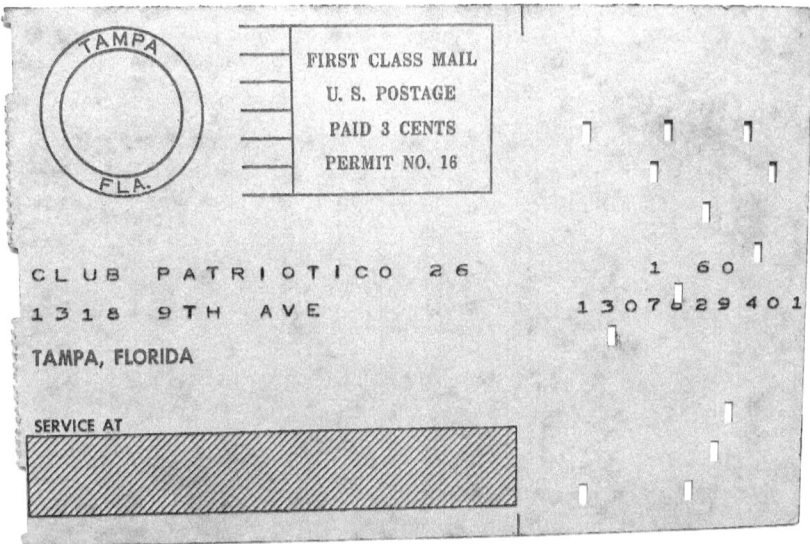

Front side of TECO bill gives customer name of "Club Patriotico 26" and clubhouse address 1318 9th Avenue. It also has the numbers "1 60" above the account number, which may be the date the account was opened, which would coincide with the clubhouse's January 28, 1960, inaugural ceremony. Tampa (Ybor City), Florida (from the collection of Raul Villamia).

local standpoint, Dechard's wife, Zenaida Marrero, was the sister of Raul Moran's wife, the same Moran who was part of the radical group that caused us so much trouble over the previous year.

When the group that Anibal Velaz tried to establish in the fall of 1957 never came to fruition its members splintered in various directions. Moran, along with Someillán, revived a remnant of this group after the triumph of the revolution under the name Movimiento Amigos de la Revolución Cubana (Friends of the Cuban Revolutionary Movement). It was long in title but short on membership.

Victoriano Manteiga had a brief conversation with Dechard a few days after his arrival when he made a cursory visit to *La Gaceta*, cut short by the consul's aide interrupting him with needing to address a phone call. Manteiga was therefore unable to discuss important matters with him. Manteiga and others from the M-26-7 met with Dechard at their clubhouse at 8 p.m. on Wednesday, February 3. We informed him of the history of divisiveness in Tampa and stated that we hoped he would look to bring the community together. Dechard agreed with that sentiment, and when the meeting ended Manteiga and I thought all was well.[11]

Someone changed Dechard's mind at some point following the

Parque Amigos de José Martí with newly installed statue made by sculptor Alberto Sabas Muguercia before the planned unveiling on February 24, 1960. It had not yet been covered up in preparation for the unveiling. Note the overgrown weeds due to M-26-7 members no longer being caretakers after new Cuban Consul Rene Dechard locked them out of the park. Tampa (Ybor City), Florida, February 1960 (from the collection of Raul Villamia).

Ticket for the dinner hosted by the M-26-7 at their clubhouse in commemoration of El Grito de Baire (The Baire Outcry), to take place after the unveiling. Though the unveiling date was changed from February 24 to February 28 by Cuban Consul Dechard and the park was locked on the 24th, the dinner was well-attended nevertheless. Tampa (Ybor City), Florida, February 24, 1960 (from the collection of Raul Villamia).

meeting. Most likely it was Moran and/or one of his friends. Or perhaps he never wanted peace and lied to Manteiga. I have no proof of those accusations, but both seem plausible. In the morning, Manteiga received a written note from Dechard demanding the keys to the park, demonstrating a totally different posture from the cordial meeting we had had the prior evening. He did not even have the courage to ask for them man to man.[12]

Manteiga had no choice. The keys rightfully belonged to the Cuban consulate because the land was the property of Cuba.

The following Saturday, February 6, the club volunteers went to the park to clean, plant flowers, and maintain the grounds as they always had, but the gate was padlocked with a new lock. The consulate was closed on weekends, so we could not ask why we were being kept out of the park. Normally, when we had custody of the keys, we would open the park daily to allow visitors to enter. We held a meeting at our headquarters the following day, and some members said that they had heard rumors that the new consul had been stating that he was changing the date of the unveiling from February 24 to February 28. This was an odd choice, as that day had no historical significance. Plus, the ceremony was our idea. How could a man not involved with it change the date? We decided at the meeting that four of us would visit the consul on Monday.

That morning, we visited the consulate and asked Dechard why he padlocked the park. He simply responded that he wanted the doors locked but did not wish to offer any reasons for his decision. We suggested that the park should remain open so the public could enter at will and so the club members could continue to maintain it and so Martí would not look like he was being held prisoner. He again denied our request, further stating that our planned ceremony on February 24 had indeed been changed to February 28. Furthermore, we were told that we were not invited to the event and that the park would be padlocked on February 24 to prevent us from holding our ceremony without permission. Legally, he had every right to lock the park: it was officially run by the consulate. Ethically, however, he was wrong. Then, shortly after the meeting, white rose bushes the M-26-7 had planted were removed per orders from Dechard.

After the keys had been handed to Dechard on February 4, Dorta and Berdeal went to see him and compliantly accorded with him to dispense with the M-26-7's involvement and change the unveiling date. Though Manteiga was on the José Martí Memorial Foundation committee when founded in 1949 and now at this juncture representing the M-26-7, it seems clear that all parties were working together to thwart what had already been put in place by us.

The situation was getting out of hand.

Around the time Manteiga and I were initially discussing having a

Martí likeness installed at the park and considering options, he recalled that, in 1952, as a committee member of the José Martí Memorial Foundation, he had commissioned Fidalgo to erect a bronze statue for Tampa, but when his studio was raided by Batista's henchmen, no one knew what happed to the statue. It was not at the studio and assumed destroyed.

Manteiga reached out to Juan Orta Cordova, Director General of the Office of the Prime Minister, to inquire if they could possibly investigate the matter of that missing statue and confirm whether it might exist somewhere or was in fact destroyed. Orta agreed to make inquiries. Granted, the new government had only been in place about 10 months, with new President Osvaldo Dorticós Torrado in office only three months, so there was much going on at the time Manteiga approached Orta with this request.

This was before Sabas was commissioned to erect the statue. We were trying to determine the probability of Cuba finding that original statue made by Fidalgo and sending it to Tampa for its unveiling at the Martí Park on February 24. We received a letter from Orta detailing that, after carrying out multiple investigations, he learned that the bronze statue was found abandoned in a public works workshop. The Revolutionary Police Command who discovered it there (and knew nothing about it) requested and obtained its transfer to the slopes of the Castillo de Atares in Habana, the site of their headquarters, where the statue remained. Reference to this letter appears in the February 26 *La Gaceta*.

When Dechard locked the Martí Park, Manteiga sent a telegram to Cuban Foreign Minister Raúl Roa García explaining the circumstances. Roa replied that the park was under the jurisdiction of the consulate but that he hoped Dechard would compromise with us. Manteiga on M-26-7 letterhead also sent a February 9 three-page letter to Dechard in response to a derogatory letter the consul had sent the M-26-7. In our letter we enumerated points proving our history in maintaining and beautifying the formerly neglected park, our having commissioned sculptor Alberto Sabas to erect the Martí statue, the history of the M-26-7 obtaining the keys to and custody of the park while I served as interim consul and up to that present moment, etc.

At some point after having received Juan Orta's letter confirming the Fidalgo statue had been found, we asked Orta if the statue could be transferred from Castillo de Atares to Tampa to be placed on the Ybor factory steps for the historically significant February 24 date. We received a February 18 telegram from him stating that "insurmountable difficulties" made it impossible to transfer the statue to Tampa by the desired date.[13]

By February 19, a press release was sent out by the "José Martí Memorial Foundation c/o Cuban Consulate," which states in part: *"In the*

24. Battling the Consul    237

```
AB2 82
A CDU458 HA76 4X41 40/39   INTL FR CUBAN GOVT=CD HABANA
VIA ALLAMERICA 18 1119AM=         1960 FEB 18  'V 2 23
ETAT VIMEA= MANTEIGA 1
     2015-15 ST TAMPA (FLO)=

DIFICULTADES INSUPERABLES IMPIDEN TRASLADO ESTATUA DEL
APOSTOL ESA CIUDAD PARA FECHA QUE PRETENDE PUNTO CORREO
AEREO AMPLIO DETALLES PUNTO SALUDOS=
       DR JUAN A ORTA DIRECTOR GENERAL JEFE DE
       DESPACHO OFICINAS DEL PRIMER MINISTRO.

ETAT
```

Western Union telegram from Juan A. Orta, Director General of the Office of the Prime Minister (Castro), to Victoriano Manteiga, advising: *"Insurmountable difficulties prevent the transfer of the Apostle's statue to that city for intended date."* An attempt was made by Victoriano Manteiga and Raul Villamia to inquire about the whereabouts of the José Martí statue made by sculptor Jose Manuel Fidalgo Rodriguez in Cuba, which was to have been sent to Tampa for installation at the steps of the Vicente Martinez Ybor cigar factory where Martí gave his 1893 speech. The statue was never sent due to Fidalgo's studio being ransacked by Fulgencio Batista y Zaldívar's henchmen, and the statue went missing. Tampa (Ybor City), Florida, February 18, 1960 (from the collection of Raul Villamia).

*Friends of José Martí Park ... on Sunday February 28th at 12 noon, the unveiling of the statue of the Apostle José Martí, which at the initiative of the José Martí Memorial Foundation, has been installed there, will take place."*[14]

It further states: *"The José Martí Memorial Foundation was organized in Tampa in May 1949, and started at the initiative of Ruben Fabelo."* Then it mentions 31 member names in which Dorta, Pizzo, Berdeal, and Manteiga are included.

It continues: *"Said committee remained inactive for a number of years until the end of last year when they accepted the offer of Cuban sculptor Alberto Sabas to create the statue of the Apostle; a meeting was held and the executive committee composed of Armando Dorta, president; Rogelio*

*Berdeal, treasurer; and Pedro Ramirez Moya, authorized the completion of the work, that once executed, will officially be given to the Honorable Rene Dechard de la Torriente, Cuban Consul of Tampa, as a gift to the Cuban government."*

Whether it was Dechard or the foundation members who composed the release, it was clear that the M-26-7 and all our efforts were totally ignored, even to the point of making it sound like the foundation's "executive committee" were the ones who authorized Sabas to do the work. As for the mention of Fabelo as the initiator, I am not sure where Dechard was getting his information.

Having had no response to our February 9 letter, as a last-ditch effort of good faith, I, along with Ray Delgado, Maria Luisa Gervac, and Humberto Baez, made an impromptu February 23 visit to the consulate to try reasoning with Dechard. We asked him to please open the park gates so people would be able to visit and bring flowers on the 24th in honor of El Grito de Baire.

Dechard, under the guise of negotiation, told us that he was willing to meet with M-26-7 member Ray Delgado later that evening to discuss the matter. The meeting was a waste of time. Dechard had Delgado come in simply to tell him that he would not open the park on February 24.

We were upset but decided we would not let Dechard dictate when we would celebrate the statue. On February 24, despite a light rain, the M-26-7, accompanied by a young cameraman and reporter from WTVT Channel 13, gathered outside the chained fence of José Martí Park at 5:30 p.m. and placed a wreath at the gate in commemoration of El Grito de Baire. We put a note on it saying the wreath was there because the Cuban consul refused to open the park's doors to the M-26-7. The wreath would have been placed at the statue had we been able to access the park.

Manteiga then spoke about Dechard's decision, stating that he could keep us out of the park but could not break our spirits. He said we were driven by the strength of our founder, Castro, and would continue to support the cause of a free Cuba no matter how many obstacles men like Dechard placed in our way. We then returned to our headquarters, where, along with approximately 100 guests, we dined on yellow rice and chicken prepared by the Columbia Restaurant. Such a great turnout proved that Dechard had failed. He could not dampen our support.

He continued to try, however.

At some point between February 24 and 28, Dechard was interviewed by Ruben Fabelo on his radio show and by the *Tampa Times*. He declared that the M-26-7 was "nothing" in Cuba and that he was considering abolishing it in Tampa. He further stated that Manteiga was an "agitator" who was always looking to cause problems. He never once mentioned sculptor Sabas

## 24. Battling the Consul

M-26-7 wreath that would have been placed at the Martí statue for its originally planned unveiling ceremony on February 24, 1960, but since Cuban Consul Rene Dechard locked the M-26-7 out of the park and changed the unveiling date to February 28, the wreath was placed on the park's gates with a sign saying, *"This wreath is here because the Cuban Consul refuses to open the doors of this park to the 26th of July Movement."* Tampa (Ybor City), Florida, February 24, 1960 (courtesy of *La Gaceta*).

and then gave credit for the statue to the "The José Martí Memorial Foundation," the committee that had commissioned the Fidalgo bronze statue that never made it to Tampa in 1952. And that is all they did. Some members of this committee then became part of the José Martí Pro-Monument Committee that created the park in 1957 and dissolved soon after.

Even odder is that Manteiga, one of the leaders of this committee, was the very man Dechard was seeking to discredit. As stated earlier, it was at that Circulo Cubano meeting on May 19, 1945, that Manteiga proposed Tampa erect a statue or bust of Martí. The May 21 *La Gaceta* published the resolutions made at that meeting, which had been attended by representatives from all mutual aid societies, journalists, the Cuban consul Guillermo Bolivar, and vice consul Eliseo Pérez.

On February 28, at the statue's unveiling, he continued his assault on the M-26-7.

The ceremony began at noon and was broadcast live on Fabelo's *Fiesta en Tampa* program. Several people who had nothing to do with the statue spoke, Dechard being the final one to address the audience. He spoke of Martí for the first quarter of his speech, as he should have, but he never once mentioned Castro or any of the positive things the revolution was doing for Cuba. He then talked about himself and his family and their history as revolutionaries and patriots. Only Dechard's cat and dog were omitted from mention.[15]

The final portion of his speech was used to insult Manteiga, my brother Mario, and me. Dechard said, "*If in Cuba there had been traitors like the Díaz Lanzes, the Urrutias and the Huber Matoses, there were also the Manteigas ... the denouncers of expeditions and accusers of Cubans for their revolutionary activities.*" Of my brother and me, he continued: "*The Villamias, when their country needed them most, they cowardly renounced their citizenship and were incapable of occupying the honorable position that young Cubans should embrace, one of whom, his brother Mario along with Urrutia had to leave the palace for being counterrevolutionaries.*"[16]

Dechard finished his speech as follows: "*Be assured that I will defend [the revolution] from traitors both there and here, because this revolution, which cost the great Cuban family so much blood, is the revolution of my elders, my children, my wife and mine.*"[17]

Calling Manteiga a traitor to the cause of Cuban independence was laughable. No one in Tampa had done more for it.

Dechard's belief that Mario and I were turncoats because we had become American citizens was equally ridiculous. I believe people should become citizens of that country to which they immigrate and in which they plan to spend the rest of their lives. I criticize neither those who wish to maintain the citizenship of their country of origin nor those who choose not to. I do not believe the love of and devotion to a country where one was born and raised can ever be lost.

No one believed Dechard's accusations. The city rallied behind the M-26-7 rather than turning on us, and many asked us to do something about Dechard.

## 24. Battling the Consul

Our first form of retaliation was through *La Gaceta* newspaper. Manteiga published columns stating the truth on March 4, 1960, the first edition following Dechard's comments.

One of the columns defended Manteiga by listing his numerous affiliations throughout his years fighting for freedom in Cuba:

Friends of the Slandered Director of La Gaceta, Victoriano Manteiga
These are some of Victoriano Manteiga's friends, including some who passed away some time ago:
Eduardo Chibás, with whom along with Dr. Roberto Agramonte, he celebrated in this city in 1930 and helped to fight the tyranny of Gerardo Machado.
Dr. Fernando Ortiz, the eminent Cuban with whom he collaborated in the Cuban League, fighting against Machado.
Dr. Ramón Grau San Martin, who was Cuba's hope in 1924 when Mr. Manteiga chaired the committee that brought him to Tampa after Batista had forced him to leave Cuba.
He is a friend of Cuban students at the University of Havana who supported Chibás in 1934.
He is one of the founders of the Committee for the Aid of Republican Spain and a friend of Don Fernando de los Rios, Don Mariano Ruiz Funes and other illustrious Spaniards.
He brought Eduardo Chibás to Tampa in 1950, along with dignified Cubans and Cuban Americans. Here, Chibás joined Dr. Manuel Bisbe, Pardo Llada, Orlando Castro, Dr. Salvador Massip and other Orthodox leaders.
He is a friend of the eminent Fidel Castro, who opened his arms to Tampa in 1955. He was also friends with Juan Manuel Márquez, one of the heroes of the Revolution against Batista, and General Alberto Bayo, a friend of many of the leaders of the Revolution.
He was never a friend of Prio, but now appreciates his desire to help the Revolution.
Manteiga's newspaper, La Gaceta, served the revolution against Machado, served against the Spanish Republic and served Fidel Castro and his people against the Batista tyranny.
Tampa knows that Manteiga has served Tampa as an honest journalist for 40 years! He has always been the defender of decent men against dictators, tyrants, politicians, thieves and their accomplices![18]

Manteiga also published a letter from a reader condemning Dechard:

Letter from Mrs. Carmen Figueroa
To the editor of La Gaceta
Dear Sir. I attended the unveiling of the José Martí statue made by the master sculptor, Alberto Sabas, on Sunday. The purpose of this event was to honor the great apostle.
I must be clear that I do not belong to a political party but I have followed the ideals of José Martí since my early childhood.

On the day that José Martí was to be honored for all that he and others sacrificed for Cuba, Rene Dechard, consul of Cuba in Tampa, used the opportunity to talk about himself and his ancestors. He was full of childish egotism, pointing to himself as a hero of our homeland, which was ironic considering we were there to honor an apostle who was full of humility.

As if this was not enough, he then publicly accused Mr. Manteiga and Mr. Villamia—who were absent—as being traitors, enemies of Cuba.

As a Martí Cuban, I am ashamed of the person representing me. I would prefer someone more humble, serene and a better diplomat. I prefer someone else as consul.

The narcissistic attitude of Mr. Dechard, who enjoys boasting of his genealogy while craftily attacking people who had previously been nice to him, shows that he is far from satisfactory or a Cuban gentleman.

For a better Cuba
without further fighting.
Carmen Figueroa del Marmol[19]

I also contributed to that edition of *La Gaceta* with a letter addressed to Manteiga:

Dear friend and comrade:

I request that this letter be published in your small but great newspaper regarding accusations made against my brother Mario and me in public and on the radio in this city by the Consul who falsely claims to be a revolutionary representing the honest people of Cuba, headed by Dr. Osvaldo Dorticos and the maximum leader of the 26th of July Movement and Prime Minister Dr. Fidel Castro.

This phony will have to answer to the Cuban authorities for his false accusations and for apparently still supporting his former boss Batista. I hope we expose this schemer shortly. I thank you in advance.

Raul Villamia[20]

If anyone in the community still doubted the authenticity of Tampa's M-26-7 and our allegiance to a free Cuba, Manteiga also published a history of our organization, beginning with Castro's visit to Ybor City in 1955, detailing the victory, our occupation of the consulate, how we cleaned the park and commissioned the sculptor to create the statue of Martí, and ending with the false accusations Dechard made against us.

I had recorded the speech on audiotape and transcribed it so there was a written version that I then sent to Raul Roa Garcia along with a letter summarizing our problems with Dechard. On our behalf, Miami's M-26-7 also sent him a letter, explaining how Dechard had attempted to smear the good name of Manteiga, who had dedicated the past 40 years to fighting for a free Cuba. Miami's M-26-7 echoed our belief that Dechard was looking to splinter Tampa's Cuban population and was still an agent of Batista despite his claims to the contrary.

Less than a month later, Dechard was out.

## 24. Battling the Consul

Manteiga happily published the following news in the March 25 edition of *La Gaceta*:

New Consul of Cuba in Tampa
 The Revolutionary Government of Cuba has named Mr. Ramiro Ortiz Planos, veteran of the consular service, as the temporary consulate of Cuba in this city.
 Planos was born in Cardenas in the province of Matanzas on August 6, 1898 and was appointed chancellor of the consulate in Rome, Italy in July 1920.
 He was previously in Tampa as chancellor in 1930.
 Planos also served in Charleston, Chicago, Detroit and elsewhere.[21]

And like that, Dechard was gone from the consulate, a victim of his own ignorance and ego.

Unfortunately, his family was not done with us yet.

# 25

# The End of Tampa's M-26-7

The accusations of being Communists dogged us.

I became a father for a second time to my daughter Denise at the end of March 1960, but the events that had transpired over the previous three months dominated my life outside my home more than I had imagined. And they continued.

It started in March, soon after Rene Dechard y de la Torriente had been taken out of office.

Miguel Alamo tried to run down Roberto de los Rios and Orlando Bueno on March 8 as they were crossing 14th Street and 9th Avenue. He then came back and pumped three shots at them. Bueno and de los Rios fortunately were unharmed. Alamo was charged with two counts of assault but fled to Cuba immediately following the incident. Charges were dropped.

Those sympathizing with the revolution received threatening phone calls. People threw red paint at houses, *La Gaceta*'s office, our clubhouse, and the clubhouse of the Patriotic Movement of Tampa for Aid to the Cuban Farmer.

The situation for us worsened in May when Fidel Castro Ruz announced that Cuba was establishing diplomatic relations with the Soviet Union and the two nations signed a trade agreement.

Soon after, Manteiga again stepped down as president and the M-26-7 quietly ceased day-to-day operations. We voted to temporarily terminate our activities in support of the Cuban revolution until relations between the nations improved but to continue meeting on a regular basis. We also continued collecting items to send to Cuba, and boxes of supplies would be stored in our clubhouse until there were enough to send in one shipment.

Then, in June, I had co-workers lie to my boss that I was Communist to get me fired. It did not work. My boss, Sherwood Hillier, called me to his office and asked if it was true. When I said no, he replied, "You are a good worker and as long as you are a good worker you will be working here."

## 25. The End of Tampa's M-26-7

Inside the M-26-7 clubhouse with boxes of goods to be sent to Cuba. Carmelo Bueno, Raul Villamia, Humberto Baez, and Juan M. Perez. Tampa (Ybor City), Florida, 1960 (from the collection of Raul Villamia).

The following month I made my last trip to Cuba before relations were severed. There is an undated photo I have at the Habana airport tarmac of us just having arrived. In the photo is also Esperanza Chediak, a well-known Cuban singer who was living in Tampa and often performed in shows at the theaters of Tampa's various mutual aid societies.

Around that time, for wearing a "26th of July" hat to practice, Carlos Carbonell's oldest son, Hector, was fired from his job at the post office because the government claimed he was Communist. And his younger son, George, was kicked off his West Tampa All-Star Baseball Team just prior to the team leaving to compete in the national all-star tournament in California.[1]

George Carbonell said the most humiliating moment for the family was the night someone threw an open bucket of red paint at their home. The guilty party did so while driving by, missed their home, and hit their neighbor's car. His mother tried all night to clean the car and apologized to the neighbor for a week straight.[2]

September was an especially dreadful month for United States–Cuba relations. That was when Castro announced that Cuba was seizing all cigar and cigarette factories and tobacco warehouses, including a few that belonged to Tampa residents: Garcia y Vega, Cuba Tobacco Company, and Cuesta-Rey.

At the end of that same month—possibly in response—vandals attacked and shattered the glass windows at *La Gaceta*, our clubhouse, and El Movimiento Patriótico's clubhouse, all on the same day.

Either directly before or after that act of destruction—it's hard to remember all these years later—Raul Moran and some of his group showed up in front of our clubhouse, making provocative gestures, challenging us to come out.

When we stepped outside, Moran, yelling and pacing in front of us, began to hurl insults and obscenities at us, calling us Communists and cowards. He continued with his menacing posture, becoming increasingly more aggressive and physical. Moran was tall and strong and had been a boxer. He must have thought we were afraid of him. He was mistaken. Out of self-defense, I punched him in the face. Before we could throw more punches, club members separated us.

Also in September, there were other altercations, which Manteiga detailed in *La Gaceta* on September 23, 1960:

> Two thugs armed with "bats" jumped out of a car and ran into the Patriotic Movement's meeting room swinging their weapons. They inflicted injuries upon several members of the organization who were merely talking to each other.
> Members of the Patriotic Movement quickly armed themselves with chairs and after several minutes of head busting proceeded to beat the hell out of the Batista thugs.
> At least five persons required medical treatment.
> Several days later, rotten eggs were thrown from a speeding car at a peaceful family who lives nearby the 26th of July Club room.
> Yesterday, in the early morning hours, a large window of this newspaper office was broken again by a thrown rock.
> And in broad daylight yesterday at noon, a man ran into the Patriotic Movement clubroom holding a razor blade. He slashed a member of the organization while he sat at a table within the room. Luckily, the man suffered no serious injuries.

In that article, Manteiga went on to plead with local law enforcement to do something to prevent further attacks.

> You represent the leadership of law enforcement in the progressive City of Tampa.
> We wish to bring to your attention what we regard to be a serious situation which may break into open bloodshed within weeks unless law enforcement agencies step in and use a strong and firm hand against the vandalism and strong-arm tactics of several non-citizens. Here are the facts of the case:
> For the past several months a handful of ex-Cuban dictator Batista's supporters have come to Tampa and have tried to impose a "reign of terror" upon a number of people living and working in the Ybor City sector. Several of these "jackals" served in Batista's army.

## 25. The End of Tampa's M-26-7

About two months ago this "reign of terror" began to slowly unfold and in the last two weeks it has grown in greater proportions. First it was the destruction of property. Breaking the windows of this newspaper office and at the 26th of July and the Patriotic Movement meeting rooms.

Like delinquents, they used the cover of night to protect their withdrawal from the scene of the crime....

... Things have gone too far. There is talk of retaliation. There is now talk of arming with revolvers for self-protection. Unless law enforcement agencies step in now and give the proper protection to those being attacked ... blood will flow more freely. Tampa will acquire another black eye.

We ask and encourage you gentlemen to give your attention to this situation which may become a serious problem for the authorities within weeks unless proper steps are taken to protect the property and person of citizens of this city.[3]

Finally, decades later, I learned through FBI records that, by September, Enrique Someillán was providing the federal law enforcement agency with intel on everything going on in Tampa to do with the conflict in Cuba.[4]

His nephew Felix Someillán would say he did this because he had grown discontent with the direction Castro had taken the Cuban government and felt it betrayed the revolution's purpose to bring freedom to the island.[5]

On October 19 the United States began to impose a trade embargo against Cuba, prohibiting all exports to the island except food and medicines. Cuba responded a week later by nationalizing remaining United States properties left on the island. In subsequent days, signs criticizing Castro's friendship with Nikita Khrushchev, and others saying "Americans ... do not allow in the United States those who defend Castro's Communism" appeared near our clubhouses.

In Cuba, my brother Mario was making his plans to leave. By then he had left his position with the United Press International office and traveled throughout the various provinces of Cuba with his old friend and arms acquisition partner Pablo Fernandez Alegre, who was an official in the Ministry of Agriculture. When Mario left the United Press International office at the palace, he was given the equivalent of unemployment compensation, since he was technically out of a job. Thus, Fernandez invited Mario to join him as he traveled throughout Cuba carrying out his responsibilities as sub-minister.[6]

By July, Mario's wife, Carmen, was seven months pregnant with their third daughter, Deborah, and Mario did not want her to be born in Cuba. Her two older sisters had been born in the United States, and he wanted this child to be born an American citizen as well. So, he sent them back to the states. Prior to this, Howard K. Davis had flown a few rescue flights for a group with which Rafael del Pino was affiliated. Davis showed up one day at Mario's apartment, offering to fly him out via a clandestine airstrip on the road to Varadero Beach being used to smuggle those mostly in high-level positions who wanted to leave.[7]

Mario might have risked it were he a bachelor, but with a family it was not worth the possible tragic consequences. But given Carmen's advanced pregnancy and the fact that she and their daughters were born in America, he wanted to have this third child enjoy that privilege. So, this is the posture he assumed in at least getting his family out of Cuba while he figured out how and when he would leave.[8]

Then, Jesús Montané Oropesa, who was Minister of the Instituto Nacional de la Industria Turística (National Institute of Tourism) or INIT, made Mario a very tempting offer. He wanted to name Mario the director of tourism for Habana Province. It was ironic that this would be happening then considering that that was the position my brother had originally wanted, but on a national level as Minister of Tourism.[9]

Montané brought Mario by the building being constructed for this ministry and pointed to the floor that would be his office. He told Mario he could pick whatever house he wanted for his family. But, by that point, Mario had sent his family back to the United States. In order not to appear ungrateful, he told Montané that he would accept Montané's offer if Carmen was willing to return to Cuba after the baby was born but decline if not.[10]

My brother Fernando, who had been in Cuba since July 1959 when we brought the M-2 down in his car, was also preparing to leave. Mario was seeing the writing on the wall as Communism appeared to be the new language spoken. He wanted no part of this system. So, he planned to leave in late October by joining Fernando on the ferry, using the assumed name of Frank Guzman (his wife Carmen's brother's name), accompanied by forged documents.[11]

It was risky. It would not reflect well on Cuba if Mario left. He had been a staunch supporter of the revolution from barely a month after Batista's coup in 1952, achieved the position as arms acquisition coordinator of the M-26-7 in exile, and was President Manuel Urrutia Lleó's chief of security at the palace. Entering the United States with someone else's identity would be helpful since he had broken parole by leaving it in 1959, and he was expecting he would be arrested and forced to serve his sentence. He hoped an assumed name would keep him below the radar under the strained diplomatic relations.[12]

Mario believed that might have been the last ferry to leave Cuba before relations were severed.[13]

When the ferry docked in Key West, Mario was baffled that the FBI was not there to take him into custody for breaking parole. Obviously, leaving the United States to assume a high position in the Cuban government was not in keeping with the agreement he had made as a condition for his early release from prison. He was surprised no agents were there.[14]

Mario stopped in Tampa on his way to New York.

During that Tampa pit stop, Davis called my home for Mario, requesting they get together. We always wondered how Davis knew Mario's whereabouts, and thought he might be a government intelligence operative, something he has denied to us to this day. When I shared this with Davis while writing this book, he chuckled and responded that he does not blame us for thinking that, but does not know how he knew Mario's whereabouts, adding that perhaps he had heard it from one of our Cuban contacts. He simply said, "Nothing happens in secret."[15]

Davis recalls flying into Tampa International Airport and parking near the office that oversaw private planes. Mario and I picked him up from there. I considered where I could take them so they could have a private conversation. Both Davis and I remember that I took them to a bridge, and the bridge that comes to my mind is the Lafayette Street Bridge near the University of Tampa, which is today the Kennedy Boulevard Bridge. That bridge has wide sidewalks and a couple areas where it curves out into the Hillsborough River in a semicircle so people could stand or sit, like the periodic curves one sees along South Tampa's Bayshore Boulevard.[16]

I parked within walking distance and waited while they made their way to the bridge to talk privately. Then the three of us went to the luncheonette at the Woolworth five and dime downtown to have a bite. Mario later shared with me that Davis had asked him if he wanted to participate in an operation that came to be known as the 30 November Revolutionary Movement. This counterrevolutionary movement was founded in Cuba on March 13, 1960, in honor of those martyred in the presidential palace attack that day in 1957. It sought to follow the ideals of Frank País García and those murdered in the November 30, 1956, uprising led by País in Santiago de Cuba, as well as those of the men and women who fought to restore Cuba's 1940 Constitution in trying to end Castro's Communist dictatorship.[17]

Mario succinctly told Davis that he was not going to do anything but go meet his new daughter, Deborah, who had been born the previous month. Mario was done with revolutionary activities. He joined no groups that were either in favor of or against Castro. He had invested over 20 years of his life for the Cuban cause of freedom, and this is where the buck stopped.[18]

Tampa residents continued to take out their anger on M-26-7 members, with the most visible target being Manteiga.

By this point, we were having few activities at our clubhouse. One of these was a celebration of Manteiga's birthday on November 2. Despite the political tensions between our two countries and the local unrest because of it, we wanted to honor the life of the man who had done so much for so many.

According to an article in *La Gaceta* on December 9, 1960, written by Roland Manteiga, such individuals were sending anonymous letters to the newspaper's advertisers, threatening to boycott those establishments if they continue to do business with "Communists":

> Since July this newspaper has been subject to subversive and sneak attacks by a small band of pro Batista thugs who apparently entered this country less than a year ago.
>
> The windows of La Gaceta's offices have been broken on two occasions; the exterior walls of the building have been smeared with paint on three different occasions; then there have been the usual phone threats and other types of un-American activities.
>
> These Cuban "bully boys" have always struck under the cover of night.
>
> Recently a new twist has been added to the harassment which now lends

At the M-26-7 clubhouse celebrating Victoriano Manteiga's birthday. Standing: Ramon Lebron, Alberto Nunez Bordon, Billy Lima, Mario Garcia Montalvo, Ray Delgado, Alfredo Valdivia, unidentified man, Juan Valdivia, Carmelo Bueno. Sitting: Raul Villamia, Humberto Baez, Manteiga, Carlos Carbonell, Gilberto Valdivia. Tampa (Ybor City), Florida, November 2, 1960 (courtesy of *La Gaceta*).

support to a story coming out of Miami, that top Batista generals consider this humble newspaper a serious obstacle in their path towards organizing the Cuban American community here in their favor by whatever means necessary; by force, threats and other strong arm methods.

We are proud that we have this type of people as our enemies.

Here is the text of a mimeographed letter which was mailed to all our advertisers on October 27 and again this week, December 6. Needless to say, the letter was not signed.

TO WHOM IT MAY CONCERN

By this letter I would like to inform you that in days gone by I was really shocked when reading in the Spanish Weekly paper, "La Gaceta," that your commercial advertisements appeared in one of their pages. I say shocked, because that is exactly what happened to me in reading that a place of business in these United States would advertise their merchandise in a communist paper. Yes, I say communist, because the Editor of "La Gaceta," Mr. Victoriano Manteiga, defends the murderer of America who tries to influence his communist ideas throughout the continent.

As a merchant you should not continue to help those who are defending a communist government like the Cuban government which has confiscated a great majority of Cuban commerce, leaving in ruins and misery hundreds of honest merchants and industries which after so many years of labor have lost everything they worked for.

Unite with the Cuban commerce and do not benefit any longer with your advertisements in a weekly paper which is inducing communism into the United States. For your acknowledgement I would like for you to know that on Friday, October 14, 1960, the government that this paper defends seized 382 Cuban and American enterprises.

In closing I hope that I will not have to read in the following edition of this weekly paper your commercial ads.

Sincerely, An Anti-Communist Cuban[19]

Roland replied:

Now there are a few misplaced Cubans (they should be in jail in Habana) living "high on the hog" in this great country and they would like to silence the voice of a newspaper which has served this community for over thirty-eight years.

It was because of this type of people (of the Batista category) and their reactionary tactics that helped bring about the bloody revolution in Cuba.

This group of foreign opportunists who are playing the "anti-communist" game would have intelligent merchants of this city believe that they have a great interest in the United States.

While the leaders of this Batista mob were down in Cuba stealing from the poor, this reporter was serving as a line company rifleman for 30 months in the South Pacific with the 132nd Infantry during World War II (Bougainville, Leyte, Ticao and Cebu).

La Gaceta has always been the object of attacks from different groups and individuals throughout the years, and this is quite understandable.

In the first place, small subversive groups seldom attack powerful newspapers because the large dollars have too many resources.

The groups always strike at the small newspapers because of their economic weakness and their lack of strong resources.

And in the second place the editor of La Gaceta has always expressed his opinion quite openly and to the point.

He has been critical often and openly of any and all whom he thought he should be critical of. Quite often, because of his editorial policy, La Gaceta has suffered financially, but at this late date neither he nor this writer intend to change this policy of expressing opinions.

During the late thirties and early forties this newspaper was honored by being the main object in a strong and consistent attack by the Communist Party, then legal in the United States when this newspaper opposed them. They were trying to gain control of several of the local unions in Tampa.

We still have the leaflets, circulars and economic scars from this fight with the Communists. The leaflets circulated by the Communists attacked the editorial policy of this newspaper and branded the editor with the name "Hitler." It was more popular in those days to label your enemies fascist or Nazi. Today, these terms have gone out of style.

Today, the worst name you can label your enemy is communist.

The "anti-this" and "anti-that" groups have come and gone in Tampa and the little newspaper "La Gaceta" is still here. Our files are open to the public to check. We have always expressed our opinion. We shall continue to do so.

We repeat this for the benefit of our beloved enemies ... the individual or individuals who hide behind the curtain of anonymity is or are cowards, in fact they are nothing.[20]

A weekly newspaper in Miami called *El Avance Criollo* then attacked *La Gaceta* in late December, according to an article by Manteiga that was published on December 23, 1960.

The article in *El Avance*, wrote Manteiga, was as follows:

> La Gaceta, subsidized and paid for by Fidel Castro, figures as a front-line spokesman for these elements. Its directors and editorial writers have frank Fidel-communist tendencies and proclaim a political feeling that is frankly anti–American. Their names are Victoriano and Rolando Manteiga, father and son.

In response, Manteiga wrote:

> We are going to ask the Federal Bureau of Investigation, in whose honesty we trust, to investigate:
> 1. If this newspaper is subsidized and paid for by Fidel Castro because by being so we would be violating a Federal Law.
> 2. That the files of La Gaceta be reviewed in search of writings that are frankly anti–American. (Our director has been an American citizen since 1928). His son, veteran of the Second World War, and two daughters were born here, as were his grandchildren.
>
> These represent forty (40) years of clean history in Tampa, history that cannot be stained by these individuals that have taken refuge in Florida and

believing themselves aided by the authorities, which we do not believe, lie with the greatest of cynicism.[21]

The vandalism returned on Christmas Eve, when the Cuban consulate was ransacked. Eight gallons of red paint was splashed throughout the office. Typewriters and the air conditioning unit were smashed. The safe was opened and documents plus $150 stolen.

But the criminals made a mistake. They did not break the door or a window to get in and didn't have to crack the safe. They had a key and the combination.

On January 4, 1961, three men were arrested for the attack on the consulate: Miguel Alamo, Enrique Someillán, and Raul Moran, who, as Rene Dechard y de la Torriente's relative, had access to the key and combination.

Cuban Consul Armando Sacassas at the consulate after Christmas Eve 1960 vandalism, speaking to a reporter in the presence of two Tampa policemen assigned to guard him. Note the smeared red paint on the walls. Tampa, Florida, January 8, 1961 (photograph by Dan Hightower, courtesy of *Tampa Bay Times*).

They were also linked to the other acts of vandalism carried out on homes and businesses in the prior months. I do not remember if those individuals were found guilty.²²

It ultimately mattered little that they were even arrested. Three days prior, on New Year's Day, Castro showed off Cuba's new Soviet tanks in a military parade.

The Patriotic Movement of Tampa for Aid to the Cuban Farmers shuttered its organization that same day.

The day earlier, on January 3, President Eisenhower broke off diplomatic relations with Cuba.

Shortly after hearing the news, the M267 members cleared all our belongings out of the clubhouse, expecting an attack. It came on January 6. Using hatchets, a group of men smashed the windows and then sliced up what little furniture we left behind.

When the January 13 edition of *La Gaceta* was published, it contained the public announcement that the M267 in Tampa was officially dissolved:

> In a meeting that took place a few days ago, we decided to close the 26th of July Club, not for the depredations of some individuals that call themselves anti-communists in order to carry out criminal acts in Tampa, but because the government of the United States has broken off its relations with Cuba.
>
> Everyone was in complete accord with this decision to dissolve the Club and pray for better relations between the people and the governments of Cuba and the United States.
>
> In the 26th of July Club there were no communists but only civic-minded men, enemies of violence and defamation.
>
> Those who in Tampa and other places wish to defeat Fidel Castro by throwing stones and paint, destroying furniture and window glass, are fascists and anti-democratic. As far as the case of Consul Sacassas goes, he has said that since last October he has been "turning over the secrets" of the government that paid his salary and to which he had promised his loyalty.
>
> Any man can stop sympathizing with another person, party, or government, but it is "ugly," nauseating, that he be living off the man, business or government and at the same time, stabbing him in the back.
>
> With a hope for better relations between Cuba and the United States, we salute all, and especially the tobacco factory workers classified as communist by Sacassas and other individuals that have come to this city during the last few months to disturb the tranquil life of Ybor City, West Tampa and of Tampa.
>
> The Tampa 26th of July of Movement²³

26

# The End to My Revolutionary Days

The FBI began pestering us midway through 1961, despite the M-26-7 being shuttered.

I was interviewed by the federal agents twice in a month, once in their office and once while sitting in the rear of their car as they cruised through the city.

The two instances blend, so it is difficult to remember when what was asked and answered.

One agent did most of the talking each time while the other sat quietly holding an attaché case that I would bet contained a tape recorder.

It was a standard back and forth for the most part.

They asked if I believed Cuba was Communist, to which I replied yes.

They grilled me on whether I was part of an intelligence operation on behalf of Cuba, and I repeatedly said I was not.

They asked what I thought of Fidel Castro Ruz, and I explained that I do not like Communism, but I do favor some of the things he has brought to Cuba, such as building more schools and homes for the peasants and ridding the island of gambling.

They had obviously been following me for a while because they knew about the time that I punched Raul Moran.

What stands out the most to me, however, is the foolish question they asked about Raúl Castro: did I think that he was a homosexual?

I maintained a straight face and replied, "That is a question I cannot answer because I do not know Raúl Castro personally, but I have never heard he is homosexual. However, I have heard rumors that your boss Mr. J. Edgar Hoover is. Is that true?" My question received no answer.

The FBI agent looked annoyed and tried to intimidate me with body language, but I was not scared. I knew my rights. I had done nothing wrong.

The FBI would interview all the former members of the M-26-7.

My wife, Nora, was called into her supervisor's office at Broadway Bank where she worked. She was told two FBI agents wanted to speak with her, and she was instructed to go into the conference room where they were waiting for her.

The agents identified themselves when she entered the room and immediately asked her if she sympathized with Communism. She answered no. Was she a Christian? Yes. Did she go to church on Sundays? Yes. What school did her daughter attend? Our Lady of Perpetual Help, a Catholic school. Did her husband go to church? Sometimes. Was her husband opposed to her daughter attending a Catholic school? No.

Although the interrogation had been brief, Nora was very humiliated. The FBI had no reason to interrogate Nora at her job on a matter that had nothing to do with her employment.

And, routinely, we were followed. On many mornings a car would be parked at the end of our block, which at that time was a dead-end. Seven out of the 10 houses on it were family, so an unfamiliar car was obvious.

My neighbors and co-workers were interrogated. My family's every move was watched.

Victoriano Manteiga's conversation with the agents went the same. He told them little because there was little to tell. We supported Castro because Fulgencio Batista y Zaldívar was a tyrant. Castro turned to Communism, and the United States cut off relations with Cuba. So, we no longer supported Castro or his government.

Carlos Carbonell's answers differed slightly when he was questioned in October. He still refused to admit that Cuba was Communist and defended the country's ties to Russia as economically necessary.

Felix Someillán would later detail that by then his uncle Enrique was one of many sporting a new bumper sticker on his car, a 1954 Buick, that read, "Cuba yes, Russia no."

Tired of the needling I took at work for a bumper sticker with the likeness of Castro that I had on the back of my Plymouth Cambridge car, I removed it in October. And with it, ties to my former life as a Cuban revolutionary were severed.

27

# Saying Goodbye to Cuban Cigars

The revolution brought about the end of Ybor City's vaunted rolled cigar industry.
Factories had already begun to close because of the growth in popularity of cigarettes and because the advent of rolling machines meant fewer people were needed to create the same number of cigars as in previous years.
Still, according to a *New York Times* article on February 4, 1962, the year 1961 was a record-breaking year for Tampa's tobacco industry with 750 million cigars rolled by machine.[1]
But this industry flourished due to the popularity of Cuba's fine tobacco, and Tampa had a virtual monopoly on the crop.
As relations between the United States and Cuba continued to be strained, Carlos Fuente Sr., then-head of the Arturo Fuente Cigar Company and in his 20s, had a hunch that tobacco imports from the island would soon be cut off.[2]
So, in early January 1961, Fuente borrowed money from a friend, promising the investment would be well worth it, and then left for Cuba to purchase a large shipment of Cuban tobacco. The amount and the cost had long been forgotten years later when the Fuente family recalled this history.[3]
On February 3, 1962, President John F. Kennedy signed the Cuban embargo, but, according to legend, before he did, he asked an aide to purchase 1,000 Cuban cigars.
The Fuentes recalled that their father told them he was worried over the next few days because his tobacco had not yet arrived, and all Cuban imports had been cut off.[4]
Then, a few days later, they were contacted by the federal government. The boat failed to reach Tampa's port before the embargo began. The government confiscated the tobacco, saying its purchase was in violation of the embargo.[5]

But Fuente was able to prove he paid for it with cash before the presidential proclamation. The government turned the tobacco over to him a few weeks later.[6]

It may have been the last shipment of Cuban tobacco to arrive in the United States, and the Fuentes used it to grow their empire.[7]

Other cigar companies begged the Fuente family to sell some of their tobacco even as the price rose from the embargo, but they refused, becoming a "premiere cigar family." Their wisdom prevailed and propelled their brand to new heights.[8]

Once most of their competitors were gone and cigar smokers had switched to the Fuente brand, they slowly withdrew Cuban tobacco from their cigars, replacing it with quality tobacco from other regions of the world, and moved their operations to the Dominican Republic, where they grow their own tobacco. Still, they kept their corporate headquarters in Ybor City.[9]

But they are a rare happy ending for Ybor's cigar industry. Post embargo, only two cigar families remained—the Fuentes and the Newmans, who continue to run J. C. Newman Cigar Company. The rest were shuttered. It was the end of an era.

Years later, the Fuente family became neighbors of mine. My wife, Nora, grew up in Ybor not far from the Arturo Fuente home where the company had its humble beginnings rolling cigars in the back of the house. They eventually moved to West Tampa, and in the early 1970s, Carlos and Anna Lopez Fuente built their new home a block from where we lived. Their backyard faced Nora's cousin's backyard across the street from us.

My daughters were friends with their children, Carlito, Cynthia, and Ricky, and they had carved a path in the grass between our houses from going back and forth so often. All through the years, our families were friends, and, to this day, Cynthia remains someone especially dear to me.

28

# The Cuban Missile Crisis

The Cuban Missile Crisis split the Carbonell family.
Tired of the harassment from the FBI and neighbors, Carlos Carbonell and his family would relocate to Cuba in December 1961. There, Carbonell worked as a pressman for *Bohemia*.[1]
But his daughter Daisy Carbonell Rocamora remained in Tampa rather than uproot her American-born kids.[2]
George Carbonell said 75 percent of Cuba was pro-Castro, but it became apparent within weeks of moving to the island that they were in more danger there due to opposition forces than in Tampa.[3]
They lived near the coast and often saw small-scale American military attacks against Cuba. During one offensive, George Carbonell said, U.S. gunfire sprayed an apartment building and nearly killed an infant in a crib.[4]
Life became even tenser after the United States discovered the Soviet missiles on October 16, 1962, and the nations moved toward the brink of nuclear war.
George Carbonell watched as the Cuban military assembled on the beach near his home and later ducked for cover when tanks shot at a U.S. spy plane.[5]
He wondered if he would survive an American invasion, while his sister back in Florida worried that the nuclear missiles might be fired at Florida.[6]
And with phone service between the nations cut off, the family members could not check up on one another.[7]
Of course, the Soviet Union eventually agreed to move its nuclear weapons, and the crisis eased. But the Carbonells sought a return to Tampa. They did not agree with Communism and were tired of the threat from the United States.[8]
George Carbonell said his mother, Isabel, did not want to do it on a rinky-dink boat under the veil of darkness, though. That was too risky. Instead, they asked the Cuban government for permission to return to the

United States. George and his mother were granted the opportunity. Carlos was not. It would have been an embarrassment to the Cuban government for a revolutionary and employee of its official magazine to leave the country.[9]

In late 1962, a day before George Carbonell and his mother were scheduled to leave Cuba, the G2, Cuba's political police, visited the Carbonells' home and took inventory of what they owned. They were told they could take a few pairs of clothes to the United States. The rest of their belongings, including George Carbonell's gold chain and his mother's jewelry, were confiscated. The next day, they boarded a plane and landed in Miami an hour later. They were questioned by the FBI but were allowed to return to Tampa and resume their lives because it was apparent that they knew nothing of the inner workings of the Cuban government.[10]

Six months later, George Carbonell enlisted in the military for a two-year term. During his time in the military—the exact month and year escaped George—his father slipped out of Cuba and returned to the United States.[11]

He said his father had friends in the Cuban secret police who felt bad for him because he was separated from his family. Carbonell's friends knew of a flight leaving for Mexico late one night and told Carlos to be at the terminal. His friends then led him onto the plane, using their credentials to convince the airline that Carbonell was to be given a seat because he had important "press business" to tend to in Mexico.[12]

Carbonell went right to the U.S. embassy when he arrived in Mexico, asked for asylum, and was allowed to return to Tampa.[13]

George Carbonell said that his father was questioned off and on by the FBI over the next few years, but the Cubans who once bullied the family left them alone. Over the next few decades, according to George Carbonell, his father rarely spoke of the Cuban Revolution or his work with the M-26-7. In 1992, Carlos passed away. His obituary only listed him as a cigar maker and a native of Cuba.[14]

29

# The Assassination of JFK

The assassination of President John F. Kennedy on November 22, 1963, in Texas brought scrutiny upon Tampa. The president had been in Tampa just four days prior on November 18.

From the start, there were questions whether Cuba was involved, so the FBI increased surveillance on those communities with Cuban populations that had been sympathetic to Castro.

In 2018 when U.S. President Donald Trump released more of the FBI's JFK files, I learned that the federal law enforcement agency stopped by the home of Marcelino Golan the day after the assassination, but no one was there.[1]

Why? Why would Golan be of such interest in the wake of the murder of our president?

His son Ernesto Golan later suggested that perhaps it was because of a man who had stayed with them for a couple of weeks a few years earlier.[2]

Ernesto Golan could not recall the man's name, only that he appeared to be hiding from someone and said the FBI had been pestering him. A white American slightly on the heavy side and with a receding hairline, he distributed pro-Fidel Castro Ruz publications on behalf of Fair Play for Cuba Committee.[3]

This organization was thrust into the public eye on April 6, 1960, when it took out a full-page ad in the *New York Times*.[4]

The ad, titled "What Is Really Happening in Cuba," maintained that some of the charges against Cuba being made by the United States government were untrue and laid out its arguments in a question-and-answer format.[5]

For example, the ad explained that American landowners were offered payment for their nationalized property through 20-year Cuban government bonds at an interest rate of four percent and had not just been seized, but the U.S. government said no.[6]

Of course, in the ad, the committee stated it does not believe Cuba leans Communist. We know now that was not true.[7]

261

Among those who signed the ad were Truman Capote, Allen Ginsberg, Simone de Beauvoir, and Carleton Beals.[8]

The committee held their first public meeting on April 24, 1960, at the Community Church in New York City, where they restated much of what was in the ad.[9]

That same full-page ad later appeared in the Sunday edition of the *Tampa Tribune* on May 15, 1960.

The Fair Play for Cuba Committee was officially established in Tampa in early 1961.

The organization did much of the same work the M-26-7 once did: it hosted rallies, usually at José Martí Park, and published editorials in the local newspapers advocating for better relations with Cuba.

I attended one meeting at a church on Platt Street near Bayshore Boulevard shortly after the M-26-7 dissolved. They showed some pro–Cuba movie, leaders gave some speeches, and they planned future rallies. I noticed a couple of very obvious-looking FBI agents in the audience, who at the end of the film were seen going throughout the parking lot making note of people's license plate numbers. That was my one and only experience with the Fair Play Committee.

Ernesto Golan attended one meeting also, doing so with his father and the man who was staying at their home. The strange man, said Ernesto, was a keynote speaker that night, but it was not clear if he was a leader or just an outspoken member.[10]

When the man left his home, he gifted a chessboard to Ernesto and was then never seen again.[11]

Fair Play ceased to exist in 1963.

A year later, Vincent T. Lee—who once headed up the Tampa chapter—became a nationally known figure when he testified before the Warren Commission in April 1964 about his correspondence with Lee Harvey Oswald, who was interested in setting up a New Orleans chapter of the Fair Play Committee.

Another familiar name in the Warren Commission report was that of Silverio Mario Villamia, my brother. He earned that placement for working with Robert McKeown in Texas to run guns to Cuba as part of the Carlos Prío Socarrás-funded expedition that resulted with him and four others being arrested and jailed. McKeown owned the house where the arms were being stored. Jack Ruby heard of the arms smuggling operation and reached out to McKeown to see if he needed assistance. Nothing ever came of it, though.[12]

But that alone was enough for Mario's name to be attached to one of the most infamous reports in U.S. history.

Also of interest in the JFK files released under President Donald Trump was what came of Enrique Someillán.

## 29. The Assassination of JFK

Along with former Tampa M-26-7 member Raul Moran, Someillán formed an organization called the Anti-Communist Group to Help in the Liberation of Cuba that later became part of another organization, Insurrectional Movement for Revolutionary Recovery, with Someillán heading the Tampa branch.[13]

Also known as MIRR, Movimiento Insurreccional de Recuperación Revoluciónario, the group's Miami affiliate was run by its founder Orlando Bosch Avila, a CIA-backed Cuban exile the FBI once declared an anti-Castro "terrorist" for, among other acts, firing a bazooka at a Polish ship in Miami and bombing a Cuban airliner on October 6, 1976, on which all 73 passengers were killed.[14]

Miami's MIRR would assimilate into yet another organization, Cuba Power, that threatened actions against any country doing business with Cuba.

Cuba Power would admit to planting explosives that detonated on board the Japanese freighter *Asaka Maru* in Tampa on May 30, 1968. The ship was damaged in the explosion, but no one was injured, according to news archives. The assassination records reveal that an explosives expert from MacDill Air Force Base determined that it was set off by a "chemical long-delay detonator."

Informants, according to the records, told the FBI that the Tampa wing of MIRR was peaceful and mostly dealt with the dissemination of propaganda.

The FBI also wrote that Bosch had not been in Tampa during the year before the bombing of the ship.

Still, Someillán of the Tampa branch was his "natural friend," and they were known to talk on the phone, according to the assassination records. Moreover, they reveal, two of Bosch's top aides visited the city less than two weeks before the explosion.

That Someillán would work with a man like Bosch saddens me. Bosch killed innocent people. This is inexcusable.

## 30

# My Brother Comes Home

I was no longer a revolutionary, but I guess someone forgot to tell the FBI.

According to the FBI files for myself, Victoriano Manteiga, and the M-26-7, the law enforcement agency continued to document our comings and goings for years, at times falsely accusing us of remaining active supporters of Fidel Castro Ruz. But none of that was true, well, at least on my part.

From time to time, some sort of pro–Castro activity would arise. In October 1964, for instance, offices, homes, and automobiles of anti–Castro activists were bombed with Molotov cocktails. A month later, the Ybor City church Our Lady of Perpetual Help was slightly torched in the same manner and the words "Viva Fidel" were painted on the wall.

As for my brother Mario, he returned to New York and got a job as a tool and die maker. But, within a couple months early in 1961, Mario decided to move with his family to Tampa.

By then, his oldest daughter, Natacha, was in third grade and attended Our Lady of Perpetual Help with my daughter Rhonda, who was in first grade. His third daughter, Deborah, was a baby.

I took Mario to see Cosmo Re, a friend who at the time was in a supervisory position at the Port of Tampa. But there were no openings available. So, after a short while with no luck finding the type of employment he wanted, he and his family returned to New York. He went to his former employer, and they gave him his job once again. A few days after having been back at work, a couple FBI agents showed up at his job and arrested him for having violated parole.

Remember, after being arrested in Houston in 1958 for arms possession and sentenced to two years, he was released on parole. However, when he left for Cuba in January 1959, he broke parole.

So, he had to complete the remainder of his sentence for violating this.

Federal Judge Allen Burroughs Hannay had placed him on a

22-month probation beginning on August 22, 1958. Mario was supposed to report monthly to the Miami probation office, but when he moved to Cuba and did not report in February, March, or April 1959, a probation violator warrant was issued on May 18, 1959. His hearing before Judge Hannay was held on November 17, 1961, and he was sentenced to 13 months in a Seagoville, Texas prison.[1]

But he was able to transfer to a correctional facility in Danbury, Connecticut, which was closer to his family, and, with good behavior, he was eligible for release by September 24, 1962. After his release, he remained in New York until 1967 and then moved to Miramar, Florida. By then he had had two more children: son Michael and youngest daughter Elizabeth. He moved back up to the northeast for a season, eventually moving back south to Sunrise, Florida.

Angel Pérez-Vidal had sought to resign from his chief of staff and financial administrator positions at the presidential palace about three weeks prior to President Manuel Urrutia Lleó's July 17, 1959, impeachment. From the beginning of Urrutia's term, there had been much tension caused by the secretary to the president, Luis Buch Rodriguez, who was covertly undermining the work of the president. Pérez-Vidal observed this and tried to make Urrutia aware of the situation, but the president refused to accept that anything sinister was occurring.[2]

In his book *Historia Íntima de la Revolución Cubana* (*An Intimate History of the Cuban Revolution*), Pérez-Vidal elaborates on the many things he witnessed that caused him to suspect Buch was slowly inserting the political dagger into Urrutia, per Fidel Castro's directives. By the end of June when it became apparent that his insight was being ignored and things continued status quo, he gave his resignation, effective June 30. It was only at the personal request of Urrutia's wife, Esperanza Llaguno Aguirre, that he agreed to remain an additional 30 days until July 31 so a replacement could be found. But by July 17, Urrutia was no longer president. Buch, the Castros, the cabinet, and whatever other co-conspirators were involved in making Urrutia appear treasonous had succeeded.[3]

Pérez-Vidal occupied other lesser positions outside the palace once President Osvaldo Dorticós Torrado replaced Urrutia. He was not in agreement with the Communist ideology that had slowly infiltrated the Revolutionary Government, so he had determined he would take steps to leave Cuba. Since his wife, Alma Rivera, was American, she had been offered numerous opportunities to leave the island nation. But she refused to leave if her husband could not be by her side. Of course, Cuba was not going to allow someone as important as Pérez-Vidal to go into exile. So, they quietly continued to explore options for their mutual departure.[4]

Ironically, as things were lining up to have their exit together become reality, he was offered the position of Minister of Education that Armando Hart Dávalos had occupied from the triumph of the revolution. It sounds like a familiar tactic, offering attractive high-level positions to revolutionaries who were about to flee Cuba. He was told that Hart was going to be occupying another position, so Pérez-Vidal was offered the opportunity to be Hart's successor. Pérez-Vidal never learned whether Hart was ever aware of this plan to remove him as Minister of Education. Pérez-Vidal was already planning to leave the country when the offer was made.[5]

He left Cuba on January 18, 1963, aboard one of the last Red Cross flights. He and Alma went to her native New York City to start a new life. Though he had been an accountant in Cuba prior to the revolution, he became a social worker in New York, earning a master of social work and a master of arts in arts and literature. He also earned a master of science in psychology when he moved to Miami. He continued his education until ultimately attaining a doctorate in psychology and was a clinical psychologist at the University of Miami School of Medicine until retirement.[6]

In January 2010, my daughter Rhonda orchestrated a visit between

Old friends reunite in Miami after 50 years. Raul Villamia, Howard K. Davis, and Mario Villamia share a precious visit together, reminiscing about their days in the M-26-7. Howard assisted Mario in arms acquisition for the M-26-7 in exile, opening a new rebel front in the Sierra, and piloting a weapon-filled flight to Raúl Castro. Miami, Florida, January 12, 2010 (from the collection of Rhonda Villamia).

## 30. My Brother Comes Home

Raul Villamia, Angel Perez-Vidal, and Mario Villamia share a long overdue visit, and many memories. Angel and Mario were friends since 1946, when both had moved to New York City, and then were part of the first anti–Batista club in the United States, Acción Cívica Cubana, established in April 1952. Hialeah, Florida, January 11, 2010 (from the collection of Rhonda Villamia).

Mario and Howard K. Davis. They had not seen each other since that meeting they had in Tampa in 1960 when Mario had just returned from Cuba. I had not seen Davis since then either. Mario had been in phone touch with Davis over the previous years and was always saying they were going to get together, but they had never gotten around to doing it.

Since Pérez-Vidal was near Miami in Hialeah and Mario had also been in phone touch with him but had not seen him since their revolutionary days, Rhonda arranged a reunion for them as well.

So, when, in January 2010, Rhonda and I drove to Sunrise to help my sisters Irene and Marta pack and move to Tampa, she seized this opportunity to have these old friends reunite after so many years. It was a very special moment for all of us. Although Mario never saw Davis or Pérez-Vidal again, they continued to converse by phone. Mario's last few years of life were spent in Holliston, Massachusetts, near his daughter Liz. He died in February 2013, just four months short of his 90th birthday.

I have seen Davis a few times since that initial 2010 visit. Interestingly, from our exchanges, I learned he had been the technical advisor for the 1991 Oliver Stone movie *JFK*.[7]

Davis had also been a member of InterPen (Intercontinental

Penetration Force), established by Gerald Patrick Hemming in 1961 to provide training to anti-Castro group members.[8]

I only got to see Pérez-Vidal once after our 2010 reunion. He passed away in May 2015.

Even though the revolution had played such a large role in our lives, Mario and I rarely spoke of our efforts to support Castro in those early years after relations between our countries were severed. We both just wanted to move on.

I think I best summed it up during one of my initial meetings with the FBI when they asked what I thought of Communist Cuba.

I replied that I was not in favor of Cuba because the United States is accusing it of being Communist, but I am not against Castro because part of my family still lives in Cuba.

At the time of that FBI interrogation, I was concerned about my brother Miguel and two sisters Irene and Marta, who had been living in Cuba after having moved back from the United States where each of them at one point or another lived in Ohio, New York, and Florida since the mid-1940s.

Cubans who had family members move to America were often harassed, especially if the person was someone who had been a well-known revolutionary leader like Mario. So, both Mario and I adopted a neutral posture, neither supporting nor against Castro, for the sake of our family still living there. And when Pérez-Vidal wrote his *Historia Intima de la Revolución Cubana* in 1989, Mario specifically requested that he please not include Mario's name in the book, for that very reason.[9]

It only appears on a small May 7, 1957, hand-written letter from Pedro Miret Prieto and Gutavos Arcos Bergnes addressed to "General." The note was to have been hand delivered to General Alberto Bayo Giroud, with instructions that, upon his arrival in Miami, he was to "go to the address of Mario Villamia, 1443 NE Miami Place, and present him with the note." Faustino Pérez Hernández had requested that Bayo be sent to Cuba to train the rebels, and they were trying to make arrangements for that, but only Mario and Pablo Fernandez Alegre were savvy as to the details.[10]

So, although Mario's name appears in Pérez-Vidal's book, it is only mentioned as part of a historical artifact, the photo of which he used as an illustration.

I do not believe our family in Cuba would have been harassed for this. But we just did not know what might trigger retaliations.

## 31

# Viva Cuba Libre

As the decades passed, I admit I at times forgot why it was that I ever supported Fidel Castro Ruz. I recalled his words and how he reminded me and countless others of José Martí Pérez, but the bombardment of anti-Castro propaganda clouded those memories.

Then, in late July 2010, I took a trip to Cuba with my daughter Rhonda and two grandsons Wynter and Javan Galindez.

Wynter had done a six-week study abroad program in Habana the summer of 1998. He was part of a pioneer group of 10 students from Duke University, which included Washington Alcebo Duke, son of Anthony Drexel Duke and Maria "Luly" de Lourdes Alcebo Duke, a Habana native. Luly founded an organization called "Fundacion Amistad" in 1997 dedicated to fostering understanding between the people of the United States and Cuba. Duke University was making its first trip to Cuba post–revolution. During his stay, Wynter developed a rapport with one of his professors at Casa de las Americas, the educational institute in Habana founded by Haydée Santamaría Cuadrado where they had their classes. Professor Gerardo Hernandez Bencomo was a walking encyclopedia of Cuban history, with an endearing personality. When we were planning our 2010 visit, Wynter reached out to Hernandez to let him know he would be coming with his family. Gerardo was instantly adopted into our family.

He took us on a tour of the former palace, which now houses the Revolutionary Museum, where details of the struggle against Fulgencio Batista y Zaldívar are preserved.

The savage-looking photos of men tortured under the Batista regime reminded me why that dictator needed to be overthrown.

At one point, Hernandez's speech about Batista's many crimes against Cuba became so impassioned that a crowd formed around him and hung on his every word.

He then looked at me and, with his voice breaking with emotion, informed the onlookers that, from Tampa, I supported Castro and his fight against Batista.

In the big picture, what I did for the revolution was small. I did not put my life on the line like so many young men did. I only collected money and supplies.

Still, the men and women in that museum room clapped and cheered for me. I wept, as did my daughter. My grandsons beamed with pride.

For that one moment, I was transported back in time to January 1, 1959, when all of Tampa applauded the efforts of the M-26-7, when what we did for Castro was noble. Viva Cuba libre.

# Chapter Notes

## Chapter 2

1. Eusebio Leal Spengler, Email to Rhonda Villamia, August 7, 2012; *El Cerro...Llave de la Ciudad—Enero*; "Cuban Student Is Killed in Gunfight With Police," Associated Press, *Chicago Tribune*, January 16, 1933, 5; "Spain Protests to Cuba About Killing of Student," Associated Press, *St. Louis Post-Dispatch*, January 21, 1933, 6; "Cuba Gets Notes From Spain Protesting Slaying of Citizen," Associated Press, January 20, 1933.
2. "Last of Machado Henchmen Killed," *The Brownsville Herald*, September 2, 1933, 1; "Last One of Machado's Strong-Arm Squad Killed," *Baltimore Sun*, September 2, 1933, 7.

## Chapter 4

1. Mario Villamia, Interviewed by Rhonda Villamia, February 7, 2007 to October 24, 2010.
2. Mario Villamia, interview.
3. Mario Villamia, interview.
4. Mario Villamia, interview.
5. Mario Villamia, interview.
6. Mario Villamia, interview.
7. Mario Villamia, interview.
8. Mario Villamia, interview.
9. Mario Villamia, interview.
10. Mario Villamia, interview.
11. Mario Villamia, interview.
12. Tad Szulc, *Fidel: A Critical Portrait* (Harper Perennial, 2000), 274–279.
13. Szulc, *Fidel*, 274–279.
14. Szulc, *Fidel*, 274–279.
15. Szulc, *Fidel*, 274–279.
16. Szulc, *Fidel*, 274–279.
17. Szulc, *Fidel*, 274–279.
18. Mario Villamia, interview.
19. Mario Villamia, interview; Vicente Cubillas, "Cubanos En Nueva York...Los Verdaderos Heroes De La Revolución Son, En Este Momento," *Bohemia*, 46–49, 76–77.
20. Mario Villamia, interview.
21. Heberto Norman Acosta, *La Palabra Empenada, Tomo 1* (Oficina de Publicaciónes del Consejo de Estado, 2005), 132–133.
22. Acosta, *La Palabra*, 132–133.
23. Acosta, *La Palabra*, 132–133.
24. Alberto Bayo, *Mi Aporte a la Revolución Cubana* (Ejército Rebelde, 1960).
25. Alvaro Pérez, Letter to Mario Villamia, September 6, 1955.
26. Angel Pérez-Vidal, *Historia Íntima de la Revolución Cubana* (Ediciones Universal, 1997), 40–59; Acosta, *La Palabra*, 298.
27. Pérez-Vidal, *Historia*, 40–59; Acosta, *La Palabra*, 298.
28. Pérez-Vidal, *Historia*, 40–59; Acosta, *La Palabra*, 298.
29. Pérez-Vidal, *Historia*, 40–59; Acosta, *La Palabra*, 298.
30. Pérez-Vidal, *Historia*, 40–59; Acosta, *La Palabra*, 298.
31. Pérez-Vidal, *Historia*, 40–59; Acosta, *La Palabra*, 298.
32. Pérez-Vidal, *Historia*, 40–59; Acosta, *La Palabra*, 298.
33. Pérez-Vidal, *Historia*, 40–59; Acosta, *La Palabra*, 298.
34. Mario Villamia, interview; Acosta, *La Palabra*, 302–305.
35. Mario Villamia, interview; Acosta, *La Palabra*, 302–305.
36. Mario Villamia, interview; Acosta, *La Palabra*, 302–305.

37. Mario Villamia, interview; Acosta, *La Palabra*, 302–305.
38. Mario Villamia, interview; Acosta, *La Palabra*, 302–305.
39. Mario Villamia, interview; Acosta, *La Palabra*, 305–313.
40. Mario Villamia, interview; Acosta, *La Palabra*, 305–313.
41. Mario Villamia, interview; Acosta, *La Palabra*, 305–313.
42. Mario Villamia, interview; Acosta, *La Palabra*, 305–313.
43. Mario Villamia, interview; Acosta, *La Palabra*, 305–313.
44. Mario Villamia, interview; Acosta, *La Palabra*, 305–313.
45. Mario Villamia, interview; Acosta, *La Palabra*, 305–313.
46. Mario Villamia, interview; Acosta, *La Palabra*, 305–313.
47. Mario Villamia, interview; Acosta, *La Palabra*, 313–315.
48. Mario Villamia, interview; Acosta, *La Palabra*, 313–315.
49. Fidel Castro, New York City speech, Office of Historic Affairs, Habana, Cuba, October 28, 1953.
50. Mario Villamia, interview; Acosta, *La Palabra*, 316.
51. Fidel Castro, New York City speech, October 28, 1953.
52. Fidel Castro, New York City speech, October 28, 1953.
53. Fidel Castro, New York City speech, October 28, 1953.
54. Mario Villamia, interview; Acosta, *La Palabra*, 316, 319.
55. Mario Villamia, interview; Acosta, *La Palabra*, 316, 319.
56. Mario Villamia, interview; Acosta, *La Palabra*, 316, 319.
57. Acosta, *La Palabra*, 323–329.
58. Acosta, *La Palabra*, 323–329.
59. Acosta, *La Palabra*, 323–329.
60. Acosta, *La Palabra*, 323–329.
61. Acosta, *La Palabra*, 323–329.
62. Acosta, *La Palabra*, 343–349.
63. Acosta, *La Palabra*, 343–349.
64. Acosta, *La Palabra*, 348–350.
65. Acosta, *La Palabra*, 348–350.
66. Acosta, *La Palabra*, 348–350.
67. Acosta, *La Palabra*, 348–350.
68. Acosta, *La Palabra*, 348–350.
69. Acosta, *La Palabra*, 348–350.
70. Acosta, *La Palabra*, 348–350.

## Chapter 5

1. Tony Pizzo, "The Cigar That Sparked a Revolution," *Sunland Tribune* 6, no. 5 (1980): 32–35.
2. Pizzo, "The Cigar."
3. Paul Guzzo, "Memorial Planned in Tampa for Civil War Hero Clara Barton of the Red Cross," *Tampa Bay Times*, August 31, 2017, 1.
4. Victoriano Manteiga, "Chungas y No Chungas," *La Gaceta*, October 21, 1950, 1.
5. Victoriano Manteiga, "Chungas y Chungas," *La Gaceta*, October 21, 1950, 1.
6. Patrick Manteiga, Interviewed by Paul Guzzo, 2017.
7. Manteiga, interview.
8. Manteiga, interview.
9. Manteiga, interview.
10. Manteiga, interview.
11. Manteiga, interview.
12. Manteiga, interview.
13. Manteiga, interview.
14. Manteiga, interview.
15. Rhonda Villamia, "Building José Martí Park," *Cigar City Magazine*, September/October 2008, 18–21; Bob Denley, "Somewhere in Cuba ... Long Lost Statue and Sculptor Sought," *Tampa Times*, January 1, 1959, 1.
16. Rhonda Villamia, "Building José Martí Park"; Denley, "Somewhere."
17. Fidel Castro, "Asaltado y Destruido el Estudio Del Escultor Fidalgo," *Bohemia*, February 8, 1953, www.granma.cu/cuba/2018-07-12/asaltado-y-destruido-el-estudio-del-escultor-fidalgo-12-07-2018-19-07-25.
18. Castro, "Asaltado y Destruido el Estudio Del Escultor Fidalgo."
19. Castro, "Asaltado y Destruido el Estudio Del Escultor Fidalgo."
20. Castro, "Asaltado y Destruido el Estudio Del Escultor Fidalgo."
21. José Manuel Fidalgo, Letters to Victoriano Manteiga, October 14, 1955; FBI Record: Participants: Nestor Suarez Feliu, Lauro Blanco, and Jacob Canter: May 22, 1953, U.S. Department of State Confidential Memorandum of Conversation, Page 1 of Encl No. Desp. No. 1832 from Habana; "Solución de un Presunto Secuestro Como Polizón Llego a N. York, el Dia 19 el Escultor J.M. Fidalgo," *Prensa Libre*, May 22, 1953; FBI Record: May 25, 1953, Foreign Service Dispatch from American Embassy,

Habana Cuba, Desp. No. 1832, Subject: José Manuel Fidalgo, Stowaway Arrival in New York, re: *Havana Herald* February 1, 1953 "Sculptor Sought as Prio Agent."

## Chapter 6

1. Ernesto Golan, Interviewed by Rhonda Villamia and Paul Guzzo, November 24, 2017.
2. Pete Arnade, Interviewed by Paul Guzzo, December 2016.
3. Arnade, interview.
4. Arnade, interview.
5. Acosta, *La Palabra*, 353–354.
6. Acosta, *La Palabra*, 353–354.
7. Tom O'Connor, "Anti-Batista Cuban Comes to Seek Revolt Here," *Tampa Tribune*, November 26, 1955, 1; Flyer: "Invitamos a Todos los Cubanos de Tampa" invitation to Fidel Castro's speech November 27, 1955.
8. Tom O'Connor, "Italian Club Bars Theatre to Leader of Cuban Revolt," *Tampa Tribune*, November 27, 1955, 1.
9. Tom O' Connor, "Cubans Here Give Funds to Aid Revolt Against Batista," *Tampa Tribune*, November 28, 1955, 12; "Demanda Fidel Castro Que Batista Renuncíe," *La Gaceta*, December 2, 1955, 2.
10. Paul Guzzo, "Some from Tampa were Shocked over Castro's Rise," *Tampa Bay Times*, December 3, 2016, B-1.
11. Guzzo, "Some from Tampa."

## Chapter 7

1. Acosta, *La Palabra*, 363–373.
2. Acosta, *La Palabra*, 363–373.
3. Acosta, *La Palabra*, 363–373.
4. Acosta, *La Palabra*, 363–373.
5. Acosta, *La Palabra*, 363–373.
6. Acosta, *La Palabra*, 363–373.
7. Acosta, *La Palabra*, 363–373.
8. Acosta, *La Palabra*, 363–373.
9. Acosta, *La Palabra*, 363–373.
10. Acosta, *La Palabra*, 363–373.
11. Acosta, *La Palabra*, 363–373.
12. Acosta, *La Palabra*, 363–373.
13. Estes Kefauver, *Crime in America* (Doubleday & Company, 1951).
14. Kefauver, *Crime in America*.
15. Kefauver, *Crime in America*.
16. Fidel Castro, Letter to Mario Villamia, December 15, 1955.
17. Fidel Castro, Letter to Mario Villamia, December 20, 1955.

## Chapter 8

1. Juan M. Pérez, Interviewed by Rhonda Villamia, August 3, 2010.
2. Pérez, interview.
3. Rafael García Bárcena, Interviewed by Rhonda Villamia, September 15, 2018, to July 2, 2019.
4. Bárcena, interview.
5. Bárcena, interview.
6. Bárcena, interview.
7. Bárcena, interview.
8. Bárcena, interview.
9. Bárcena, interview.
10. Bárcena, interview.
11. Bárcena, interview.
12. Bárcena, interview.
13. Pérez, interview.
14. Pérez, interview.
15. Pérez, interview.
16. Bárcena, interview.
17. Pérez, interview.
18. Bárcena, interview.
19. Bárcena, interview.
20. Bárcena, interview.
21. Bárcena, interview.
22. Bárcena, interview; Johan Moya Ramis, "Entre la Memoria y el Olvido," Fondos Bibliograficos de la Biblioteca Nacional de Cuba José Martí; Luis Alberto Pérez-Llody, *Rafael García Barcena: el sueño de la gran nación* (Editorial Oriente, 2007).
23. Bárcena, interview.
24. Fidel Castro, Letter to Victoriano Manteiga, December 13, 1955.
25. Fidel Castro, Letter to Raul Villamia, January 2, 1956.
26. Jesús Montané, Letter to Raul Villamia, January 5, 1956.
27. "Protestan Detención en Mexico Dr. Fidel Castro," United Press, June 24, 1956; "Exilados Veran al Consul en Nueva York," United Press, June 24, 1956.
28. "Protestan Detención en Mexico Dr. Fidel Castro"; "Exilados Veran al Consul En Nueva York."
29. Victoriano Manteiga, "Chungas y No Chungas," *La Gaceta*, June 29, 1956, 1.
30. Victoriano Manteiga, "Fidel Castro Sets His Conditions," *La Gaceta*, November 23, 1956, 1.

31. Szulc, *Fidel*, 366–367.
32. Szulc, *Fidel*, 366–367.
33. Szulc, *Fidel*, 366–367.
34. Szulc, *Fidel*, 371–377.
35. Szulc, *Fidel*, 371–377.
36. Szulc, *Fidel*, 371–377.
37. Szulc,. *Fidel*, 371–377.
38. Szulc, *Fidel*, 371–377.
39. Szulc, *Fidel*, 371–377.
40. Szulc, *Fidel*, 371–377.
41. Szulc, *Fidel*, 371–377.
42. Szulc, *Fidel*, 371–377.
43. Szulc, *Fidel*, 371–377.
44. Szulc, *Fidel*, 371–377.
45. Szulc, *Fidel*, 371–377.
46. Szulc, *Fidel*, 371–377.
47. Mario Villamia, interview.
48. "Cuba Planes, Troops Annihilate 40 Invaders," *New York Times*, December 3, 1956, 2.
49. Szulc, *Fidel*, 371–377.
50. Szulc, *Fidel*, 371–377.
51. Szulc, *Fidel*, 371–377.

## Chapter 9

1. Victoriano Manteiga, "Chungas y No Chungas," *La Gaceta*, December 14, 1956, 1.
2. Mario Villamia, interview.
3. Mario Villamia, interview.
4. Mario Villamia, interview.
5. Mario Villamia, interview.
6. Mario Villamia, interview.
7. Mario Villamia, interview.
8. Mario Villamia, interview.
9. Mario Villamia, interview.
10. Mario Villamia, interview.
11. Mario Villamia, interview.
12. Mario Villamia, interview.
13. Herbert Matthews, "Cuban Rebel Is Visited in Cuba," *New York Times*, February 24, 1957, 1.
14. Matthews, "Cuban Rebel."
15. Matthews, "Cuban Rebel."
16. Mike Garvey, Interviewed by Rhonda Villamia and Paul Guzzo, February 1, 2019.
17. Garvey, interview.
18. Garvey, interview.
19. Garvey, interview.
20. Garvey, interview.
21. Garvey, interview.
22. Garvey, interview.
23. Garvey, interview.
24. Garvey, interview.
25. Garvey, interview.
26. Garvey, interview.
27. Garvey, interview.
28. Garvey, interview.
29. Garvey, interview.
30. Garvey, interview.
31. Garvey, interview.
32. Garvey, interview.
33. Garvey, interview.
34. Garvey, interview.
35. Garvey, interview.
36. Garvey, interview.
37. Garvey, interview.
38. Garvey, interview.
39. Garvey, interview.
40. Garvey, interview.
41. Garvey, interview.
42. Garvey, interview.
43. Garvey, interview.
44. Garvey, interview.
45. Garvey, interview.
46. Garvey, interview.
47. Habana Embassy, Dispatch to the Department of State, May 29, 1957; "Misa Por el Alma de Jorge Prieto," *La Gaceta*, June 14, 1957, 4; Captioned photo of group in front of Our Lady of Perpetual Help Church with Mario Prieto, brother of murdered victim Jorge Prieto after Mass was celebrated in his honor, *La Gaceta*, June 28, 1957.
48. "Contra La Tiranía—A los Cubanos y sus Amigos de Tampa," *La Gaceta*, June 28, 1957, 2; "Batista Foes Rally Here," *Tampa Morning Tribune*, July 1, 1957, 6; "Asamblea de los Amigos de Fidel Castro y de la Libertad de Cuba," *La Gaceta*, June 28, 1957; "Acto de Adhesión a Fidel Castro y a los Que Combaten por la Libertad de Cuba," *La Gaceta*, July 5, 1957.
49. Paul Guzzo, "New JFK files feature a few surprises about intrigue in Tampa as Castro rose to power," *Tampa Bay Times*, November 2, 2017, A-1.
50. Guzzo, "New JFK files."
51. Guzzo, "New JFK files."
52. Guzzo, "New JFK files."
53. Guzzo, "New JFK files."

## Chapter 10

1. Raul Villamia, M-26-7 Meeting Minutes, July 16, 1957.
2. Raul Villamia, M-26-7 Meeting Minutes, July 16, 1957.

3. Raul Villamia, M-26-7 Meeting Minutes, July 16, 1957.
4. Raul Villamia, M-26-7 Meeting Minutes, July 16, 1957.
5. Victoriano Manteiga, "Incident on the Cuban Club Patio," *La Gaceta*, July 19, 1957, 1.
6. Manteiga, "Incident on the Cuban Club Patio."
7. Raul Villamia, M-26-7 Meeting Minutes, July 21, 1957.
8. Raul Villamia, M-26-7 Meeting Minutes, July 21, 1957.
9. Raul Villamia, M-26-7 Meeting Minutes, July 21, 1957.
10. Raul Villamia, M-26-7 Meeting Minutes, July 21, 1957.
11. Victoriano Manteiga, "Celebration at the Cuban Club," *La Gaceta*. August 9, 1957, 4; "Mitin del 26 de Julio en W. Tampa," *La Gaceta*, July 26, 1957; "Acto de Unidad Revoluciónaria en Miami," *La Gaceta*, July 26, 1957.
12. Raul Villamia, M-26-7 Meeting Minutes, August 14, 1957.
13. Raul Villamia, M-26-7 Meeting Minutes, July 21, 1957.
14. Raul Villamia, M-26-7 Meeting Minutes, August 20, 1957.
15. Raul Villamia, M-26-7 Meeting Minutes, September 4, 1957.
16. Raul Villamia, M-26-7 Meeting Minutes, September 4, 1957.
17. El Comité Pro Unidad Revoluciónario de Tampa booklet.
18. Chuck Hendrick, "Two Arrested in Ruckus Over Cuban Revolt Here," *Tampa Tribune*, September 21, 1957, 4.
19. Hendrick, "Two Arrested."
20. Hendrick, "Two Arrested."
21. Guzzo, "New JFK Files."
22. Angel Pérez-Vidal, *Historia Íntima de la Revolución Cubana*; Angel Pérez-Vidal, Letter to Consulate General of the United States in Montreal, Canada, August 15, 1963.
23. Pérez-Vidal, *Historia*; Angel Pérez-Vidal, Letter to Consulate General of the United States in Montreal, Canada; Angel Pérez-Vidal, Interviewed by Rhonda Villamia, May 1, 2008 to April 20, 2015.
24. Pérez-Vidal, *Historia*; Angel Pérez-Vidal, Letter to Consulate General of the United States in Montreal, Canada; Pérez-Vidal, interview.
25. Pérez-Vidal, *Historia*; Angel Pérez-Vidal, Letter to Consulate General of the United States in Montreal, Canada; Pérez-Vidal, interview.
26. Victoriano Manteiga, "Mitin del Consejo Cubano de Liberación," *La Gaceta*, November 22, 1957, 1.
27. Victoriano Manteiga, *La Gaceta*, November 8, 1957, 1.
28. Victoriano Manteiga, "Camioneta del 26 de Julio," *La Gaceta*, November 8, 1957; Victoriano Manteiga, "La Camioneta Con las Canas," *La Gaceta*, November 15, 1957, 2.
29. Victoriano Manteiga, "Dos Años de la Visita a Tampa del Dr. Fidel Castro," *La Gaceta*, November 29, 1957, 1, 11.
30. "Manifesto del Ejecutivo del Movimento 26 de Julio," *La Gaceta*, December 20, 1957, 10.
31. "Urrutia is Anti-Communist, Pro-U.S.," United Press International, January 3, 1959, www.upi.com/Archives/1959/01/03/Urrutia-is-anti-communist-pro-US/6149212204416.

## Chapter 11

1. Victoriano Manteiga, "Miami Unity Pact letter," *La Gaceta*, January 17, 1958, 1.
2. Victoriano Manteiga, "Notice of M-26-7 Meeting," *La Gaceta*, February 21, 1958, 1.
3. Virgilio Jacas Quintana, Letter to Raul Villamia, March 30, 1958.

## Chapter 12

1. Mario Villamia, interview.
2. FBI, Record Number 124-90061-10016, March 13, 1958, Released November 14, 2017.
3. Mario Villamia, interview.
4. Mario Villamia, interview.
5. Mario Villamia, interview.
6. Howard K. Davis, Interviewed by Rhonda Villamia, August 18, 2014, May 2, 2017, and September 20, 2018.
7. Davis, interview.
8. Davis, interview.
9. Davis, interview.
10. Davis, interview.
11. Davis, interview.
12. Davis, interview.

13. Davis, interview; Mario Villamia, interview.
14. Davis, interview; Mario Villamia, interview.
15. Davis, interview; Mario Villamia, interview.
16. Davis, interview; Mario Villamia, interview.
17. Davis, interview; Mario Villamia, interview.
18. Davis, interview.
19. Davis, interview; Mario Villamia, interview.
20. Davis, interview; Mario Villamia, interview.
21. Davis, interview; Mario Villamia, interview.
22. Davis, interview; Mario Villamia, interview.
23. Davis, interview; Mario Villamia, interview.
24. Davis, interview; Mario Villamia, interview.
25. Davis, interview; Mario Villamia, interview.
26. Davis, interview; Mario Villamia, interview.
27. Davis, interview; Mario Villamia, interview.
28. Davis, interview; Mario Villamia, interview.
29. Letter from Mario Villamia to Fidel Castro, May 22, 1958.
30. Mario Villamia, interview.
31. Mario Villamia, interview.
32. Pérez-Vidal, *Historia*, 128–133.
33. Pérez-Vidal, *Historia*, 128–133; Mario Villamia, interview; David Shaftel, "The Black Eagle of Harlem," *Air & Space Magazine*, January 1, 2009, www.smithsonianmag.com/air-space-magazine/the-black-eagle-of-harlem-95208344; "Exile Is Planning U.S. Laetrile Operations," *New York Times*, June 18, 1977, 9.
34. Pérez-Vidal, *Historia*, 128–133; Mario Villamia, interview; Shaftel, "The Black Eagle."
35. Pérez-Vidal, *Historia*, 128–133; Mario Villamia, interview; Shaftel, "The Black Eagle."
36. Pérez-Vidal, *Historia*, 128–133; Mario Villamia, interview; Shaftel, "The Black Eagle."
37. Pérez-Vidal, *Historia*, 128–133; Mario Villamia, interview; Shaftel, "The Black Eagle."
38. Pérez-Vidal, *Historia*, 128–133; Mario Villamia, interview; Shaftel, "The Black Eagle."
39. Pérez-Vidal, *Historia*, 128–133; Mario Villamia, interview; Shaftel, "The Black Eagle."
40. Pérez-Vidal, *Historia*, 128–133; Mario Villamia, interview; Shaftel, "The Black Eagle."
41. Pérez-Vidal, *Historia*, 128–133; Mario Villamia, interview; Shaftel, "The Black Eagle."
42. Pérez-Vidal, *Historia*, 128–133.
43. Pérez-Vidal, *Historia*, 128–133.
44. Pérez-Vidal, *Historia*, 128–133.
45. Pérez-Vidal, *Historia*, 128–133.
46. Pérez-Vidal, *Historia*, 128–133.
47. Pérez-Vidal, *Historia*, 128–133.
48. Mario Villamia, interview; Davis, interview.
49. Mario Villamia, interview; Davis, interview.
50. Mario Villamia, interview; Davis, interview.
51. Mario Villamia, interview; Davis, interview.
52. Mario Villamia, interview; Davis, interview.
53. Mario Villamia, interview; Davis, interview.
54. Davis, interview; "La Expedición de El Corojo," *Diario Granma*, Numero 103, April 28, 2008.
55. Davis, interview; "La Expedición de El Corojo."
56. Davis, interview; "La Expedición de El Corojo."
57. Davis, interview; "La Expedición de El Corojo."
58. Davis, interview; "La Expedición de El Corojo."
59. Davis, interview; "La Expedición de El Corojo."
60. Davis, interview.
61. Davis, interview.
62. Davis, interview.
63. Davis, interview.
64. Davis, interview.
65. Davis, interview.

## Chapter 13

1. M-26-7 Flyer, A Los Obreros de las Fábricas de Tabaco.
2. Hector Arturo, "Con Fidel Voy

Adonde Sea," *Verde Olivo*, October/November 2010.
3. Arturo, "Con Fidel."
4. Arturo, "Con Fidel."
5. Arturo, "Con Fidel."
6. Arturo, "Con Fidel."
7. M-26-7 Flyer, A la Colonia Cubana y al Pueblo de Tampa, Gabriel Gil Delegate, July 1958.
8. "FBI Arresto a Tres Hispanos En Houston," Associated Press, February 18, 1958; "Cubans Held After Arms Are Seized," Associated Press, February 19, 1958; "Agentes Federales Retienen Yate Bajo Sospecha de Otra Expedición Rebelde a Cuba," United Press, February 19, 1958; "Investigan En Houston la Frustrada Expedición Contra Cuba," United Press, February 19, 1958; "Three Cuban Residents of Miami Held In Texas On Plot to Invade Cuba," United Press, *Diario de Las Américas* Miami Springs, February 19, 1958; "U.S. Agents Seize Yacht, Arms and Ammunition from Cubans In Houston, Texas," United Press, *Diario de las Américas* Miami Springs, February 19, 1958; "Buscan A Complicado En Plan De Invasión," *El Mundo*, February 20, 1958; "Confiscan Armas Para Fidel, Cubanos Detenidos," *El Diario De Nueva York*, February 21, 1958; "Dictaran Sentencia Contra Otros 5 Cubanos en Texas el Próximo Once de Julio," United Press, June 21, 1958; "Cuban Exile Pleads For Group Sentenced Here," *The Houston Post*, July 26, 1959; "5 In Cuban Arms Cache Case Free On Probation," *The Houston Post*, August 13, 1958; "Sentences Of 5 Gun-Runners Are Suspended," *Chronicle*, August 13, 1958; Front-page photo, *Diario de Las Américas* Miami Springs, August 15, 1958; "Mario Villamia en Libertad," *La Gaceta*, August 22, 1958.
9. "FBI Arresto a Tres Hispanos en Houston; "Cubans Held After Arms Are Seized"; "Agentes Federales Retienen Yate Bajo Sospecha de Otra Expedición Rebelde a Cuba"; "Investigan en Houston la Frustrada Expedición Contra Cuba"; "Three Cuban Residents of Miami Held In Texas On Plot To Invade Cuba"; "U.S. Agents Seize Yacht, Arms And Ammunition From Cubans In Houston, Texas"; "Buscan a Complicado en Plan de Invasión"; "Confiscan Armas Para Fidel, Cubanos Detenidos"; "Dictaran Sentencia Contra Otros 5 Cubanos en Texas el Próximo Once de Julio"; "Cuban Exile Pleads For Group Sentenced Here"; "5 In Cuban Arms Cache Case Free On Probation"; "Sentences Of 5 Gun-Runners Are Suspended"; Front-page photo; "Mario Villamia en Libertad."
10. "FBI Arresto a Tres Hispanos En Houston; "Cubans Held After Arms Are Seized"; "Agentes Federales Retienen Yate Bajo Sospecha de Otra Expedición Rebelde a Cuba"; "Investigan En Houston la Frustrada Expedición Contra Cuba"; "Three Cuban Residents of Miami Held in Texas On Plot To Invade Cuba"; "U.S. Agents Seize Yacht, Arms And Ammunition From Cubans In Houston, Texas"; "Buscan a Complicado en Plan de Invasión"; "Confiscan Armas Para Fidel, Cubanos Detenidos"; "Dictaran Sentencia Contra Otros 5 Cubanos En Texas el Próximo Once De Julio"; "Cuban Exile Pleads For Group Sentenced Here"; "5 In Cuban Arms Cache Case Free On Probation"; "Sentences Of 5 Gun-Runners Are Suspended"; Front-page photo; "Mario Villamia en Libertad."
11. Pérez-Vidal, *Historia*, 163–164; Pérez-Vidal, interview; "4 Seized with Arms Here...Cache Destined for Castro Discovered in Brooklyn," *New York Times*, 6.
12. Pérez-Vidal, *Historia*, 163–164.
13. Pérez-Vidal, *Historia*, 163–164.
14. Pérez-Vidal, *Historia*, 163–164.
15. Pérez-Vidal, *Historia*, 163–164.
16. Davis, interview.
17. Davis, interview.
18. Davis, interview.
19. Davis, interview.
20. Davis, interview.
21. Davis, interview.
22. Davis, interview.
23. Davis, interview.
24. Davis, interview.

## Chapter 14

1. Tom Dunkin, "Fidel Castro's Ybor Underground," *St. Petersburg Times Sunday Magazine*, January 18, 1959, 3, 27.
2. Dunkin, "Fidel Castro's Ybor Underground."
3. Dunkin, "Fidel Castro's Ybor Underground."
4. Dunkin, "Fidel Castro's Ybor Underground."
5. Paul Guzzo, "Tampa Helped Arm

Castro's Revolution," *Tampa Tribune*, May 5, 2013.
6. Guzzo, "Tampa Helped Arm Castro's Revolution."
7. Guzzo, "Tampa Helped Arm Castro's Revolution."
8. Pérez, interview.
9. Pérez, interview.
10. Pérez, interview.
11. Pérez, interview.
12. Bárcena, interview.
13. Bárcena, interview; "José Prieto Rodriguez," *Archivo Historico Provincial de Granma Biografias*, May 14, 2014.
14. Golan, interview; "José Prieto Rodriguez."
15. Bárcena, interview.
16. Paul Guzzo, "The Odyssey of Carlos Carbonell," *Cigar City Magazine*, November 2010, 28–41.
17. Golan, interview.
18. Guzzo, "New JFK files."
19. Guzzo, "New JFK files."

## Chapter 15

1. José Llanusa, Western Union telegram to Gabriel Gil Alfonso, January 2, 1959.
2. "Tampans Make Bid to Seize Consulate," *Tampa Times*, January 2, 1959, 1.
3. Cecil Mann, "Rebels Here Fail in Bid for Consulate," *Tampa Tribune*, January 3, 1959, 5.
4. Mann, "Rebels Here Fail."
5. Tom Inglis, "Castro's Men Get Foot in Consulate," *Tampa Times*, January 3, 1959, 1.
6. Inglis, "Castro's Men Get Foot in Consulate."
7. Charles Hendrick, "Tampa Followers of Castro Make Peaceful Invasión of Cuban Consulate Here," *Tampa Tribune*, January 4, 1959, 11.
8. Gerardo Pérez Puelles, Western Union telegram to Gabriel Gil Alfonso, January 7, 1959.

## Chapter 16

1. Tom Dunkin, "Another Gun—Another Soldier," *La Gaceta*, January 9, 1959, 1.
2. Roland Manteiga, "As We Heard It," *La Gaceta*, January 16, 1959, 16.

3. Roland Manteiga, "As We Heard It," *La Gaceta*, January 16, 1959.
4. Frank Ragano, *Mob Lawyer* (Scribner, 1994), 51.
5. Roland Manteiga, "As We Heard It," *La Gaceta*, January 16, 1959.
6. Victoriano Manteiga, "Chungas y No Chungas," *La Gaceta*, January 23, 1959, 1.

## Chapter 17

1. Davis, interview; Mario Villamia, interview.
2. Davis, interview; Mario Villamia, interview.
3. Davis, interview; Mario Villamia, interview,.
4. Davis, interview; Mario Villamia, interview.
5. Davis, interview; Mario Villamia, interview.
6. Davis, interview; Mario Villamia, interview.
7. Davis, interview; Mario Villamia, interview.
8. Davis, interview; Mario Villamia, interview.
9. Davis, interview; Mario Villamia, interview; State of Florida Corporate Stock Certificate #8 Naming Mario Villamia Owner Of 33,000 Shares Of EXECUTIVE AIR SERVICE, INC, Signed by the 2 Other Owners Howard K. Davis, President, and Paul Lazar, Secretary, December 30, 1958.
10. Mario Villamia, interview.
11. Mario Villamia, interview.
12. Mario Villamia, interview.
13. Mario Villamia, interview.
14. Pérez-Vidal, interview.
15. Official Order from PNR (Policía Nacional Revoluciónaria) Commander Efigenio Ameigeira Delgado, Naming José Luis Cuza Tellez de Giron Chief of Police at Presidential Palace, March 4, 1959.

## Chapter 18

1. Cecil Mann "Castro Regime Fires Cuban Consul Here, In Office for 15 Years," *Tampa Tribune*, October 28, 1959, 8.
2. John Sellers, "Does Cuba Own José Martí Park?" *Sunland Tribune* 3, no. 1 (1977); Tony Pizzo, "Tampa's Cuban Heritage," *Sunland Tribune* 16, no. 1 (1994); *Traduccion Prensa*, "Se Inaugurara el 11

de Abril," October 16,1956; "Cuba to Raze Martí House to Build Garden Sanctuary," October 21, 1956, Special Collections, University of South Florida, Tony Pizzo Collection, Box 57, Folder Martí-Maceo.
3. José Martí, *Versos Sencillos* (New York: Louis Weiss & Co., 1891).
4. Victoriano Manteiga, "Comisiones Del Movimiento 26 de Julio," *La Gaceta*, March 27, 1959, 1.
5. Pedro Aguilera, Letter to Raul Villamia, May 19, 1959; Delfa Lines invoice for baby food shipped to Cuba, May, 19, 1959; "Visita de Distinguidos Cubanos," *La Gaceta*, May 1, 1959, 2.
6. Juan M. Leon, Letter to Raul Villamia, August 4, 1959.
7. Juan Almeida Bosque, Letter to Raul Villamia, June 18, 1959.
8. El Movimiento Patriótico de Tampa de Ayuda al Campesino Cubano, Letter to Carlos Carbonell, December 19, 1959.
9. Juan M. Fidalgo, "Complots Contra Fidel," *La Gaceta*, April 10, 1959, 5.
10. Victoria Esperanza Lydia Urrutia, Baptismal Certificate, April 7, 1959.
11. Pérez-Vidal, *Historia*, 207–212; Pérez-Vidal, interview.
12. Pérez-Vidal, *Historia*, 207–212; Pérez-Vidal, interview.
13. Pérez-Vidal, *Historia*, 207–212; Pérez-Vidal, interview.
14. Victoriano Manteiga, "Chungas y No Chungas," *La Gaceta*, April 17, 1959, 11.
15. Roland Manteiga, "As We Heard It," *La Gaceta*, June 12, 1959, 12.
16. "7 Indicted in Miami in Arms-Smuggling," *New York Times*, June 6, 1959, 6.
17. "7 Indicted in Miami in Arms-Smuggling."
18. Roland Manteiga, "As We Heard It," *La Gaceta*, July 3, 1959, 12.
19. "Detenidos En Cuba Santo Trafficante, Henry Saavedra y Oscar Reguera," *La Gaceta*, June 12, 1959, 1; "El Caso de S. Trafficante," *La Gaceta*, June 19, 1959, 1.
20. Roland Manteiga, "As We Heard It," *La Gaceta*, July 3, 1959, 12.

## Chapter 19

1. Mario Villamia, interview.
2. Mario Villamia, interview.
3. Mario Villamia, interview.

4. Mario Villamia, interview.
5. Pérez-Vidal, *Historia*, 244–249.
6. Mario Villamia, interview.
7. "Recibimiento Al Compañero," *La Gaceta*, July 31, 1959, 1.

## Chapter 20

1. *Ecos*, July 1959, 8.
2. *Ecos*, July 1959, 8.
3. *Ecos*, July 1959, 8.
4. *Ecos*, July 1959, 1, 8, 9.
5. *Ecos*, July 1959, 1, 8, 9.

## Chapter 21

1. "Cienfuegoes Rumored in Tampa," *Tampa Tribune*, November 18, 1959, 1.
2. Cecil Mann, "If Cienfuegoes Hiding in Ybor City, He's Doing Good Job of Staying Hidden," *Tampa Tribune*, November 19, 1959, 6D.
3. "Attacked Man Says He'll Resume Ybor City Hunt for Cienfuegos," *St. Petersburg Times*, November 19, 1959, 4.
4. "Attacked Man Says He'll Resume Ybor City Hunt for Cienfuegos."

## Chapter 22

1. Ragano, *Mob Lawyer*.
2. Paul Guzzo, "Tampa Helped Arm Castro's Revolution," *Tampa Tribune*, May 5, 2013, 7.
3. Guzzo, "Tampa Helped."
4. Guzzo, "Tampa Helped."
5. Guzzo, "Tampa Helped."
6. Guzzo, "Tampa Helped."

## Chapter 23

1. Bob Delaney, "How Popular Is Fidel Castro in Ybor City?" *Tampa Times*, November 17, 1959, 1.
2. M-26-7 Flyer "Al Pueblo de Tampa! En Defensa del Honrado Gobierno de Cuba," Announcing Car Parade September 12. 1959.
3. *La Gaceta*, February 26, 1969, 1.

## Chapter 24

1. Paul Guzzo, "The Odyssey of Carlos Carbonell."

2. "Max Garcia Multado en $4,300," *La Gaceta*, December 11, 1959, 1.
3. Ruby Hart Phillips, "Planes Again Raid Cuban Cane Crop; Drops Fire Bombs On Fields—Havana Charged They Came From U.S.," *New York Times*, January 20, 1960, 8.
4. Phillips, "Planes Again Raid."
5. Phillips, "Planes Again Raid."
6. Manuel De Paz-Sanchez, "Zona Rebelde: La Diplomacia Espanola Ante la Revolución Cubana (1957–1960)," Centro de la Cultura Popular Canaria, January 1, 1997.
7. Guzzo, "Some from Tampa."
8. Guzzo, "Some from Tampa."
9. "Martí Statue Erected," *Tampa Times*, February 4, 1960, 1.
10. "Martí Statue Erected."
11. Victoriano Manteiga, "Carta Del M. 26 de Julio Para Rene Dechard," *La Gaceta*, March 4, 1960, 1.
12. "Cuban Consul Rene Dechard Requesting Martí Park Key Returned by M-26-7," *La Gaceta*, February 19, 1960, 1.
13. Juan Orta, A Western Union to Victoriano Manteiga, February 18, 1960.
14. "El Develamiento de la Estatua Del Apostol Anunciada Para el Domingo En el Parque de la Octava y Calle 13," *Traduccion Prensa*, February 23, 1960; Press Release from José Martí Memorial Foundation c/o Cuban Consulate February 19, 1960; "Nota Del Movimiento 26 De Julio," *La Gaceta*.
15. Rene Dechard "Transcript of Speech at Martí Statue Unveiling Ceremony," February 28, 1960.
16. Dechard, "Transcript of Speech."
17. Dechard, "Transcript of Speech."
18. Victoriano Manteiga, "Friends of the Slandered Director Of La Gaceta," *La Gaceta*, March 4, 1960, 12.
19. Carmen Figueroa, "Letter from Mrs. Carmen Figueroa," *La Gaceta*, March 4, 1960, 1.
20. Raul Villamia, "Carta del Compañero Villamia, Secretario Del Movimiento 26 de Julio de Tampa," *La Gaceta*, March 4, 1960, 2.
21. "New Consul of Cuba in Tampa," *La Gaceta*, March 25, 1960, 1.

## Chapter 25

1. Guzzo, "The Odyssey of Carlos Carbonell."
2. Guzzo, "The Odyssey of Carlos Carbonell."
3. Victoriano Manteiga, "Nota del 26 de Julio de Tampa," *La Gaceta*, September 23, 1960, 1; Raul Villamia, "Carta Del Compañero Villamia, Secretario del Movimiento 26 de Julio de Tampa," March 4, 1960, 2; "Cuban Ideas in Food and Entertainment—and Politics Are Reflected in Ybor City," *St. Petersburg Times Sunday Magazine*, October 9, 1960, 10; "Fidelistas de Tampa Se Desmandan, Ybor City, Último Bastión del Fidelo-Comunismo En Florida," *El Avance Criollo*, December 23, 1960, 18.
4. FBI, Record Number 124-90041-10035, September 16, 1960, Released August 18, 2017.
5. Guzzo, "New JFK files."
6. Mario Villamia, interview.
7. Mario Villamia, interview.
8. Mario Villamia, interview.
9. Mario Villamia, interview.
10. Mario Villamia, interview.
11. Mario Villamia, interview.
12. Mario Villamia, interview.
13. Mario Villamia, interview.
14. Mario Villamia, interview.
15. Davis, interview; Mario Villamia, interview.
16. Davis, interview; Mario Villamia, interview.
17. Davis, interview; Mario Villamia, interview.
18. Davis, interview; Mario Villamia, interview.
19. Roland Manteiga, "As We Heard It," *La Gaceta*, December 9, 1960, 12.
20. Roland Manteiga, "As We Heard It," *La Gaceta*, December 9, 1960.
21. Roland Manteiga, "As We Heard It," *La Gaceta*, December 9, 1960.
22. Duana Bradford, "Cuba Consul Here Packs As He Awaits Close Order," *Tampa Tribune*, January 5, 1961, 1; Fred Smith, "Tension Still Runs High In Tampa Latin Quarters," *Tampa Tribune*, January 5, 1961, 1; Fred Smith, "Former Cuban Consul Here, Armando Sarcassas Seeks Asylum," *Tampa Tribune*, January 8, 1961, 1; "Three Arrested In Vandalism Spree," *St. Petersburg Times Sunday Magazine*, January 8, 1961, 2.
23. Victoriano Manteiga, "Public announcement," *La Gaceta*, January 13, 1961, 1; "Families Arrange Return To

Cuba, Consulate Here Closing," *Tampa Times*, January 5, 1961, 1.

## Chapter 27

1. John Durant, "Tampa's Old and New Unite For Fair Time," *New York Times*, January 4, 1962, 285.
2. Carlos Fuente Jr., Interviewed by Paul Guzzo, December 2014.
3. Fuente Jr., interview.
4. Fuente Jr., interview.
5. Fuente Jr., interview.
6. Fuente Jr., interview.
7. Fuente Jr., interview.
8. Fuente Jr., interview.
9. Fuente Jr., interview.

## Chapter 28

1. Guzzo, "The Odyssey of Carlos Carbonell."
2. Guzzo, "The Odyssey of Carlos Carbonell."
3. Guzzo, "The Odyssey of Carlos Carbonell."
4. Guzzo, "The Odyssey of Carlos Carbonell."
5. Guzzo, "The Odyssey of Carlos Carbonell."
6. Guzzo, "The Odyssey of Carlos Carbonell."
7. Guzzo, "The Odyssey of Carlos Carbonell."
8. Guzzo, "The Odyssey of Carlos Carbonell."
9. Guzzo, "The Odyssey of Carlos Carbonell."
10. Guzzo, "The Odyssey of Carlos Carbonell."
11. Guzzo, "The Odyssey of Carlos Carbonell."
12. Guzzo, "The Odyssey of Carlos Carbonell."
13. Guzzo, "The Odyssey of Carlos Carbonell."
14. Guzzo, "The Odyssey of Carlos Carbonell."

## Chapter 29

1. FBI, Record Number 124-10173-10436, November 23, 1963, Released October 12, 2017.
2. Golan, interview.
3. Golan, interview.
4. FBI, Record Number 124-10184-10319, July 30, 1964, Released October 4, 2017.
5. FBI, Record Number 124-10184-10319.
6. FBI, Record Number 124-10184-10319.
7. FBI, Record Number 124-10184-10319.
8. FBI, Record Number 124-10184-10319.
9. FBI, Record Number 124-10184-10319.
10. Golan, interview.
11. Golan, interview.
12. Warren Commission Volume XXVI:CE 3066 Report, April 17, 1964, www.aarclibrary.org/publib/jfk/wc/wcvols/wh26/pdf/WH26_CE_3066.pdf.
13. FBI, Record Number 124-90041-10035, September 16, 1960, Released August 18, 2017.
14. FBI, Record Number 124-10209-10485, October 22, 1968, Released August 18, 2017.

## Chapter 30

1. FBI, Record Number 124-10209-10485, October 22, 1968, Released August 18, 2017.
Mario Villamia, Probation System, U.S. Courts, District Court Of The United States, Southern District Of Texas, Docket #C-13,313.
2. Pérez-Vidal, interview; Pérez-Vidal, *Historia*, 230–250.
3. Pérez-Vidal, interview; Pérez-Vidal, *Historia*, 230–250.
4. Pérez-Vidal, interview; Pérez-Vidal, *Historia*, 230–250.
5. Pérez-Vidal, interview; Pérez-Vidal, *Historia*, 230–250.
6. Pérez-Vidal, interview; Pérez-Vidal, *Historia*, 230–250.
7. Howard K. Davis, imdb.com/name/nm0204710/ referencing him as Technical Director of 1991 Oliver Stone Film *JFK*.
8. John Simpkins, "Assassination of John F. Kennedy," *Spartacus Educational*, www//spartacus-educational.com.
9. Mario Villamia, interview; Pérez-Vidal, *Historia*, 230–250.
10. Mario Villamia, interview; Pérez-Vidal, *Historia*, 230–250.

# Bibliography

## Books

Acosta, Heberto Norman. *La Palabra Empeñada, Tomo 1*. Oficina de Publicaciónes del Consejo de Estado, 2005.
Bayo, Alberto. *Mi Aporte a la Revolución Cubana*. Ejército Rebelde, 1960.
Kefauver, Estes. *Crime in America*. Doubleday & Company, 1951.
Martí, José. *Versos Sencillos*. Louis Weiss & Co., 1891.
Paz-Sanchez, Manuel de. *Zona Rebelde: La Diplomacia Española Ante la Revolución Cubana (1957-1960)*. Centro de la Cultura Popular Canaria, 1997.
Perez Llody, Luis Alberto. *Rafael Garcia Barcena: el sueno de la Gran Nacion*, Editorial Oriente, 2007.
Pérez-Vidal, Angel. *Historia Íntima de la Revolución Cubana*. Ediciones Universal, 1997.
Ragano, Frank. *Mob Lawyer*. Scribner, 1994.
Szulc, Tad. *Fidel, A Critical Portrait*. Harper Perennial, 2000.

## Interviews

Arnade, Pete. Interviewed by Paul Guzzo. December 2016.
Davis, Howard K. Interviewed by Rhonda Villamia. August 18, 2014, to September 20, 2019.
Fuente, Carlos, Jr. Interviewed by Paul Guzzo. December 2014.
Garcia Barcena y Valladares, Rafael. Interviewed by Rhonda Villamia. September 15, 2018, to July 2, 2019.
Garvey, Mike. Interviewed by Rhonda Villamia and Paul Guzzo. February 1, 2019.
Golan, Ernesto. Interviewed by Rhonda Villamia and Paul Guzzo. December 2017.
Manteiga, Patrick. Interviewed by Paul Guzzo. 2017.
Pérez, Juan M. Interviewed by Rhonda Villamia. August, 3, 2010.
Pérez-Vidal, Angel. Interviewed by Rhonda Villamia. May 1, 2008 to April 20, 2015.
Villamia, Mario. Interviewed by Rhonda Villamia. February 7, 2007 to October 24, 2010.

## Correspondence and Minutes

Aguilera, Pedro. Letter to Raul Villamia. May 19, 1959.
Almeida, Juan. Letter to Raul Villamia. June 18, 1959.
Castro, Fidel. Letter to Angel Perez-Vidal. September 19, 1955.
Castro, Fidel. Letter to Angel Perez-Vidal. October 11, 1955.
Castro, Fidel. Letter to Victoriano Manteiga. December 13, 1955.
Castro, Fidel. Letter to exile community. December 14, 1957.
Castro, Fidel. Letter to Mario Villamia. December 15, 1955.
Castro, Fidel. Letter to Mario Villamia. December 20, 1955.
Castro, Fidel. Letter to Raul Villamia. January 2, 1956.
Castro, Fidel. Letter to Mario Villamia. February 14, 1956.

Castro, Fidel. Proclamation letter to New York City M-26-7. November 3, 1955.
Castro, Fidel. Western Union telegram to Angel Perez-Vidal. October 6, 1955.
Castro, Fidel. Western Union telegram to Angel Perez-Vidal. October 14, 1955.
Castro, Fidel. Western Union telegram to Angel Perez-Vidal. October 15, 1955.
Castro, Fidel. Western Union telegram to Jesus Montane. October 20, 1955.
Durant, John. "Tampa's Old and New Unite for Fair Time." *New York Times*. January 4, 1962.
Fidalgo, José Manuel. Letters to Victoriano Manteiga. October 14, 1955.
Figueroa del Marmol, Carmen. Letter to La Gaceta. March 4, 1960.
Habana Embassy. Dispatch to the Department of State. May 29, 1957.
Jacas, Virgilio. Letter to Raul Villamia. March 30, 1958.
Jose Marti Memorial Foundation c/o Cuban Consulate. Press Release. February 19, 1960.
Leal Spengler, Eusebio. Email to Rhonda Villamia. 2010.
León, Juan M. Letter to Raul Villamia. August 4, 1959.
Llanusa, Jose. Report on Trip to Haiti. April 16, 1958.
Llanusa, Jose. Western Union telegram to Gabriel Gil Alfonso. January 1, 1959.
Llanusa, José. Telegram to Gabriel Gil Alfonso. January 2, 1959.
Lopez Fernandez, Antonio. Letter to Mario Villamia. November 11, 1954.
Manteiga, Victoriano. Letter to Fidel Castro. December 31, 1955.
Manteiga, Victoriano. Letter to Raul Villamia. January 19, 1959.
Manteiga, Victoriano. Letter to Rene Dechard. February 9, 1960.
Montané, Jesús. Letter to Mario Villamia. September 6, 1955.
Montané, Jesús. Letter to Raul Villamia. January 31, 1956.
El Movimiento Patriótico de Tampa de Ayuda al Campesinado Cubano. Letter to to Carlos Carbonell. December 10, 1959.
Nuccio, Nick. Letter to Fidel Castro. February 11, 1959.
Orta, Juan. Western Union telegram to Victoriano Manteiga. February 18, 1960.
Pando, Emilio. Western Union telegram to Guillermo Bolivar. January 1, 1959.
Pérez Pulles, Gerardo. Western Union telegram to Gabriel Gil Alfonso. January 7, 1959.
Pérez-Vidal, Angel. Letter to Consulate General of the United States in Montreal, Canada. 1957.
Rodriguez Luloaga, Rafael. Letter to Raul Villamia. November 24, 1960.
Villamia, Mario. Letter to Fidel Castro. May 22, 1958.
Villamia, Raul. Letter to Fidel Castro. January 5, 1956.
Villamia, Raul. Letter to La Gaceta. March 4, 1960.
Villamia, Raul. Letter to Bohemia. November 20, 1960.
Villamia, Raul. M-26-7 Meeting Minutes. July 16, 1957.
Villamia, Raul. M-26-7 Meeting Minutes. July 21, 1957.
Villamia, Raul. M-26-7 Meeting Minutes. August 14, 1957.
Villamia, Raul. M-26-7 Meeting Minutes. August 20, 1957.
Villamia, Raul. M-26-7 Meeting Minutes. September 4, 1957.

## Newspapers, Magazines, and Journals

"Agentes Federales Retienen Yate Bajo Sospecha De Otra Expedición Rebelde a Cuba." United Press, February 19, 1958.
Arturo, Hector. "Con Fidel Voy Adonde Sea." *Verde Olivo*, October/November 2010.
"Attacked Man Says He'll Resume Ybor City Hunt for Cienfuegos." *St. Petersburg Times*, November 19, 1959.
"Batista Foes Rally Here." *Tampa Morning Tribune*, July 1, 1957.
Bradford, Duana. "Cuba Consul Here Packs as He Awaits Close Order." *Tampa Tribune*, January 5, 1961.
"Buscan A Complicado En Plan De Invasión." *El Mundo*, February 20, 1958.
"El Caso de S. Trafficante." *La Gaceta*, June 19, 1959.
Castro, Fidel. "Asaltado Y Destruido El Estudio Del Escultor Fidalgo." *Bohemia*, February 8, 1953. www.granma.cu/cuba/2018-07-12/asaltado-y-destruido-el-estudio-del-escultor-fidalgo-12-07-2018-19-07-25.

# Bibliography 285

"Cienfuegoes Rumored in Tampa." *Tampa Tribune*, November 18, 1959.
"Confiscan Armas Para Fidel, Cubanos Detenidos." *El Diario De Nueva York*, February 21, 1958.
"Contra La Tiranía—A los Cubanos y sus Amigos de Tampa." *La Gaceta*, June 28, 1957.
"Cuba Gets Note from Spain Protesting Slaying of Citizen." Associated Press, January 20, 1933.
"Cuba Planes, Troops Annihilate 40 Invaders." *New York Times*, December 3, 1956.
"Cuba To Raze Martí House to Build Garden Sanctuary." Special Collections, University of South Florida. Tony Pizzo Collection, Box 57, Folder Martí-Maceo. October 21, 1956.
"Cuban Consul Rene Dechard Requesting Martí Park Key Returned by M267." *La Gaceta*, February 19, 1960.
"Cuban Exile Pleads for Group Sentenced Here." *The Houston Post*, July 26, 1959.
"Cuban Ideas in Food and Entertainment—and Politics Are Reflected in Ybor City." *St. Petersburg Times Sunday Magazine*, October 9, 1960.
"Cuban Student Is Killed in Gunfight With Police." Associated Press. *Chicago Tribune*, January 16, 1933.
"Cubans Held After Arms Are Seized." Associated Press, February 19, 1958.
Delaney, Bob. "How Popular Is Fidel Castro in Ybor City?" *Tampa Times*, November 17, 1959.
"Demanda Fidel Castro Que Batista Renuncíe." *La Gaceta*, December 2, 1955.
Denley, Bob. "Somewhere In Cuba ... Long Lost Statue and Sculptor Sought." *Tampa Times*, January 1, 1959.
"Detenidos En Cuba Santo Trafficante, Henry Saavedra y Oscar Reguera." *La Gaceta*, June 12, 1959.
"Dictaran Sentencia Contra Otros 5 Cubanos en Texas El Próximo Once de Julio." United Press, June 21, 1958.
Dunkin, Tom. "Another Gun—Another Soldier." *La Gaceta*, January 9, 1959.
Dunkin, Tom. "Fidel Castro's Ybor Underground." *St. Petersburg Times Sunday Magazine*, January 18, 1959.
Durant, John. "Tampa's Old and New Unite For Fair Time." *New York Times*, January 4, 1962.
*Ecos*, July 1959.
"Exilados Veran Al Consul En Nueva York." United Press, June 24, 1956.
"Exile Is Planning U.S. Laetrile Operation." *New York Times*, June 18, 1977.
"La Expedición Del Corojo." *Diario Granma*, Numero 103. April 28, 2008.
"Families Arrange Return to Cuba, Consulate Here Closing." *Tampa Times*, January 5, 1961.
"FBI Arresto a Tres Hispanos En Houston." Associated Press, February 18, 1958.
Fellows, Bob. "Break In Relations with Cuba Brings Mixed Reactions Here." *Tampa Tribune*, January 4, 1961.
Fidalgo, Jose M. "Complots Contra Fidel." *La Gaceta*, April 10, 1959.
"Fidelistas de Tampa Se Desmandan, Ybor City, Último Bastión del Fidelo-Comunismo En Florida." *El Avance Criollo*, December 23, 1960.
Figueroa, Carmen. "Letter from Mrs. Carmen Figueroa." *La Gaceta*, March 4, 1960.
"5 In Cuban Arms Cache Case Free on Probation." *The Houston Post*, August 13, 1958.
*La Gaceta*, February 26, 1969.
Guzzo, Paul. "Memorial Planned in Tampa for Civil War Hero Clara Barton of the Red Cross." *Tampa Bay Times*, August 31, 2017.
Guzzo, Paul. "New JFK Files Feature a Few Surprises About Intrigue in Tampa as Castro Rose to Power." *Tampa Bay Times*, November 2, 2017.
Guzzo, Paul. "Some from Tampa were shocked over Castro's Rise." *Tampa Bay Times*, December 3, 2016.
Guzzo, Paul. "Tampa Helped Arm Castro's Revolution." *Tampa Tribune*, May 5, 2013.
Guzzo, Paul. "The Odyssey of Carlos Carbonell." *Cigar City Magazine*, November 2010.
Hendrick, Charles. "Tampa Followers of Castro Make Peaceful Invasión of Cuban Consulate Here." *Tampa Tribune*, January 4, 1959.
Hendrick, Charles. "Two Arrested in Ruckus Over Cuban Revolt Here." *Tampa Tribune*, September 21, 1957.

Inglis, Tom. "Castro's Men Get Foot in Consulate." *Tampa Times*, January 3, 1959.
"Investigan En Houston La Frustrada Expedición Contra Cuba." United Press, February 19, 1958.
"José Prieto Rodriguez." *Archivo Historico Provincial De Granma Biografias*, May 14, 2014.
"Last of Machado Henchmen Killed." *The Brownsville Herald*, September 2, 1933.
"Last One of Machado's Strong-Arm Squad Killed." *Baltimore Sun*, September 2, 1933.
"Manifesto Del Ejecutivo Del Movimiento 26 de Julio." *La Gaceta*, December 20, 1957.
Mann, Cecil. "Castro Regime Fires Cuban Consul Here, In Office for 15 Years." *Tampa Tribune*, October 28, 1959.
Mann, Cecil. "If Cienfuegoes Hiding in Ybor City, He's Doing Good Job Of Staying Hidden." *Tampa Tribune*, November 19, 1959.
Mann, Cecil. "Rebels Here Fail in Bid For Consulate." *Tampa Tribune*, January 3, 1959.
Manteiga, Roland. "As We Heard It. " *La Gaceta*, January 16, 1959.
Manteiga, Roland. "As We Heard It." *La Gaceta*, June 12, 1959.
Manteiga, Roland. "As We Heard It." *La Gaceta*, July 3, 1959.
Manteiga, Roland. "As We Heard It." *La Gaceta*, December 9, 1960.
Manteiga, Victoriano. "Carta Del M. 26 de Julio Para Rene Dechard." *La Gaceta*, March 4, 1960.
Manteiga, Victoriano. "Celebration at the Cuban Club." *La Gaceta*, August 9, 1957.
Manteiga, Victoriano. "Chungas y No Chungas." *La Gaceta*, October 21, 1950.
Manteiga, Victoriano. "Chungas y No Chungas." *La Gaceta*, June 29, 1956.
Manteiga, Victoriano. "Chungas y No Chungas." *La Gaceta*, January 23, 1959.
Manteiga, Victoriano. "Chungas y No Chungas." *La Gaceta*, December 14, 1956.
Manteiga, Victoriano. "Chungas y No Chungas." *La Gaceta*, April 17, 1959.
Manteiga, Victoriano. "Comisiones Del Movimiento 26 de Julio." *La Gaceta*, March 27, 1959.
Manteiga, Victoriano. "Dos Años de la Visita a Tampa Del Dr. Fidel Castro." *La Gaceta*, November 29, 1957.
Manteiga, Victoriano. "Fidel Castro Sets His Conditions." *La Gaceta*, November 23, 1956.
Manteiga, Victoriano. "Friends Of the Slandered Director of La Gaceta." *La Gaceta*, March 4, 1960.
Manteiga, Victoriano. "Incident on the Cuban Club Patio." *La Gaceta*, July 19, 1957.
Manteiga, Victoriano. "La Camioneta con las Canas." *La Gaceta*, November 15, 1957.
Manteiga, Victoriano. "Meeting of the Cuban Liberation Council." *La Gaceta*, November 22, 1957.
Manteiga, Victoriano. "Miami Unity Pact letter." *La Gaceta*, January 17, 1958.
Manteiga, Victoriano. "Nota Del 26 De Julio De Tampa." *La Gaceta*, September 23, 1960.
Manteiga, Victoriano. "Notice of M267 Meeting." *La Gaceta*, February 21, 1958.
Manteiga, Victoriano. "Public announcement." *La Gaceta*, January 13, 1961.
"Mario Villamia En Libertad." *La Gaceta*, August 22, 1958.
"Martí Statue Erected." *Tampa Times*, February 4, 1960.
Matthews, Herbert. "Cuban Rebel Is Visited in Cuba." *New York Times*, February 24, 1957.
"Max Garcia Multado En $4,300." *La Gaceta*, December 11, 1959.
"New Consul of Cuba in Tampa." *La Gaceta*, March 25, 1960.
O'Connor, Tom. "Anti-Batista Cuban Comes to Seek Revolt Here." *Tampa Tribune*, November 26, 1955.
O'Connor, Tom. "Cubans Here Give Funds to Aid Revolt Against Batista." *Tampa Tribune*, November 28, 1955.
O'Connor, Tom. "Italian Club Bars Theatre to Leader Of Cuban Revolt." *Tampa Tribune*, November 27, 1955.
Orta, Juan. "A letter to Victoriano Manteiga." *La Gaceta*, February 18, 1960.
Phillips, Ruby Hart. "Planes Again Raid Cuban Cane Crop; Drops Fire Bombs On Fields—Havana Charged They Came From U.S." *New York Times*, January 20, 1960.
Pizzo, Tony. "Tampa's Cuban Heritage." *Sunland Tribune* 16, no. 1 (1994). digitalcommons.usf.edu/tampabayhistory/vol16/iss1/5.

# Bibliography

Pizzo, Tony. "The Cigar That Sparked a Revolution." *Sunland Tribune* 6, no. 5 (1980): 32–35. https://digitalcommons.usf.edu/cgi/viewcontent.cgi?article=1043&context=sunlandtribune.
"Protestan Detención En Mexico Dr. Fidel Castro." United Press, June 24, 1956.
Ramis, Johan Moya. "Entre la Memoria y el Olvido." Fondos Bibliograficos de la Biblioteca Nacional de Cuba José Martí.
"Recibimiento Al Compañero." *La Gaceta*, July 31, 1959.
"Se Inaugurara el 11 de Abril." *Traduccion Prensa*. October 16, 1956.
Sellers, John. "Does Cuba Own José Martí Park?" *Sunland Tribune* 3, no. 1 (1977). www.digitalcommons.usf.edu/sunlandtribune/vol3/iss1/7.
"Sentences Of 5 Gun-Runners Are Suspended." *Chronicle*, August 13, 1958.
"7 Indicted in Miami in Arms-Smuggling." *New York Times*, June 6, 1959.
Shaftel, David. "The Black Eagle of Harlem." *Air & Space Magazine*, January 1, 2009. www.smithsonianmag.com/air-space-magazine/the-black-eagle-of-harlem-95208344.
Simpkins, John. "Assassination of John F. Kennedy." *Spartacus Educational*. www./-spartacus-educational.com.
Smith, Fred. "Former Cuban Consul Here, Armando Sarcassas Seeks Asylum." *Tampa Tribune*, January 8, 1961.
Smith, Fred. "Tension Still Runs High in Tampa Latin Quarters." *Tampa Tribune*, January 5, 1961.
"Spain Protests to Cuba About Killing of Student." *St. Louis Post-Dispatch*, January 21, 1933.
"Tampans Make Bid to Seize Consulate." *Tampa Times*, January 2, 1959.
"Three Arrested in Vandalism Spree." *St. Petersburg Times Sunday Magazine*, January 8, 1961.
"Three Cuban Residents of Miami Held in Texas On Plot to Invade Cuba." *Diario De Las Americas Miami Springs*, February 19, 1958.
"Urrutia is Anti-Communist, Pro-U.S." United Press International, January 3, 1959. www.upi.com/Archives/1959/01/03/Urrutia-is-anti-communist-pro-US/6149212204416.
"U.S. Agents Seize Yacht, Arms and Ammunition from Cubans In Houston, Texas." *Diario De Las Americas Miami Springs*, February 19, 1958.
Villamia, Raul. "Carta Del Compañero Villamia, Secretario Del Movimiento 26 de Julio de Tampa." *La Gaceta*, March 4, 1960.
Villamia, Rhonda. "Building José Martí Park." *Cigar City Magazine*, September/October 2008.
"Visita de Distinguidos Cubanos." *La Gaceta*, May 1, 1959.

## Miscellaneous

Castro, Fidel. New York City speech. Office of Historic Affairs in Habana Cuba. October 28, 1953.
Dechard, Rene. "Transcript of Speech at Martí Statue Unveiling Ceremony." February 28, 1960.
Delfa Lines invoice for baby food shipped to Cuba. May 19, 1959.
FBI. Record Number 124-90061-10016. March 13, 1958.
FBI. Record Number 124-90041-10035. September 16, 1960.
FBI. Record Number 124-10184-10319. July 30, 1964.
FBI. Record Number 124-10209-10485. October 22, 1968.
M-26-7 Flyer: *Invitamos A Todos los Cubanos de Tampa…Y A Todos Los Hombres Que Aman La Libertad* (invitation to Fidel Castro's address to the people of Tampa). November 27, 1955.
M-26-7 Flyer: *A Todos Los Cubanos De Tampa* (invitation to join the M-26-7). 1955.
M-26-7 Flyer: *Contra La Tirania, A Los Cubanos Y Sus Amigos de Tampa* (invitation to an event at the Boulevard Restaurant, commemorating the fallen heroes of the Moncada, Goicuria, the Presidential Palace, the *Corinthia* expedition, Holguin, and Humboldt No. 7). June 20, 1957.

M-26-7 Flyer: *A Los Obreros De Las Fabricas De Tabacos* (invitation for the cigarmakers to donate to the M-26-7). July 1957.
M-26-7 Flyer: *A la Colonia Cubana Y Al Pueblo De Tampa* (invitation to an event commemorating the 5th anniversary of the Moncada Barracks attack. July 25, 1958.
M-26-7 Flyer: *Al Pueblo De Tampa! En Defensa Del Honrado Gobierno De Cuba* (invitation to participate in car caravan). September 12, 1959.
Official Order from PNR (Policía Nacional Revoluciónaria) Commander Efigenio Ameigeira Delgado, Naming José Luis Cuza *Téllez* de Ciron Chief of Police at Presidential Palace. March 4, 1959.
State Of Florida Corporate Stock Certificate #8 Naming Mario Villamia Owner Of 33,000 Shares of EXECUTIVE AIR SERVICE, INC. Signed by the 2 Other Owners Howard K. Davis, President, and Paul Lazar, Secretary. December 30, 1958.
Urrutia, Victoria Esperanza Lydia. Baptismal Certificate. April 7, 1959.
Villamia, Arlene. Baptismal Certificate. June 20, 1959.
Villamia, Mario. Probation System. U.S. Courts, District Court of the United States, Southern District of Texas. Docket #C-13,313.

# Index

Numbers in **_bold italics_** indicate pages with illustrations

Abascal, Armando  30, 31, 38, 125
Abascal, Casin  31
Abay, Rolando  91
Abraham Lincoln Brigade  50
Abreu, Reinaldo  213, 214
Acción Cívica Cubana (ACC) (Cuban Civic Action)  30–32, *31*, 36, 38, *38*, 40, 42, 44, 97, 101, 102, 122, 123, 267
Acosta, Ruben  194, *194*
Afanador, José Q.  58
African slaves  17
Agramonte y Pichardo, Roberto, Jr.  30, 119, 142, 193
Aguilera Gonzalez, Pedro Celestino  34, 193
Aguirre, Esperanza Llaguno  185, 208, 265
Aguirre, Hilda  90
Air Force Reserves  131
Alamo, Miguel  115–118, 121, 122, 244, 253
Alcalde Valls, Oscar  32, 33
Alegre, Pablo Fernandez  *200*
Alegría de Pío  103
Alexander City, Alabama  21, 23
Alfonso, Gabriel Gil  *155*
Allied Building, New York City, New York  159
Almeida Bosque, Juan  103, 150, 183, 184, 193
Almendares (section of Habana, Cuba)  90
Aloma, Tony  100
Alvarez, Rafael  115
Alvarez, Socartes  81
Amador Rodriguez, Juan  52, 53
American Can Company  24, 71
American Legion  82, 116, 117
American/U.S. Embassy  178, 179
Amsterdam Avenue, New York City, New York  30, 38, 39
Anastasia, Albert  217, 218

Anti-Communist Group to Help in the Liberation of Cuba  263
A.P. Leto High School  3
Apollo Beach, Florida  25
Apostle of Cuba/Cuba's George Washington  23, 43, 220
Arawak Tribe  16
Archer, Evelyn Eleanor  134
Arcos Bergnes, Gustavo  105, 106
Armenia Avenue, Tampa, Florida  86
Arnade, Charles  67
Arques, Manuel  133, 134
Arteaga, Abelardo  195
Arturo Fuente Cigar Company  257, 258
As We Heard It (*La Gaceta* newspaper column)  54
*Asaka Maru*  263
Asencio Duque de Heredia, Oscar  113
El Ateneo Cubano de Nueva York (The Cuban Athenaeum of New York)  28
*El Avance Criollo*  252
El Azteca printing company  38
Avellanal, Concepción Jimenez  231, 232
Avellanal, Jose Ramon  231
Ayers Diner  67

Baez, Humberto  231, 238, 245, 250
*Bahía de Mariel*  55
*Bahia de Nipe*  122
Banco Nacional de Cuba (National Bank of Cuba)  107
Banos, Angel  134
Barcena y Valladares, Rafael Garcia  **88**
Barroso Dorta, Enrique  81
Barton, Clara  49
baseball  15, 20, 21, 23, 24–26
Batabano, Cuba  34
Batista y Zaldívar, Fulgencio  1, 2, 6, 9, 11, 12, 18, 19, 23–25, 29, 30–34, 42, 46, 47, 55,

289

# 290  Index

58, 60, 63–66, 68, 69, 71, 77–79, 82–84, 87–93, 96–111, 113, 114, 116, 119, 120, 122–129, 131, 133, 136–141, 145, 149, 152, 155, 156–160, 162–164, 166, 170, 172–177, 179–182, 185, 188, 190, 191, 193–195, 197, 200–202, 211, 212, 216, 219, 221, 222, 227, 228, 232, 236, 237, 241, 242, 246, 248, 250, 251, 256, 267, 269
Bay of Pigs Invasion 2
Bayamo, Cuba 32
Bayo Giroud, Alberto 34, 35, 54, 138, 140, 200, 203, 241, 268
Bayshore Boulevard Tampa, Florida 223, 249, 262
Beals, Carleton 262
Beatles 149
Belen (Jesuit school in Cuba) 209
Belgium 229
Berdeal, Rogelio 223, 235, 237, 238
Bergues, Gustavo Arcos **106**
Bermudez, Ramon 161, 162, 192
Betancourt, Ernesto 163
Big Springs, Texas 20
Bisbe Alberni, Manuel 52, 53, 119
The Black Eagle 136
Blanca Fernandez, Luis 122
*Bohemia* (magazine) 46, 55, 61, 92, 175, 193, 227, 228, 259
Bolivar, Rene 165
Bolivar y Morales del Castillo, Guillermo 163–170, **168**, 188, 240
Bolivia 138
Bonito Milian, Luís 34
Bonsal, Philip 229
Borjas, Abelardo 39
Borjas, Carlos 213
Bosch Avila, Orlando 263
El Boulevard Restaurant 112, 113
Boy Scouts 174
Bradenton, Florida 216
Bradford, John 216
Bravo, Ricardo 224
Bridgeport, Connecticut: baseball 21; M-26-7 35, 37, 39, 41
Bridgers, Barney (baseball player) 20
Broadway Bank 54, 224, 256
Bronx, New York 136
Brooklyn Dodgers (baseball team) 21
Brown, Neil 216
Brown, Norman 164, 169
Buch Rodriguez, Luis 183
*Buddy Dee* 133
Buehlman, Victor 108–110
Bueno, Carmelo 4, 67, 86, 87, 92, 119, 147, 156, 157, 191, 192, 194, 209, 224, 231, 245, 250

Bueno, Ofelia Perez 87, 224
Bueno, Orlando 231, 244

Caballero, Gilberto 67
Caballo Blanco (White Horse war name) 132
La Cabana 198
Cabañas Pazos, Julio 81
Cabo Cruz, Cuba 101
Cabrera, Israel 103
Cabrera, José A. 191, 194, 209
Caceras, Antonio 30, 31
Caimanera, Cuba 108, 109
Calle Apodaca, Habana, Cuba 34
Calle Auditor, Habana, Cuba 27, 230
Calle Carvajal, Habana, Cuba 14
Calle Corrales, Habana, Cuba 36
Calle Doce (12th), Habana, Cuba 90
Calle Factoria, Habana, Cuba 34
Calle Fuego, Mexico City, Mexico 85
Calle Humboldt, Habana, Cuba 111, 112
Calle Leonor, Habana, Cuba 14
Calle Mariano, Habana, Cuba 27
Calle Monserrate, Habana, Cuba 205
Calle Risco, Mexico City, Mexico 85
Calle Salud, Habana, Cuba 156
Calle San Paolo, Habana, Cuba 27
Calle Setenta y Ocho (78th), Habana, Cuba 90
Calle Siete (7th), Habana, Cuba 90
Calle Vento, Habana, Cuba 14
Calle Zapata, Habana, Cuba 230
Camaguey, Cuba 211, 212, 215
Cambria, Joe (baseball scout) 20
Camp Columbia Barracks/Camp Rebel/ Ciudad Escolar Libertad 87, 89, 156, 174, 181, 184; Post 6 90; Post 13 90
Campanella, Roy (baseball player) 21
Canada 50, 136
Canadian Armed Forces 135
Canadian Consulate 137
Canedo Garcia, Luis 45
Capitolio 209
Capote, Truman 262
Capri Hotel Casino, Habana, Cuba 84
Caraballo Orraca, José 90
Carbo Servia, Juan Pedro 111
Carbonell, Carlos 70, 86, 94, 116, 119, 147, 157, 191, 195, 224, 227, 228, 231, 245, 250, 256, 259, 260
Carbonell, George 157, 245
Carbonell, Hector 245
Carbonell, Isabel 259
Carbonell Alfonso, Manuel 155, 156
Carbonell Duque, Manuel "Manolito" 157
Cárdenas, Lázaro 99, 221

## Index

Caribbean 22
Carillo La Guardia, Mercedes 189
Carlos de Céspedes Medal of Honor 211
Carpenters' Association 82
Carrera, Julio 81
Carrillo Hernández, Justo 149
Cartaya, Raul 115, 118
Casa de las Americas, Habana, Cuba 269
La casa de piedras (stone house), Miami, Florida 130
Casa Dominicana/The Dominican Club 37
La Casa Loma Restaurant 86, 147, 148, 212
Casals, Violeta 150
Casanova, Joseph A. 194
Casino Theatre 192
Cass Street 219
Castane, Graciela Frances 196
Castillo, Conrado 115, 118
Castillo, Luis 41
Castillo de Atares, Habana, Cuba 236
Castro, Angel 33
Castro, Emma 111
Castro, Fidel, Jr. 37
Castro, Juanita 131, 199, *200*
Castro, Lydia 111
Castro Garcia, Orlando 27, 28, 52, 53
Castro Ruz, Fidel: *41, 42, 62, 63, 77, 186*; Communism 244; fleeing to Mexico 34, 35; forming Cuba's M-26-7 34; forming Tampa's M-26-7 69; Granma expedition 99–103; Guantanamo Boys 109, 110; Herbert Matthews 107; letters from 36, 44, 45, 84, 85, 93, 94, 95–97, 101, 123; Manuel Urrutia Lleo 125, 126, 208, 265; Mexico arrest 97, 99; Moncada Barracks attack 32, 33, 91, 92; morning of Tampa speech 73, 74, 76; nationalizing properties 228–230, 245; planning Tampa speech 57–59, 61, 62, 69, 71–73; planning trip to Tampa 55–57; prison 33, 34; Rafael Garcia Barcena 87–92; rise 31, 32; Tampa arrival 59–61; Tampa speech 76–79; Tampa tour 62–67; trial 33; trip to Bridgeport, Connecticut 41; trip to Key West, Florida 81–83; trip to Miami, Florida 45–47; trip to New York 35–47; trip to Union City, New Jersey 39; trip to United States to meet the president 196–198; victory 172–176
Castro Ruz, Raúl 32, 103, 131, 132, 150–152, 182–185, *184*, 209, 255, 266
Cates, Bill (Miami Tourists coach) 20
Caton, Delia 31
Catskill Mountains, New York 149
Cayo Largo, Cuba 215

CBS 107, 109, 110
Central Park, New York City, New York 39, 196
Centro Asturiano 22
Centro Espanol 22, 192
Cerro (section of Habana), Cuba 14, 23, 27, 183, 208, 230
The Cerro Municipal Museum 14
Cerro Stadium, Habana, Cuba 206
Cervantes, Gilberto 185
Cesar Rodriguez, Diego 139
Cessna (airplane) 137, 151, 180
Chamberlain High School 3
Chapman, Mark David 149
Charleston, South Carolina 243
Chaumont Portocarrero, Arturo 45
Chediak, Esperanza 245
Chestnut Street, Tampa, Florida 67
Chibás y Ribas, Eduardo 27–30, *29*, 32, 50–54, *52, 53*, 56, 57, 73, 98, 117, 119, 200, 219, 241
Chibas y Ribas, Raul 72, 73
Chicago, Illinois 243; M-26-7 111
Chomón Mediavilla, Faure 150
Christmas/Christmas Eve 5, 94, 253
Chungas y No Chungas (*La Gaceta* newspaper column) 54
Church of the Angel (Iglesia de el Angel) 196
Cienfuegos, Cuba 122
Cienfuegos Gorriarán, Camilo 103, 109, 152, 159, 187, 200, 202, 215, 216
Cigar City 22
cigars 3, 49, 52–54, 66, 67, 110, 245, 257, 258
Cincinnati, Ohio 204
CIO Center 71, 73, 74, 76–79
Circulo Cubano (Cuban Club) 22
Citizen's Building, Tampa, Florida 24
City of Tampa Traffic Department 25, 158
Civilian Resistance Movement 124
Clearwater, Florida 107
Clifton, Ellis 154, 217, 218
CMQ-TV 203
Coble, Dave (Miami Tourists manager) 20
Cojimar (section of Habana), Cuba 207
Colonial League (baseball) 25
Columbia Centennial Museum 128
Columbia Music and Appliance 62, 161, 162
Columbia Restaurant 51, 128, 129, 193, 238
Columbus, Christopher 16, 223
Columbus Avenue, New York City, New York 30, 38

Columbus Drive, Tampa, Florida 68, 86, 158, 219
Comité Obrero Democratico de Exiliados y Emigrados Cubanos (Democratic Workers Committee of Cuban Exiles and Emigrants) 36, 40
Comité Ortodoxo (Orthodox Committee) 36, 40, 42, 44
El Comité Pro-Monumento a José Martí (The Jose Marti Pro-Monument Committee) 220
*Comite Pro-Unidad Revolucionaria* booklet *120, 121*
El Comité Pro Unidad Revoluciónario de Tampa (The Pro-Unity Revolutionary Committee of Tampa) 118
Committee for the Aid of Republican Spain 241
Commodoro (hotel), Habana, Cuba 84
Communism/Communist 2, 10, 30, 52, 53, 82, 97, 173, 179, 182, 198, 208, 215, 227, 230, 244, 245, 246- 252, 254–256, 259, 261, 263, 265, 268
Community Church 262
Company B 184
Colonia Juarez, Mexico 95
*Con Todos Y Para El Bien De Todos (With All and for the Good of All)* 48
Concepción, Hipolito 3, 73, 160
Concepcion, Maria Coniglio 3, 59, 160
Coniglio, Alfonso 3
Coniglio, Anthony "Chino" 3
Coniglio, Anthony Sr. 3
Conte Agüero, Luis 46, 130, 196, 200, 203
Contreras, Juan 194
Convento Santa Brigida, Habana, Cuba 15
Copcheck, Bill (baseball player) 20
*Corinthian* 111
*El Corojo* 139
Corral Wodiska (cigar factory) 24, 66, 67
Costa Broom Works 25, 54
*La Coubre* (Belgian ship) 229
Coutin, Leoncio 168
Cozumel, Mexico 139
La Crema Bakery 86, 148
Cremata Valdes, Radio 216
Crespo, Moises 41
Cruz, Ramon 191
Cruz, Ursula 191
Cuatro Caminos Café 68
Cuba Power 263
Cuba Tobacco Company 245
Cuban Air Force 218, 230
Cuban Ambassador to Brazil 157
Cuban Ambassador to El Salvador 132
Cuban Club guestbook page *65*

Cuban Constitution 2, 30
Cuban Consulate 31, 110, 115, 116, 163–171, 190, 235, 236, 253, *253*
Cuban Foreign Minister 221, 236
Cuban House of Representatives (La Camara) 139
Cuban League 241
Cuban Liberation Junta Pact/Unity Pact/ Miami Unity Pact (Junta de Liberacion Cubana) 123, 133, 155
Cuban Missile Crisis 2, 259, 260
Cuban police/G 2 14, 16, 23–25, 33, 39, 78, 82, 90, 110, 111, 149, 174, 175, 177–179, 184, 185, 204, 205, 236, 260
Cuban Revolution 6, 9, 11, 13, 27, 197, 244, 260
Cuban Senate (El Senado) 27, 138
Cuba's Ellis Island 202
Cuba's First War of Independence, 1868/ Ten Years War/Grito de Yara 17, 18, 82, 190, 191, 225
Cuba's National War College 88, 91
Cuba's Second War of Independence, 1895/Grito de Baire 1, 49, 225, 231, 234, 238
Cubillas, Vicente, Jr. 39
Cuellar, Benny 162
Cuellar, Charlie (baseball player) 24, 25
Cuellar, Dahlia Lopez 25
Cuervo's Restaurant 24
Cuesta-Rey Cigar Co. 245
Culbreath, Hugh 83
*Cultivo Una Rosa Blanca (I Have a White Rose to Tend)* 190, 225
Cummings, David 141
Cummings, Mervin 172
Cunningham, Paul 129
Cuscaden Park, Tampa, Florida 51
Customs and Immigration 204
Cuza Téllez de Giron, José Luis 184–186, 204–206
Czech rifles 139

Dakota Building, New York City, New York 149
Danbury, Connecticut 263
Davis, Howard K. ("Davy") 131–135, 138–141, 150–152, 180–182, 247–249, **266**
Deauville (hotel), Habana, Cuba 84, 176, 178
de Beauvoir, Simone 262
de Cardenas, José A. 191, 194
de Cardenas, Maria Teresa 221
de Cespedes, Carlos Manuel 18
Dechard y de la Torriente, Rene 191, 232–244, 253

## Index

Deland, Florida 21, 23
de la Parte, Melchor 227
de la Rosa, Alicia Perez 87
de la Rosa, Juan 87, 147
de la Torre, Amable 112
del Conde, Antonio "El Cuate" 99
Delfa Lines (shipping company) 193
Delgado, Billy 77
Delgado, Dalia Mas 59-63
Delgado, Mary 31
Delgado, Raul 30, 38
Delgado, Ray 191, 192, 194, 209, 223, 224, 231, 238, 250
Dellunde Puyans, Buenaventura 52, 53
de Lojendio e Irure, Juan 229
de los Rios, Fernando 241
de los Rios, Roberto 194, 195, 231, 244
del Pino, Rafael 66, 77, 78, 248
de Menecis, Ivo A. 190
Demmi, John 128
Demmi, Stephen 128
Department of Assistance to War Victims and their Families 193
de Poo, Julio 81
de Quesada, Gonzalo 49
Detroit, Michigan 243
de Yurre, Anthony "Tony" 196
de Yurre, Clayton Victor Formerio 196
*Diario Las Americas* 45
Diaz, Armando 224
Diaz, Delia 59
Diaz, Domingo 118
Diaz, Orlando 81
Diaz, Rafael "Felo" 31
Diaz, Waldo 53
Díaz-Balart, José 37
Díaz-Balart, Lincoln 37
Diaz-Balart, Mario 37
Díaz-Balart, Mirta 37
Diaz-Balart, Rafael, Jr. 37
Díaz-Balart, Rafael, Sr. 37
Diaz Gonzalez, Pablo 36-38, 42
Díaz Lanz, Pedro Luis 150, 181, 182
Dilio Nunez, Matias 91
Dirección de Publicidad Palacio Presidencial (Presidential Palace Public Relations Office) 184-186
Director General of the Office of the Prime Minister 236, 237; secretary 202
Director of Immigration 194
Directorio Obrero Revoluciónario (Revolutionary Workers Directorate) 123
Directorio Revoluciónario (DR) (Revolutionary Directorate) 110, 111, 118, 122, 123, 150, 180

Dirigente del Municipio de la Habana (Director of the Municipality of Habana) 154
Dlugokecki, Henry (baseball player) 20
Dominican Republic/Dominicans 37, 173
Dorta, Armando 223, 235, 237
Dorticós Torrado, Osvaldo 208, 226, 236, 242, 265
Drimal, Arlene Villamia 130, 198, 199
Dublin, Georgia 21, 23, 24
Duenas, Luis 231
Duke, Anthony Drexel 269
Duke, Maria "Luly" de Lourdes Alcebo 269
Duke, Washington Alcebo 269
Duke University 196, 269
Dunkin, Tom 153, 154
Duque de Estrada, Miguel Angel 49
Duran, Rafael 115, 119, 147
Duval Street, Key West, Florida 81
Duvalier, François "Papa Doc" 136, 137

Easter Monday 89
Easter Sunday 87, 89; Conspiracy 87-92
Echeverria Bianchi, Jose Antonio 110
*Ecos* 212-214
ECOS newsletter *213*
Eighteenth (18th) Avenue, Tampa, Florida 54, 61
Eighteenth (18th) Street, Tampa, Florida 24
Eighth (8th) Avenue, New York City, New York 36-38
Eighth (8th) Avenue, Tampa, Florida 65, 190, 219, 220, 227
Eisenhower, Dwight 109, 196, 198, 229, 254
El Salvador 132
Eleventh (11th) Avenue, Tampa, Florida 74
11th Police Precinct, Habana, Cuba 14
Eleventh (11th) Street, Tampa, Florida 51
Elizabeth Street, Key West, Florida 81
Elías, Lino 45, 46, 62, 63, 65, 66, 77, 78, 116
Elmuza Agaisse, Félix 45, 62, 105
England/Great Britain 17, 89, 136, 173
El Ensanche de la Habana 14
Erickson, Robert B. 99
Ermisch, Howard "Red" (baseball player) 20
Escalona Gonzalez, Pedro 30, 38
Escambray Mountains, Cuba 1, 2
*La Escoba* 54, 55
Espín Guillois, Vilma 183, 184
Esquinaldo, Enrique 82
Estrada Palma, Tomás 18, 64

Europe 28
Executive Air Service, Inc. 182

Fabelo, Ruben 51, 53, 63, 64, 74, 147, 148, 161, 162, 211–214, 237–240
Fair Play for Cuba 195, 261, 262
Fascism 30
FBI 11, 41, 247–249, 255, 256, 259–264, 268
Federación Estudiantil Universitaria (FEU) (University Student Federation) 31, 32, 55, 87, 110, 123, 157, 180
Fernandez, Belarmino 153
Fernandez, Conchita 200, 203
Fernández, Ismael Ricondo 144
Fernandez, José L. 91
Fernandez, Juan 81
Fernández, Leovigildo 222
Fernandez, Mancilo 200
Fernandez, Manuel 116
Fernandez, Marta 64, 181
Fernandez, Rose Coniglio 3
Fernandez Alegre, Pablo 107, 130–132, 185, 199, 247, 268
Fernandez de la Nuez, Francisco 162
Fernandez Pendas, Jaime 112
Ferrara, Molly 62, 161, 162
Ferrara, Sam 62, 161
Ferreiro Mora, Julio 52, 53
Ferrer, Victor 115, 117
Fidalgo Rodriguez, Jose Manuel. 54–56, 121, 195, 200, 202, 221, 223, 236, 237, 239
Fidel Castro letter to Raul Villamia *96, 97*
Fiesta en Tampa 63, 64, 161, 211, 213, 240
Fifteenth (15th) Street, Tampa, Florida 54, 62, 93, 98, 227
Fifty-sixth (56th) Street, Tampa, Florida 158
Figueroa del Marmol, Carmen 241, 242
Fiorini, Frank/Sturgis, Frank 141, 150
Flagler Building, Tampa, Florida 164, 167
Flagler Street, Miami, Florida 46
Flagler Theater 45–47, 57, 59, 116, 183
Florida Avenue, Tampa, Florida 158
Florida International League (baseball) 22, 25
Florida Keys 153
Florida Printing 71, 192
Ft. Benning, Georgia 138
Ft. Jackson, South Carolina 154
Fourteenth (14th) Avenue, Tampa, Florida 59, 60, 71, 127
Fourteenth (14th) Street, Tampa, Florida 62, 64, 74, 86, 127, 143, 194, 231, 232, 244
Fourth (4th) Avenue, Tampa, Florida 25, 54

Franco, Francisco 49, 50, 58
Franklin Street, Tampa, Florida 24
Franqui, Carlos 202
Frisco Printing 192
Frisco, Tony 192
Fuente, Anna Lopez 258
Fuente, Carlos, Sr. 257
Fuente, Carlito 258
Fuente, Cynthia 258
Fuente, Ricky 258
Fuentes Alfonso José 39
Fuentes Alfonso Mario 39
Fuentes, Manuel 123, 124, 194
Fundacion Amistad 269

*La Gaceta* 23, 52–54, 56–62, 67, 71, 76–80, 86, 93–95, 98, 99, 102, 104, 113, 116, 117, 121–124, 127–129, 143, 147, 148, 153, 160–163, 165, 167, 172, 174–180, 191, 192, 194, 195, 199, 200–203, 209, 210, 223, 231, 233, 236, 239, 240–244, 246, 250–252, 254
*La Gaceta* office, Tampa, Florida *94*
Gadea, Hilda 95
Gainza, Melba Ortega 106
Galindez, Javan 5, 154, 269
Galindez, Wynter 5, 154, 196, 269
Galveston Bay, Texas 133
Garcia, Benigno 191, 209
Garcia, Francisco 149
Garcia, Israel 191
Garcia, Max 59, 86, 119, 147, 158, 191, 206, 227
Garcia, Odelio 231
Garcia, Pilar 177
Garcia, Sergio 115, 117
García Bárcena y Gomez, Jose Rafael 46, 81, 87–92, 105, 156, 157
García Bárcena y Valladares, Rafael 87–92, 157
Garcia Garcia, Reynold 97
Garcia Inclán, Guido 46
Garcia Leal, Luis 39, 42
Garcia Montalvo, Mario 231, 250
Garcia Serrano, Roberto 113
Garcia y Vega Cigar Co. 245
Garibaldi (sculpture) 223
Garroway, David 128, 203
Garvey, Mike 107–110
Gaspar, Jose 221
Gasparilla (Tampa's "Mardi Gras") 221
Gavilla, Julia 191
General Strike in Cuba 139
Gerardo Perez Pulles telegram to Gabriel Gil Alfonso *171*
Germany 67
Gervac, Maria Luisa 224, 238

Gifford, Lawrence G. 216
Gil Alfonso, Gabriel 12, 143–148, 154, 155, 158–162, 165, 166, 168, 171, 174, 185, 193, 212
Ginsberg, Allen 262
Gispert, Manuel 94
Goenaga, Gloria 39
Goenaga Barron, Arnaldo 36, 42
Goicuria Barracks/Garrison 97, 111, 112
Golan, Aida Perez 87
Golan, Ernesto 157, 262
Golan, Marcelino 86, 87, 92, 147, 157, 261, 262
Gomez, Angel 113
Gomez Olazabal, José M. "Pepin" 45, 81
Gomez y Baez, Maximo 51
Gonzalez, Alcides 46, 116
González, Aurelio "Yeyo" 76, 77
Gonzalez, Aurelio Andres "A. A." 53, 221
González, Aurelio, Jr. 77
González, Guillermo "Willie" 77
Gonzalez, Heriberto 149
González, Maria Antonia 68, 74, 80
Gonzalez, Raquel Perez 193
Gonzalez, Rene 86, 213
Gonzalez Gutierrez, Mariano 14
González Jaen, Antonio 37
Gonzalez Seijas, Carlos 35, 39, 46
Gonzalez Clinic 86, 143
Gonzmart, Cesar 193
*Granma* 7, 99, 100, 105, 106, 133, 146
Grau San Martín, Ramón 18, 19, 27, 54, 58, 241
Great Depression 19
Gualberto Gomez, Juan 49
Guantánamo Bay Naval Base 108
The Guantánamo Boys/GTMO Boys 107–110
Guastella, Vincent 58, 68
guayabera (traditional Cuban shirt) 144
Guevara de la Serna, Ernesto "Che" 35, 67, 95, 103, 104, 107, 109, 138, 150, 152, 159, 181, 185, 187, 198, 200, 206
Gutiérrez Menoyo, Eloy 150
Guzman, Frank 248
Guzzo, Paul 6, 217, 218

Habana (city) 12, 14, 15, 19, 21–23, 27, 34, 35, 46, 51, 54, 55, 63, 66, 68, 83, 87, 90, 97, 106, 107, 109, 110, 111, 113, 131, 141, 144, 154, 155–157, 159, 165, 174–178, 181–185, 187, 193, 196, 198–200, 202, 203, 205, 206, 209, 215, 225, 226, 228–230, 236, 251, 269
Habana Avenue, Tampa, Florida 67
Habana Carnival 221

Habana City Historian 14, 15
Habana Cubans (baseball team) 22
Habana Hilton (hotel), Habana, Cuba 84, 202
Habana Province, Cuba 28, 34, 248
Haiti 135–138, 141, 163
Haley, Alex 3
Hannay, Allen Burroughs 148, 264, 265
*The Harpoon* 153
Hart Dávalos, Armando 34, 87, 91, 266
Hart Davalos, Enrique 87, 156
Haynes, Charles (baseball player) 20
Hedda (woman) 60, 62, 63; mother 60
Heliodoro Martínez, Junco 138
Hemming, Gerald Patrick 268
Hendrick, Charles 170, 171
Hermida, Guillermo 115
Hernandez, Casimiro 193
Hernandez, Eddie 209
Hernandez Bacallao, José 90
Hernandez Bencomo, Gerardo 269
Hernández Rodríguez del Rey, Melba 34, 68, 91, 105
Herrera, Julio 191, 209
Herter, Charlie 228, 229
Hidalgo, Armando 39
Hidalgo Barrios, Alonso "Bebo" 87, 133, 154, 156
Hidalgo Barrios, Mario 87, 156
Hightower, Dan 253
Hillier, Sherwood 244, 245
Hillsborough Avenue, Tampa, Florida 158
Hillsborough County Sheriff 83, 218
Hillsborough County's Vice Squad 154, 217, 218
Hillsborough River, Tampa Florida 249
*Historia Intima de la Revolucion Cubana* 6, 137, 265
*La Historia Me Absolverá* (*History Will Absolve Me*) 33, 38, 39, **39**, **40**, 42, 43
Hitler, Adolf 67
Hixon, Curtis 221
Hodges, Gil (baseball player) 21
Holguin, Cuba 112
Holguin Province, Cuba 206
Holliston, Massachusetts 267
Holy Week 91
Hoover, J. Edgar 255
Hormann, Donald (baseball player) 20
Hotel Castle D' Haiti 136
Hotel Habana Riviera, Habana, Cuba 84, 178, 203
Hotel Hillsboro, Tampa, Florida 51, 52
Hotel Strathfield, Bridgeport, Connecticut 39

Houston 133–135, 148, 149, 264
Howard Avenue, Tampa, Florida 49, 219
Humboldt 7 Massacre 111

Iglesia Parroquial del S. Corpus Christi en Marianao Church (Corpus Christi Church) 198, 199
Iglesias, Mario 115, 116, 119, 147, 162, 163, 168, 188, 209, 231
Inclan Argudin, Rafael 90
Inclan Costa, Clemente 90
Inglis, Tom 172–175
Instituto Nacional de la Industria Turistica (INIT) (National Institute of Tourism) 248
Interpen (Intercontinental Penetration Force) 267, 268
Intersocial Baseball League 24
Irigoyen, Ramon 42, 62, 63, 65
Irish/Irishman 3, 80
Isla de Pinos (Isle of Pines), Cuba 33–35

Jacas Quintana, Virgilio 106, 127–130, 185, 192, 194, **194**
Jamaica 116, 136, 137
Jamaica Street, Tampa, Florida 116
Japanese 263
Jaraica, Juan 125
Jardines del Pedregal de San Angel, Mexico 85
J.C. Newman Cigar Company 258
JD's Sandwich Shop 128
Jesuit 209
*JFK* (movie) 267
Jimenez, Felipe "Indio" 194, 227, 228
Jimenez, Maximo 190
Jose Llanusa telegram to Gabriel Gil Alfonso **166**
José Martí Memorial Foundation 54, 220, 221, 223, 235–239
Jose Marti statue, Tampa, Florida **222, 234**
Juan A. Orta telegram to Victoriano Manteiga **237**
Julian Hubert Fauntleroy 136
Juventud Autentica 27

Kemah, Texas 133
Kennedy, John F. 216, 257, 261–263
Keokuk, Iowa 21, 25
Key West, Florida 2, 131, 182, 204, 205, 248; M-26-7 9, 35, 43, 55, 81, 82, 93, 110, 111, 157
*Key West Citizen* 82
Key West Kennel Club 82
Khrushchev, Nikita 247

Kilgore, Jay Allen 138–141
King Bee Grocery 3
Korea 131

Laetrile 135
Lafayette Street/Kennedy Boulevard, Tampa, Florida 67; Bridge 249
Lagos, Balbina 4, 19
Lagos, Constantino 19
Lagos, Manuela 19
Lagos, Marcelina 19
Lambright Avenue, Tampa, Florida 163
Lamothe, Humberto 103
Lansky, Meyer 84, 178
Las Coloradas Beach, Cuba 101
Las Vegas, Nevada 178
Las Villas Province, Cuba 150, 152, 159
*The Last Revolutionary* 110
latifundias (large estates in Cuba) 229
Latin American Fiesta Association (Queen's court) 221
Latin Americans 41, 67
Latin District 24
Lawton (section of Habana Cuba) 144
Lazar, Paul 180–182
Leal Spengler, Eusebio 14, 15
Lebron, Ramon 250
lector (cigar factory reader) 52
Lee, Gerardo 91
Lee, Vincent T. 262
Lennon, John (Beatles) 149
Leon Planas, Juan M. 193
León, Guillermo 142, 143
Leto, Ateo Phillip 3
Leto, Francesca "Panchita" Coniglio 3
letters: Antonio "Nico" Lopez Fernandez to Mario Villamia 34; to *Bohemia* 228; Carmen Figueroa del Marmol to *La Gaceta* 241, 242; to entire exile community 123; Fidel Castro to Angel Perez-Vidal 36; Gabriel Gil Alfonso to Ruben Fabelo (alleged) 212; to *La Gaceta* 242; Jesus Montane to Carlos Gonzalez Seijas 35; Jose Llanusa to M-26-7 report on Haiti trip 137; Jose Marti Memorial Foundation press release 236; Joseph Casanova/Roberto de los Rios to Carlos Carbonell 195; Juan Almeida Bosque to Raul Villamia 193; Juan M. Leon to Raul Villamia 193; Juan Manuel Fidalgo to Victoriano Manteiga 55, 56; to M-26-7 of New York City 44, 45; to Mario Villamia 35, 84, 85, 101; Mario Villamia to Fidel Castro 132, 135; Nick Nuccio to Fidel Castro 188; Pedro Aguilera to Raul Villamia 193;

# Index 297

Rafael Rodriguez Luloaga (*Bohemia*) to Raul Villamia 228; to Raul Villamia 94, 95, 96, 97, 180; Raul Villamia to Fidel Castro 95; to Rene Dechard 236–238; to Victoriano Manteiga 93; Victoriano Manteiga to Fidel Castro 95; Virgilio Jacas to Raul Villamia 129
Liccio, Josie 224
El Liceo Cubano 48
La Liga Nacional de Béisbol Amateur de Cuba (National Amateur Baseball League of Cuba) 20
Lima, Billy 224, 250
Lions Club 195
Little Havana section of Miami 130
Llaguno, Pedro Pablo 52
llano (Cuban rebels not in the mountains) 106
Llanusa Gobel, José 135, 149, 163
Lleó, Herminia 208
Lleo, Manuel Urrutia *125*
Longhorn League (baseball) 20
Lopez, Jose 25
Lopez, Montelongo (baseball player) 25
López Fernández, Antonio "Ñico" 33, 34
Los Caballeros Leales de América (Loyal Knights of America) 58
Los Caballeros Orden de la Luz (Order of the Knights of Light) 221
Los Cayuelos, Cuba 101
*Los Pinos Nuevos* (*The New Pines*) 48
Los Tigres de Masferrer (Masferrer's Tigers) 136
Los Venaditos (Elks Club) 82
Lowry, Blackburn 24
Loyalists 34
Lozano, Manuel 224
Luciano, Lucky 224
Lugo, Galicia, Spain 19
Luis, Miguel 41, 44

M-2 rifle 158, 159, 185, 186, 205, 206, 248
M-26-7 *66, 147, 162, 184, 185, 191, 192, 194, 211, 224, 245, 250*; announcement of Fidel Castro's speech *76*; donation bond cards *143*; donation bond commemorating the second anniversary of *Granma* landing *146*; donation bonds *145*; dues payment booklet, membership card, photo ID card *72, 75*; invitation to attend commemorative event at Boulevard Restaurant *112*; invitation to attend the 5th anniversary event in commemoration of the Moncada Barracks attack *148*; invitation to join the Tampa club *93*; invitation to participate in a caravan in defense of the Cuban government *220*; invitation to Tampa cigar workers to donate to the club *144*; meal ticket for Grito de Baire commemorative dinner at clubhouse *234*; membership application form *70*; National Directorate in Exile 105, 107, 110, 117, 118, 135, 142, 143, 145–147, 183; receipt booklet for donation collection *98*; rent receipt for clubhouse space at El Pasaje building, TECO electric bill for clubhouse space *232, 233*
MacDill Air Force Base 58, 263
Maceo y Grajales, Antonio 82
Machado Rodriguez, Jose 111
Machado y Morales, Gerardo 14–16, 18, 50, 87, 241
Madison Street, Tampa, Florida 158
Mafia 83, 84, 176–178, 201, 202, 204–206, 217, 218
Magistrate, Court of Accounts 89
Magoon, Charles 18
Main Street, Tampa, Florida 86
Malecon/Avenida de Maceo, Habana, Cuba 200
Mambi/Mambises 78
Mancebo, Gabriel 91
Manhattan Detention Center, "The Tombs" 122, 149
*Manifesto Numero 1* (*Manifest Number 1*) 35
Maniscalco, Joe 51, 58, 68,
Mann, Cecil 167, 168,
Manteiga, Roland 51, 52, 54, 76, 115, 128, 129, 174, 175, 177, 178, 191, 194, 195, 199–203, 250–252
Manteiga, Victoriano 51–59, 61, 67–73, 76–78, 80, 86, 93–99, 102, 104, 105, 111, 115–128, 142, 143, 150, 161, 174–180, 188, 191, 194, 195, 197–203, 207, 209, 210, 220–224, 231, 233, 235–244, 246, 247, 249–254, *250*, 256, 264
Manuel de Céspedes, Carlos 18
Manuel de Céspedes Barracks 32, 33
Manzanillo, Cuba 107
March, Aleida 198
Margolles, Fernando 81
Marill, Carmen 162
Marquez Rodriguez, Juan Manuel 35–39, 42, 45, 46, 57, 60, 62–68, 77, 78, 81, 82, 101–103, 105, 241
Marrero, Zenaida 233
Martí Pérez, José 23, 39, 42, 47–52, *50*, 54, 55, 57, 64–66, 79, 82, 111, 117, 144, 161, 189, 190, 195, 221, 225, 231, 242, 269

Martí-Maceo Union Society (Sociedad La Union Marti-Maceo) 51, 71, 158
Marti Theatre 35
Martinez, Felix 116
Martinez Fraga, Pedro Julio 90
Martinez Ybor, Vicente 22
Mas, Rolando 59, 60
Masferrer Rojas, Rolando 136, 137, 181
Massana, Juan 30
Massip Valdes, Salvador 52
Matanzas, Cuba 68, 97, 243
Mato Menocal, Mario 81
Matos, Huber 240
Matthews, Herbert 107, 110,
McKeown, Robert 133, 262
McNaughton, Andrew George Latta 135
McNaughton, Andrew Robert Leslie 135-137
Mejido, Juan (baseball player) 23
Mendoza, Enrique 195
Mendoza, Jorge Enrique 150
Menendez, Danilo 91
Menendez, Jose Ramon 81
Merida, Mexico 138
Mexican Coast Guard 139
Mexican police 138
Mexico City, Mexico 102
*Mi Aporte a la Revolución Cubana (My Contribution to the Cuban Revolution)* 35
Miami, Florida 1, 2, 19, 21, 22, 25, 35, 45, 55, 57, 59, 68, 78, 80-82, 97, 102, 107, 110-113, 119, 123, 127, 130-136, 138, 141, 143, 144, 146, 147, 149-155, 157, 163, 165, 166, 171, 178, 182, 183, 201, 202, 212, 242, 251, 252, 260, 263, 265, 266, 267, 268; M-26-7 9, 43, 62, 63, 77, 78, 102, 107, 111, 112, 116, 117, 123
Miami International Airport 150, 180, 201
Miami Tourists (baseball team) 20, *20*, 21
Miguel Gómez, José 18
Mijares Pujals, Eduardo 127-129, 142
Mikoyan, Anastas 229
Ministry/Minister of Agriculture 199, 207
Ministry/Minister of Education 29, 87, 206, 211, 266
Ministry/Minister of Labor 200
Ministry/Minister of Public Works 190; taxes 192, 194; workshop 236
Ministry/Minister of the Presidency/ Secretary of the Council of Ministers 183
Ministry/Minister of the Recovery of Stolen Money and Properties 200, 202
Ministry/Minister of Tourism/National Institute of Tourism (INIT) 182, 208; Habana Province 248
Miramar, Cuba 202, 203
Miramar, Florida 265
Miramar Clinic 129
Miranda, Sgt. 122, 123
Miret Prieto, Pedro 34, 105, 106, *106*, 130, 268
Miro, Ruben 202
Moa, Cuba 206
*Mob Lawyer* 177, 217
molotov cocktails 264
Moncada Barracks 32, 39, 106, 112
Montané Oropesa, Jesús 34, 35, 37, 95, 105, 183, 185, 248
Montego Bay, Jamaica 136
Montejo, Luis 39
Montreal, Canada 136
Mora, Alberto 112, 116
Mora Morales, Menelao 110
Morales (female) 162
Morales (male) 162
Morales, Carlos "Moralito" 30, 31, 38, 41, 42
Morales, Rene 82
Moran, Raul 233
Morem, Robert (baseball player) 20
Moreno, Candido 81
Moreno, Rodrigo 45, 81
Moreno, Walfrido 37
Movimiento Amigos de la Revolución Cubana (Friends of the Cuban Revolutionary Movement) 233
Movimiento Insurreccional de Recuperación Revoluciónario (MIRR) (Insurrectional Movement for Revolutionary Recovery) 263
Movimiento Nacional Revoluciónario (MNR) (National Revolutionary Movement) 81, 88-92, 105, 156
El Movimiento Patriótico de Tampa de Ayuda al Campesinado Cubano (Patriotic Movement of Tampa for Aid to the Cuban Farmer) 194, 246
Mullins, James P. 164, 168, *191*
Municipal Stadium 51
Muniz, Leonardo 45, 62, 63, 66, 81
Museo Municipal del Cerro 14

Nande, Ramon 27
Naples, Florida 215
Nassau, Bahamas 81
National Airlines 217, 218
National Bank of Cuba 107
National Firearms Act 134
National Guard 131

# Index 299

Nationalist Army 49
Nazism 30
NBC 37, 128
NE Miami Place, Miami, Florida 130, 268
Nebraska Avenue, Tampa, Florida 112, 113, 148, 219
Nee, Melvin (baseball player) 20
Negrin, Ismael 81
New Orleans, Louisiana 132, 262
New Ulm, Minnesota 21, 25
New Year's Day 160–166, 254
New York City (Manhattan), New York 1, 4, 5, 6, 12, 13, 27–31, 35–50, 55–57, 59, 61, 78, 84, 85, 97, 101, 102, 111, 117, 119, 122, 125, 126, 133, 135, 137, 138, 149, 159, 196, 197, 217, 218, 249, 262, 264, 265–268; M-26-7 9, 36–38, 43, 44–47, 78, 111, 117, 119, 122, 133, 149
New York County District Attorney Office 218
New York Police Department 122
*New York Times* 30, 31, 102, 107, 200, 201, 257, 261
Nick Nuccio letter to Fidel Castro **189**
Nineteenth (19th) Street, Tampa, Florida 66
Ninth (9th) Avenue, New York City, New York 38
Ninth (9th) Avenue, Tampa, Florida 64, 86, 112, 113, 143, 194, 231–233, 244.
Ninth (9th) Street, Miami, Florida 45
Ninth (9th) Street, Tampa, Florida 158
Niquero, Cuba 101
Nixon, Richard 198, 229
Non-Commissioned Officer in Charge (NCOIC) 131
None Such Bakery 86, 227
Nuccio, Nick 188–190, 193, 213
Nueva Gerona, Cuba 34
Nuñez, Carlos "Bigote" 194
Núñez, Pastorita 46
Nunez Bordon, Alberto 209, 224, 231, 250
NW Twenty-second (22nd) Street, Miami, Florida 130

Obregon, Francisco 134
Ochoa, Dario 131
Ochoa y Ochoa, Emilio "Millo" 28, 53
O'Connor, Tom 80
Office of the Foreign Minister 221
Oficina de Asuntos Históricos (OAH) (Office of Historic Affairs), Habana, Cuba 66, 113
O'Halloran Cigar Company 49
SS *Olivette* 51
Olmedo, Homero 162

Olympics 67
Orange Bowl Stadium 20
Organizacion Auténtica (Authentics Organization) 118, 121, 153
Oriente Province, Cuba 100–102, 124, 130, 131, 150–152, 181, 193
*El Orion* 153
Orlando, Castro Garcia **28**
Orta Cordoba, Juan A. 45, 46, 202, 203, 236, 237
Orthodox Committee 36, 40, 42, 44
Ortiz, Fernando 241
Ortiz Planos, Ramiro 243
Oswald, Lee Harvey 262
Our Lady of Perpetual Help Church 73, 74, 111, 112

País García, Frank 100, 107, 130, 249
Palm Garden Hall 36, 41–44, **44**
Pando, Emilio 165
*Para Cuba Que Sufre (For a Suffering Cuba)* 55
Pardo Llada, Jose 52, 53
Parellada Echevarria, Otto 100
Parker, George "Tiny" (Miami Tourists owner) 20
Parque Amigos de José Martí (Friends of Jose Marti Park), Tampa, Florida 190, 191, 194, 219–226, 234, 237, 238, **239**, 262
Parque Central, Habana, Cuba 23, 225
Partido del Pueblo Cubano Ortodoxo (The Party of the Cuban People—Orthodox) 28, 29, 32, 35, 36, 53
Partido Revolucionario Cubano (PRC) (Cuban Revolutionary Party) 27, 48, 123
Partido Revoluciónario Cubano Auténtico/Partido Autentico (The Cuban Revolutionary Party—Authentic/The Authentic Party) 27, 28, 78, 118, 123
El Pasaje Hotel/Cherokee Club 98, 194, 231, 232
Patriotic Movement of Tampa for Aid to the Cuban Farmer (Movimiento Patriotico de Tampa de Ayuda al Campesinado Cubano) 228, 231, 244, 254
Patterson, Frank P. 190
Paula, Jose Manuel 45, 112
Paxton, Sammy 202
Pazos Rodriguez, Felipe 107, 133
Pazos Vea, Javier 107
Pedrayes y Madera, Ofelia 51
Pedroso, Paulina 65, 66, 189, 190
Pedroso, Ruperto 65, 66, 189, 190

## 300　　　　　　　　　　　　　　Index

Pegol Cabinet Shop 86
Peñate, José 16
Pennsylvania Station 37
Peraza, Carlos G. 112, 116
Pérez, Álvaro 32, 34, 35
Pérez, Bienvenido 82
Pérez, Celida 191
Pérez, Cristo 191, 194, 209, 231
Perez, Eliseo 53, 166, 188, 225, 232, 240
Pérez, Eusebio "Silverio" (baseball player) 23, 24
Perez, Georgina Eligina 42
Pérez, Juan M. 86–87, 90, 147, 154–156, *156*, 162, 163, 164–165, 170, 188, 191, 192, 194, 206, 211, 224, 245,
Perez, Julio 125, 185
Perez, Marcelino 191
Perez, Paul D. 29
Perez, Pedro 71
Pérez Hernández, Faustino 34, 87, 91, 103, 105–107, 130, 154, 156, 185, 268
Pérez Nunez, Pedro 147, 191, 209
Pérez Puelles, Gerardo 163, 165, 171
Pérez Rosabal, Angel 101
Pérez Serantes, Enrique 33, 224
Perez-Vidal, Alma Rivera 29, 31, 183, 208, 265
Pérez-Vidal, Angel 6, 27, 29, 30, 31, 35–39, 41, 42, 44, 45, 97, 102, 122, 123, 125, 126, 135–137, 149, 150, 183, 186, 187, 196, 197, 208, 265–268, *267*
Pérez-Vidal, Ernesto 30, 97
Pérez-Vidal, Santiago 30, 31, 38, 41, 42, 97
Perrin, Bill (baseball player) 20
Peruvian Embassy 12
Petty, Gene (baseball player) 20
Philadelphia, Pennsylvania 37
Phillips, Ruby Hart 107
*Philomar III* 153
Pico, José 30, 31
Pinar del Río Province, Cuba 138, 139
Pine Street, Tampa, Florida 116
Pineiro (man) 162
*El Pinero* 34
Pino, Orquidea 85
Pioneer Parachute Company 132
Piper Cub 182
Pizzo, Tony 190, 221–223, 237
Platt Amendment 17, 18
Platt Street, Tampa, Florida 262
Plaza Civica/Plaza de la Revolucion 209
Playa Santa Fe, Cuba 28
Plaza Hotel, Habana, Cuba 206
Polish 263
Polo Grounds, Bronx, New York 196
Ponce, Ernesto 115–117

Pontevedra, Galicia, Spain 19
Poole, Samuel, Jr. 201
Popular Front 49, 50, 54
Port-au-Prince airport 137
Port Everglades, Florida 153
Port of Habana 207
Port of Tampa 264
Portales, Orestes 45, 46, 77, 81
Portsmouth, Virginia 21, 25
El Prado, Habana, Cuba 200
Presbyterian medical laboratory 156
Presidential Palace, Habana Cuba 6, 110–112, 125, 150, 180, 183–186, 205, 249, 265
Presidential Palace Publicity Department 184–186
Prieto Ibarra, Jorge 111, 112
Prieto Ibarra, Mario 111
Prieto Rodriguez, José "Pepe" 87, 91, 155, 156
Prio Socarras, Carlos 78, 97, 99, 111, 116, 118, 121, 133, 134, 138, 149, 153, 241, 262
Pujol, Rogelio 178, 179
Pujol Barrera, Abelardo 134
Punta de Palma, Cuba 139

Quesada, Elaine 222
Quevedo Jaureguízar, Manuel 189
Quinones (man) 192

Radcliff, Gus 164, 165, 167–169, 171
Radio Center 76
Radio Rebelde 150
Radio Reloj 111
Ragano, Frank 177, 217, 218
Ramirez, Oscar 45, 81, 183
Ramirez Barcega, Julio 39
Ramírez Moya, Pedro 53, 161, 162, 238
Ramos, Luis 30, 31, 38
El Ranchon (Big Ranch) 101
Ranon, Domingo 190
Rather, Dan 110
Rayneri, Rene 132, 185
Re, Cosmo 264
Red Cross 49, 266
Reese, Pee Wee (baseball player) 21
Reguera Martinez, Oscar 201
Report in Reference to Trip to Haiti (Informe Referente a Viaje a Haiti) 137
Republic of Cuba 78
La Resistencia 3
*Revolución* (newspaper) 203, 211
Revolutionary Air Force 182
Revolutionary Army 174, 176
Revolutionary Government 2, 136, 149, 163–165, 190, 201, 222, 228–230, 243, 265
Revolutionary Museum 269, 270

Revolutionary Police Command 236
Reyes García, Jesús "Chuchu" 45, 60, 77
Riera, Eliseo 45
Riestra, Luis 116, 117
Rio de Janeiro, Brazil 157
Ritz Theatre, Tampa, Florida 24
Rivero Mas, Cesar 232
Riviera Orchestra 77
Roa Garcia, Raul 54, 221, 236, 242
Robinson, Jackie (baseball player) 21
Rocamora, Daisy Carbonell 253
Roche, Miguel 115, 117
Rodriguez, Antonio "El Pollo" (baseball player) 20
Rodriguez, Eugenio 193
Rodriguez, Fernando "Trompoloco" (baseball player) 23, 24
Rodriguez, George 214
Rodriguez, Gilberto 115, 194
Rodriguez, Henry "Rod" 161, 162
Rodriguez, Johnny 130
Rodriguez, José 91, 191
Rodriguez, Noemi "Norma" Concepcion 3, 24
Rodriguez, Pérez Lester 107, 130–133, 139, 183, 184, **184**, 185
Rodriguez, Ramon 115, 118
Rodriguez, Richard Callahan 3, 24
Rodríguez Argemí, Celestino 37, 39,
Rodriguez Delgado, Oscar 45, 46, 103
Rodriguez Luloaga, Rafael 228
Rodriguez Perez, Fructoso 111
Rodriguez Rodriguez, Luis Orlando 52, 53
Rojas, Alberto 115, 118
Rojas, Eurice B. 37, 42
Rome, Italy 181, 243
Romero, Cesar 203
Roosevelt, Teddy 49
*Roots: The Saga of an American Family* 3, 4
Rough Riders 49
Royal Theatre, Tampa, Florida 24
Ruby, Jack 217, 263
Ruiz, Eva Jimenez 90, 91
Ruiz Funes, Mariano 241
Russo, Grace 66
Russo, Tony 66
Ruz, Lina 33
Ryan, Charles 108, 110

Saavedra, Henry 201
Sabas Muguercia, Alberto 222–224, **224**, 231, 232, 234, 236–238, 241
Sacassas, Armando 253
St. Petersburg, Florida 22

St. Petersburg-Clearwater International Airport 227
*St. Petersburg Times* 153, 154, 216
Salas, Osvaldo 39
Salcines, Emiliano "E.J." 1, 2
San Antonio, Texas 37
San Carlos Institute/Club San Carlos, Key West, Florida 2, 81
San Luis, Cuba 32
Sanchez, Gloria 129
Sánchez, Miguel Ángel 45
Sanchez, Pedro 52
Sanchez Alvarez, Universo 103
Sánchez Arango, Aureliano 29
Sánchez White, Calixto 11
Sanjenís Perdomo, José 149
Sans Souci Club (hotel), Habana, Cuba 84, 176, 178
Santa Clara, Cuba 152
Santamaría Cuadrado, Abel 34, 68
Santamaría Cuadrado, Aldo 68
Santamaría Cuadrado, Haydée 34, 91, 105, 106, 146, 165, 183, 269
Santiago de Cuba, Cuba 7, 33, 100, 125, 150, 197, 231, 249
Santiago de las Pena, Mexico 99
Santo Domingo, Dominican Republic 227
Santome, Inocencia 54
Santome, Jose 54
Santos, Florentino 86, 116, 119, 147
Sardinas, Felix 30, 41
Sarria Tartabull, Pedro Manuel 33
Saud, Antonio 91
Seaboard Cafeteria 66
Seabrook, Texas 133
Seagonville, Texas 265
Second (2nd) Avenue, Miami, Florida 45, 46
Second (2nd) Avenue, Tampa, Florida 66
Secret missions 105–107, 130–141, 148, 149, 151, 153–158, 182, 185, 186, 201, 206, 207
Secretary of State (Cuba) 54, 236
El Segundo Frente del Escambray (The Second Front of the Escambray) 150, 180, 184
Seijas, Arturo 20
September 11, 2001/World Trade Center (WTC)/Ground Zero 5, 6
Serrano, Edilberto 112, 116
Servicio de Inteligencia Militar/(SIM) (Military Intelligence Service) 88, 178
Setticasi, Helen 222
Seventeenth (17th) Street, Tampa, Florida 59, 60, 74
Seventh (7th) Avenue/Broadway Avenue,

## Index

Tampa Florida 24, 37, 39, 48, 51, 54, 62, 71, 74, 76, 161, 162, 227
Seventh (7th) Avenue, Miami, Florida 130
Sevilla-Biltmore (hotel), Habana, Cuba 84
Siboney Motel, Key West, Florida 81
Siboney Tribe 16, 17
Sicily/Sicilian 3
Sierra Cristal Mountains, Cuba 111, 131, 132, 150, 197
Sierra de los Organos Mountains, Cuba 140
Sierra del Rosario Mountains, Cuba 140
Sierra Maestra Mountains, Cuba 1, 2, 9, 32, 101, 104, 105, 108, 111, 116, 124, 127, 132, 140, 150, 197, 231
Silver Meteor 36, 37
Silverio, Juan 24
Sixteenth (16th) Street, Tampa, Florida 59
Sixth (6th) Avenue, Tampa, Florida 51, 158
Sixth Rural Guard Regiment "Rios Rivera" 139
Slattery, Elizabeth "Liz" Villamia 265
Snider, Duke (baseball player) 21
Sochat, Natacha Villamia 130, 264
Sociedad de Amigos de la República (SAR) (Friends of the Republic Society) 46, 47
La Sociedad del Pilar (baseball team) 20
Society of Newspaper Editors 196, 197
Sola, Tony 86, 147, 231
Someillán, Alfredo 114
Someillán, Carlos 114
Someillán, Enrique 60, 113–122, 157, 211, 230, 233, 247, 253, 256, 262, 263
Someillán, Evaristo 114, 157
Someillán, Felix 113, 114, 122, 157, 230, 247, 256
Someillan, Guillermo 230
The Someillan Building 230
Sotus Romero, Jorge 107, 130, 150, 182
Soviet Union/Soviet/Russian 151, 229, 230, 244, 254, 259
Spain 2, 16–19, 22, 23, 48–50, 51, 58, 78, 107, 190, 219
Spanish Ambassador to Cuba 229
Spanish Civil War 34, 49, 50, 54, 58, 107
Spanish Little Theatre/Spanish Lyric Theatre 86
Special Committee on Organized Crime in Interstate Commerce/Kefauver Committee 83, 84
speeches: Eduardo Chibas (Tampa, Florida) 51; Fidel Castro (Key West, Florida 82; Miami, Florida 46, 47; New York City, New York 42, 43; Tampa, Florida 69, 71, 79); Rene Dechard (Tampa, Florida) 240
Spengler, Eusebio Leal *15*
Spoto, Angelo 71, 192
Spruce Street, Tampa, Florida 116
Squad 11 of the Rural Police 33
Staggerwing Beechcraft (aircraft) 150
Stanton, William (baseball player) 20
Stark, William Ledgert 3
Statue of Liberty 117
Stock Island, Florida 82
Stone, Oliver 267
Stone and Webster 25
Suarez, Demetria 24
Suarez, José R. 216
Suarez, Roque 86, 94, 115, 119, 121, 122
Suárez Blanco, José "Pepe" 33, 34<ST><ST>
</ST></ST>Suárez Gayol, Jesús 138, 185
Suero Acosta, Abelardo 81
sugar 17, 102, 103, 123, 124, 195, 197, 228, 229
Sunrise, Florida 265, 267
Sureda, Carlos 162, 163, 168, 170

Taber, Bob 107, 109, 110
Tabernilla Palmero, Francisco 174
Taft, William 18
Taíno Tribe 16, 17
Tallahassee, Florida 21, 22, 25
Tamiami Airport 150
Tamiami Trail/Highway 91 205
Tampa Aid to Cuba Committee 190
Tampa City Clerk 3
*Tampa Daily Times* 68
Tampa Electric Company (TECO) 25, 232, 233
Tampa Fire Rescue 3
Tampa International Airport 213, 214, 249
Tampa M-26-7: building Jose Marti Park 190, 220–226, 231; celebration of Castro's victory 160–161; closing club 254; enemies 113–117, 120–123, 211–214, 227, 232, 233, 235–244, 246, 247, 253, 256; founding 1, 69, 78; founding members 86, 87, 95–97; fundraising, protests, other activities 69, 70, 92, 93, 110–113, 116, 117, 123, 142, 143, 148, 158, 159, 190–193, 199, 219, 220, 231, 250, 254; harassment 227, 244–246, 250–253, 255, 256, 264; Miami partnership 116, 119, 120; president changes 69, 126–128, 142, 146–148, 161, 162, 231; taking over Tampa's Cuban consul position 162–171; television 128, 129

Tampa Police Department 25, 74, 76, 116, 122, 163, 164, 168, 169, 170, 213, 214, 216
Tampa Public Works 25
Tampa Smokers (baseball team) 24, 25
Tampa Street, Tampa, Florida 164
*Tampa Sunday Tribune* 73
Tampa Tarpons (baseball team) 25
*Tampa Times* 167, 169, 170, 238, 239
*Tampa Tribune* 113, 121, 122, 159, 167, 168, 170, 171, 215, 216, 262
Tampa's Queen of the Cuban Agrarian Reform 195
Tarara Beach, Cuba 200
tariffs 17
Tarrero, Mary 149
Tenth (10th) Avenue/Palm Avenue, Tampa, Florida 54, 93, 122, 148, 194
Texas 20, 21, 37, 135, 153, 261, 262, 265
Tey Saint-Blancard, José "Pepito" 100
Thanksgiving Day 61
Thibedeau, Ronald 20
Third (3rd) Avenue, Miami, Florida 45
Thirteenth (13th) Street, Tampa, Florida 48, 65, 71, 76, 127, 219, 220
30 November Revolutionary Movement 249
Tiffany Tile Corp 25, 83, 207
Times Square 160
Tincup, Frank (baseball player) 20
El Titan de Bronce (The Bronze Titan) 82
*The Today Show* 128, 129
Torre, David 115, 116
Torres, Juan 170
Trafficante, Henry 83
Trafficante, Mary Josephine 202
Trafficante, Santo, Jr. 83, 84, 154, 176–178, 201, 202, 206–208, 217–219
Trelles, Jorge A. 120, 121, 221
Trelles Clinic, Tampa, Florida 120
El Tren Blindado (The Armored Train) 159
Triana, Mario 154, 155, 191
Triana, Violeta Perez 191
Trinidad, West Indies 136
Triscornia 201, 202, 207, 208, 217
Tró Rivero, Emilio 32
Tropicana Club (cabaret), Habana, Cuba 84, 175
Truman Street, Key West, Florida 81
Trump, Donald 261, 262
Tschudin, Beverly "Frank" (baseball player) 20
Tuxpan River, Veracruz, Mexico 99
Twelfth (12th) Street, Tampa, Florida 71, 76

Twenty-second (22nd) Street, Tampa Florida 51, 68, 71
Twiggs Street, Tampa, Florida 158

Ugalde Carrillo, Manuel 87, 88
Union Center 148
Union City, New Jersey M-26-7 35, 39
Unión Insurreccional Revoluciónaria (UIR) (Revolutionary Insurrectional Union) 32
Union Street, Tampa, Florida 49, 192
L'Unione Italiana (Italian Club) 22
United Nations 30
United Press International (UPI) 208
U.S. Ambassador to Cuba 229
U.S. Army 87, 131, 132, 154, 155
U.S. Border Patrol 216
U.S. Immigration Department 41, 218
U.S. Post Office 110, 158, 159, 245
U.S. Secretary of State 228
United Steelworkers of America 71, 78
University of Habana 18, 20, 31, 55, 87, 88, 90, 104, 119
University of Miami School of Medicine 266
University of Oriente 172
University of Tampa 67, 249
Urrutia, Alejandro 208
Urrutia, Jorge 208
Urrutia, Victoria Esperanza Lydia 185, 196, 208, 265
Urrutia Lleó, Manuel 33, 125, 126, 149, 165, 166, 174, 176, 180–186, 193–196, 198, 206–208, 217, 226, 240, 248, 265

V-29 VISA (29-Dayers) 28, 30
Valdes Menendez, Ramiro 103
Valdés Zambrana, Antonio 91
Valdivia, Alfredo 250
Valdivia, Gilberto 250
Valdivia, Juan 250
Valladares Abreu, Alfredo 89
Vamos a Barrer la Corrupcion (Let's Sweep Out Corruption) 28
Varadero Beach, Cuba 248
Varela, Franklin 81
Varela Castro, Manuel 91
Vasquez, Armando 46
Vazquez, Jacinto 112
Vasquez, Rodolfo 143, 144, 162
Vedado (section of Habana, Cuba) 106, 208, 230
Velaz, Anibal 115, 117–119, 148, 233
Venereo, Evaristo 140
Venezuela 173
Ventura Novo, Esteban 111, 177

Ventura Reyes, Orlando 91
Veracruz Mexico 99, 102
Verguenza Contra Dinero (Honor (Dignity) Versus Money) 28, 219
*Versos Sencillos* (*Simple Verses*) 190
Viana, Raul 116
Vicari's 222
Victory Bakery 54
Viera, Rene 116
Vila, Marc 86
Vila, Marcelino 86, 115, 119, 147, 148, 191, 231
Villamia, Arlene **200**
Villamia, Balbina Lagos 4, 19
Villamia, Barbara 4, 19, 32, 43, 44, 130, 131, 230
Villamia, Carmen Guzman 29, 31, 130, 199, 247, 248
Villamia, Deborah 247, 249, 264
Villamia, Denise 5, 206, 244
Villamia, Irene 19, 199, 230, 267, 268
Villamia, José 19
Villamia, Marta 19, 183, 199, 230, 267, 268
Villamia, Michael 265
Villamia, Nora Marie Rodriguez 24, 222, **222**, 224
Villamia, Raul **15, 28, 62, 63, 88, 124, 155, 156, 168, 191, 194, 211, 245, 266, 267**
Villamia, Rhonda 2, 3–7, 12–15, **15**, 25, 61, 88, **88**, 154, 155, 156, 186, 206, 222, 264, 266, 267, 269
Villamia Lagos, Fernando 19, 204
Villamia Lagos, Miguel 19, 23, 25, 32, 39, 41, 43, 44, 97, 130, 185, 225, 229, 230, 268
Villamia Lagos, Silverio Mario 4, 6, 19, 26–30, 32, 34, 35–39, 41–45, 84, 85, 97, 101, 102, 105–107, **106**, 112, 113, **113**, 125, **125**, 126, 128, 129, 130–138, 141, 148, 149, 152, 163, 180–187, **184, 185**, 194, 198, 199, 205, 206–208, 217, 226, 230, 240, 242, 247–249, 262, 264–268, **266, 267**
Villamia Saa, Miguel 4
Villaronga, Angel 198
Villaverde, Martin 196
Virgin of Charity shrine 144
Visbal, Gilbert L. 153
V.M. Ybor Cigar Factory 49, 50, 54, 64, 86, 221, 222, 237

WALT-AM 51, 63
Warren Commission 262
Washington, D.C. 37, 163, 165, 196, 197, 229
Washington Senators (baseball team) 20
Watergate 141
Westbrook Rosales, Joe 111
West 14th Street, New York City, New York 38
West 31st Street, New York City, New York 37
West 33rd Street, New York City, New York 37
West 50th Street, New York City, New York 36
West 52nd Street, New York City, New York 36
West 59th Street, New York City, New York 48
West 88th Street, New York City, New York 39
West 91st Street, New York City, New York 41
West 96th Street, New York City, New York 30, 38
West 137th Street, New York City, New York 37
West 138th Street, New York City, New York 37
West Tampa 2, 24, 49, 59, 61, 62, 67, 71, 73, 86, 116, 123, 124, 160, 161, 191, 192, 219, 245, 254, 258
West Tampa Sheriff Association Festival 192
Western Union/telegrams: Emilio Pando to Guillermo Bolivar 165; Fidel Castro to Angel Perez-Vidal 36; Gabriel Gil Alfonso to Ruben Fabelo (alleged) 212; Gerardo Perez Puelles to Gabriel Gil Alfonso 171; to Jesus Montane 37; Jose Llanusa to Gabriel Gil Alfonso 163, 165, 166; Juan A. Orta to Victoriano Manteiga 236, 237
Westshore Boulevard, Tampa, Florida 25
WFLA 113
Widmayer, Walt (baseball player) 20
William T. Sampson High School 108
Williers, Ray T. 195
Woolworth Co., F. W. 249
World War II 28, 135, 215, 251
WQBN-AM 86
WTVT 80, 112, 113, 238

Yang, Laureano Noa 103
Ybor City: celebration 2; history 22, 23; role in Cuban War of Independence 48, 49; role in Spanish Civil War 49, 50; support of Eduardo Chibas 50, 51
Ybor City Rotary Club 221, 222

www.ingramcontent.com/pod-product-compliance
Lightning Source LLC
Chambersburg PA
CBHW032032300426
44117CB00009B/1030